Story & Art by Tomu Ohmi

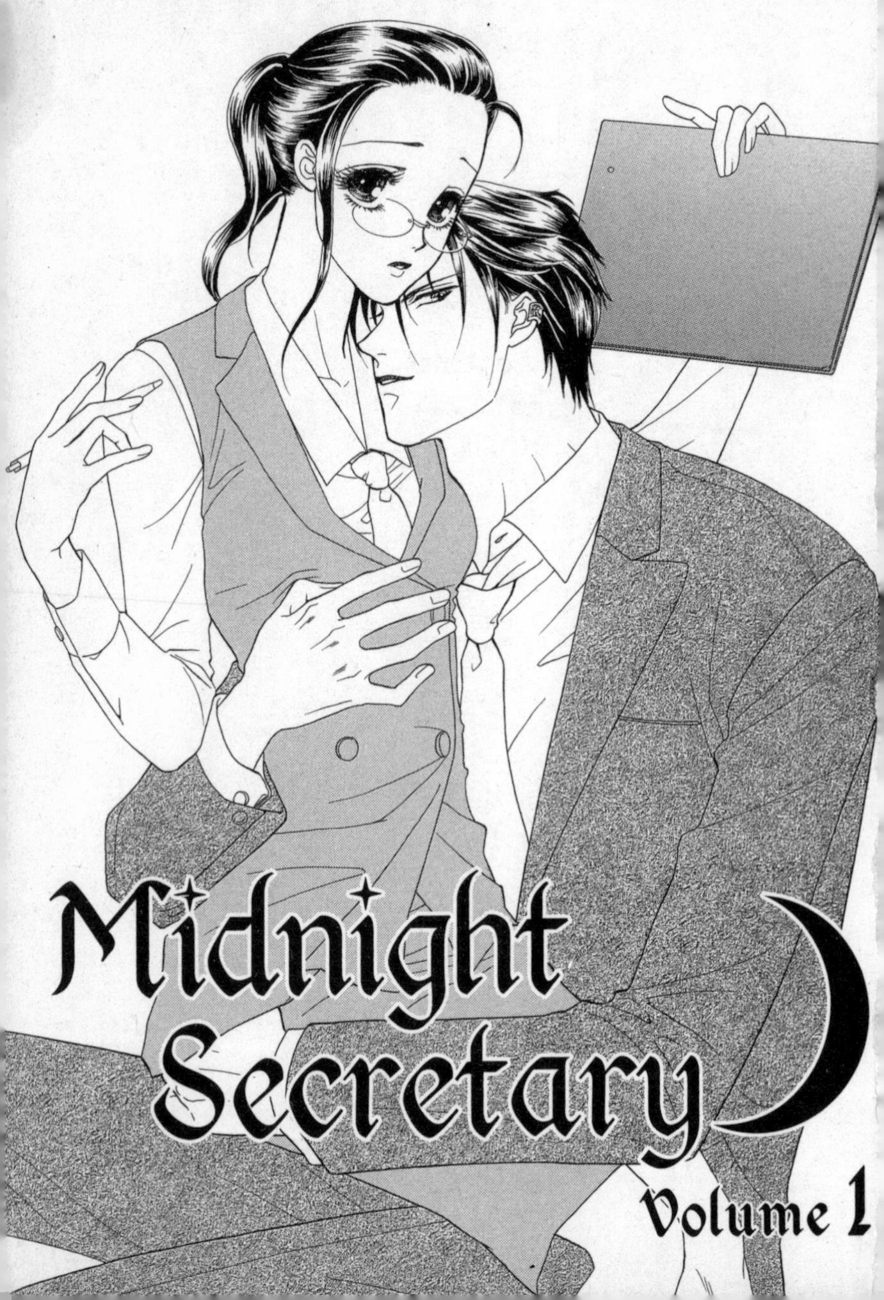
Midnight Secretary
Volume 1

Midnight Secretary

Volume 1

Contents

Night 1
Bloody Night Office
3

Night 2
Sweet Pain
49

Night 3
Brotherhood
83

Night 4
Workaholic Girl
117

Night 5
Moonlight Garden
153

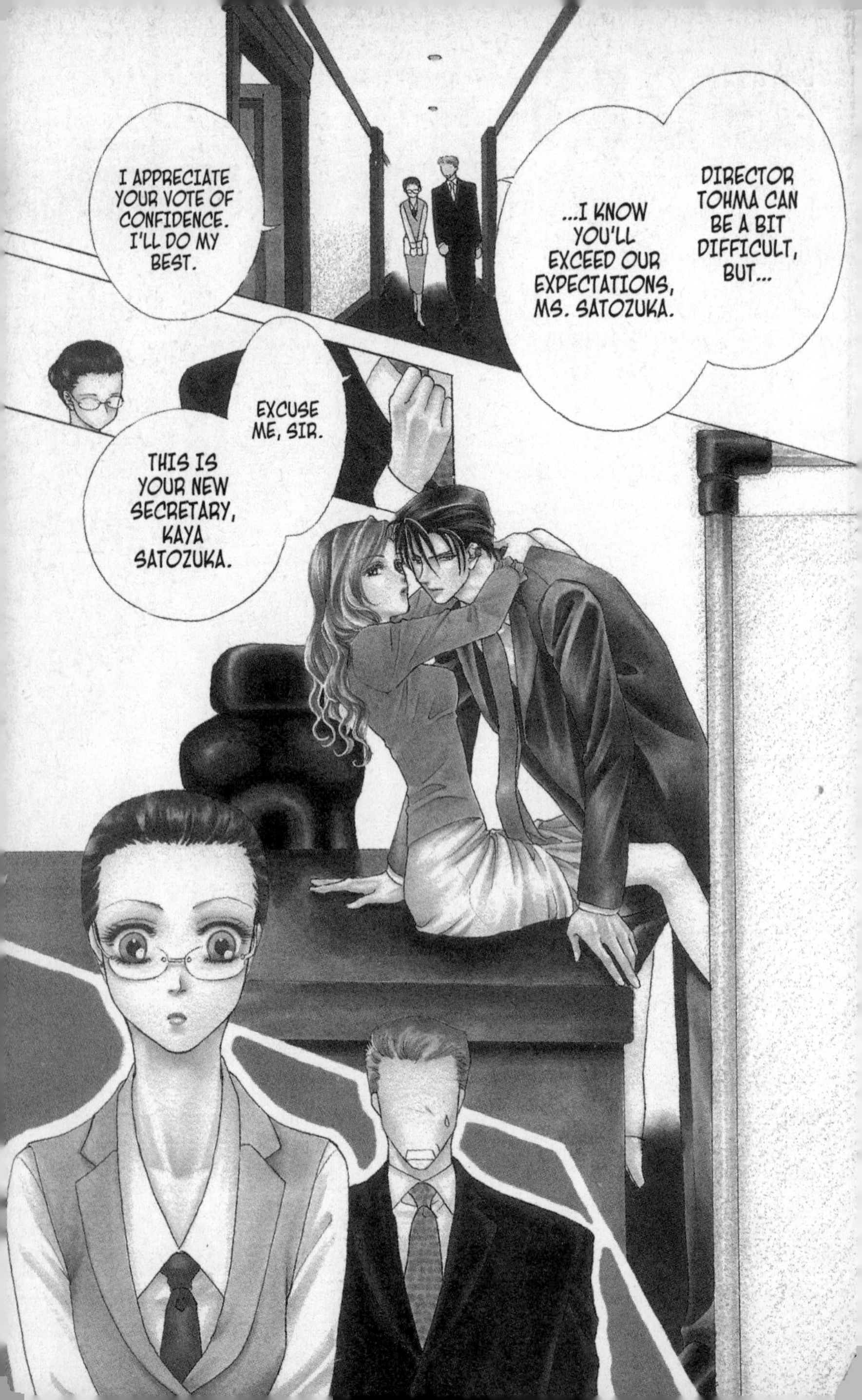
DIRECTOR TOHMA CAN BE A BIT DIFFICULT, BUT...
...I KNOW YOU'LL EXCEED OUR EXPECTATIONS, MS. SATOZUKA.
I APPRECIATE YOUR VOTE OF CONFIDENCE. I'LL DO MY BEST.
EXCUSE ME, SIR.
THIS IS YOUR NEW SECRETARY, KAYA SATOZUKA.

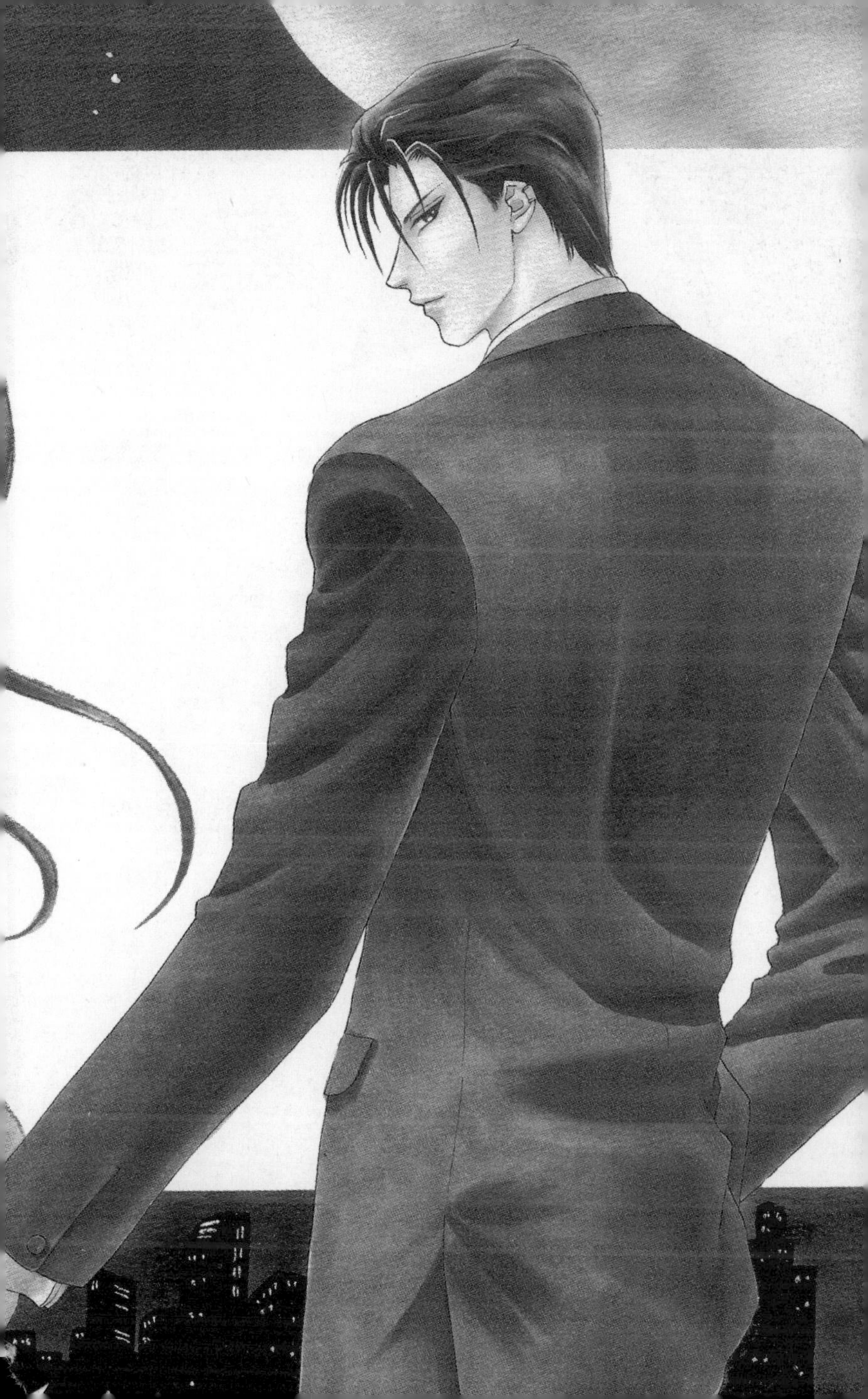

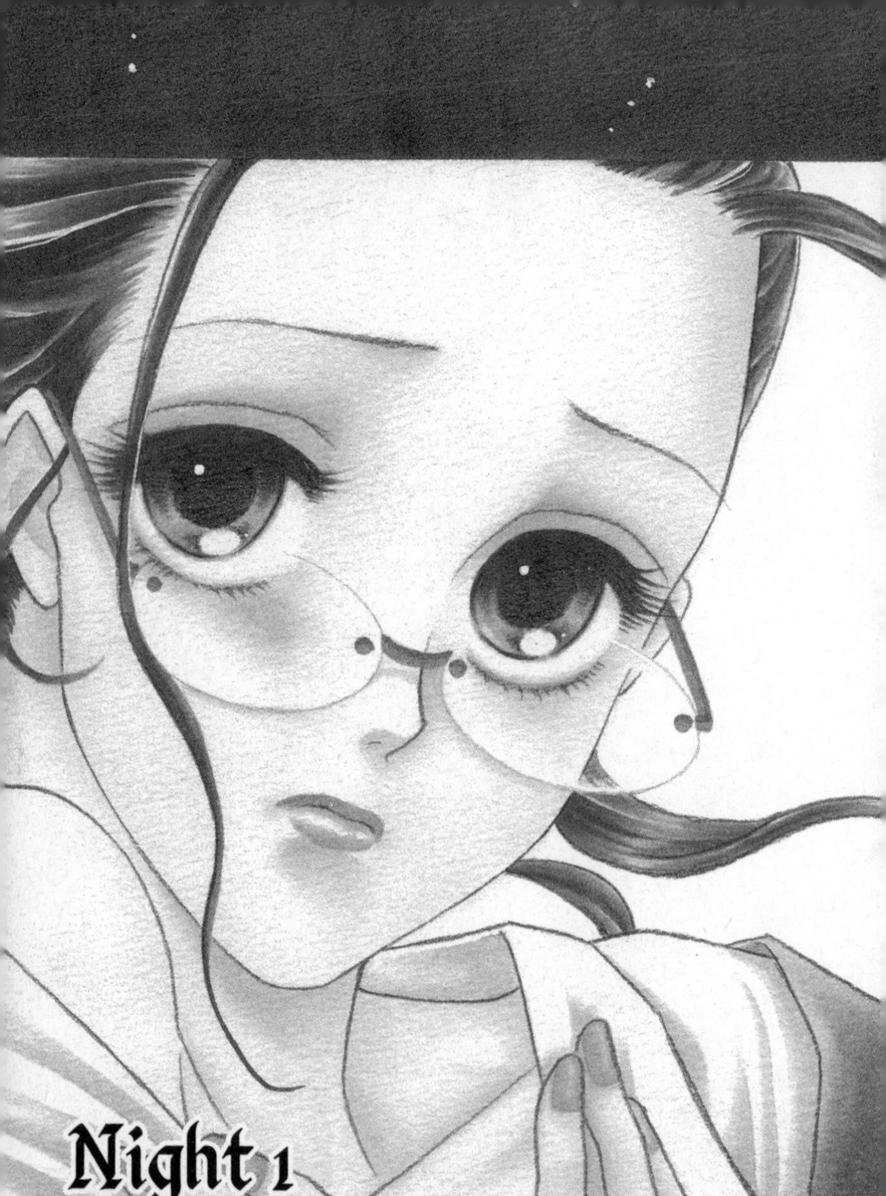
Night 1

With my new series, I have the chance to meet you all again. Thank you so much for supporting me.

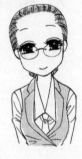

I'm so happy to see you all.
Let me be your guide.

Before I knew it, the marketing slogan had an almost love-hate feel to it. I guess that is how it is. The characters blow hot and cold. I hope you enjoy it!

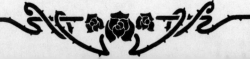

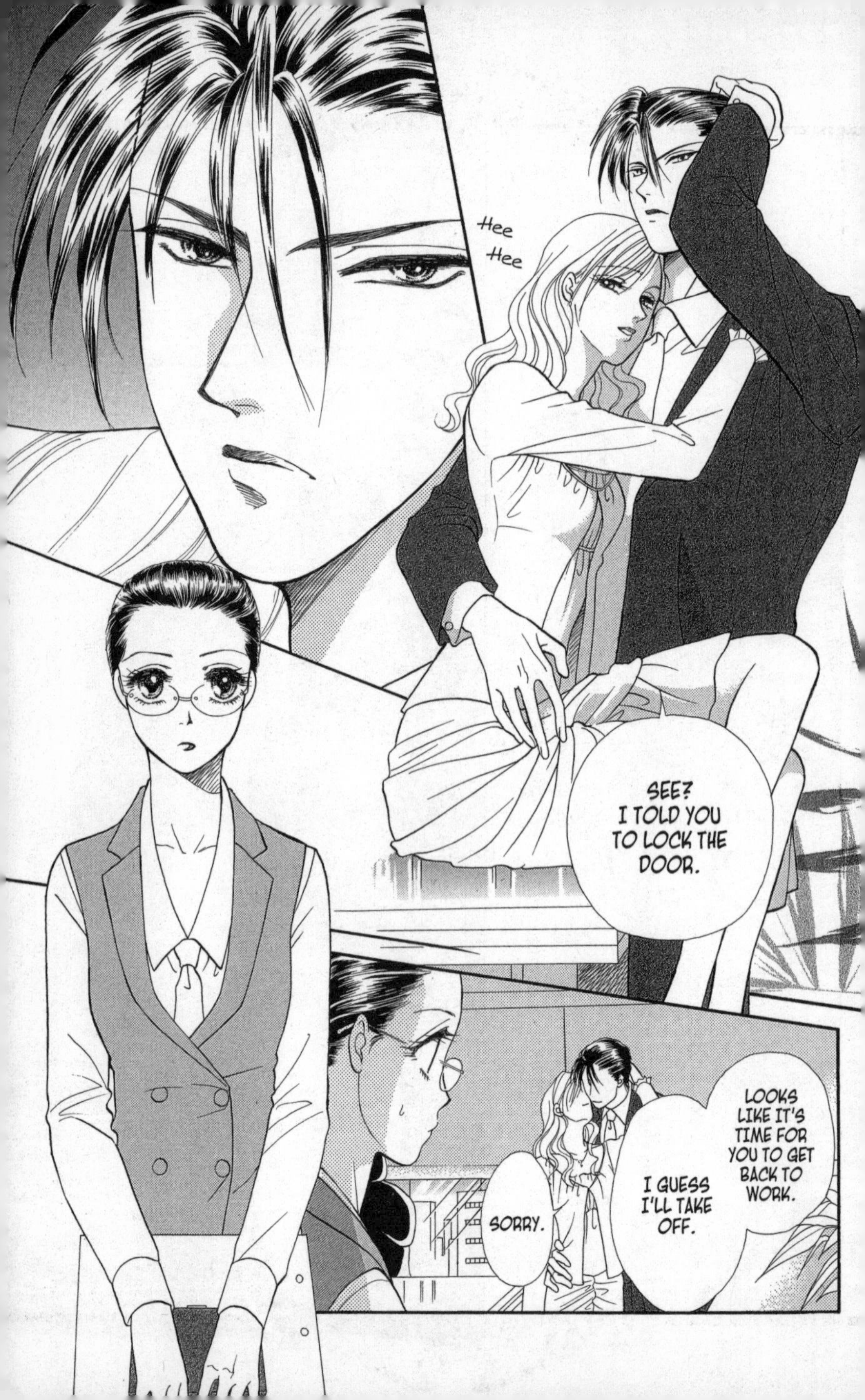
Hee Hee
SEE? I TOLD YOU TO LOCK THE DOOR.
LOOKS LIKE IT'S TIME FOR YOU TO GET BACK TO WORK.
I GUESS I'LL TAKE OFF.
SORRY.

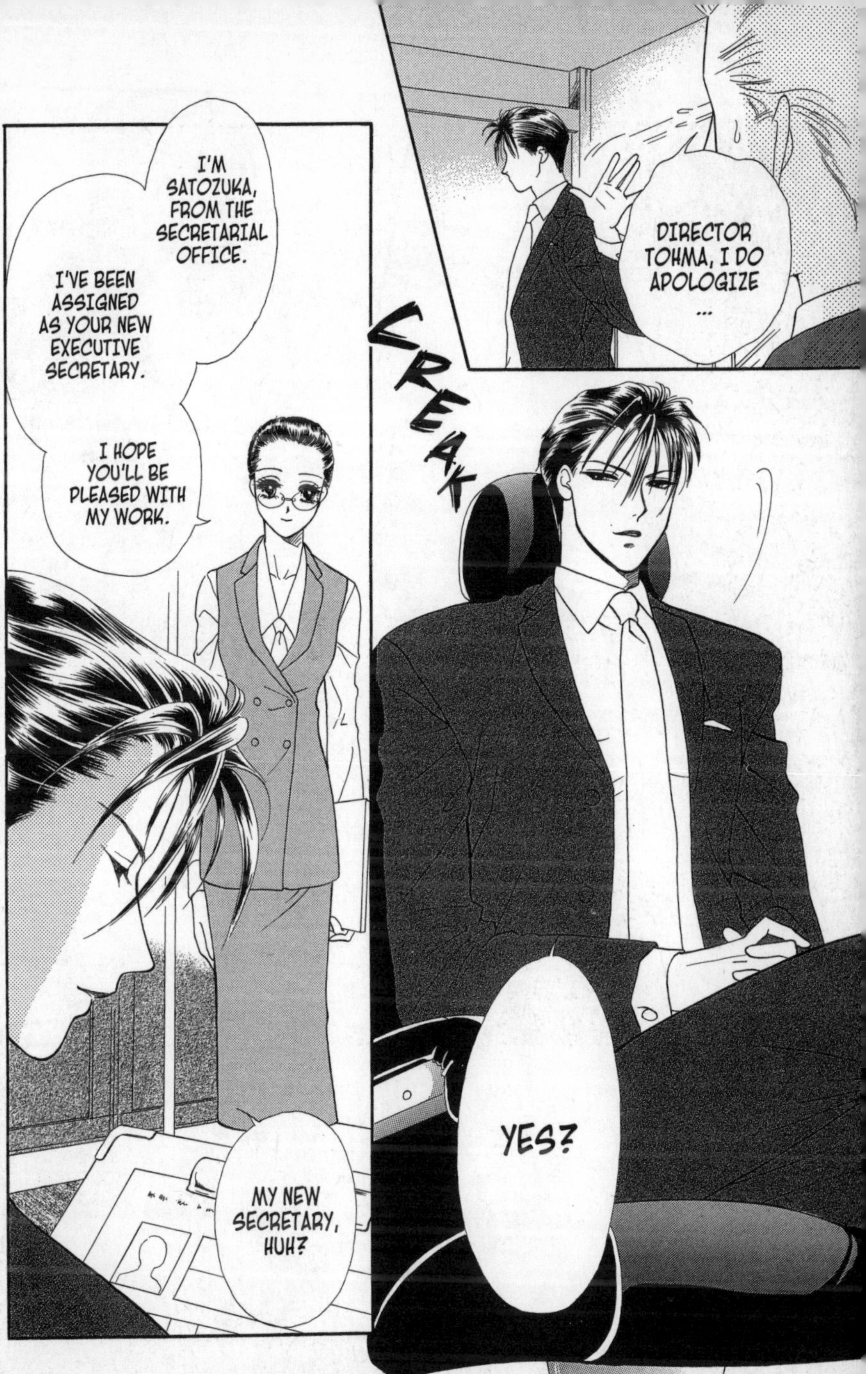
DIRECTOR TOHMA, I DO APOLOGIZE ...
CREAK
YES?
I'M SATOZUKA, FROM THE SECRETARIAL OFFICE.
I'VE BEEN ASSIGNED AS YOUR NEW EXECUTIVE SECRETARY.
I HOPE YOU'LL BE PLEASED WITH MY WORK.
MY NEW SECRETARY, HUH?

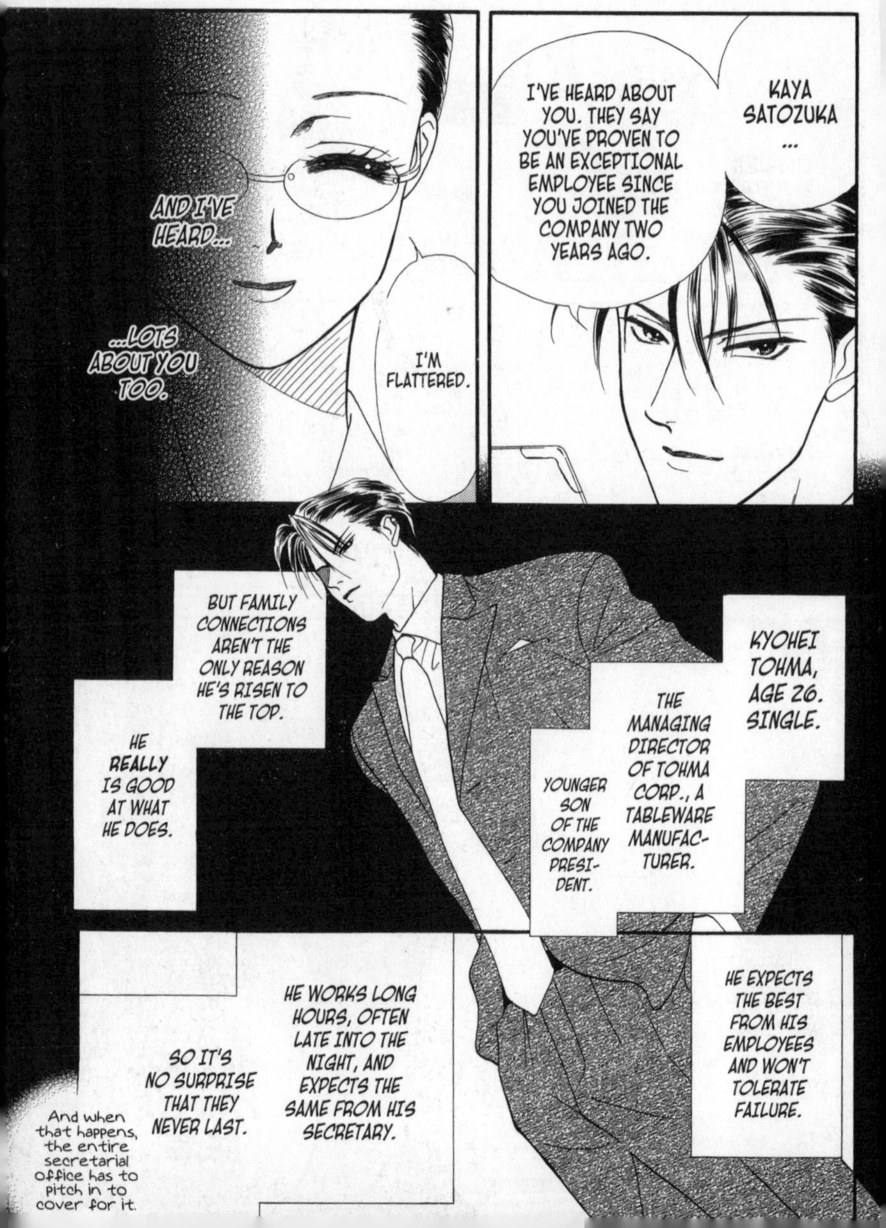
KAYA SATOZUKA ...
I'VE HEARD ABOUT YOU. THEY SAY YOU'VE PROVEN TO BE AN EXCEPTIONAL EMPLOYEE SINCE YOU JOINED THE COMPANY TWO YEARS AGO.
I'M FLATTERED.
AND I'VE HEARD...
...LOTS ABOUT YOU TOO.
KYOHEI TOHMA, AGE 26. SINGLE.
THE MANAGING DIRECTOR OF TOHMA CORP., A TABLEWARE MANUFAC-TURER.
YOUNGER SON OF THE COMPANY PRESI-DENT.
BUT FAMILY CONNECTIONS AREN'T THE ONLY REASON HE'S RISEN TO THE TOP.
HE REALLY IS GOOD AT WHAT HE DOES.
HE EXPECTS THE BEST FROM HIS EMPLOYEES AND WON'T TOLERATE FAILURE.
HE WORKS LONG HOURS, OFTEN LATE INTO THE NIGHT, AND EXPECTS THE SAME FROM HIS SECRETARY.
SO IT'S NO SURPRISE THAT THEY NEVER LAST.
And when that happens, the entire secretarial office has to pitch in to cover for it.

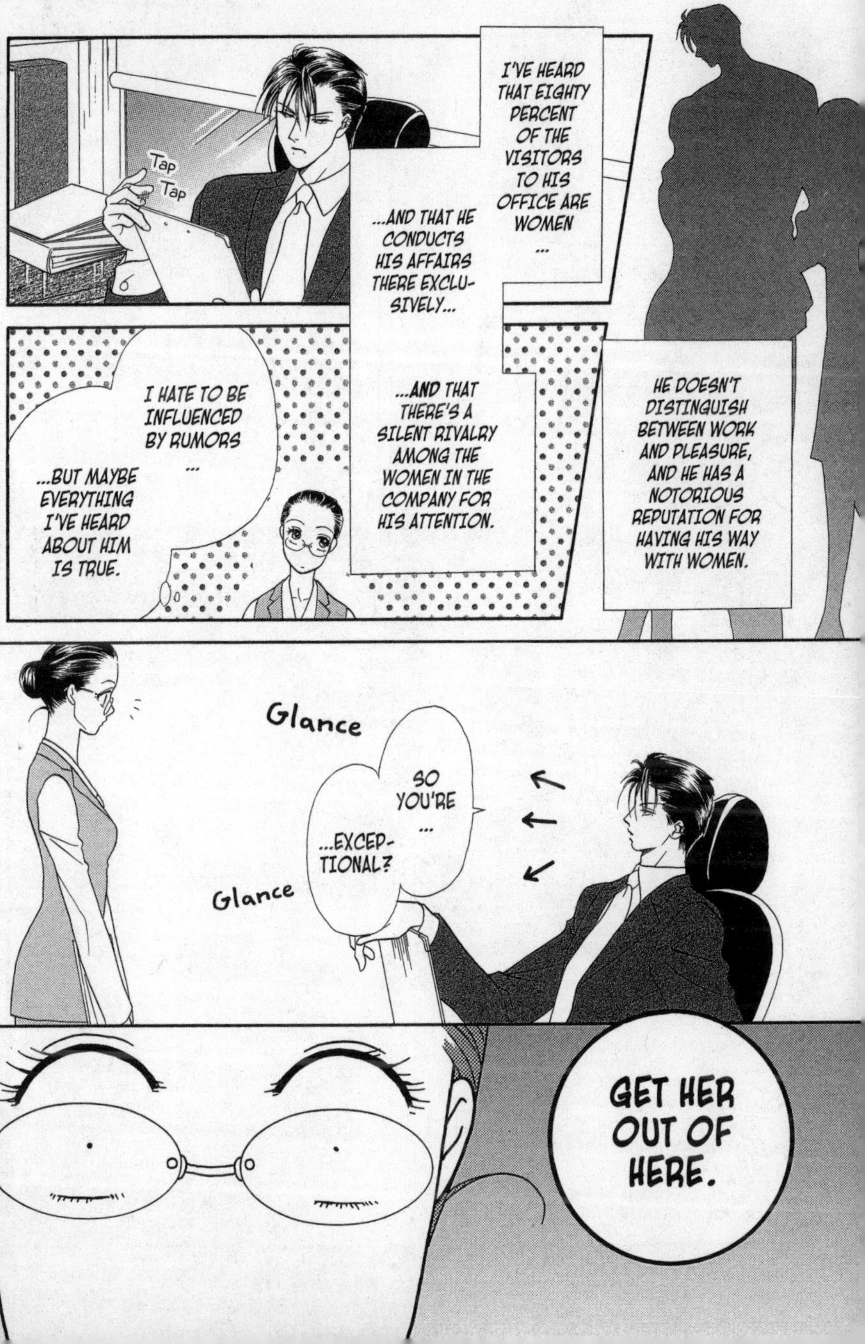
I'VE HEARD THAT EIGHTY PERCENT OF THE VISITORS TO HIS OFFICE ARE WOMEN ...
...AND THAT HE CONDUCTS HIS AFFAIRS THERE EXCLUSIVELY...
...AND THAT THERE'S A SILENT RIVALRY AMONG THE WOMEN IN THE COMPANY FOR HIS ATTENTION.
HE DOESN'T DISTINGUISH BETWEEN WORK AND PLEASURE, AND HE HAS A NOTORIOUS REPUTATION FOR HAVING HIS WAY WITH WOMEN.
Tap Tap
I HATE TO BE INFLUENCED BY RUMORS ...
...BUT MAYBE EVERYTHING I'VE HEARD ABOUT HIM IS TRUE.
Glance
SO YOU'RE ...
...EXCEPTIONAL?
Glance
GET HER OUT OF HERE.

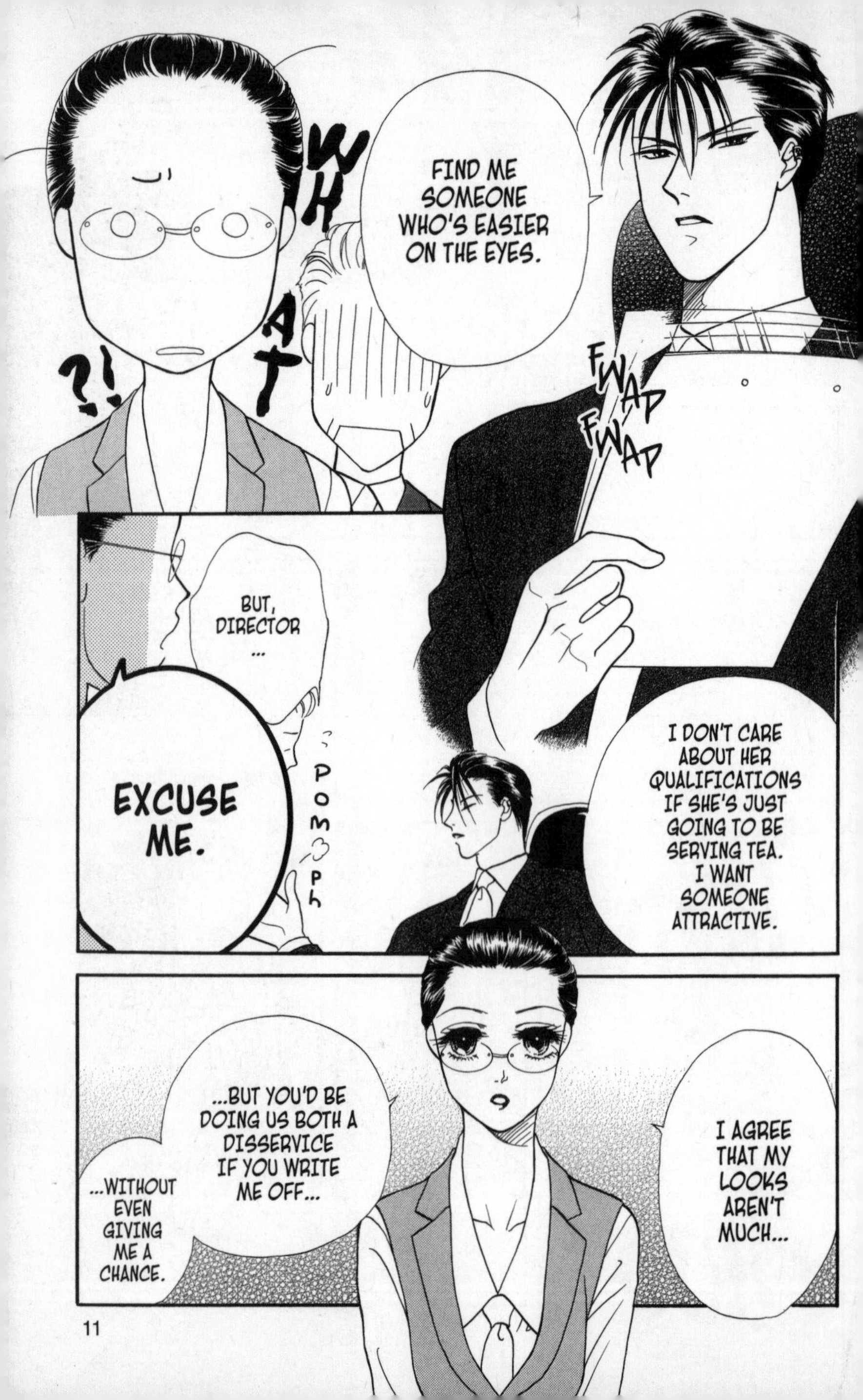
FWAP FWAP
FIND ME SOMEONE WHO'S EASIER ON THE EYES.
WHAT
?!
I DON'T CARE ABOUT HER QUALIFICATIONS IF SHE'S JUST GOING TO BE SERVING TEA. I WANT SOMEONE ATTRACTIVE.
BUT, DIRECTOR ...
POMPH
EXCUSE ME.
I AGREE THAT MY LOOKS AREN'T MUCH...
...BUT YOU'D BE DOING US BOTH A DISSERVICE IF YOU WRITE ME OFF...
...WITHOUT EVEN GIVING ME A CHANCE.

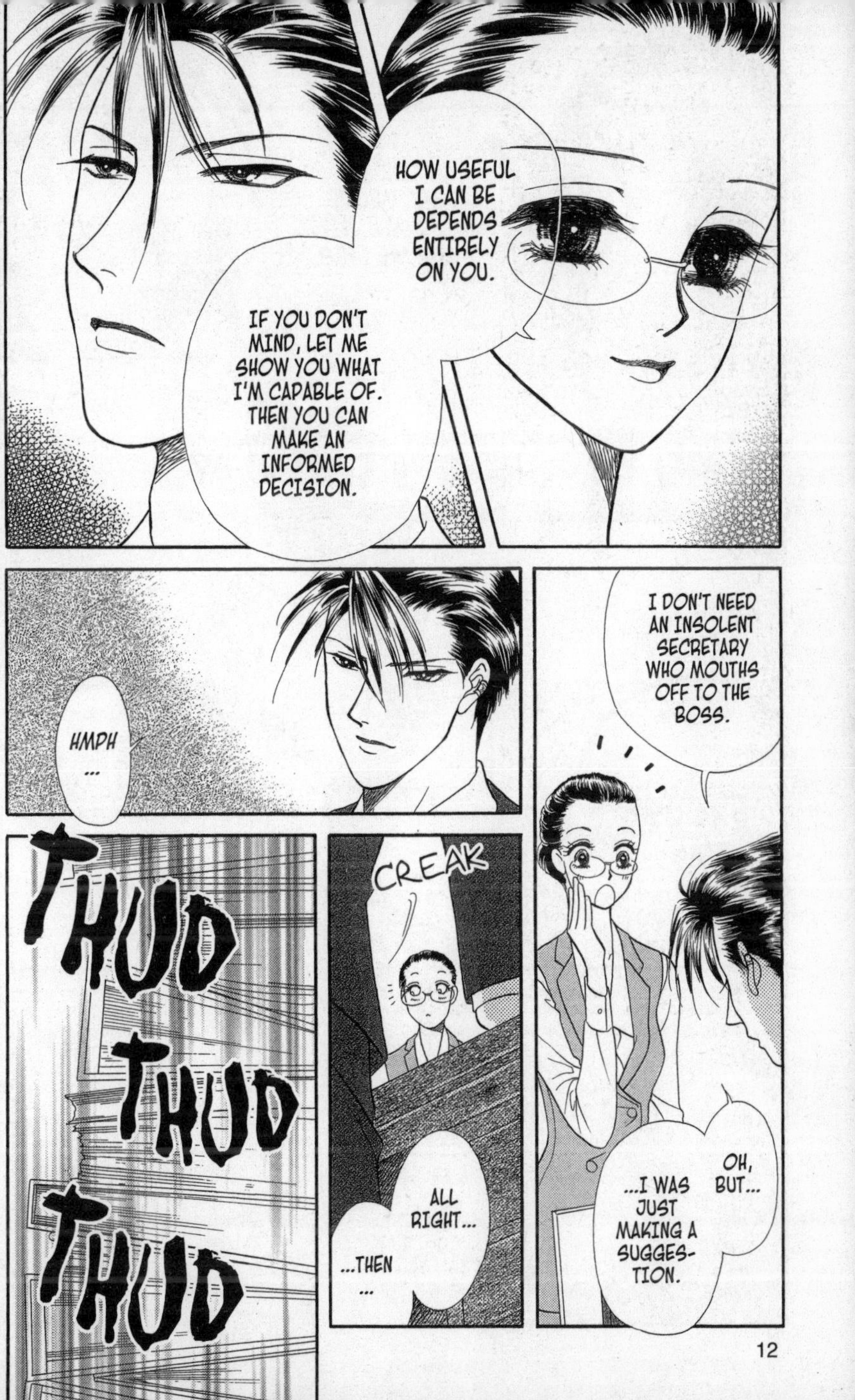
HOW USEFUL I CAN BE DEPENDS ENTIRELY ON YOU.
IF YOU DON'T MIND, LET ME SHOW YOU WHAT I'M CAPABLE OF. THEN YOU CAN MAKE AN INFORMED DECISION.
I DON'T NEED AN INSOLENT SECRETARY WHO MOUTHS OFF TO THE BOSS.
OH, BUT...
...I WAS JUST MAKING A SUGGES-TION.
HMPH ...
CREAK
ALL RIGHT...
...THEN ...
THUD THUD THUD

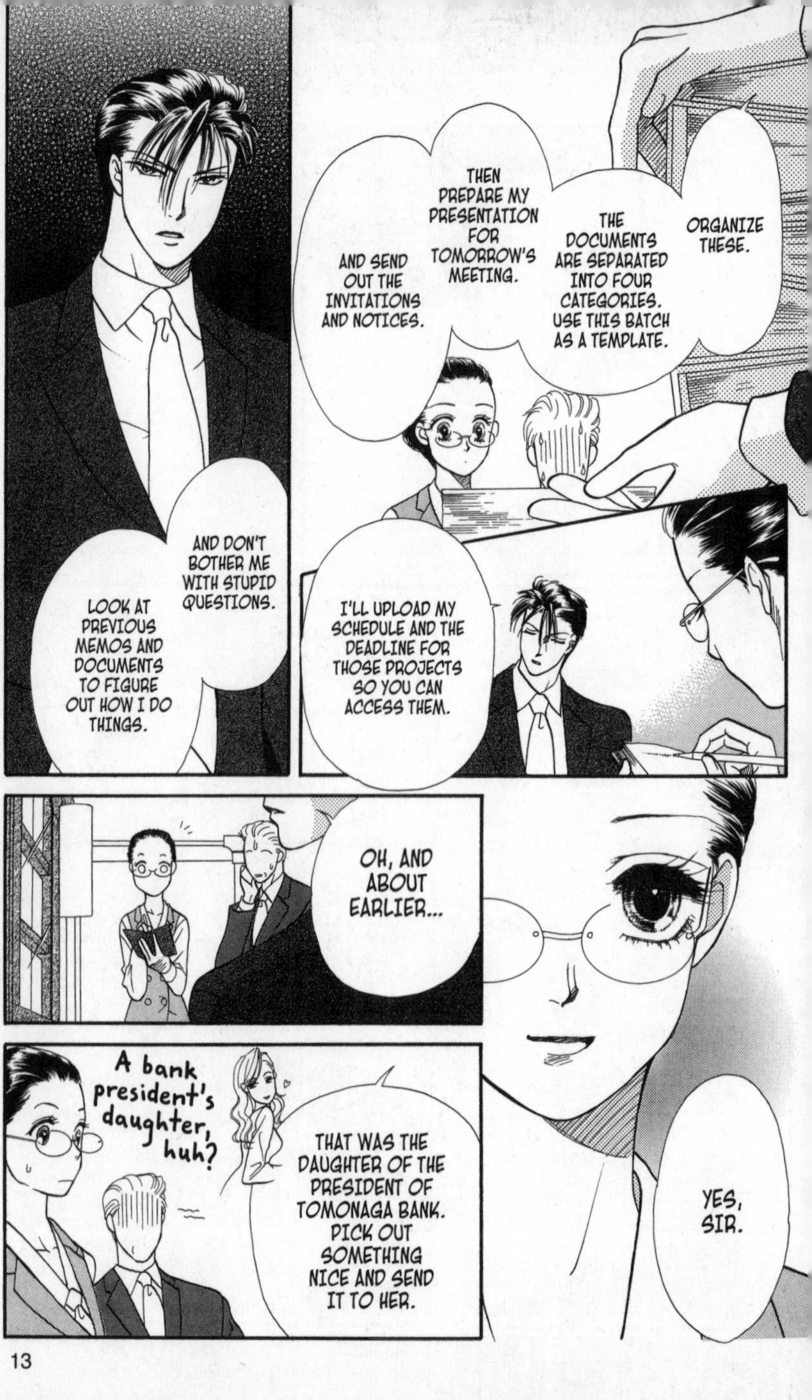
ORGANIZE THESE.
THE DOCUMENTS ARE SEPARATED INTO FOUR CATEGORIES. USE THIS BATCH AS A TEMPLATE.
THEN PREPARE MY PRESENTATION FOR TOMORROW'S MEETING.
AND SEND OUT THE INVITATIONS AND NOTICES.
I'LL UPLOAD MY SCHEDULE AND THE DEADLINE FOR THOSE PROJECTS SO YOU CAN ACCESS THEM.
AND DON'T BOTHER ME WITH STUPID QUESTIONS.
LOOK AT PREVIOUS MEMOS AND DOCUMENTS TO FIGURE OUT HOW I DO THINGS.
YES, SIR.
OH, AND ABOUT EARLIER...
THAT WAS THE DAUGHTER OF THE PRESIDENT OF TOMONAGA BANK. PICK OUT SOMETHING NICE AND SEND IT TO HER.
A bank president's daughter, huh?

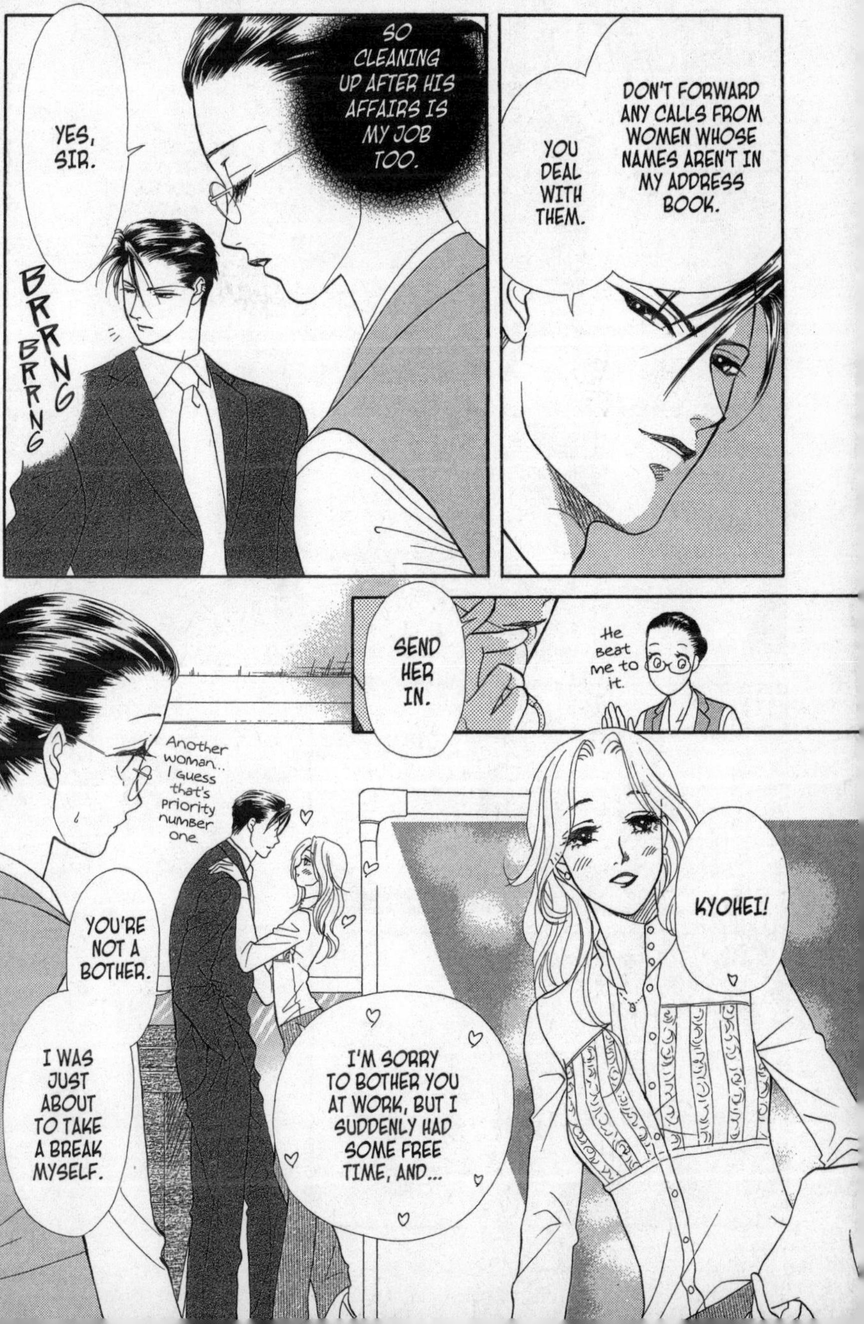
DON'T FORWARD ANY CALLS FROM WOMEN WHOSE NAMES AREN'T IN MY ADDRESS BOOK.
YOU DEAL WITH THEM.
SO CLEANING UP AFTER HIS AFFAIRS IS MY JOB TOO.
YES, SIR.
BRRRNG
BRRRNG
He Beat me to it.
SEND HER IN.
KYOHEI!
I'M SORRY TO BOTHER YOU AT WORK, BUT I SUDDENLY HAD SOME FREE TIME, AND...
YOU'RE NOT A BOTHER.
I WAS JUST ABOUT TO TAKE A BREAK MYSELF.
Another woman.. I guess that's priority number one.

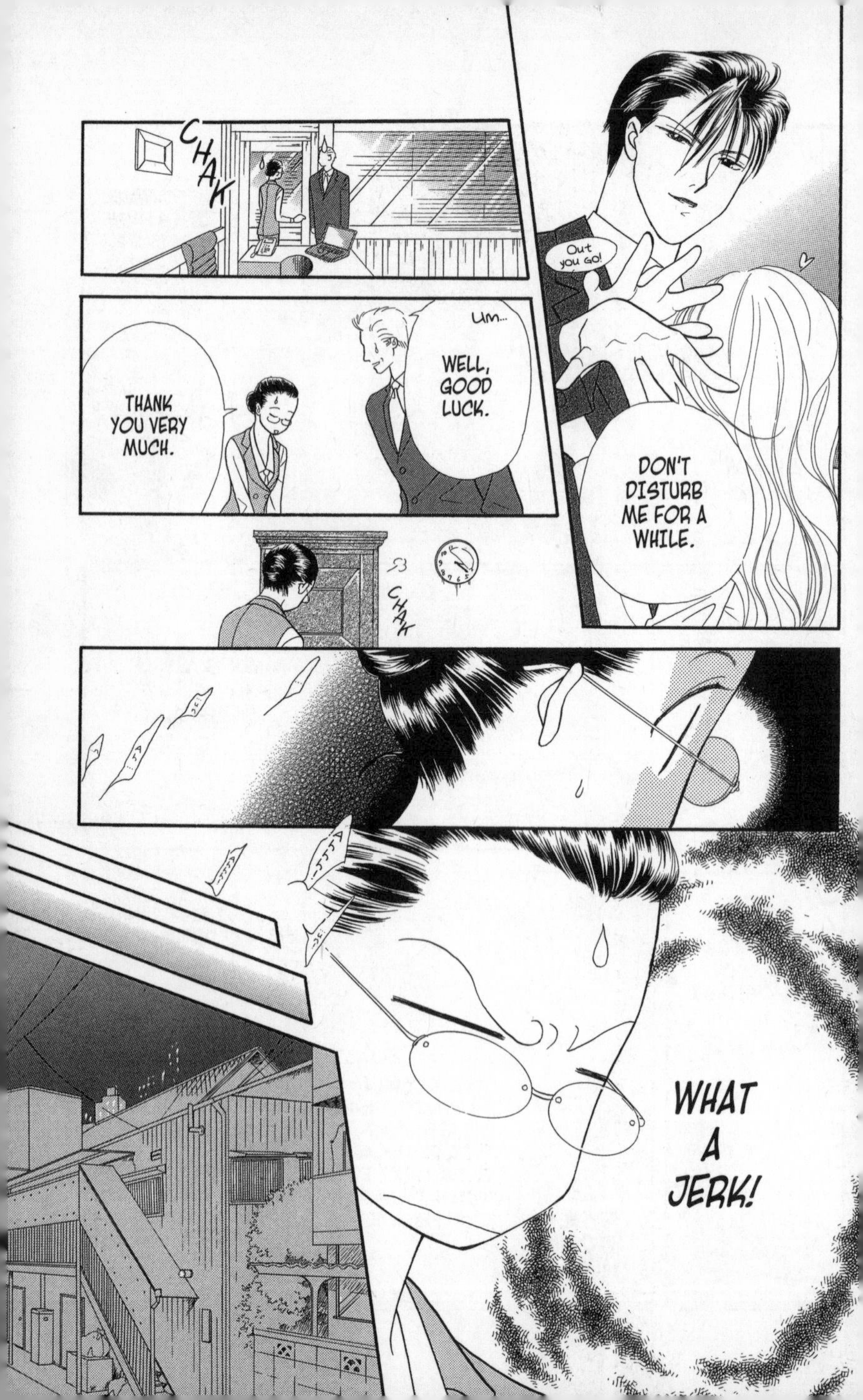
Out you go!
DON'T DISTURB ME FOR A WHILE.
CHAK
UM...
WELL, GOOD LUCK.
THANK YOU VERY MUCH.
CHAK
WHAT A JERK!

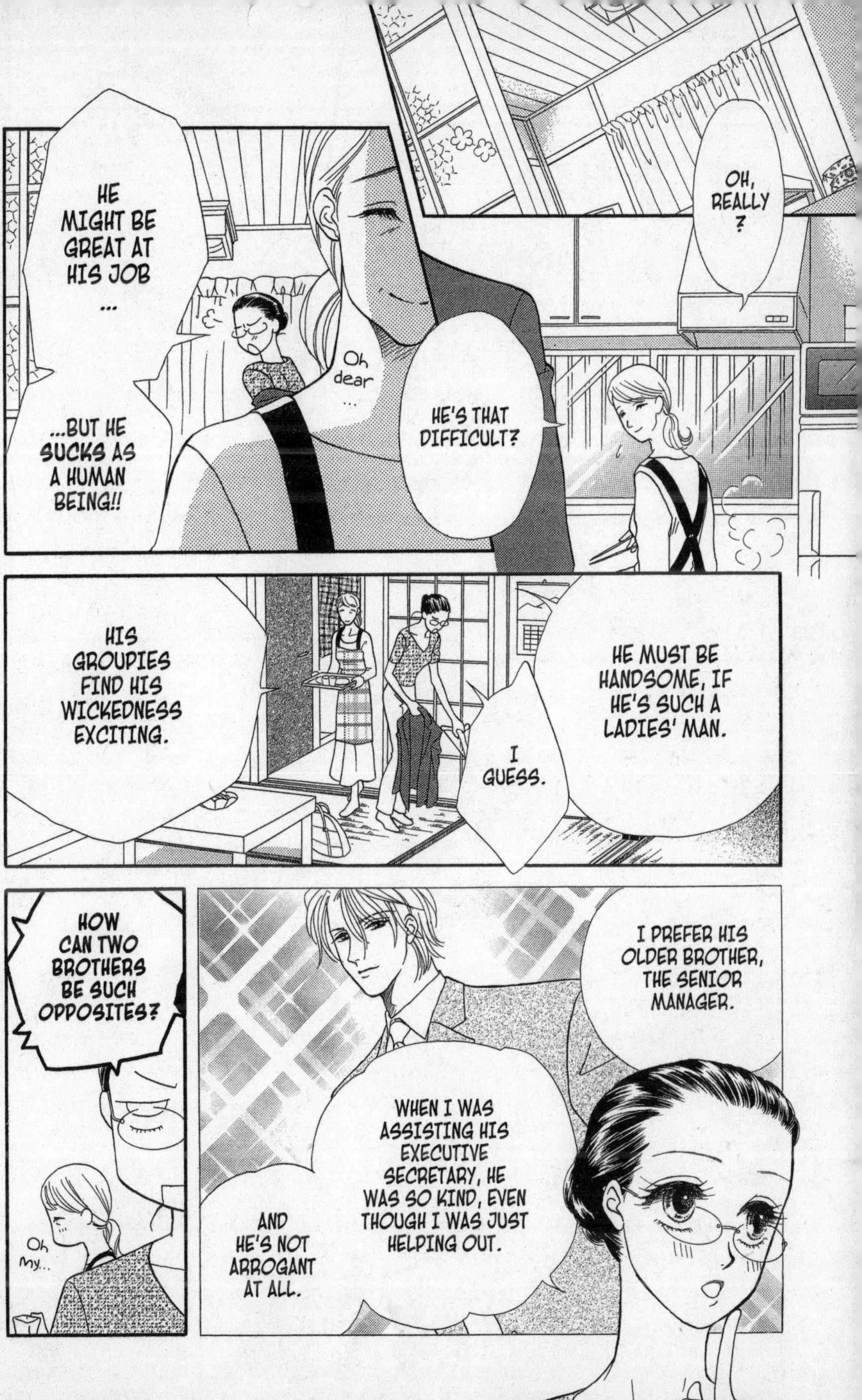
OH, REALLY?
HE'S THAT DIFFICULT?
Oh dear ...
HE MIGHT BE GREAT AT HIS JOB ...
...BUT HE SUCKS AS A HUMAN BEING!!
HE MUST BE HANDSOME, IF HE'S SUCH A LADIES' MAN.
I GUESS.
HIS GROUPIES FIND HIS WICKEDNESS EXCITING.
I PREFER HIS OLDER BROTHER, THE SENIOR MANAGER.
WHEN I WAS ASSISTING HIS EXECUTIVE SECRETARY, HE WAS SO KIND, EVEN THOUGH I WAS JUST HELPING OUT.
AND HE'S NOT ARROGANT AT ALL.
HOW CAN TWO BROTHERS BE SUCH OPPOSITES?
Oh my...

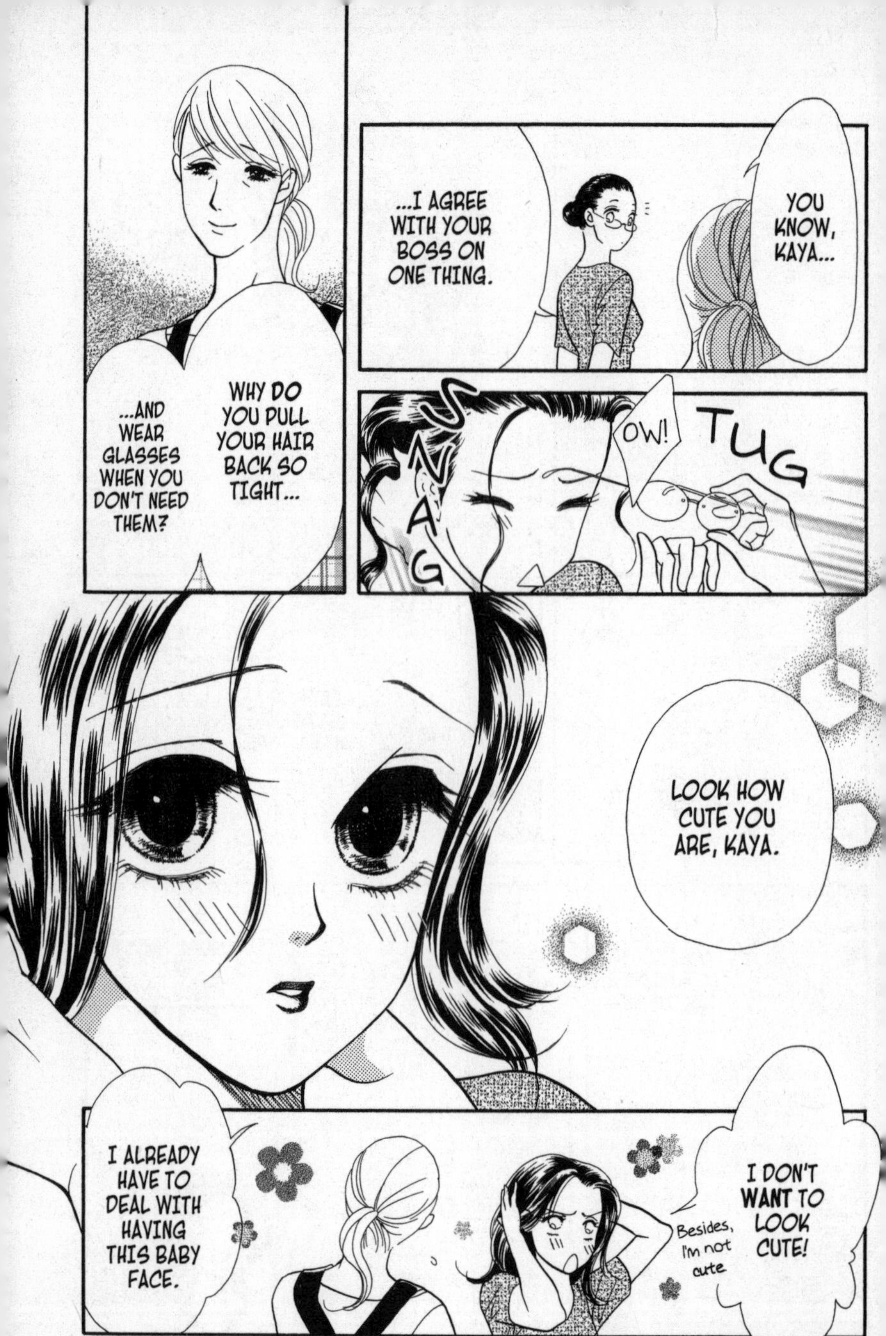
YOU KNOW, KAYA...
...I AGREE WITH YOUR BOSS ON ONE THING.
TUG
OW!
SNAG
WHY DO YOU PULL YOUR HAIR BACK SO TIGHT...
...AND WEAR GLASSES WHEN YOU DON'T NEED THEM?
LOOK HOW CUTE YOU ARE, KAYA.
I DON'T WANT TO LOOK CUTE!
Besides, I'm not cute
I ALREADY HAVE TO DEAL WITH HAVING THIS BABY FACE.

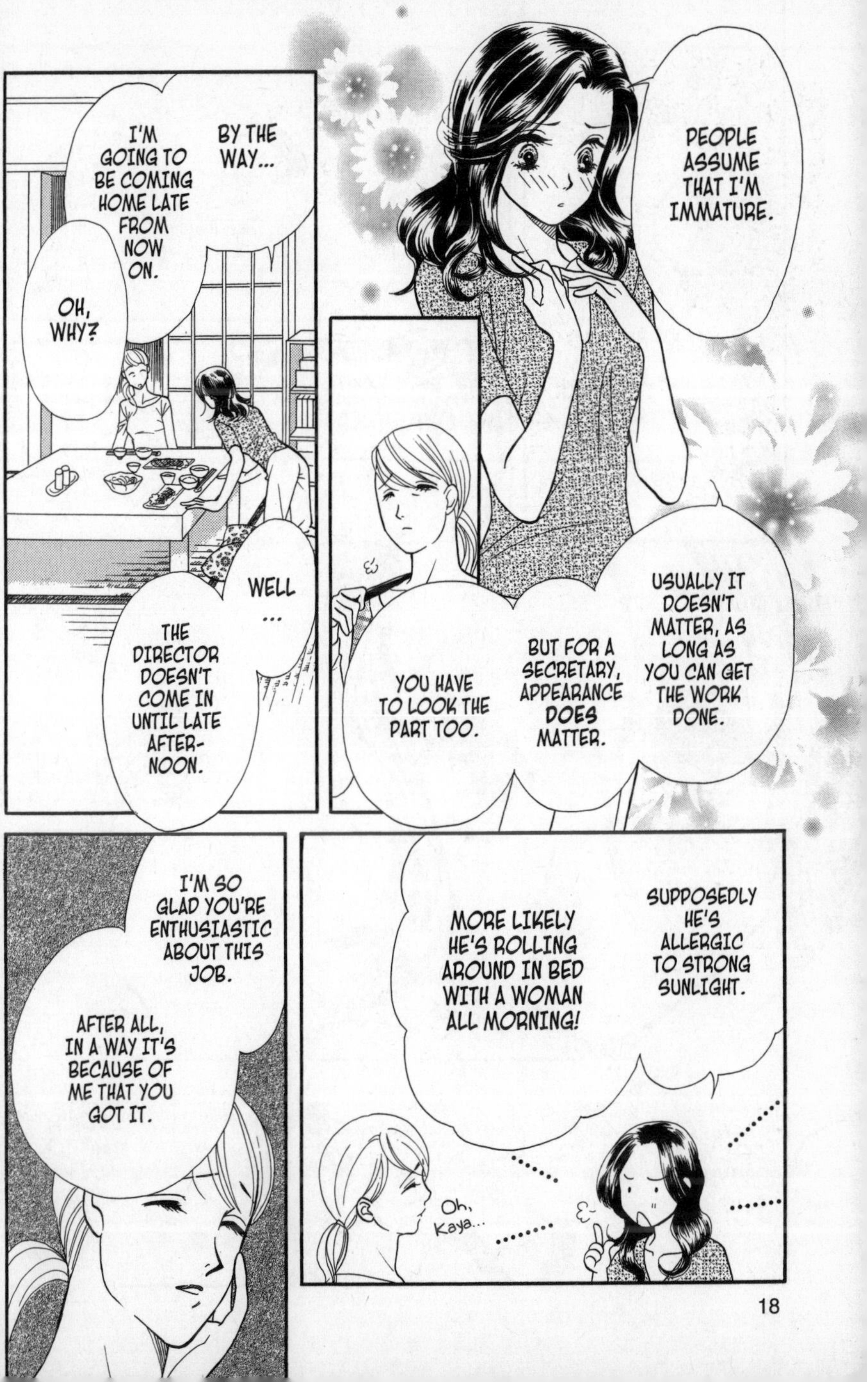
PEOPLE ASSUME THAT I'M IMMATURE.
USUALLY IT DOESN'T MATTER, AS LONG AS YOU CAN GET THE WORK DONE.
BUT FOR A SECRETARY, APPEARANCE DOES MATTER.
YOU HAVE TO LOOK THE PART TOO.
BY THE WAY...
I'M GOING TO BE COMING HOME LATE FROM NOW ON.
OH, WHY?
WELL...
THE DIRECTOR DOESN'T COME IN UNTIL LATE AFTERNOON.
SUPPOSEDLY HE'S ALLERGIC TO STRONG SUNLIGHT.
MORE LIKELY HE'S ROLLING AROUND IN BED WITH A WOMAN ALL MORNING!
Oh, Kaya...
I'M SO GLAD YOU'RE ENTHUSIASTIC ABOUT THIS JOB.
AFTER ALL, IN A WAY IT'S BECAUSE OF ME THAT YOU GOT IT.

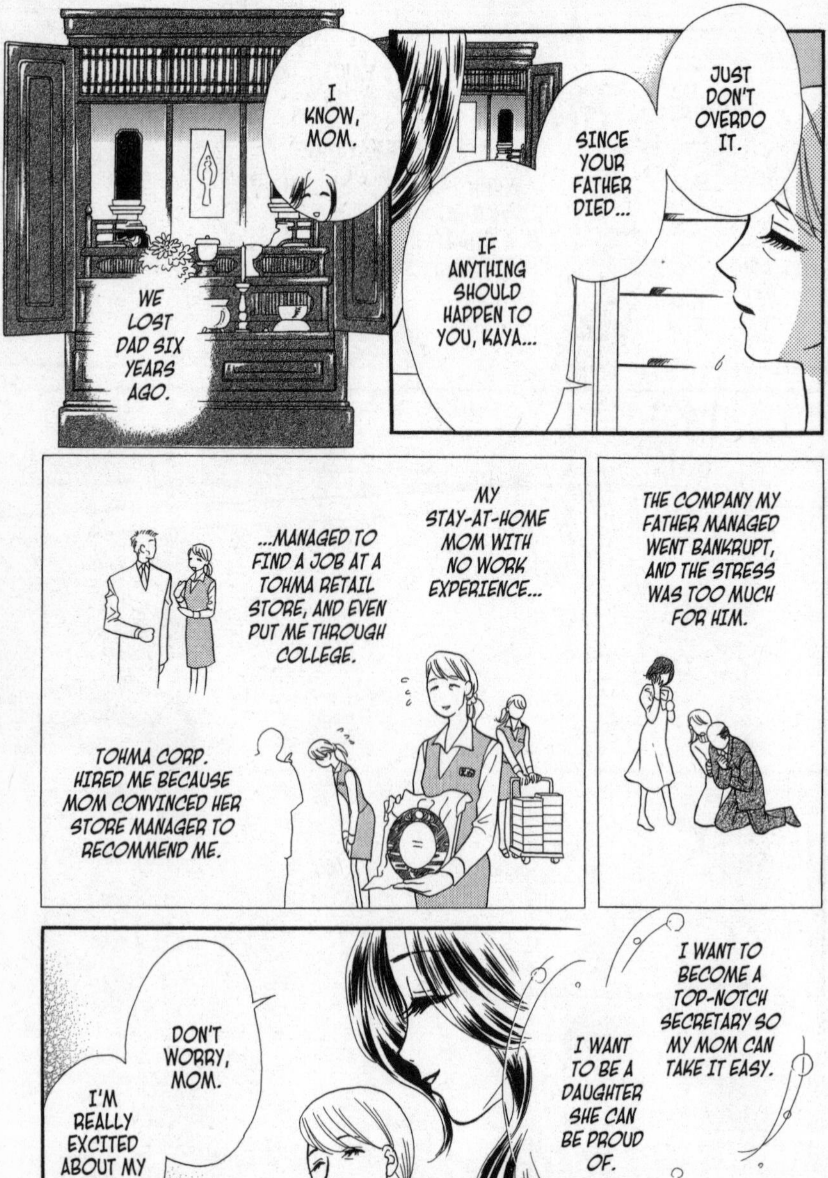
JUST DON'T OVERDO IT.
SINCE YOUR FATHER DIED...
IF ANYTHING SHOULD HAPPEN TO YOU, KAYA...
I KNOW, MOM.
WE LOST DAD SIX YEARS AGO.
THE COMPANY MY FATHER MANAGED WENT BANKRUPT, AND THE STRESS WAS TOO MUCH FOR HIM.
MY STAY-AT-HOME MOM WITH NO WORK EXPERIENCE...
...MANAGED TO FIND A JOB AT A TOHMA RETAIL STORE, AND EVEN PUT ME THROUGH COLLEGE.
TOHMA CORP. HIRED ME BECAUSE MOM CONVINCED HER STORE MANAGER TO RECOMMEND ME.
I WANT TO BECOME A TOP-NOTCH SECRETARY SO MY MOM CAN TAKE IT EASY.
I WANT TO BE A DAUGHTER SHE CAN BE PROUD OF.
DON'T WORRY, MOM.
I'M REALLY EXCITED ABOUT MY JOB.

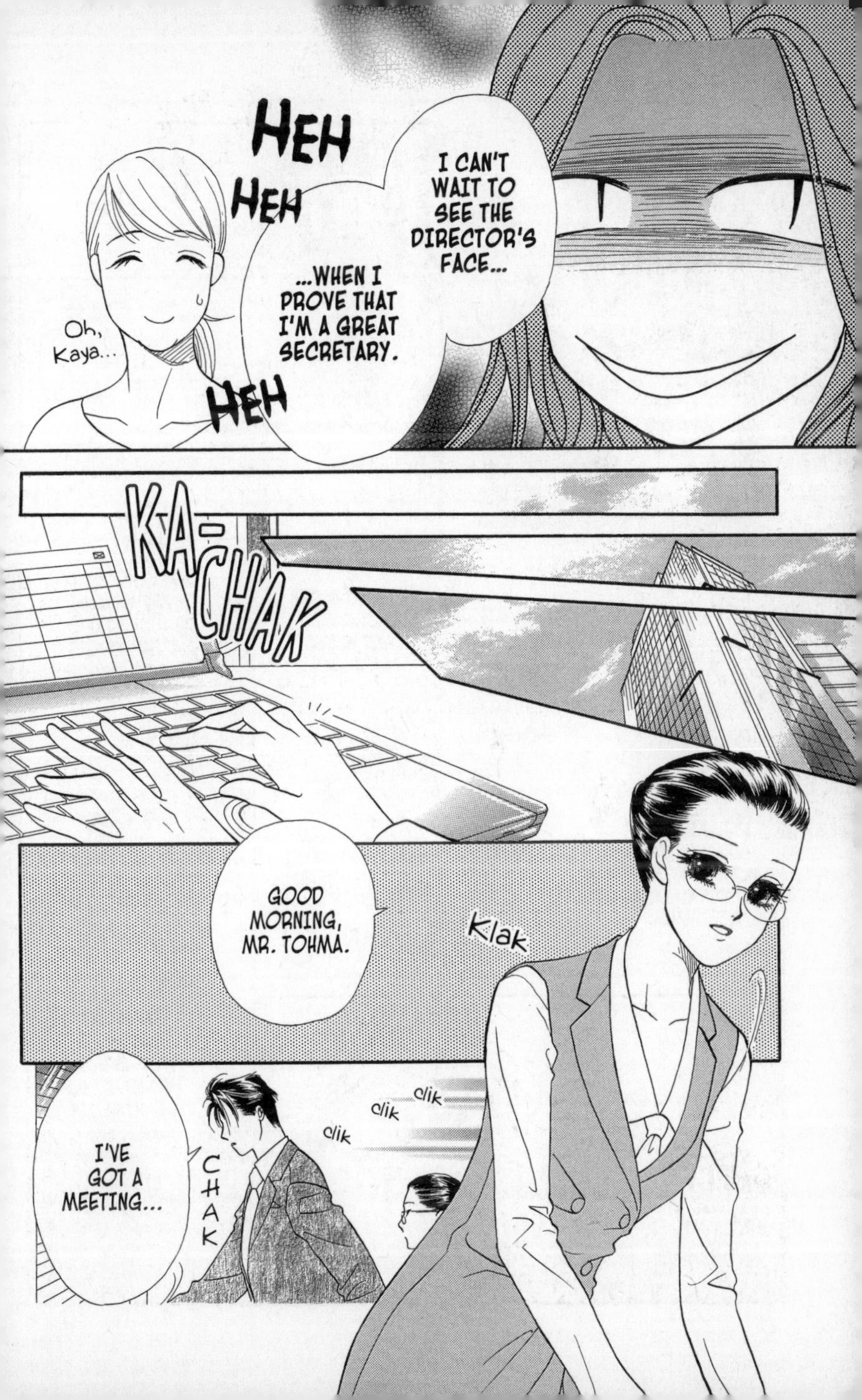
I CAN'T WAIT TO SEE THE DIRECTOR'S FACE...
...WHEN I PROVE THAT I'M A GREAT SECRETARY.
HEH
HEH
HEH
Oh, Kaya...
KA-CHAK
Klak
GOOD MORNING, MR. TOHMA.
clik
clik
clik
CHAK
I'VE GOT A MEETING...

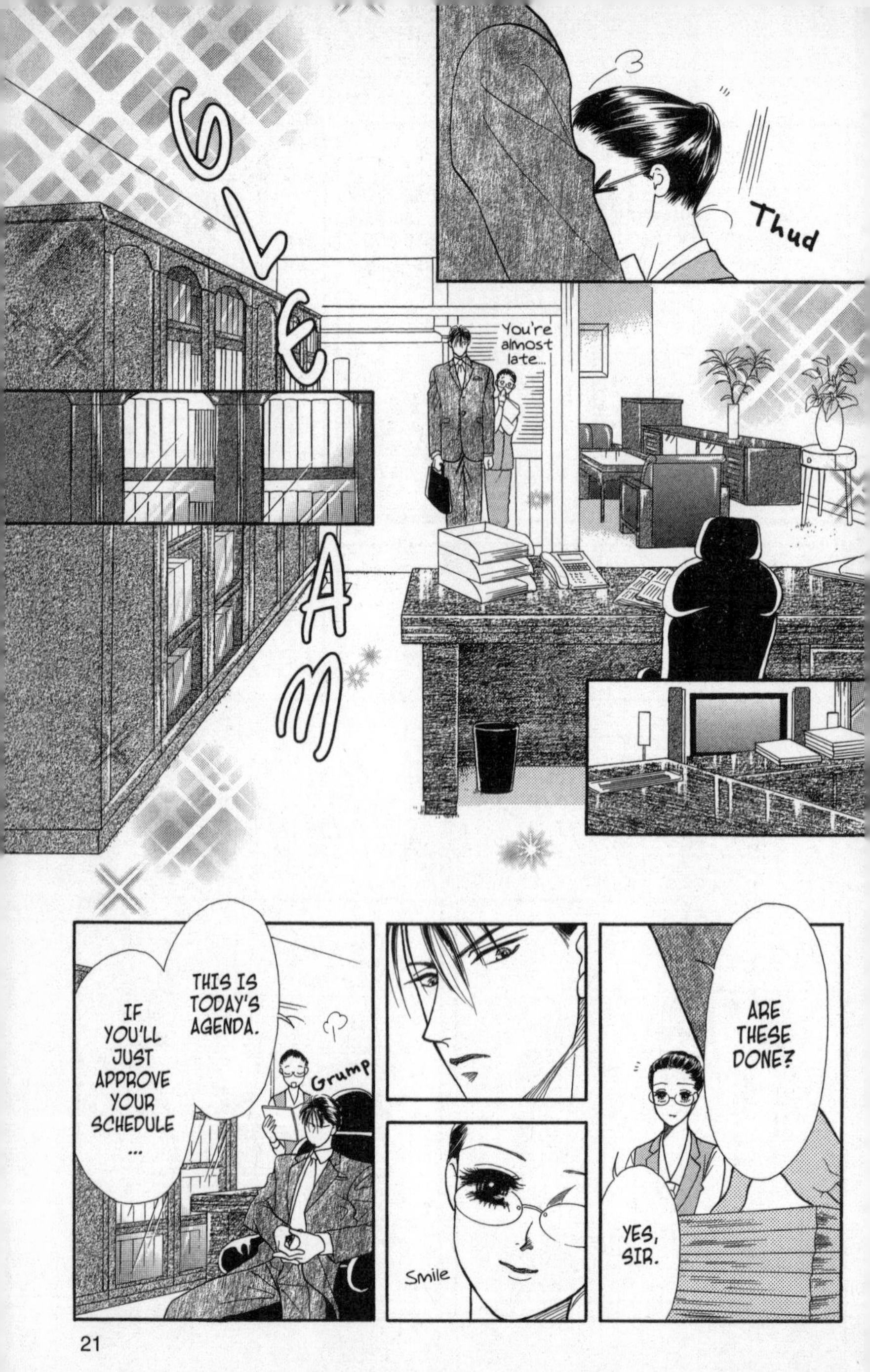
Thud
You're almost late...
GLEAM
ARE THESE DONE?
YES, SIR.
Smile
THIS IS TODAY'S AGENDA.
IF YOU'LL JUST APPROVE YOUR SCHEDULE ...
Grump

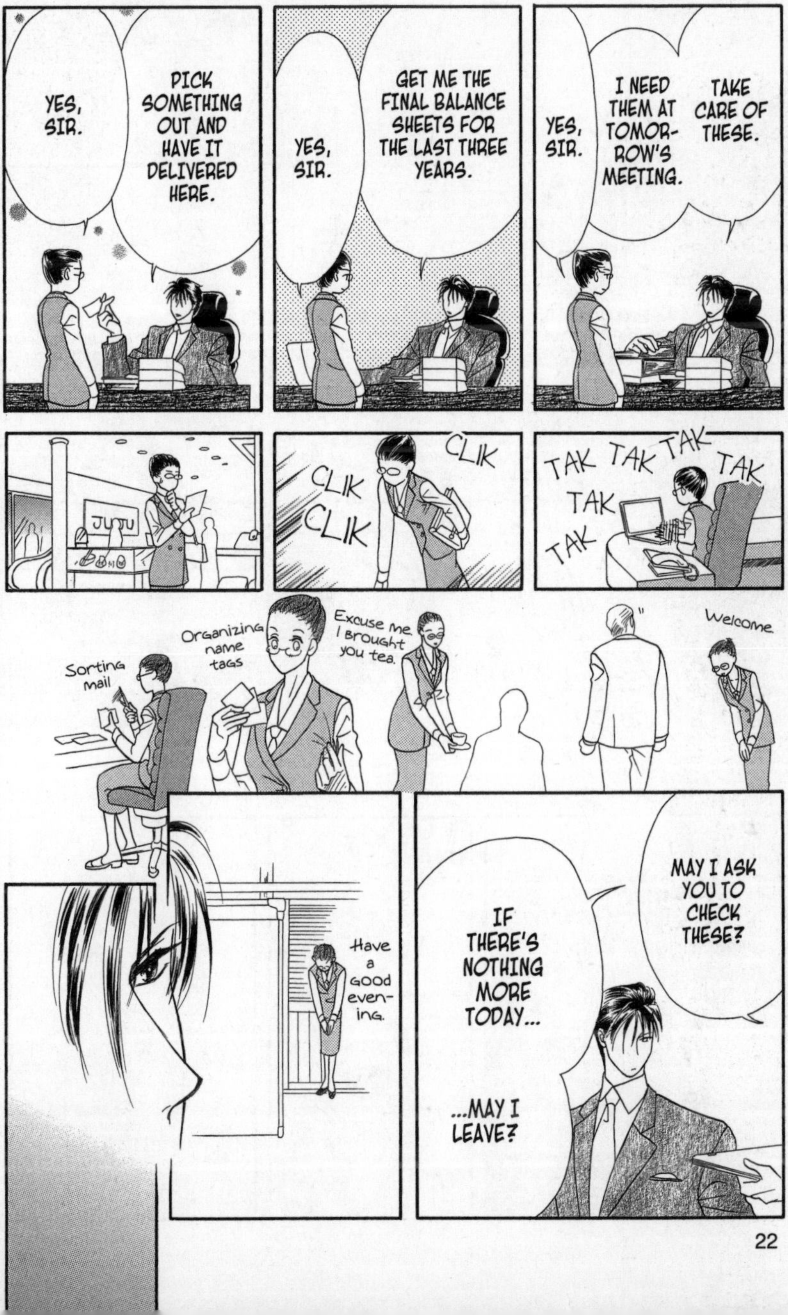
TAKE CARE OF THESE.
I NEED THEM AT TOMOR-ROW'S MEETING.
YES, SIR.
GET ME THE FINAL BALANCE SHEETS FOR THE LAST THREE YEARS.
YES, SIR.
PICK SOMETHING OUT AND HAVE IT DELIVERED HERE.
YES, SIR.
TAK TAK TAK TAK TAK TAK
CLIK CLIK CLIK
JUJU
Welcome.
Excuse me. I brought you tea.
Organizing name tags
Sorting mail
MAY I ASK YOU TO CHECK THESE?
IF THERE'S NOTHING MORE TODAY...
...MAY I LEAVE?
Have a good even-ing.

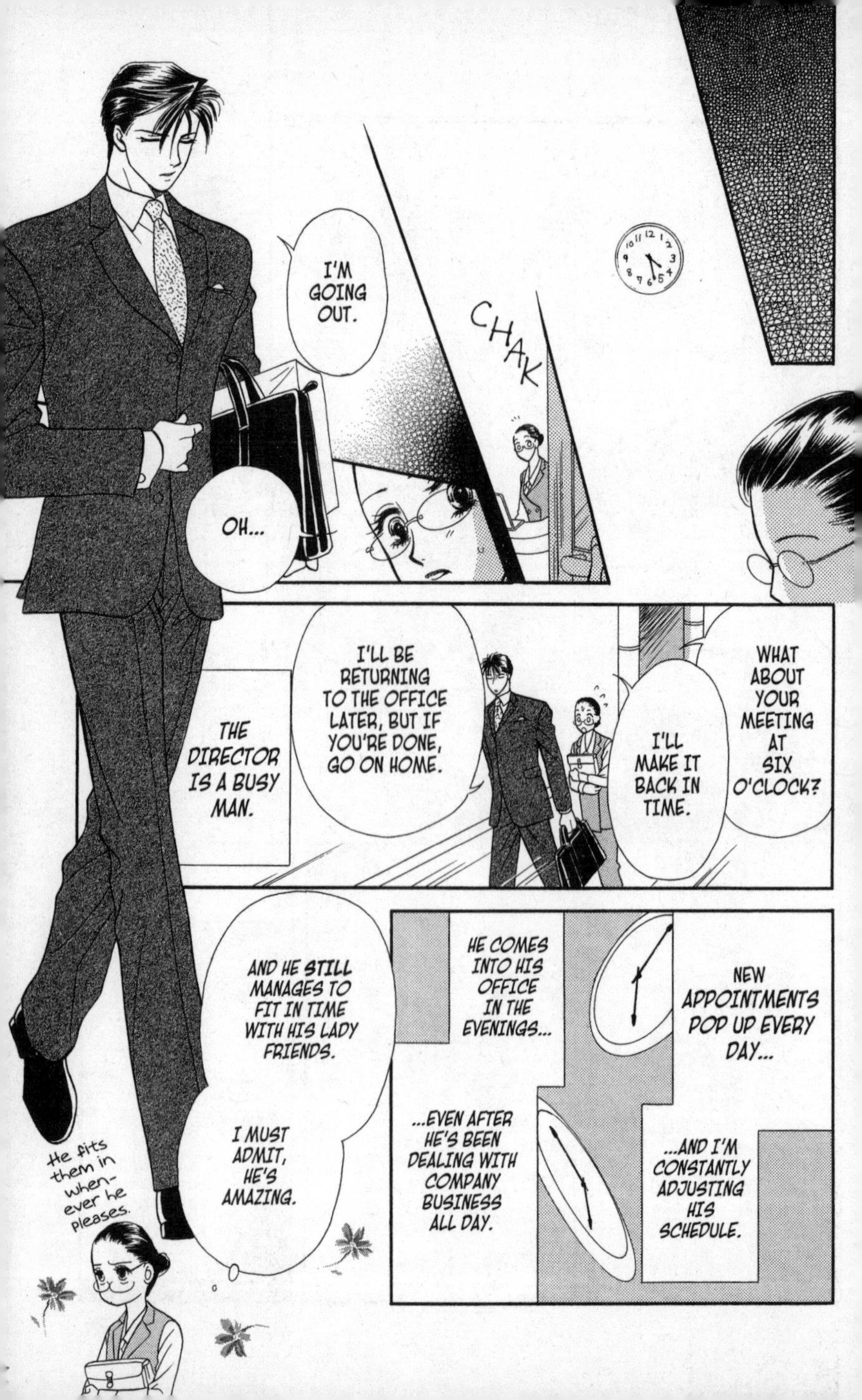
CHAK
I'M GOING OUT.
OH...
WHAT ABOUT YOUR MEETING AT SIX O'CLOCK?
I'LL MAKE IT BACK IN TIME.
I'LL BE RETURNING TO THE OFFICE LATER, BUT IF YOU'RE DONE, GO ON HOME.
THE DIRECTOR IS A BUSY MAN.
NEW APPOINTMENTS POP UP EVERY DAY...
HE COMES INTO HIS OFFICE IN THE EVENINGS...
...AND I'M CONSTANTLY ADJUSTING HIS SCHEDULE.
...EVEN AFTER HE'S BEEN DEALING WITH COMPANY BUSINESS ALL DAY.
AND HE STILL MANAGES TO FIT IN TIME WITH HIS LADY FRIENDS.
I MUST ADMIT, HE'S AMAZING.
He fits them in whenever he pleases.

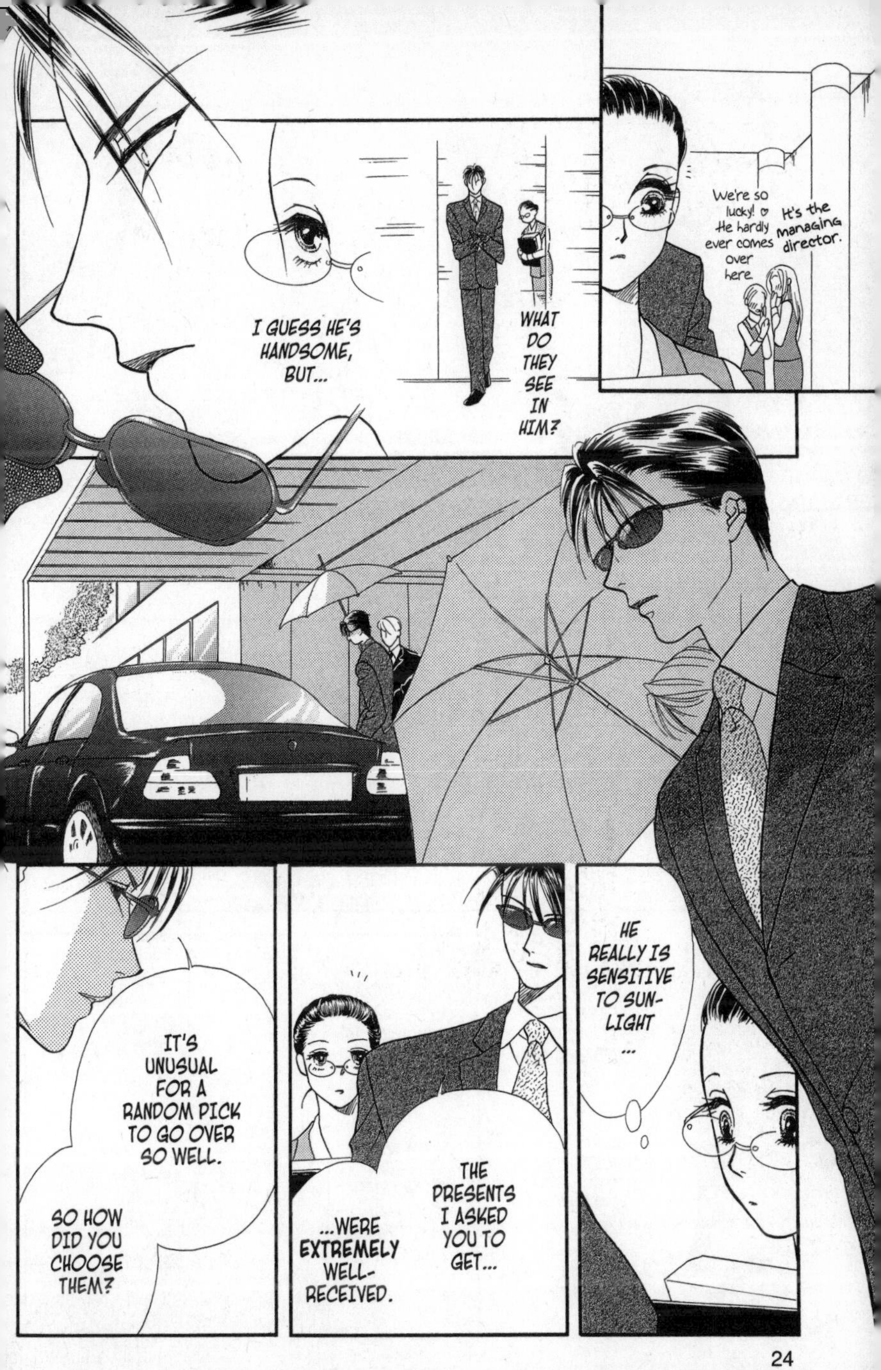
It's the managing director.
We're so lucky! ♡ He hardly ever comes over here.
WHAT DO THEY SEE IN HIM?
I GUESS HE'S HANDSOME, BUT...
HE REALLY IS SENSITIVE TO SUN-LIGHT ...
THE PRESENTS I ASKED YOU TO GET...
...WERE EXTREMELY WELL-RECEIVED.
IT'S UNUSUAL FOR A RANDOM PICK TO GO OVER SO WELL.
SO HOW DID YOU CHOOSE THEM?

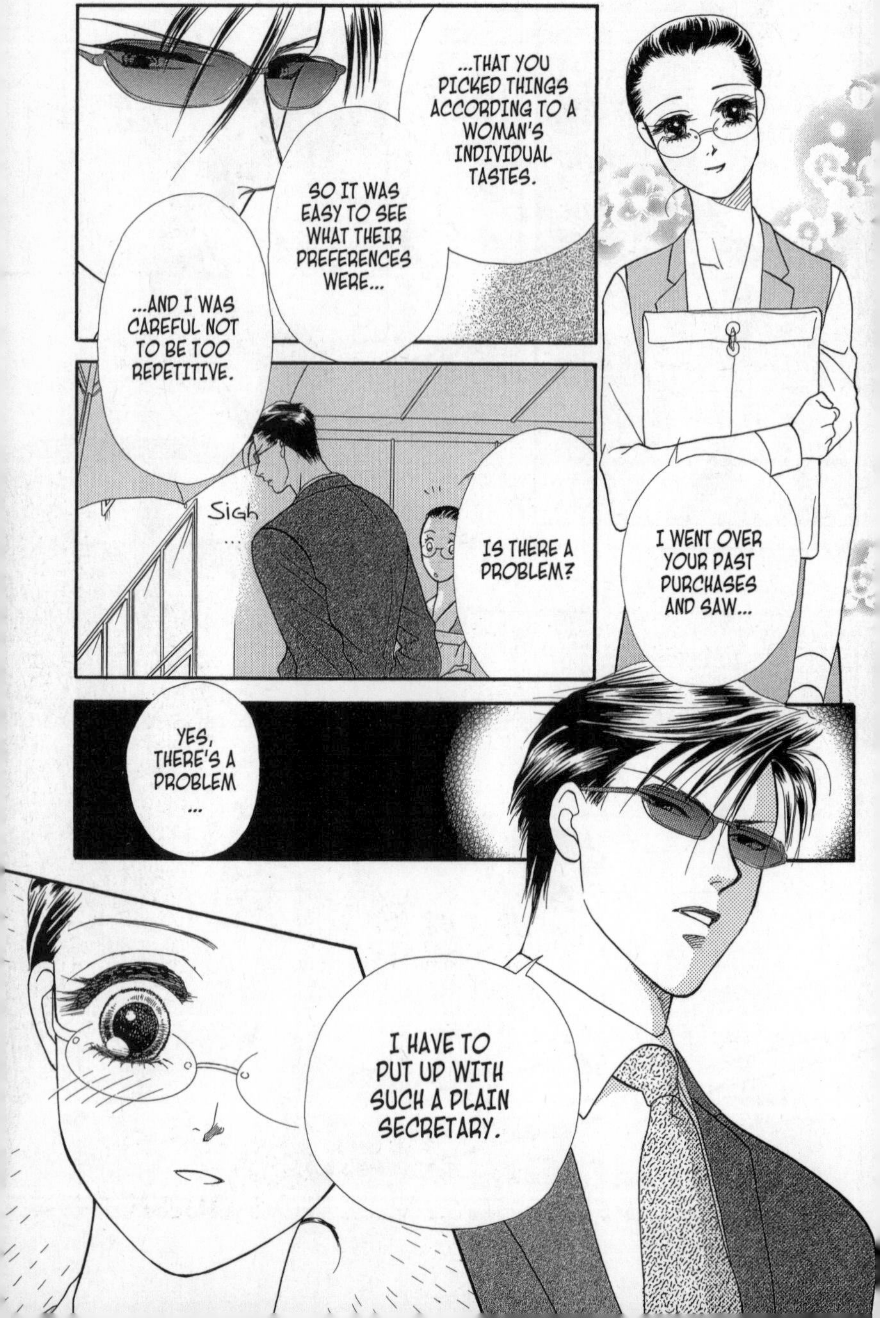
I WENT OVER YOUR PAST PURCHASES AND SAW...
...THAT YOU PICKED THINGS ACCORDING TO A WOMAN'S INDIVIDUAL TASTES.
SO IT WAS EASY TO SEE WHAT THEIR PREFERENCES WERE...
...AND I WAS CAREFUL NOT TO BE TOO REPETITIVE.
IS THERE A PROBLEM?
Sigh...
YES, THERE'S A PROBLEM...
I HAVE TO PUT UP WITH SUCH A PLAIN SECRETARY.

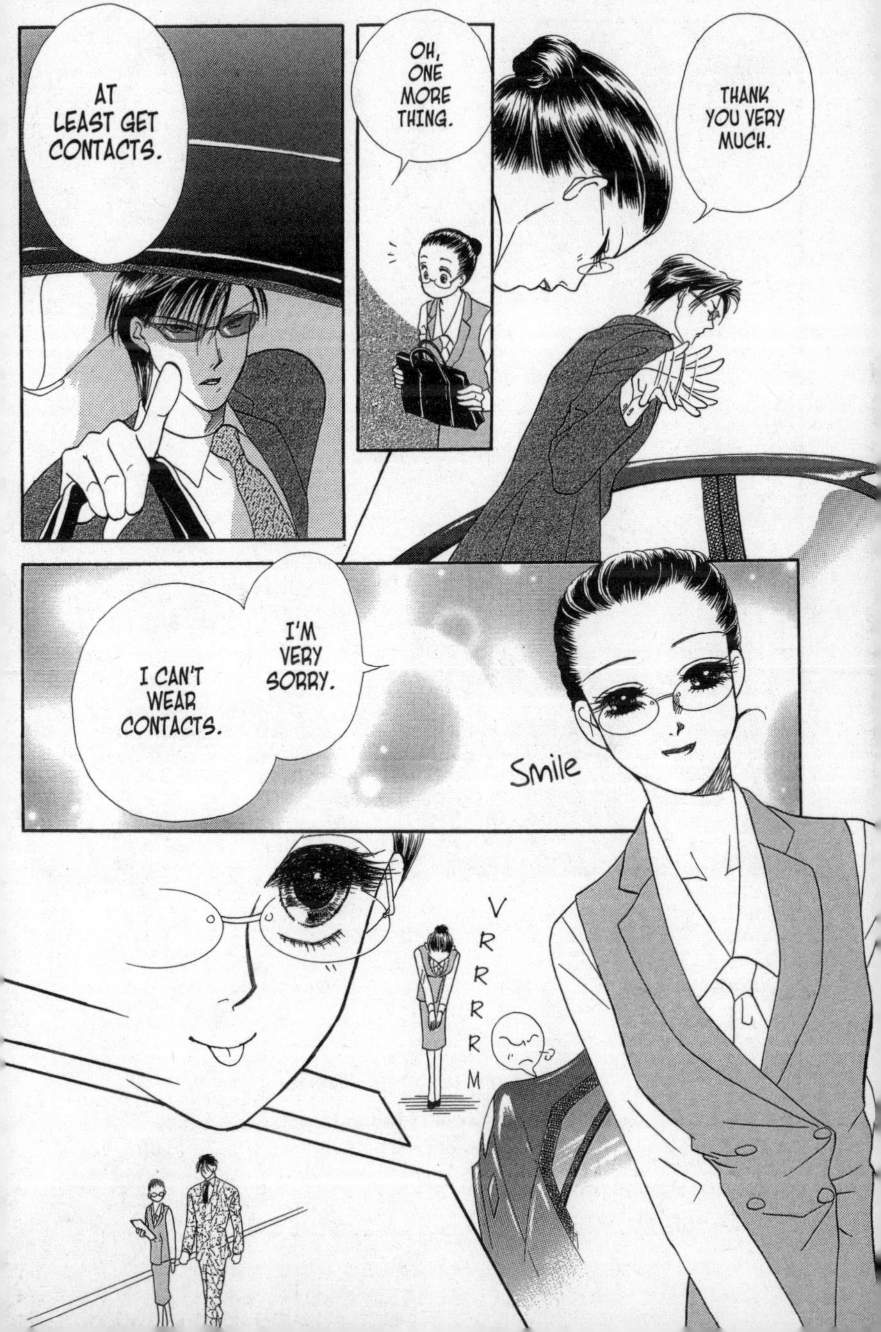
THANK YOU VERY MUCH.
OH, ONE MORE THING.
AT LEAST GET CONTACTS.
I'M VERY SORRY.
I CAN'T WEAR CONTACTS.
Smile
VRRRRM

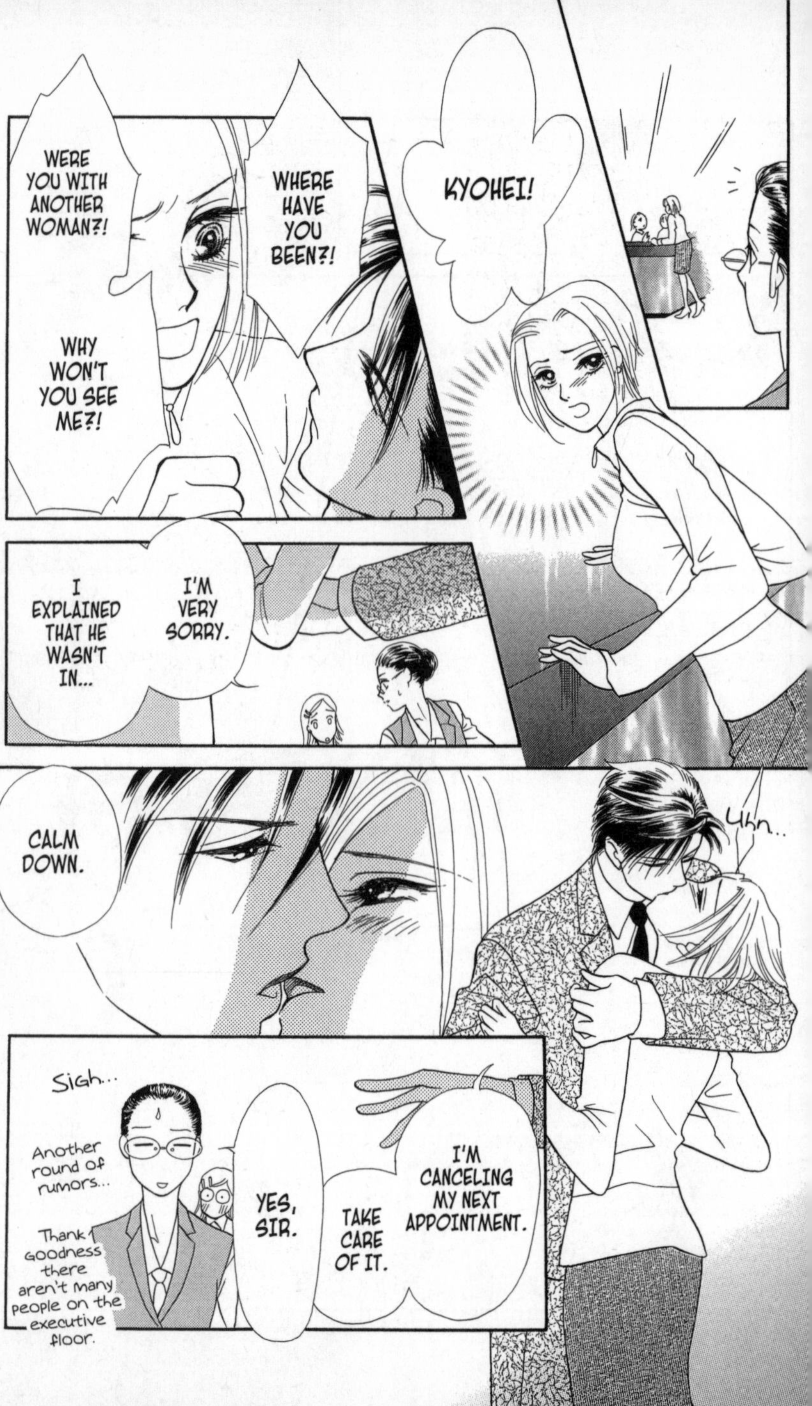
KYOHEI!
WHERE HAVE YOU BEEN?!
WERE YOU WITH ANOTHER WOMAN?!
WHY WON'T YOU SEE ME?!
I'M VERY SORRY.
I EXPLAINED THAT HE WASN'T IN...
Uhn...
CALM DOWN.
I'M CANCELING MY NEXT APPOINTMENT.
TAKE CARE OF IT.
YES, SIR.
Sigh...
Another round of rumors...
Thank goodness there aren't many people on the executive floor.

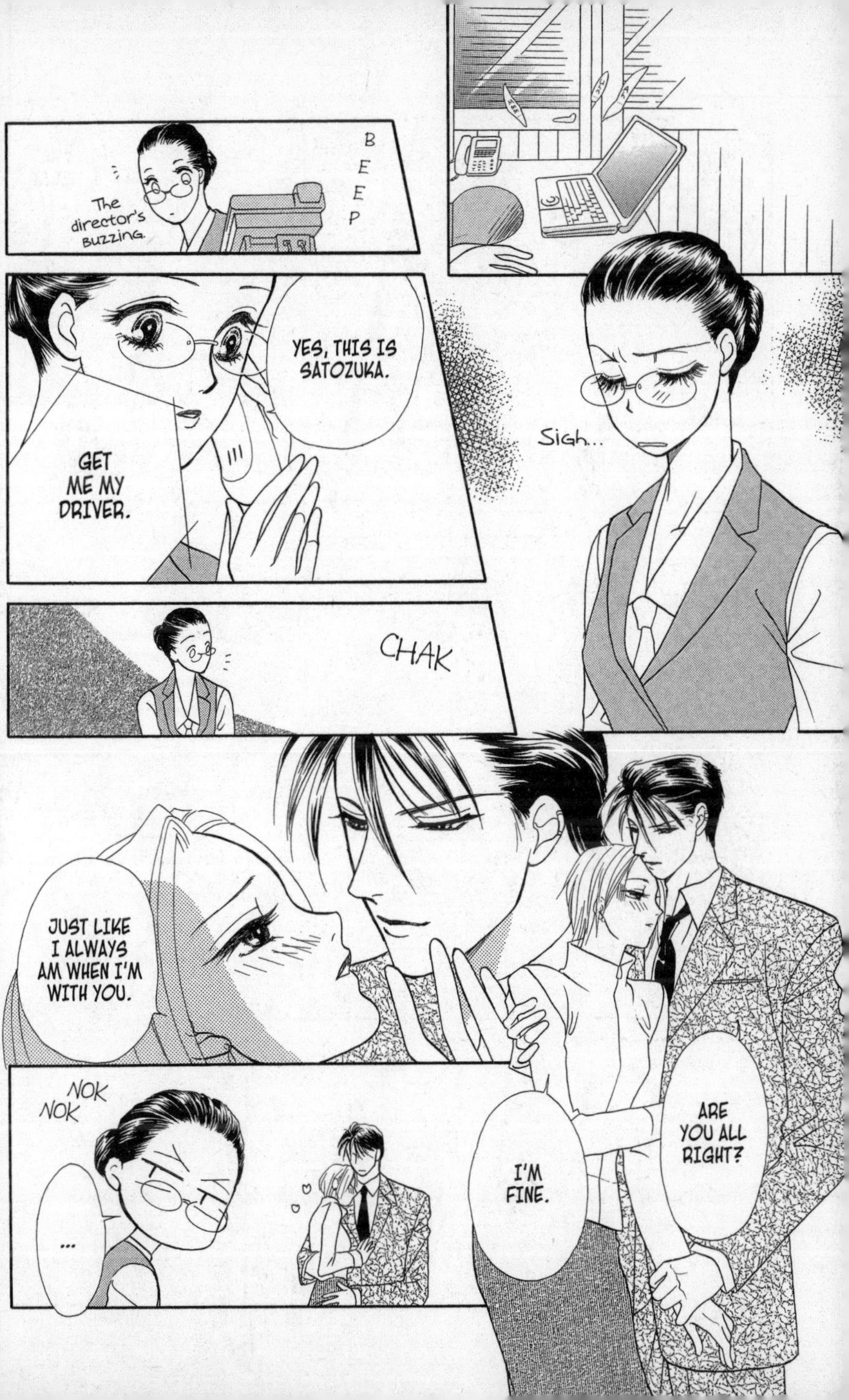

The director's buzzing.
BEEP
Sigh...
YES, THIS IS SATOZUKA.
GET ME MY DRIVER.
CHAK
ARE YOU ALL RIGHT?
I'M FINE.
JUST LIKE I ALWAYS AM WHEN I'M WITH YOU.
NOK NOK
...

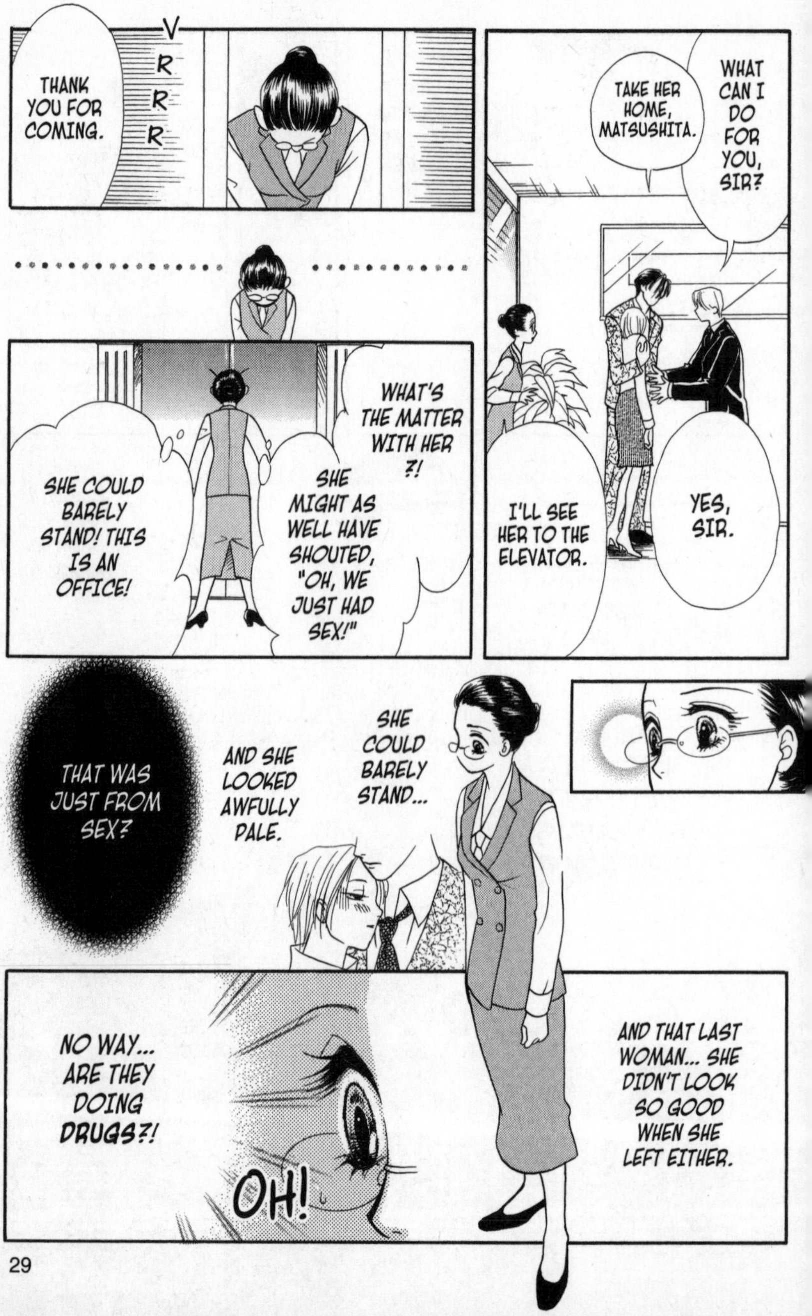
WHAT CAN I DO FOR YOU, SIR?
TAKE HER HOME, MATSUSHITA.
YES, SIR.
I'LL SEE HER TO THE ELEVATOR.
VRRR
THANK YOU FOR COMING.
WHAT'S THE MATTER WITH HER?!
SHE MIGHT AS WELL HAVE SHOUTED, "OH, WE JUST HAD SEX!"
SHE COULD BARELY STAND! THIS IS AN OFFICE!
SHE COULD BARELY STAND...
AND SHE LOOKED AWFULLY PALE.
THAT WAS JUST FROM SEX?
AND THAT LAST WOMAN... SHE DIDN'T LOOK SO GOOD WHEN SHE LEFT EITHER.
OH!
NO WAY... ARE THEY DOING **DRUGS**?!

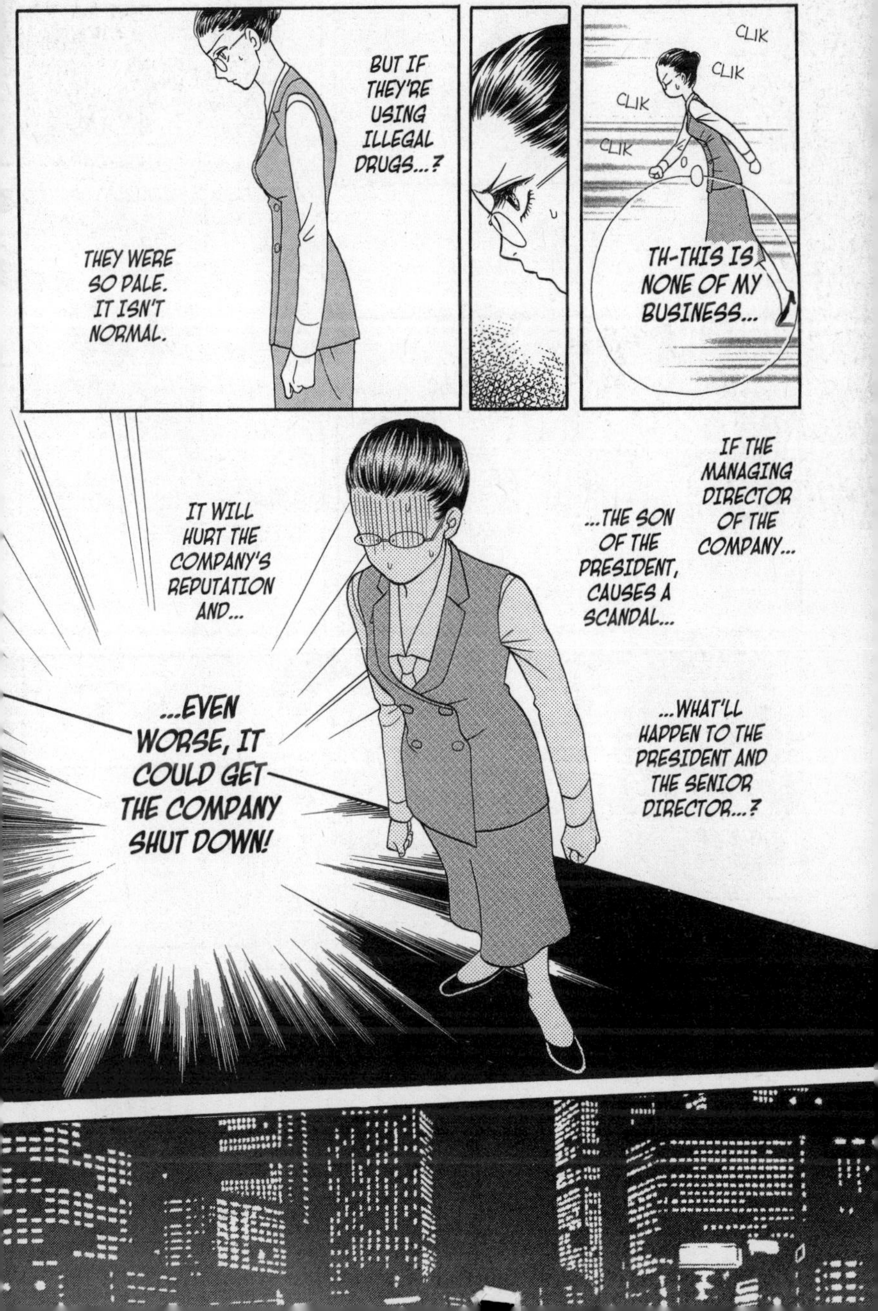
CLIK
CLIK
CLIK
CLIK
TH-THIS IS NONE OF MY BUSINESS...
BUT IF THEY'RE USING ILLEGAL DRUGS...?
THEY WERE SO PALE. IT ISN'T NORMAL.
IF THE MANAGING DIRECTOR OF THE COMPANY...
...THE SON OF THE PRESIDENT, CAUSES A SCANDAL...
IT WILL HURT THE COMPANY'S REPUTATION AND...
...WHAT'LL HAPPEN TO THE PRESIDENT AND THE SENIOR DIRECTOR...?
...EVEN WORSE, IT COULD GET THE COMPANY SHUT DOWN!

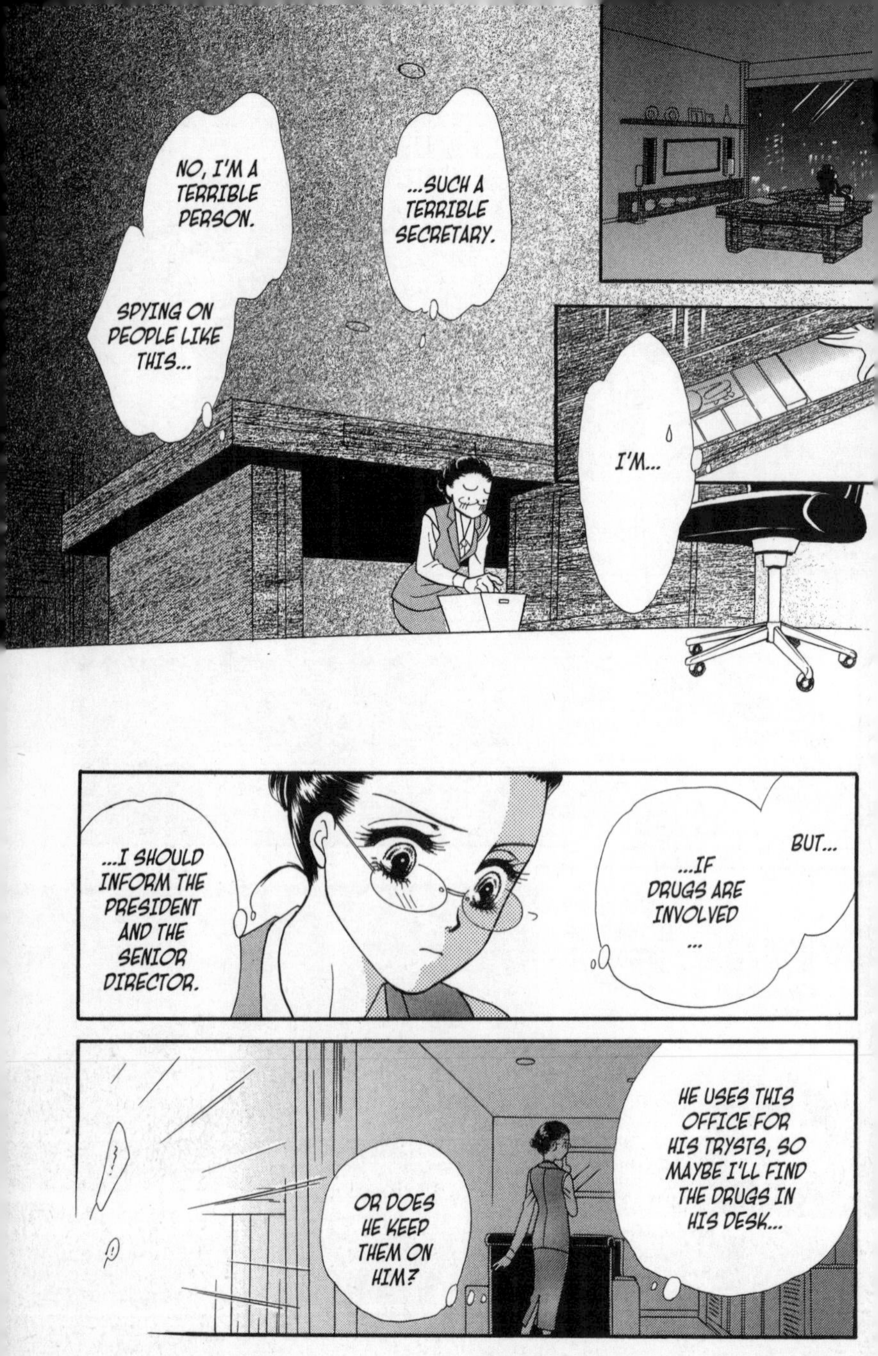
I'M...
...SUCH A TERRIBLE SECRETARY.
NO, I'M A TERRIBLE PERSON.
SPYING ON PEOPLE LIKE THIS...
BUT...
...IF DRUGS ARE INVOLVED ...
...I SHOULD INFORM THE PRESIDENT AND THE SENIOR DIRECTOR.
HE USES THIS OFFICE FOR HIS TRYSTS, SO MAYBE I'LL FIND THE DRUGS IN HIS DESK...
OR DOES HE KEEP THEM ON HIM?

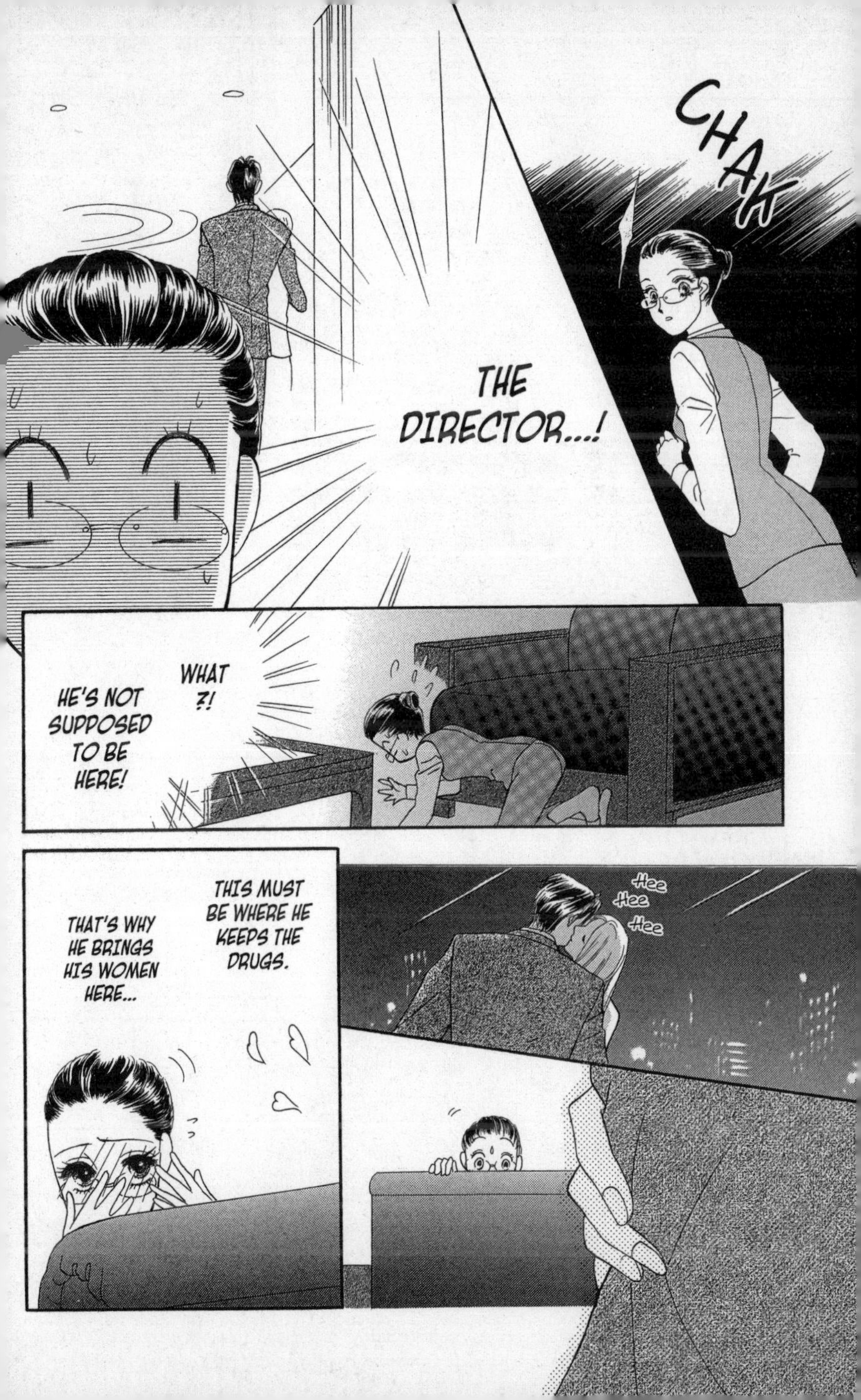
CHAK
THE DIRECTOR...!
WHAT?!
HE'S NOT SUPPOSED TO BE HERE!
Hee Hee Hee
THIS MUST BE WHERE HE KEEPS THE DRUGS.
THAT'S WHY HE BRINGS HIS WOMEN HERE...

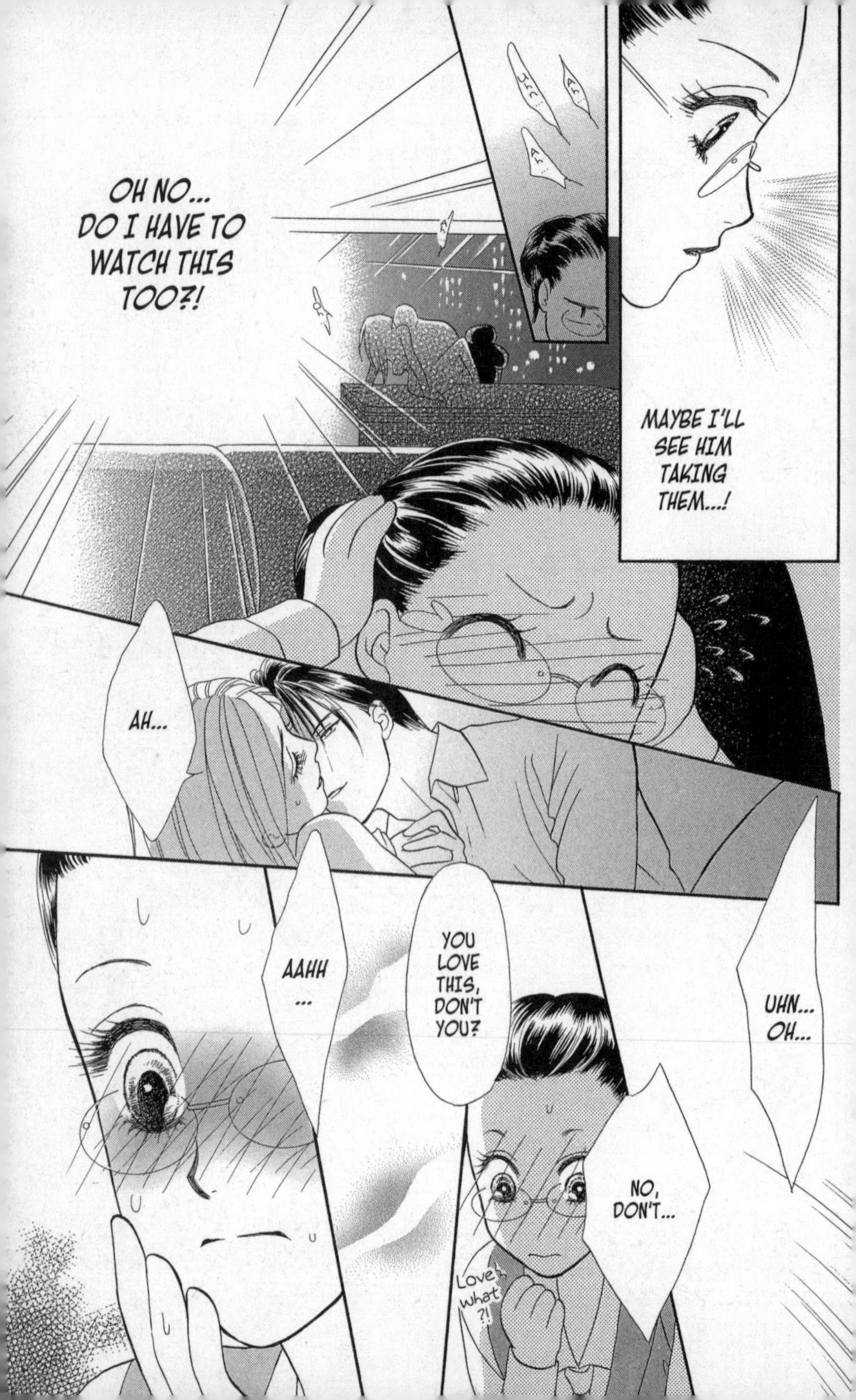
MAYBE I'LL SEE HIM TAKING THEM...!
OH NO... DO I HAVE TO WATCH THIS TOO?!
AH...
UHN... OH...
NO, DON'T...
YOU LOVE THIS, DON'T YOU?
Love what?!
AAHH ...

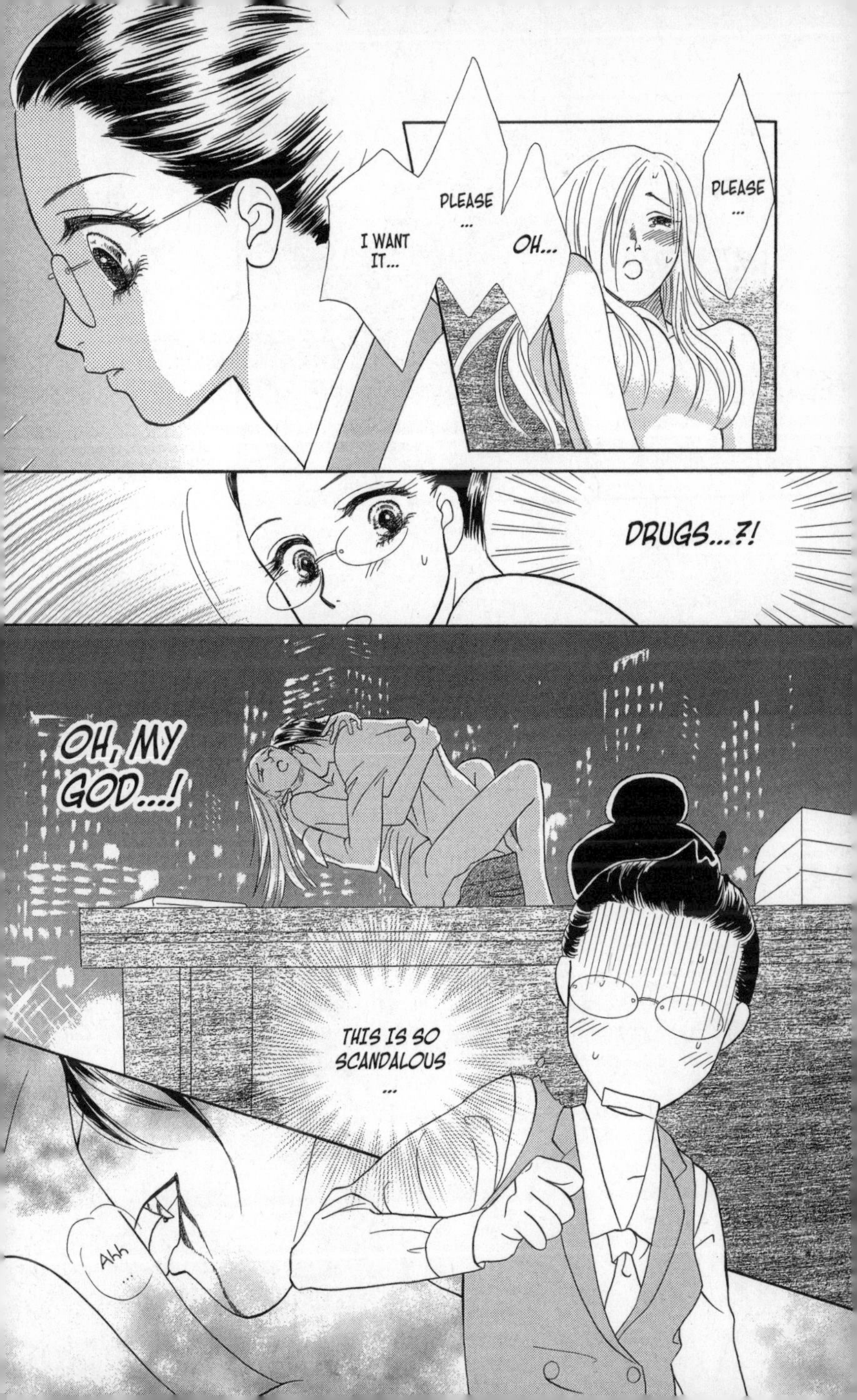
PLEASE ...
OH...
PLEASE ...
I WANT IT...
DRUGS...?!
OH, MY GOD...!
THIS IS SO SCANDALOUS ...
Ahh ...

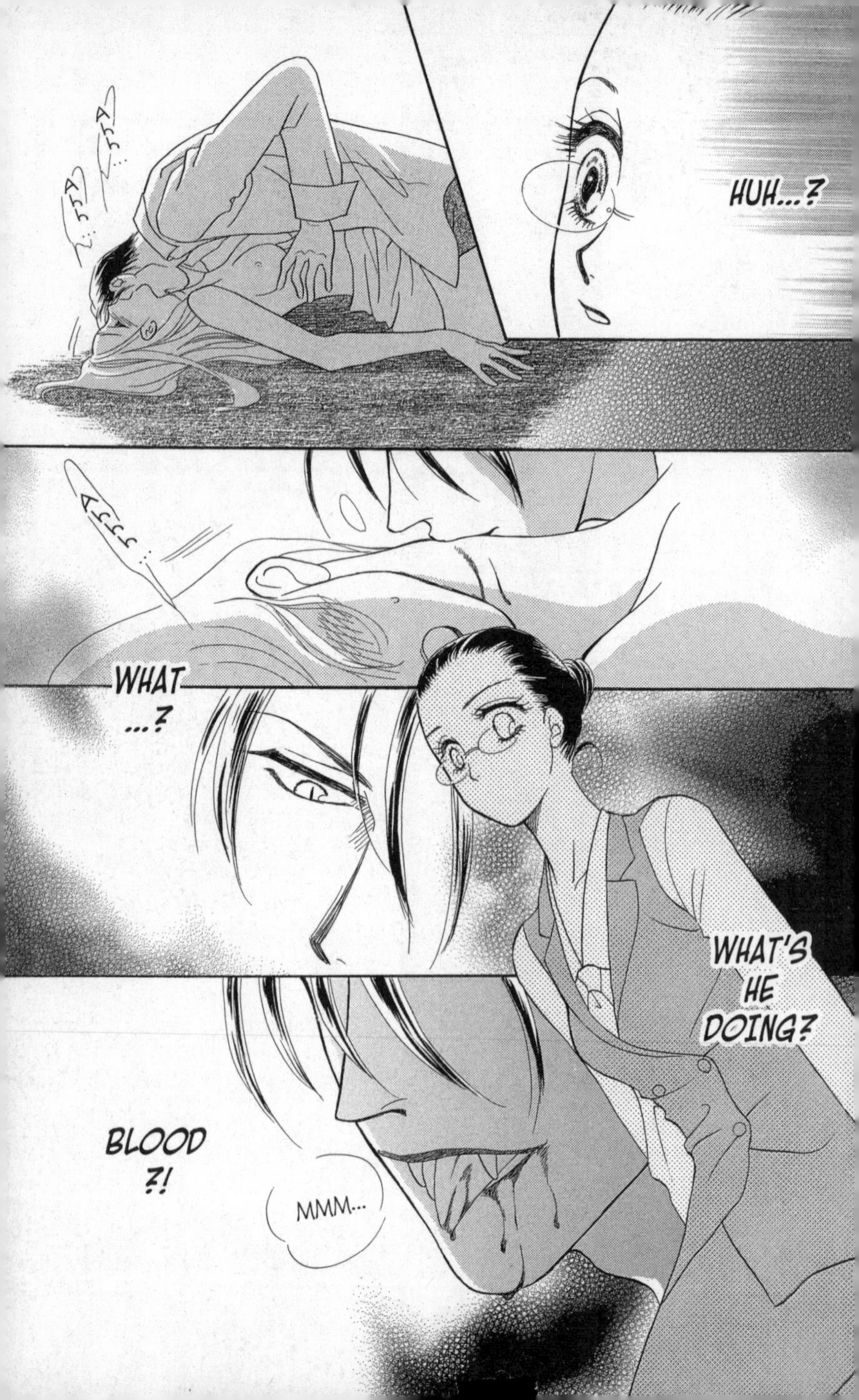
HUH...?
WHAT ...?
WHAT'S HE DOING?
BLOOD ?!
MMM...

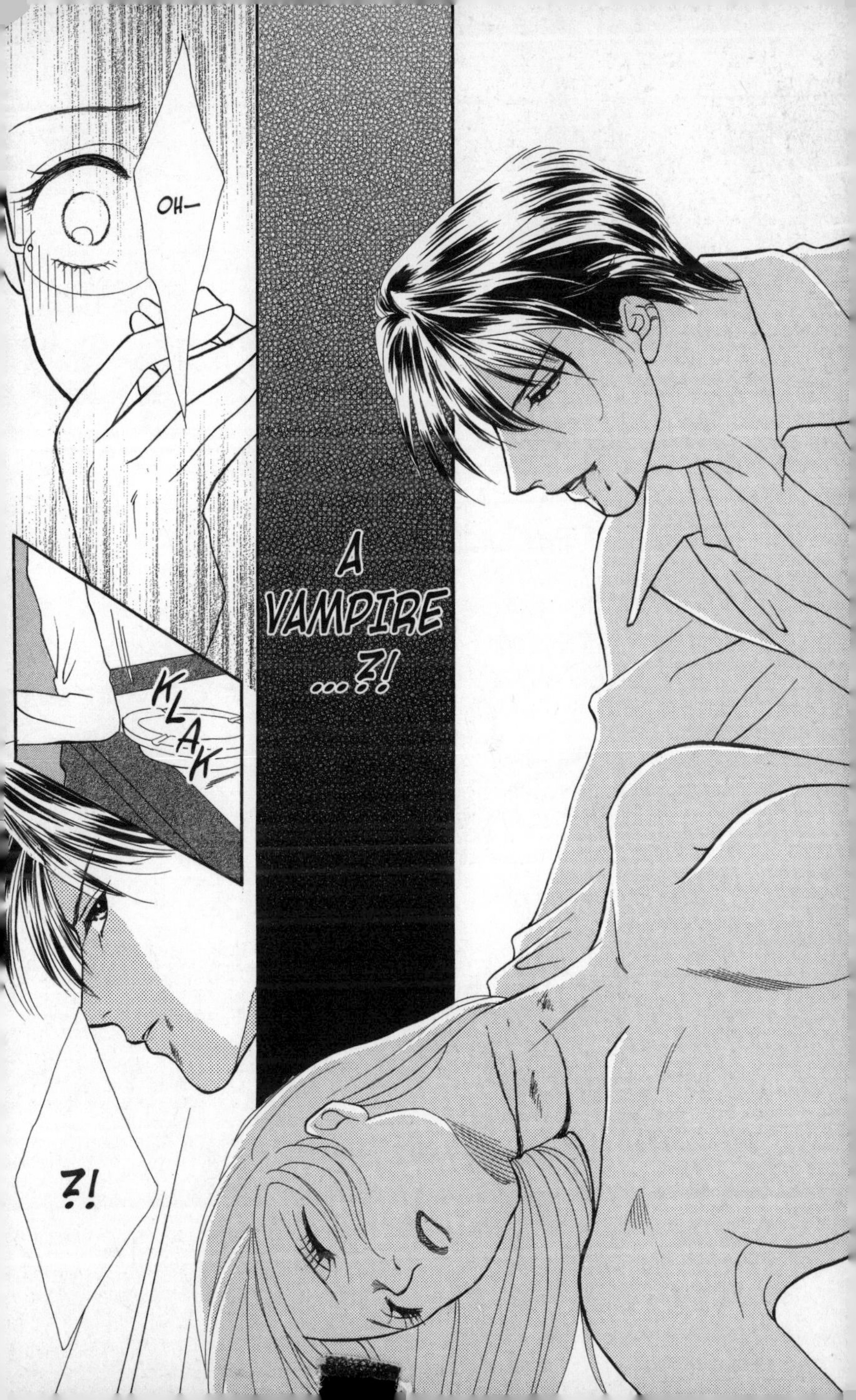
A VAMPIRE ...?!
OH—
KLAK
?!

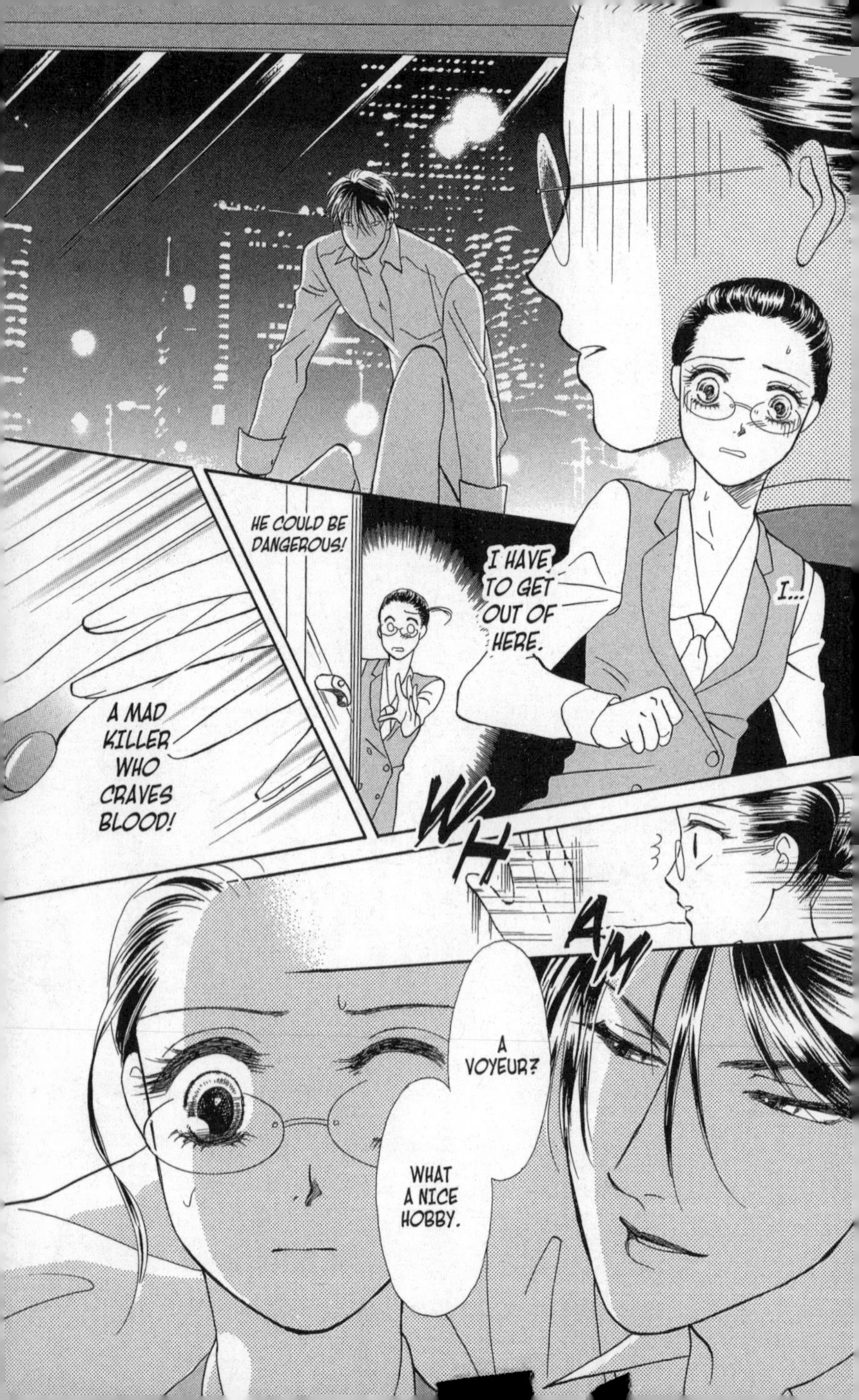
I...
I HAVE TO GET OUT OF HERE.
HE COULD BE DANGEROUS!
A MAD KILLER WHO CRAVES BLOOD!
WHAM
A VOYEUR?
WHAT A NICE HOBBY.

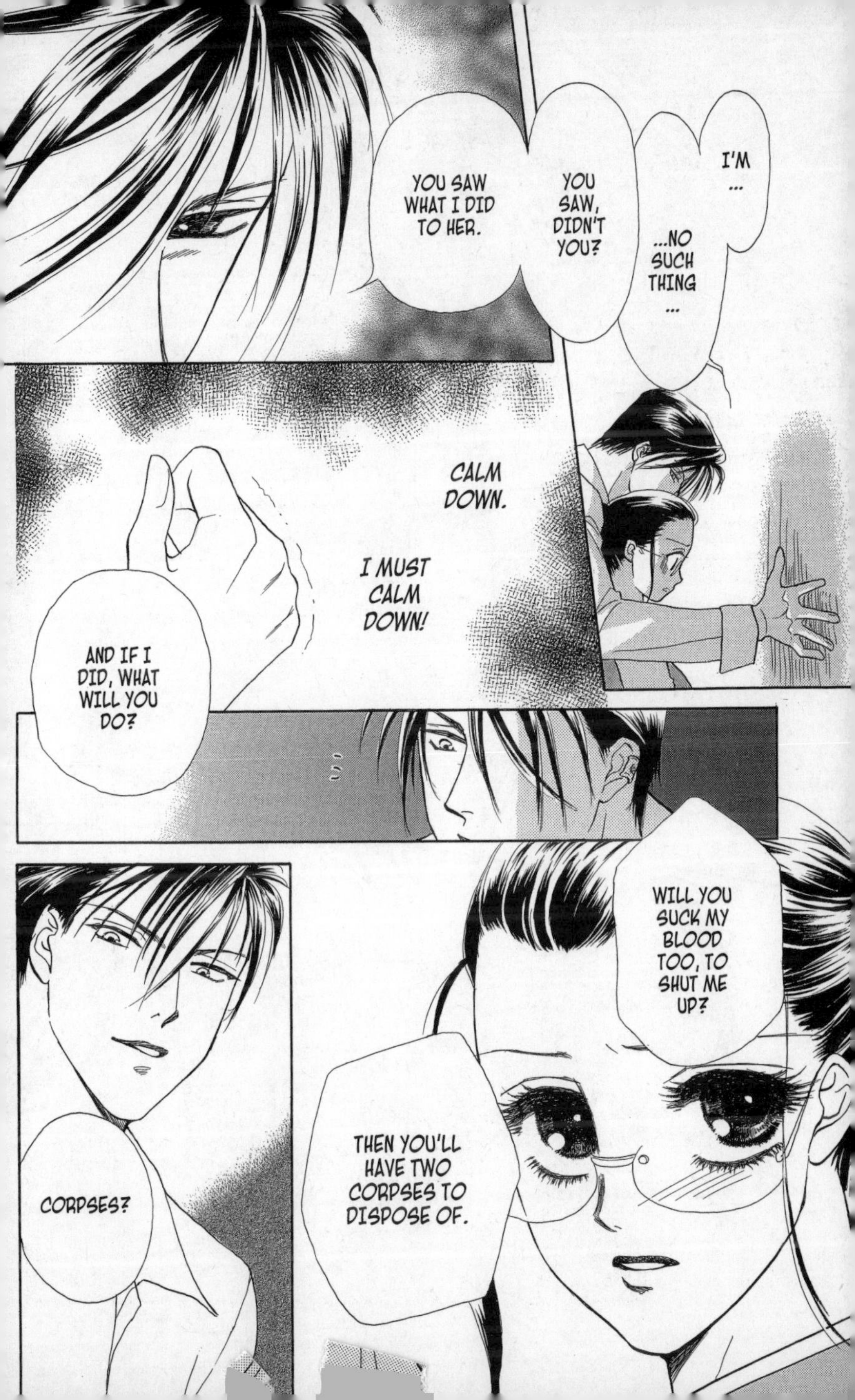
YOU SAW, DIDN'T YOU?
YOU SAW WHAT I DID TO HER.
I'M ...
...NO SUCH THING ...
CALM DOWN.
I MUST CALM DOWN!
AND IF I DID, WHAT WILL YOU DO?
WILL YOU SUCK MY BLOOD TOO, TO SHUT ME UP?
THEN YOU'LL HAVE TWO CORPSES TO DISPOSE OF.
CORPSES?

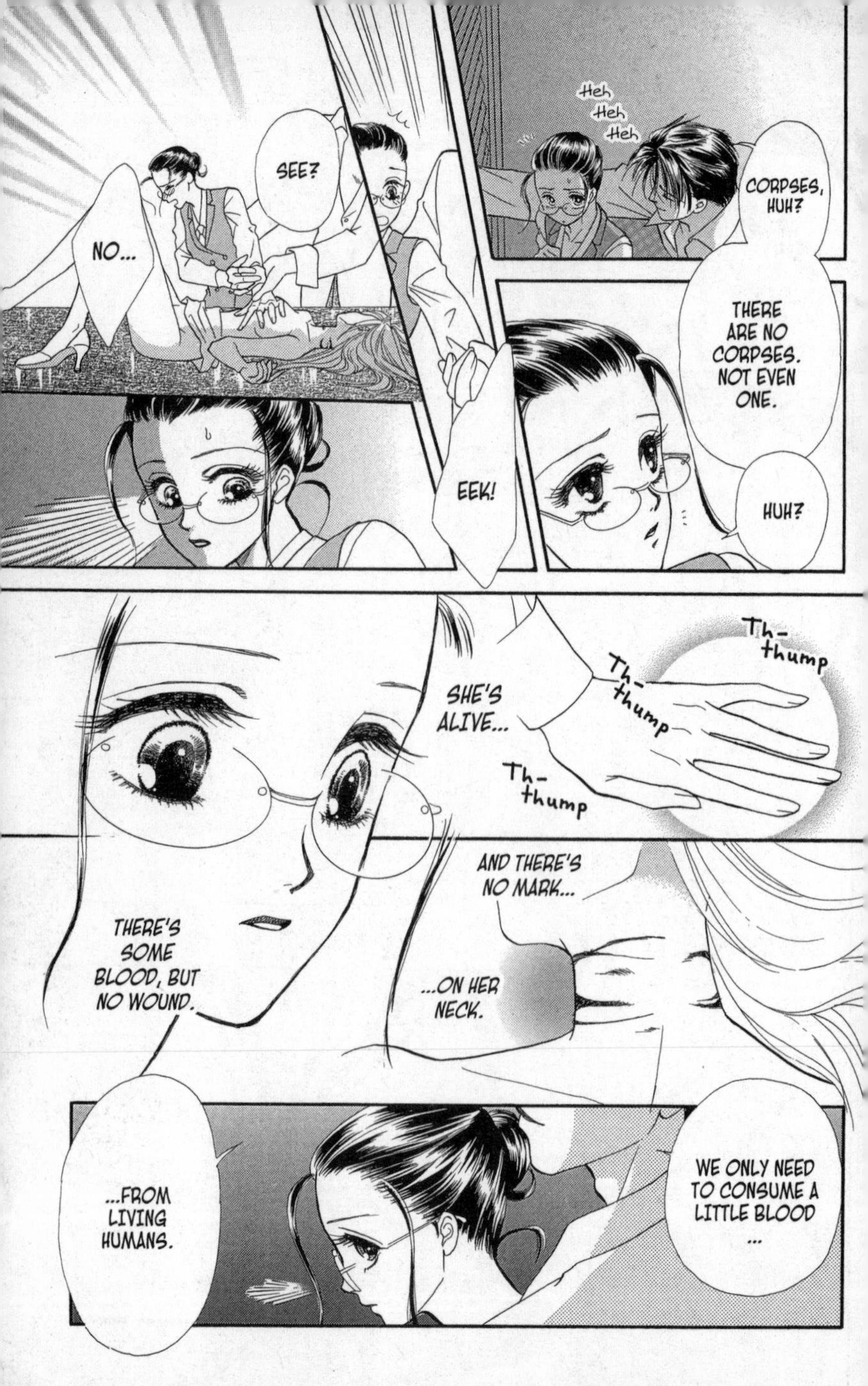
Heh Heh Heh
CORPSES, HUH?
THERE ARE NO CORPSES. NOT EVEN ONE.
HUH?
SEE?
NO...
EEK!
Th-thump
Th-thump
SHE'S ALIVE...
Th-thump
AND THERE'S NO MARK...
...ON HER NECK.
THERE'S SOME BLOOD, BUT NO WOUND.
WE ONLY NEED TO CONSUME A LITTLE BLOOD ...
...FROM LIVING HUMANS.

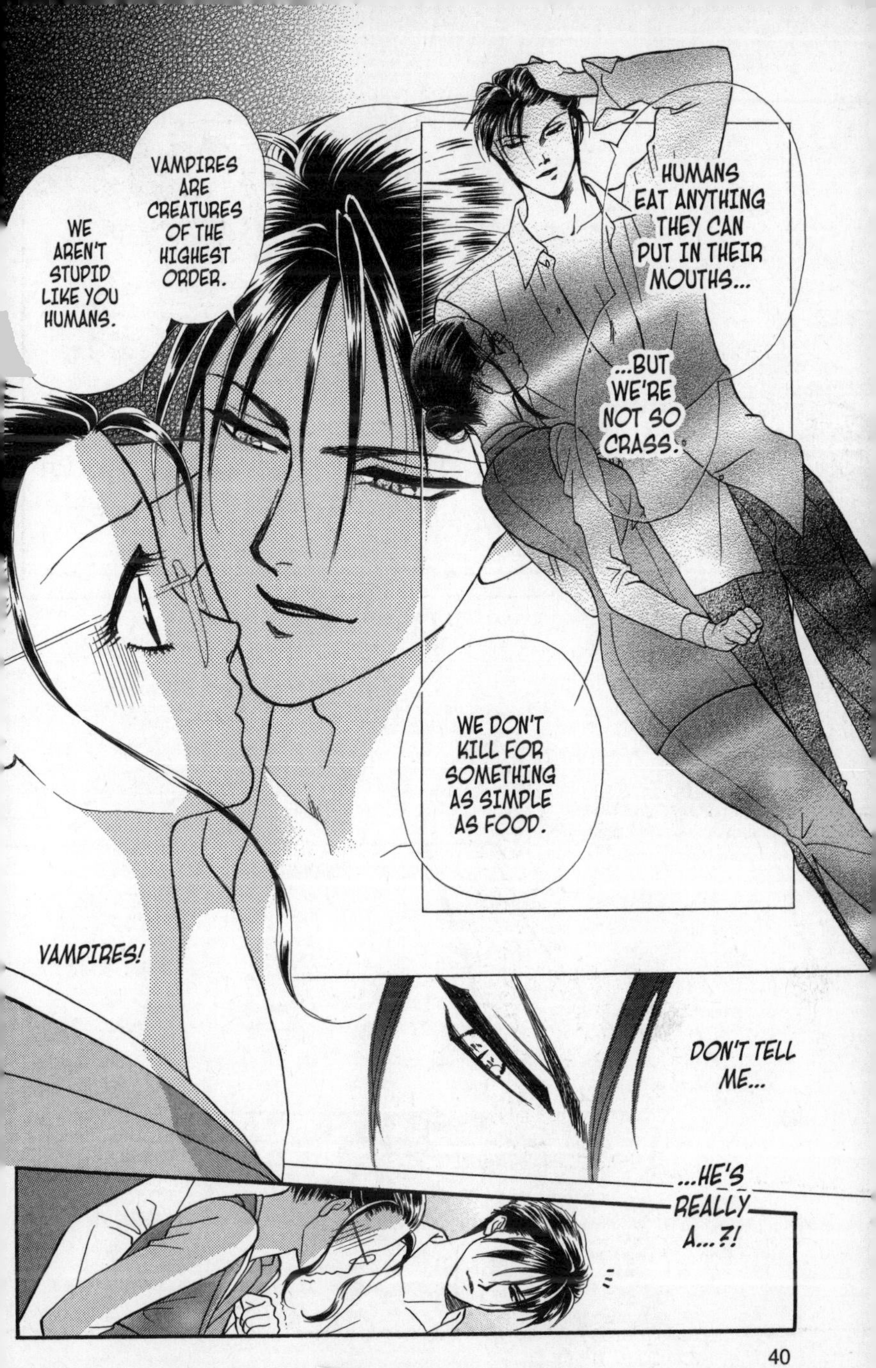
HUMANS EAT ANYTHING THEY CAN PUT IN THEIR MOUTHS...
...BUT WE'RE NOT SO CRASS.
WE DON'T KILL FOR SOMETHING AS SIMPLE AS FOOD.
VAMPIRES ARE CREATURES OF THE HIGHEST ORDER.
WE AREN'T STUPID LIKE YOU HUMANS.
VAMPIRES!
DON'T TELL ME...
...HE'S REALLY A...?!

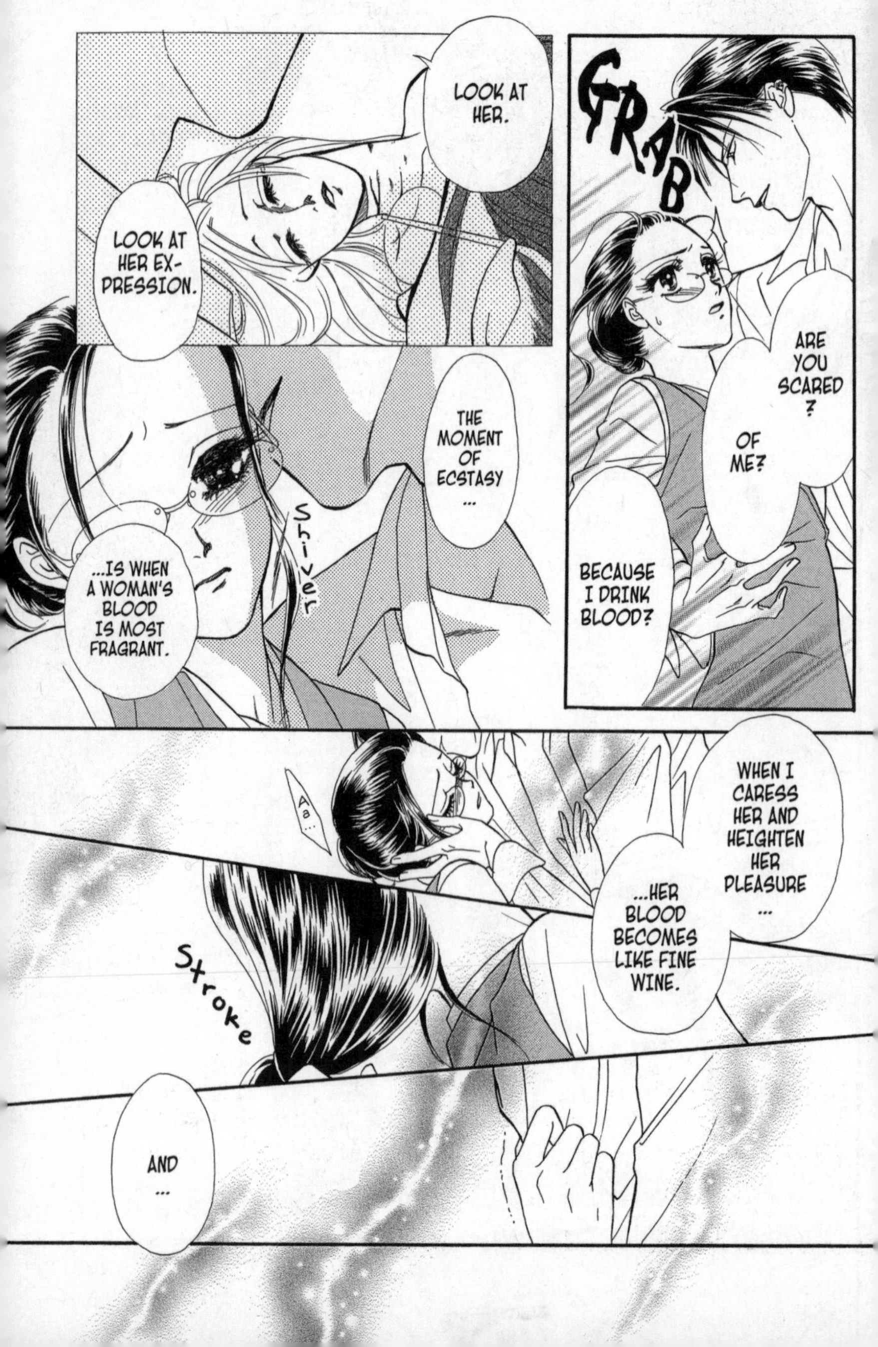
GRAB
ARE YOU SCARED?
OF ME?
BECAUSE I DRINK BLOOD?
LOOK AT HER.
LOOK AT HER EX-PRESSION.
THE MOMENT OF ECSTASY...
Shiver
...IS WHEN A WOMAN'S BLOOD IS MOST FRAGRANT.
WHEN I CARESS HER AND HEIGHTEN HER PLEASURE...
Aa...
...HER BLOOD BECOMES LIKE FINE WINE.
Stroke
AND...

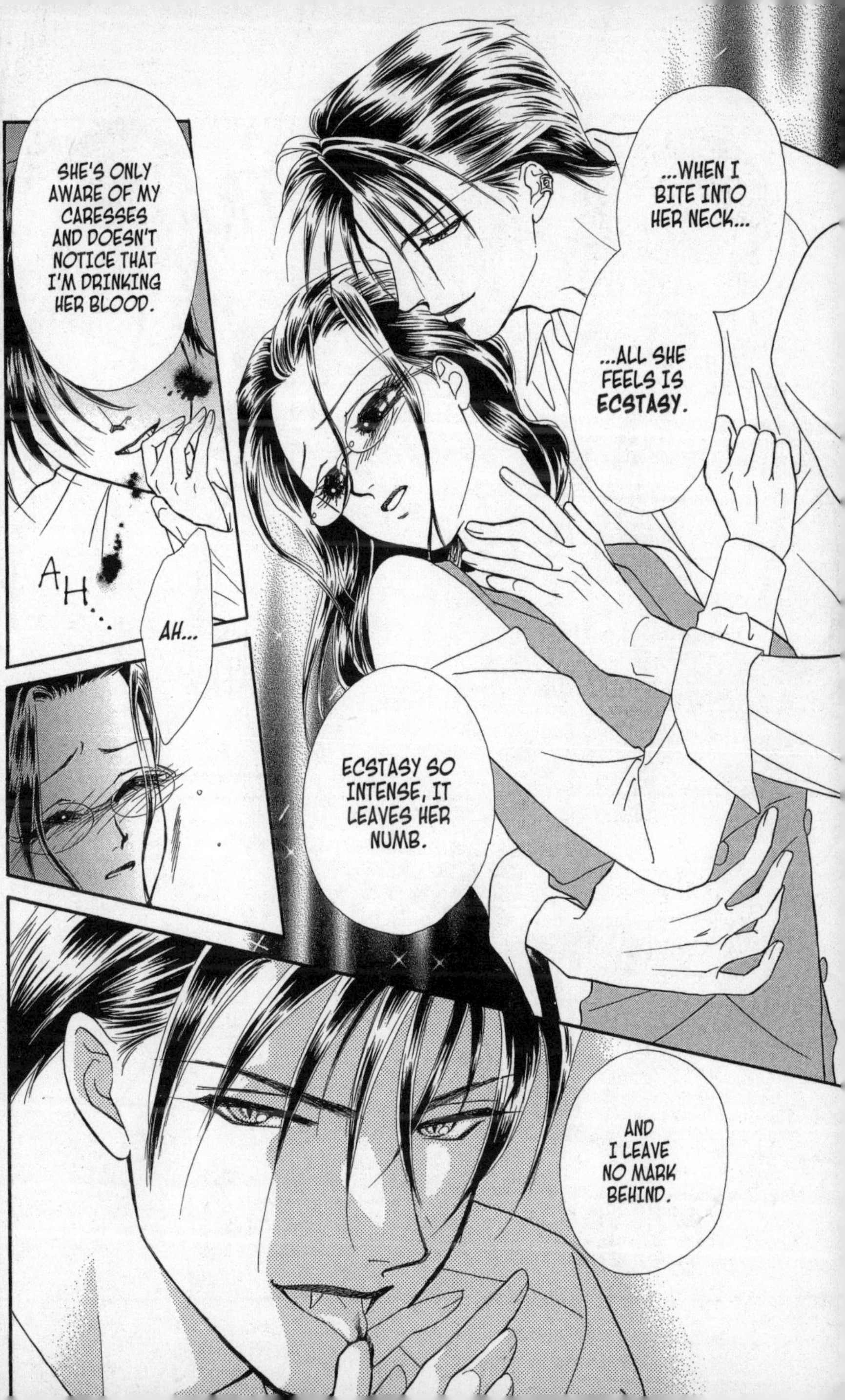
...WHEN I BITE INTO HER NECK...
...ALL SHE FEELS IS ECSTASY.
ECSTASY SO INTENSE, IT LEAVES HER NUMB.
SHE'S ONLY AWARE OF MY CARESSES AND DOESN'T NOTICE THAT I'M DRINKING HER BLOOD.
AH...
AH...
AND I LEAVE NO MARK BEHIND.

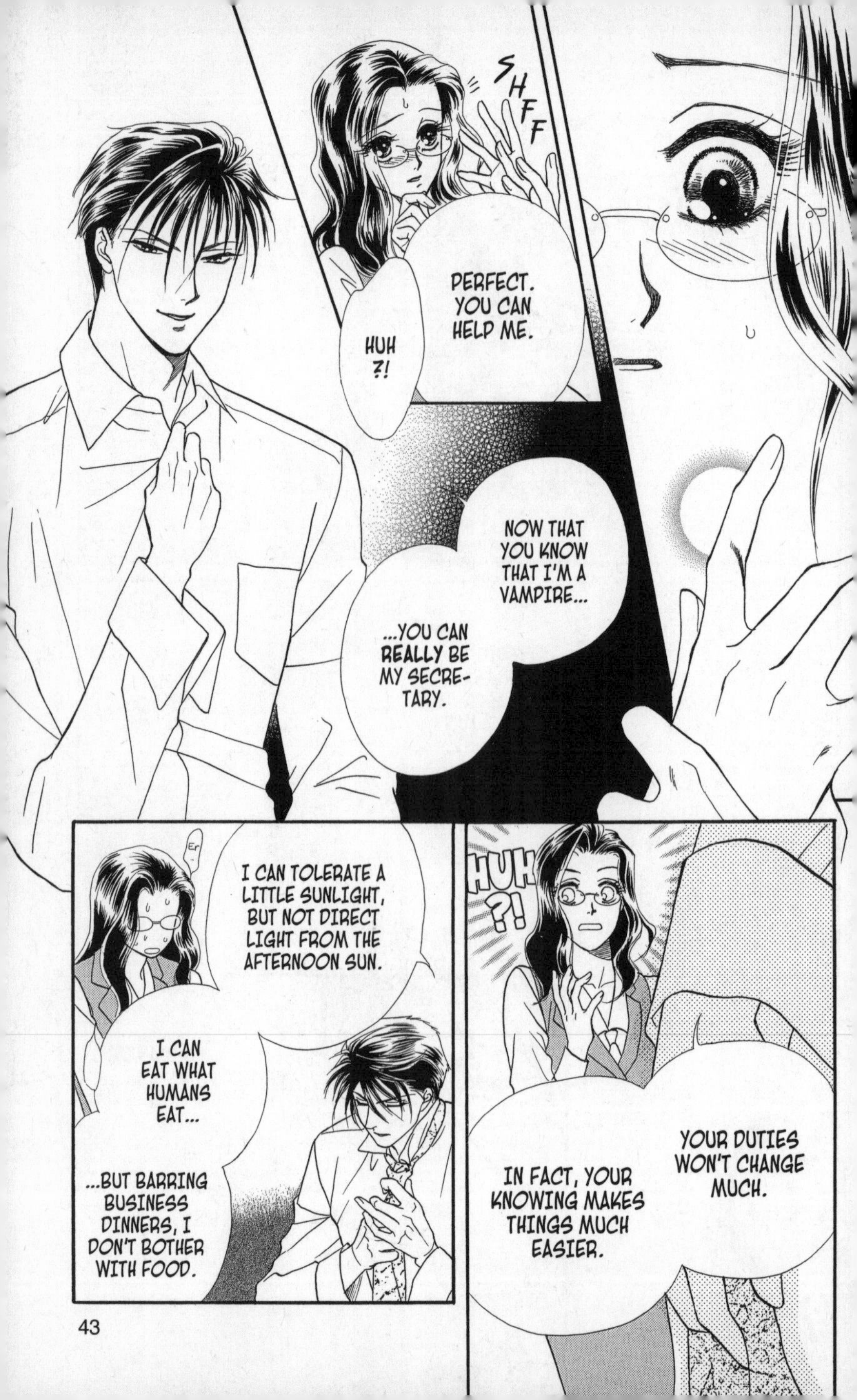
SHFF
PERFECT. YOU CAN HELP ME.
HUH?!
NOW THAT YOU KNOW THAT I'M A VAMPIRE...
...YOU CAN REALLY BE MY SECRE-TARY.
HUH?!
YOUR DUTIES WON'T CHANGE MUCH.
IN FACT, YOUR KNOWING MAKES THINGS MUCH EASIER.
Er
I CAN TOLERATE A LITTLE SUNLIGHT, BUT NOT DIRECT LIGHT FROM THE AFTERNOON SUN.
I CAN EAT WHAT HUMANS EAT...
...BUT BARRING BUSINESS DINNERS, I DON'T BOTHER WITH FOOD.

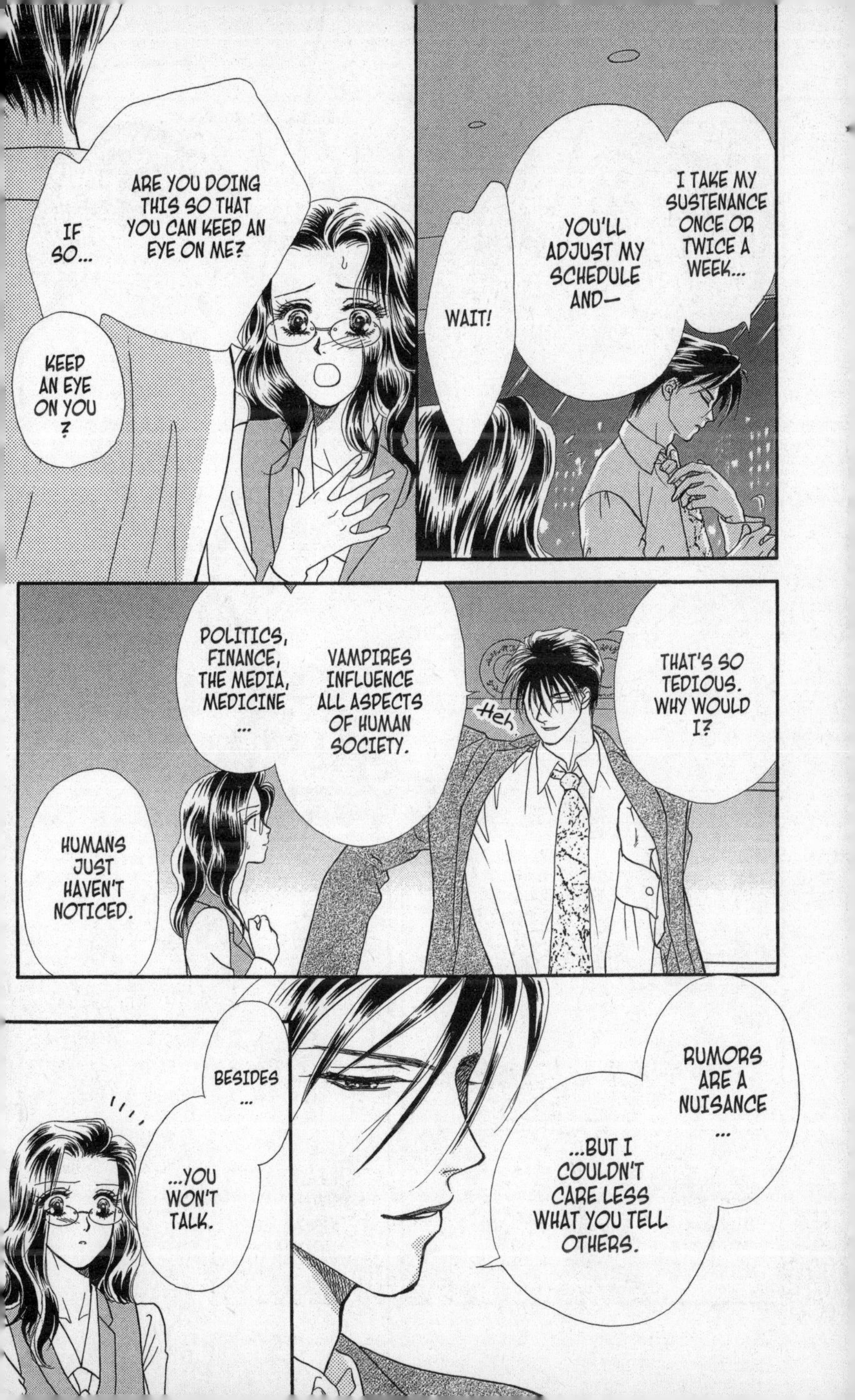
I TAKE MY SUSTENANCE ONCE OR TWICE A WEEK...
YOU'LL ADJUST MY SCHEDULE AND—
WAIT!
ARE YOU DOING THIS SO THAT YOU CAN KEEP AN EYE ON ME?
IF SO...
KEEP AN EYE ON YOU?
THAT'S SO TEDIOUS. WHY WOULD I?
Heh
VAMPIRES INFLUENCE ALL ASPECTS OF HUMAN SOCIETY.
POLITICS, FINANCE, THE MEDIA, MEDICINE ...
HUMANS JUST HAVEN'T NOTICED.
RUMORS ARE A NUISANCE ...
...BUT I COULDN'T CARE LESS WHAT YOU TELL OTHERS.
BESIDES ...
...YOU WON'T TALK.

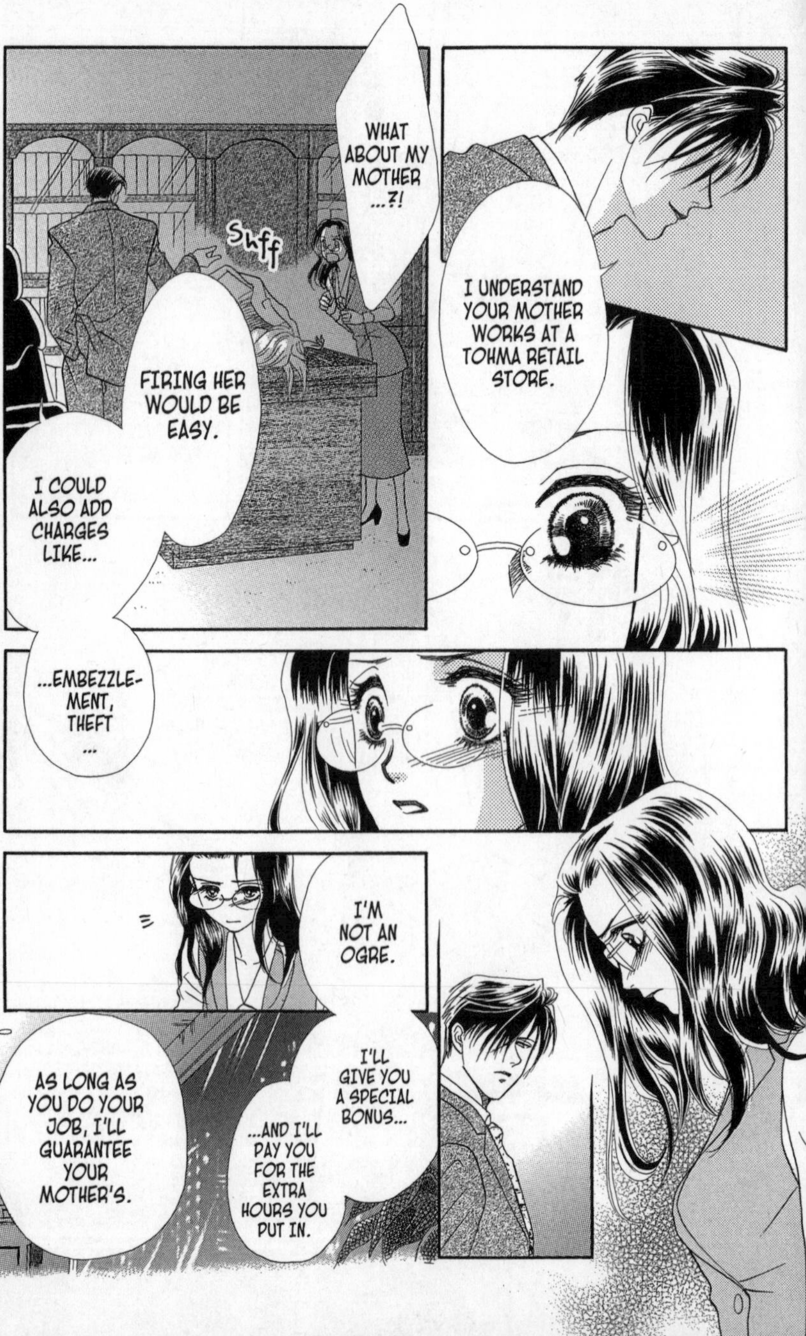
I UNDERSTAND YOUR MOTHER WORKS AT A TOHMA RETAIL STORE.
WHAT ABOUT MY MOTHER ...?!
SNFF
FIRING HER WOULD BE EASY.
I COULD ALSO ADD CHARGES LIKE...
...EMBEZZLE-MENT, THEFT ...
I'M NOT AN OGRE.
I'LL GIVE YOU A SPECIAL BONUS...
...AND I'LL PAY YOU FOR THE EXTRA HOURS YOU PUT IN.
AS LONG AS YOU DO YOUR JOB, I'LL GUARANTEE YOUR MOTHER'S.

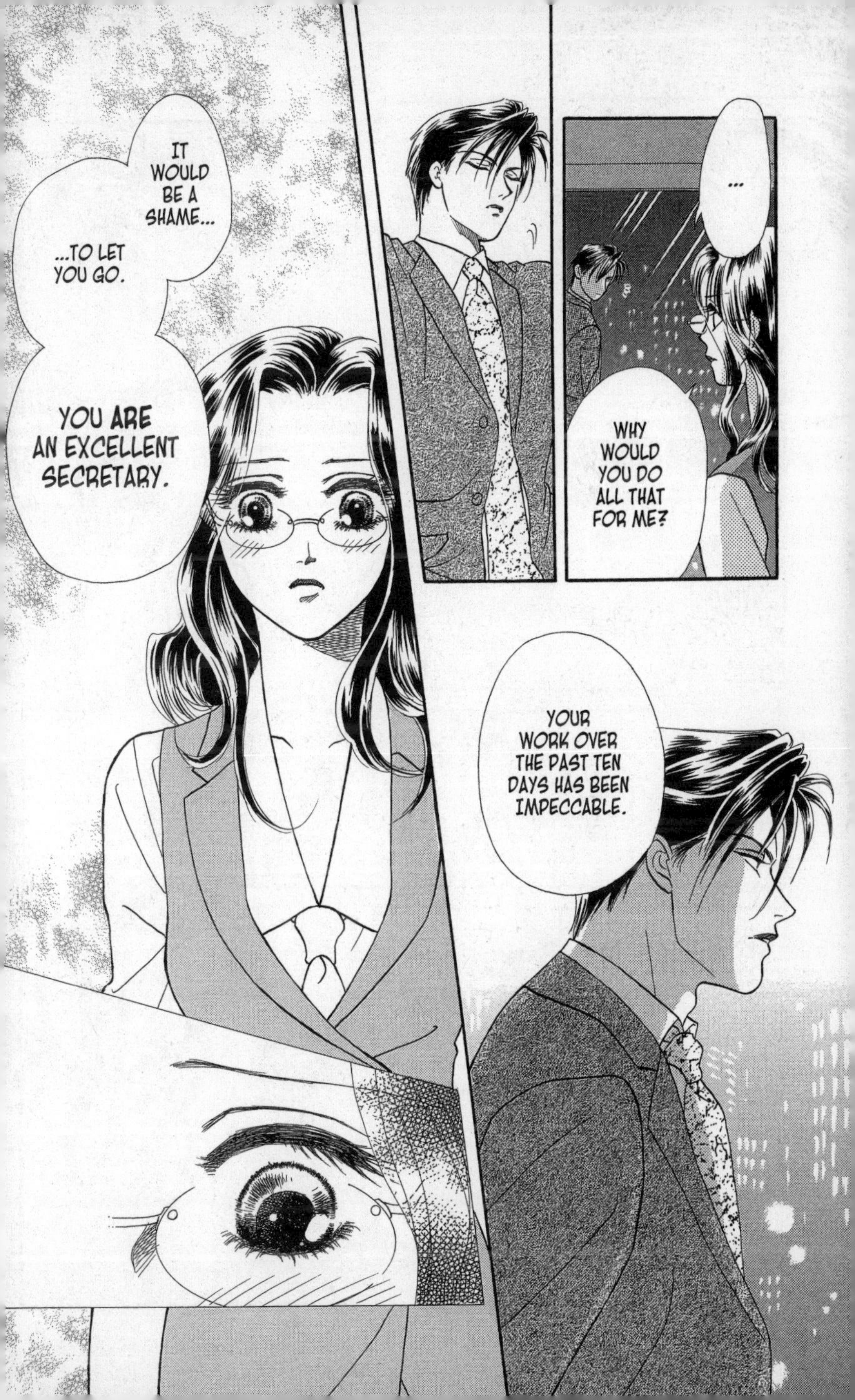
...
WHY WOULD YOU DO ALL THAT FOR ME?
YOUR WORK OVER THE PAST TEN DAYS HAS BEEN IMPECCABLE.
IT WOULD BE A SHAME...
...TO LET YOU GO.
YOU ARE AN EXCELLENT SECRETARY.

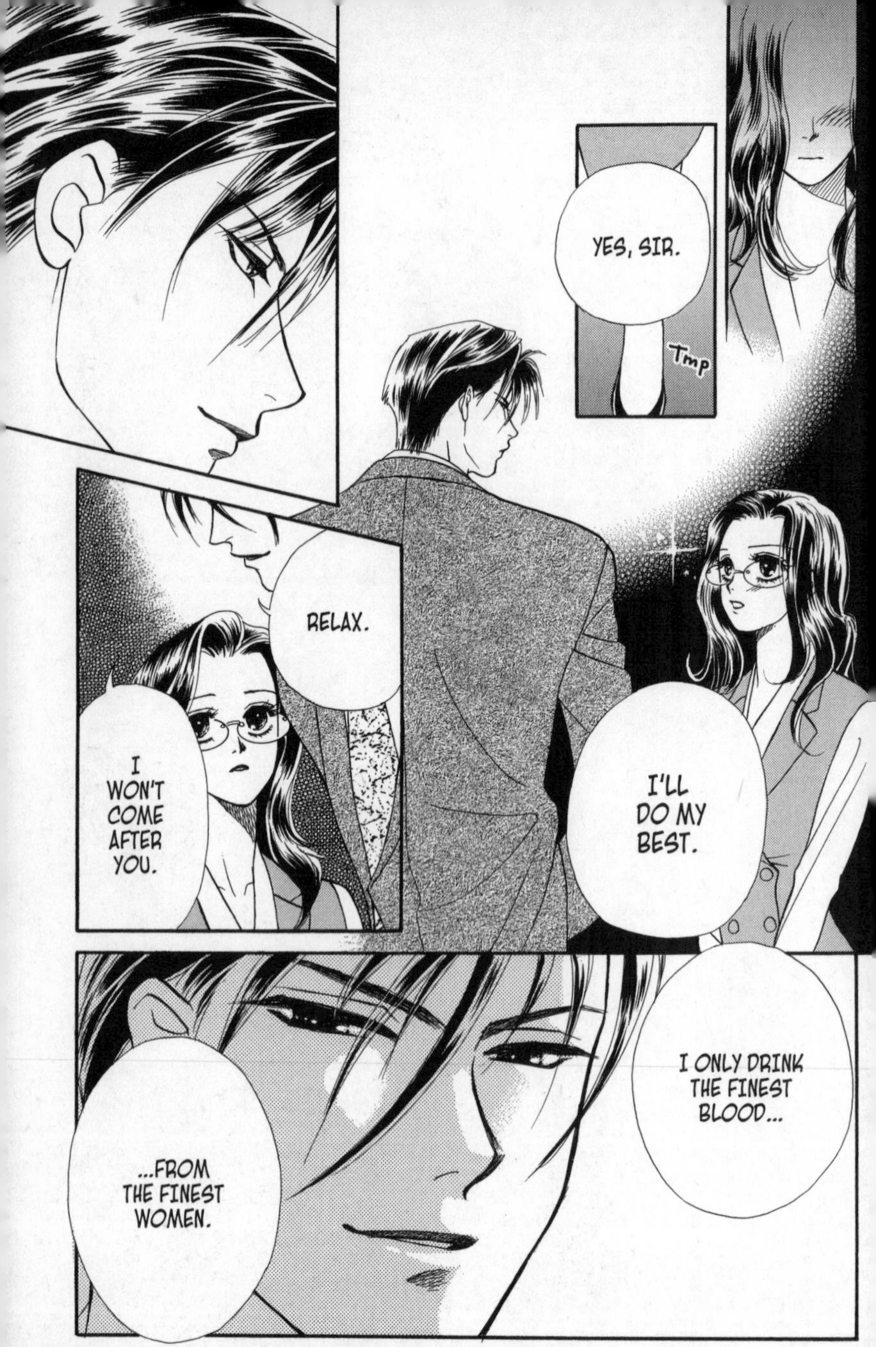
YES, SIR.
Tmp
I'LL DO MY BEST.
RELAX.
I WON'T COME AFTER YOU.
I ONLY DRINK THE FINEST BLOOD...
...FROM THE FINEST WOMEN.

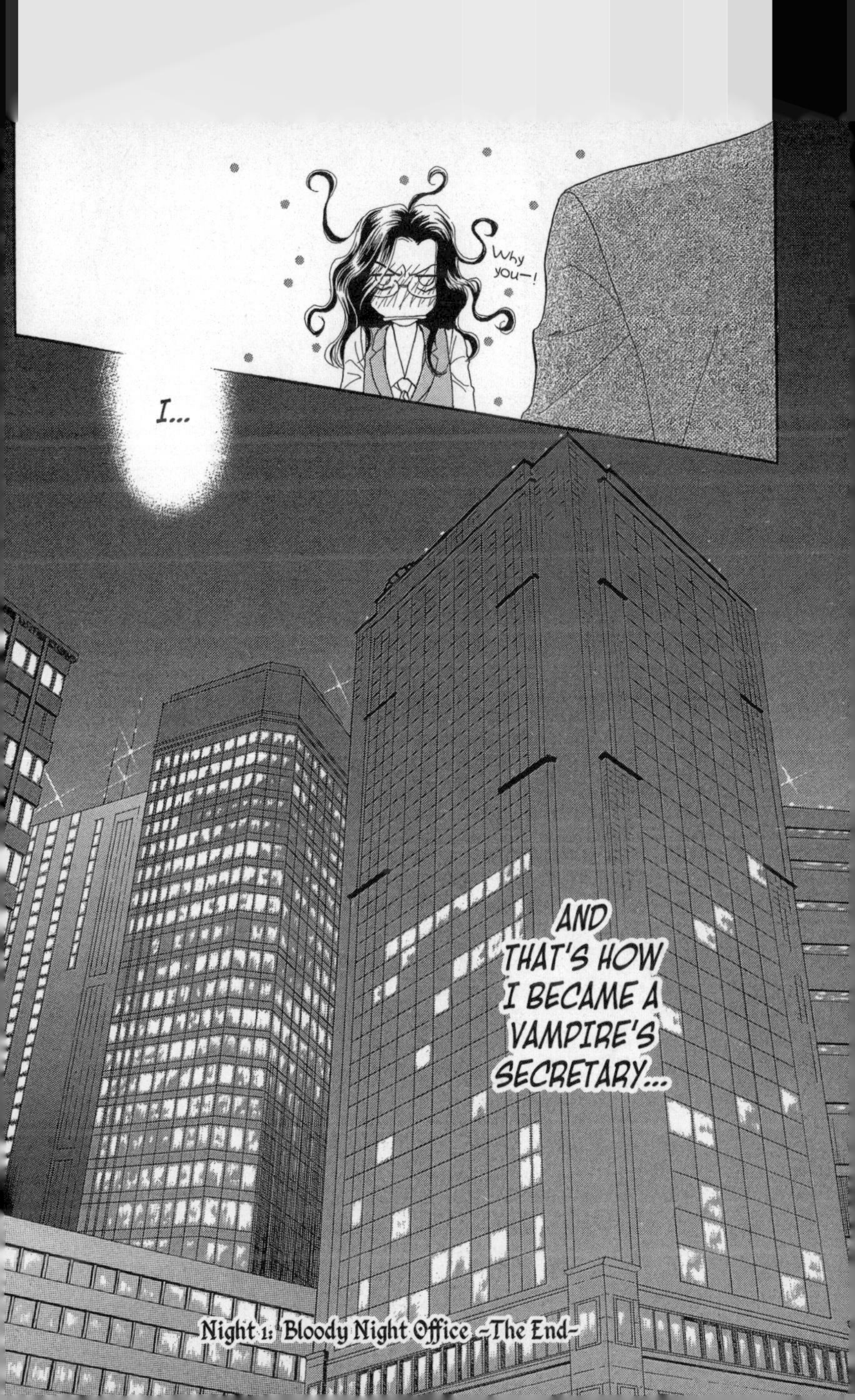
Why you—!
I...
AND THAT'S HOW I BECAME A VAMPIRE'S SECRETARY...
Night 1: Bloody Night Office ~The End~

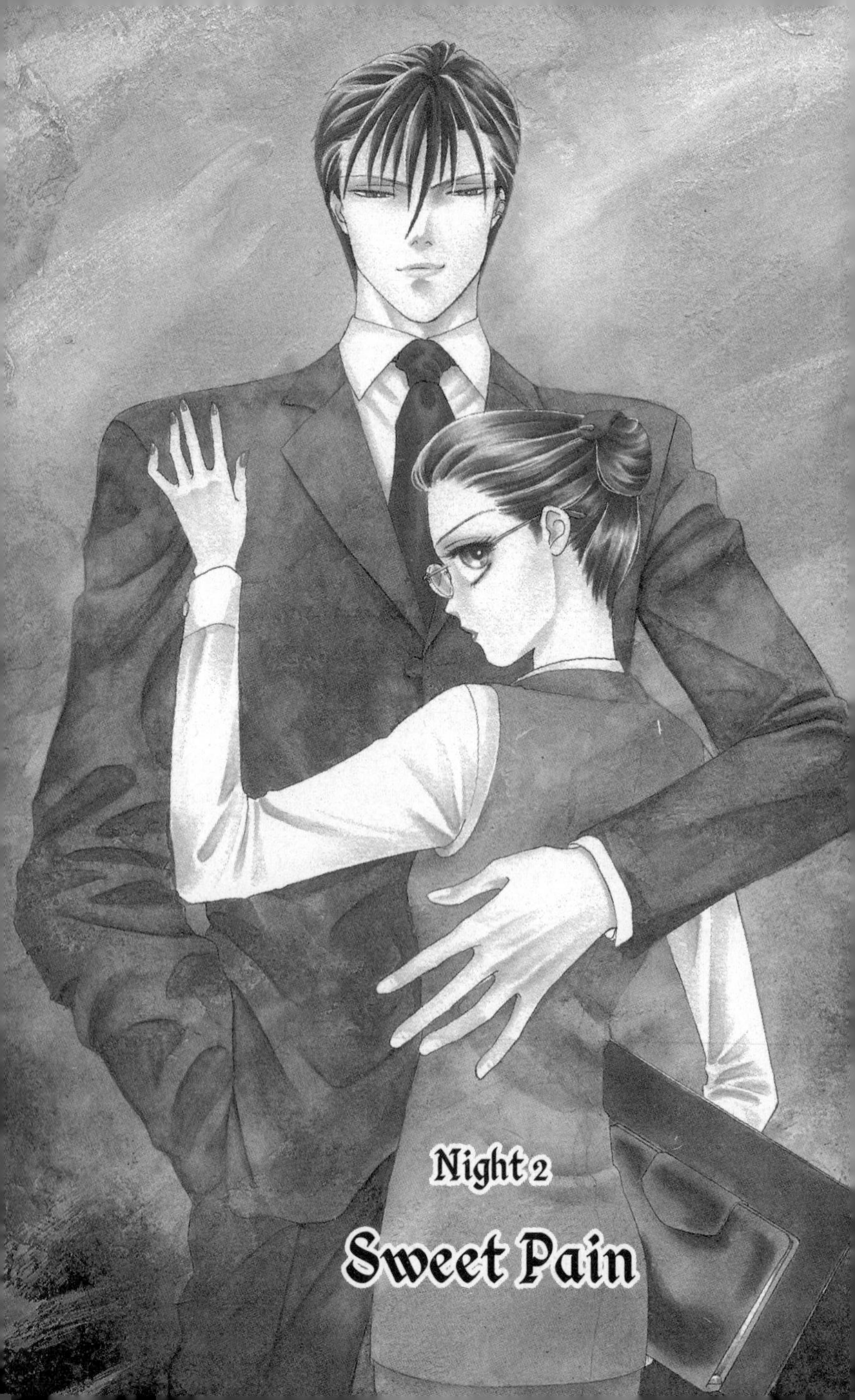
Night 2
Sweet Pain

A vampire story.

Actually, it was the first series
I did after my debut.

(It originated in "Kindan no Koi wo
Shiyo," which ran in *Flower Comics*.
I would be so pleased if you read it. ♡)
The storyline is totally different,
but it's also about a vampire clan.

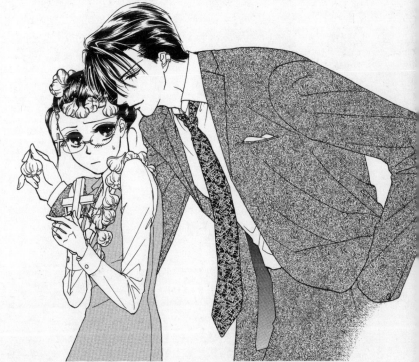

▲ Night 3: Brotherhood preview

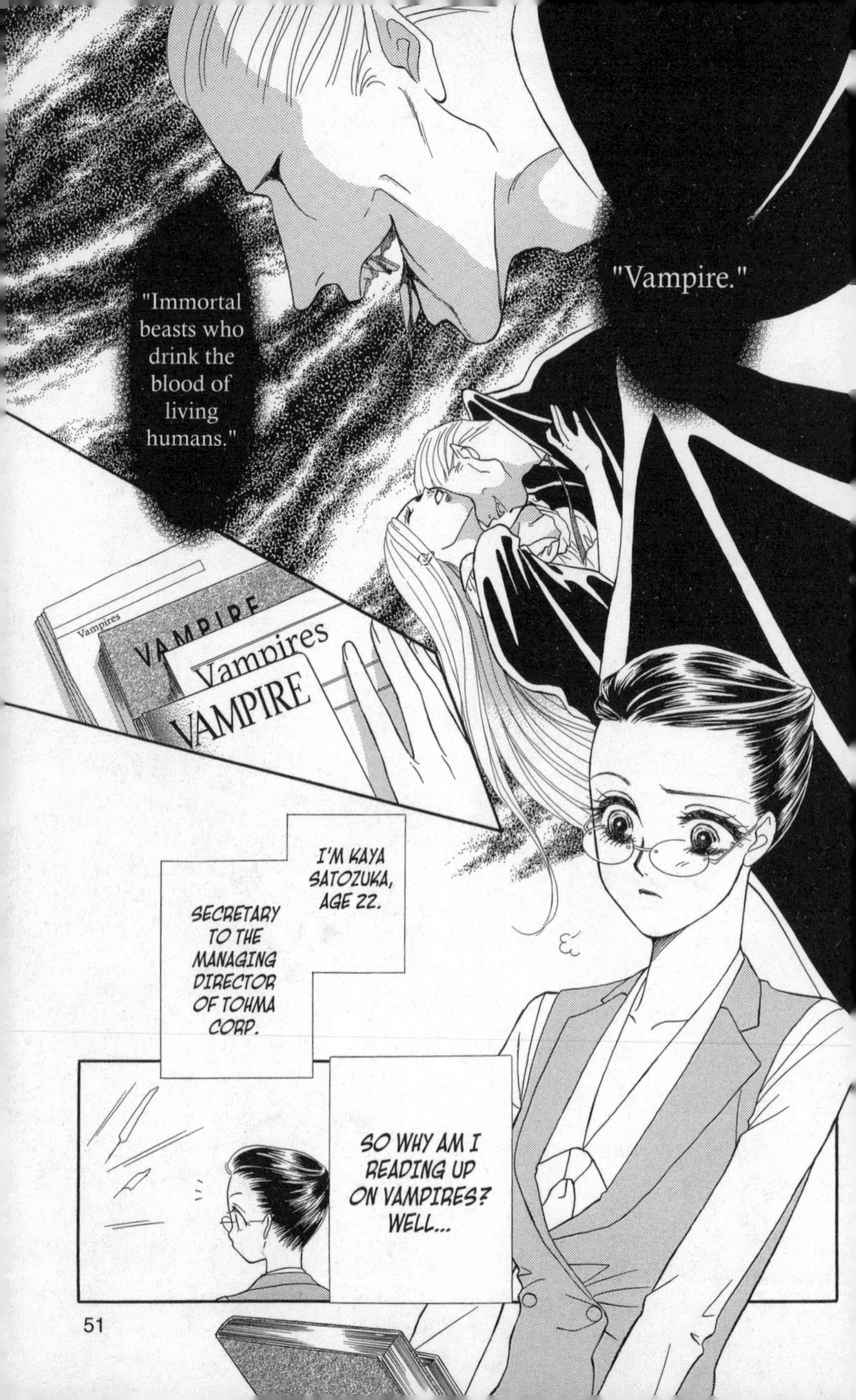
"Vampire."
"Immortal beasts who drink the blood of living humans."
Vampires
Vampires
VAMPIRE
I'M KAYA SATOZUKA, AGE 22.
SECRETARY TO THE MANAGING DIRECTOR OF TOHMA CORP.
SO WHY AM I READING UP ON VAMPIRES? WELL...

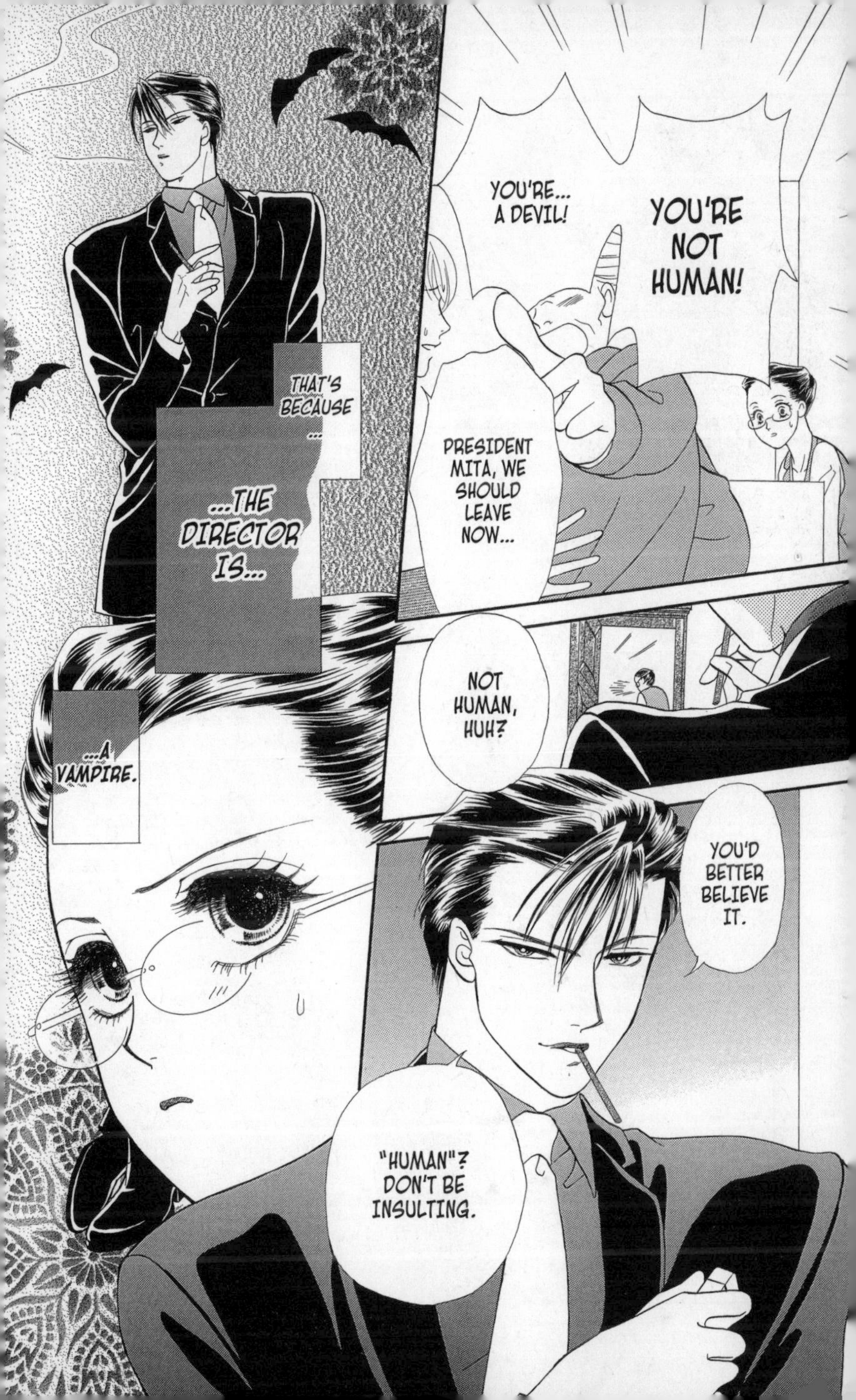
YOU'RE NOT HUMAN!
YOU'RE... A DEVIL!
PRESIDENT MITA, WE SHOULD LEAVE NOW...
NOT HUMAN, HUH?
YOU'D BETTER BELIEVE IT.
"HUMAN"? DON'T BE INSULTING.
THAT'S BECAUSE...
...THE DIRECTOR IS...
...A VAMPIRE.

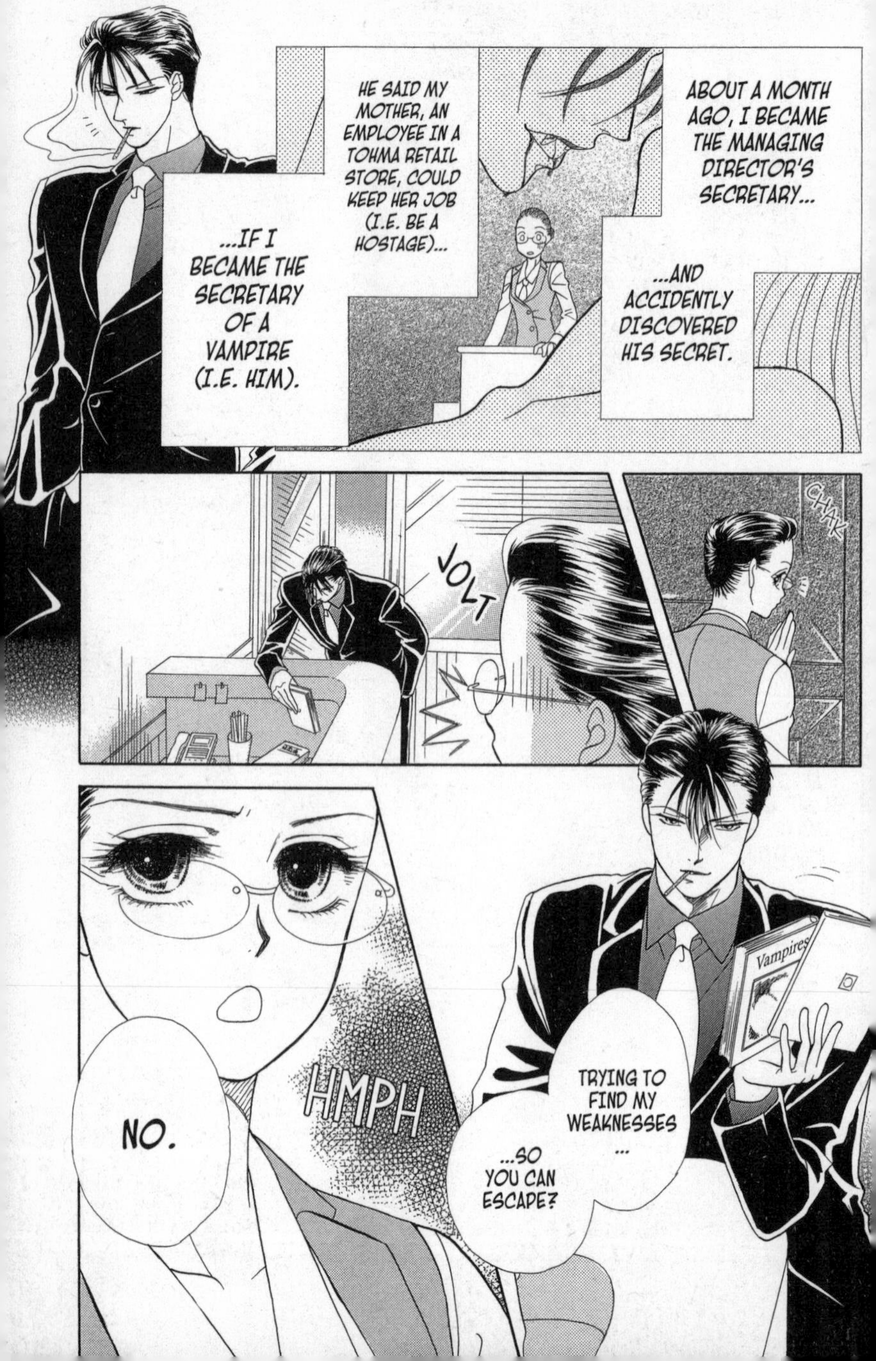
ABOUT A MONTH AGO, I BECAME THE MANAGING DIRECTOR'S SECRETARY...
...AND ACCIDENTLY DISCOVERED HIS SECRET.
HE SAID MY MOTHER, AN EMPLOYEE IN A TOHMA RETAIL STORE, COULD KEEP HER JOB (I.E. BE A HOSTAGE)...
...IF I BECAME THE SECRETARY OF A VAMPIRE (I.E. HIM).
CHAK
JOLT
Vampires
TRYING TO FIND MY WEAKNESSES ...
...SO YOU CAN ESCAPE?
HMPH
NO.

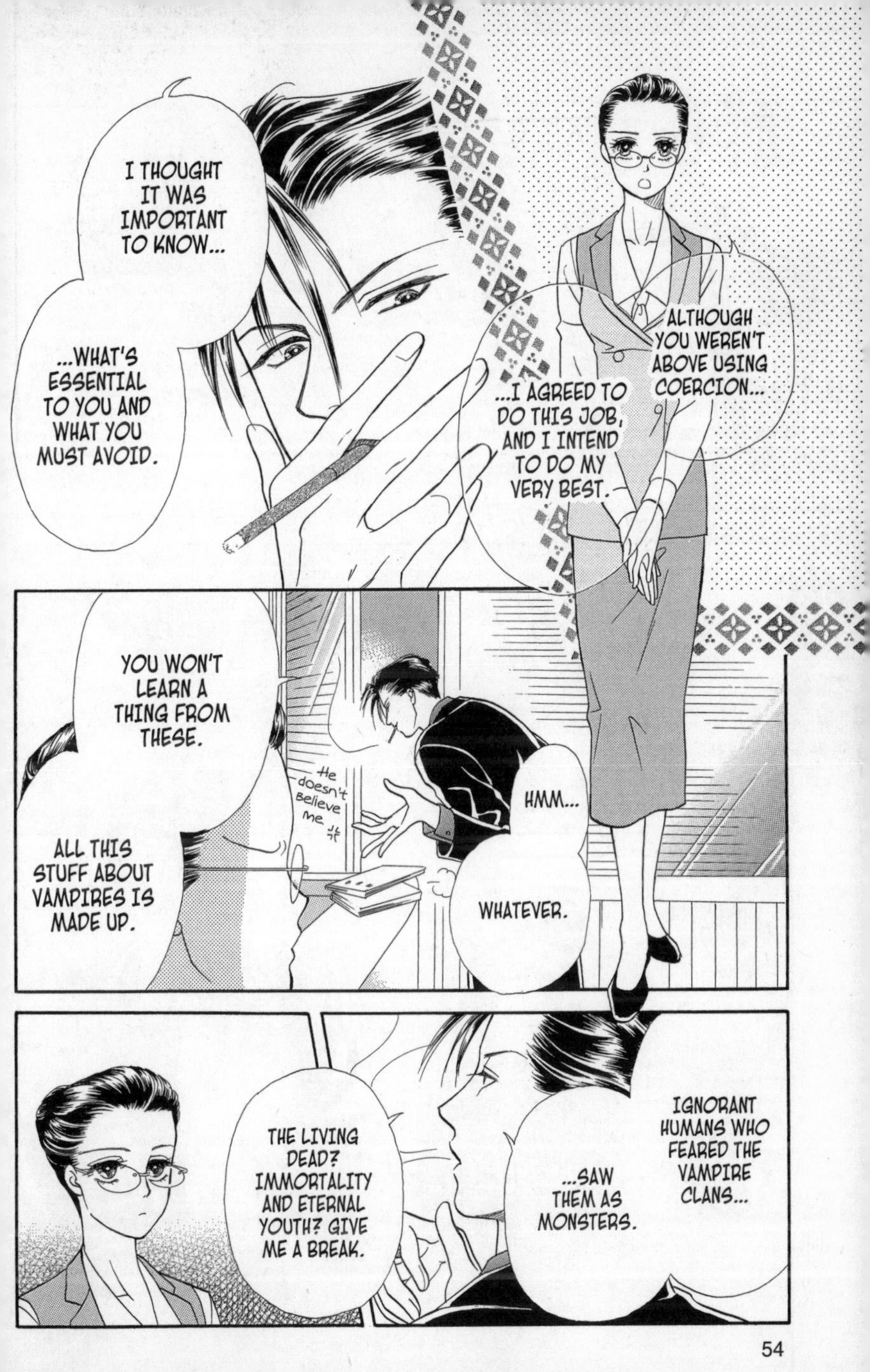
ALTHOUGH YOU WEREN'T ABOVE USING COERCION...
...I AGREED TO DO THIS JOB, AND I INTEND TO DO MY VERY BEST.
I THOUGHT IT WAS IMPORTANT TO KNOW...
...WHAT'S ESSENTIAL TO YOU AND WHAT YOU MUST AVOID.
YOU WON'T LEARN A THING FROM THESE.
HMM...
He doesn't Believe me
ALL THIS STUFF ABOUT VAMPIRES IS MADE UP.
WHATEVER.
IGNORANT HUMANS WHO FEARED THE VAMPIRE CLANS...
...SAW THEM AS MONSTERS.
THE LIVING DEAD? IMMORTALITY AND ETERNAL YOUTH? GIVE ME A BREAK.

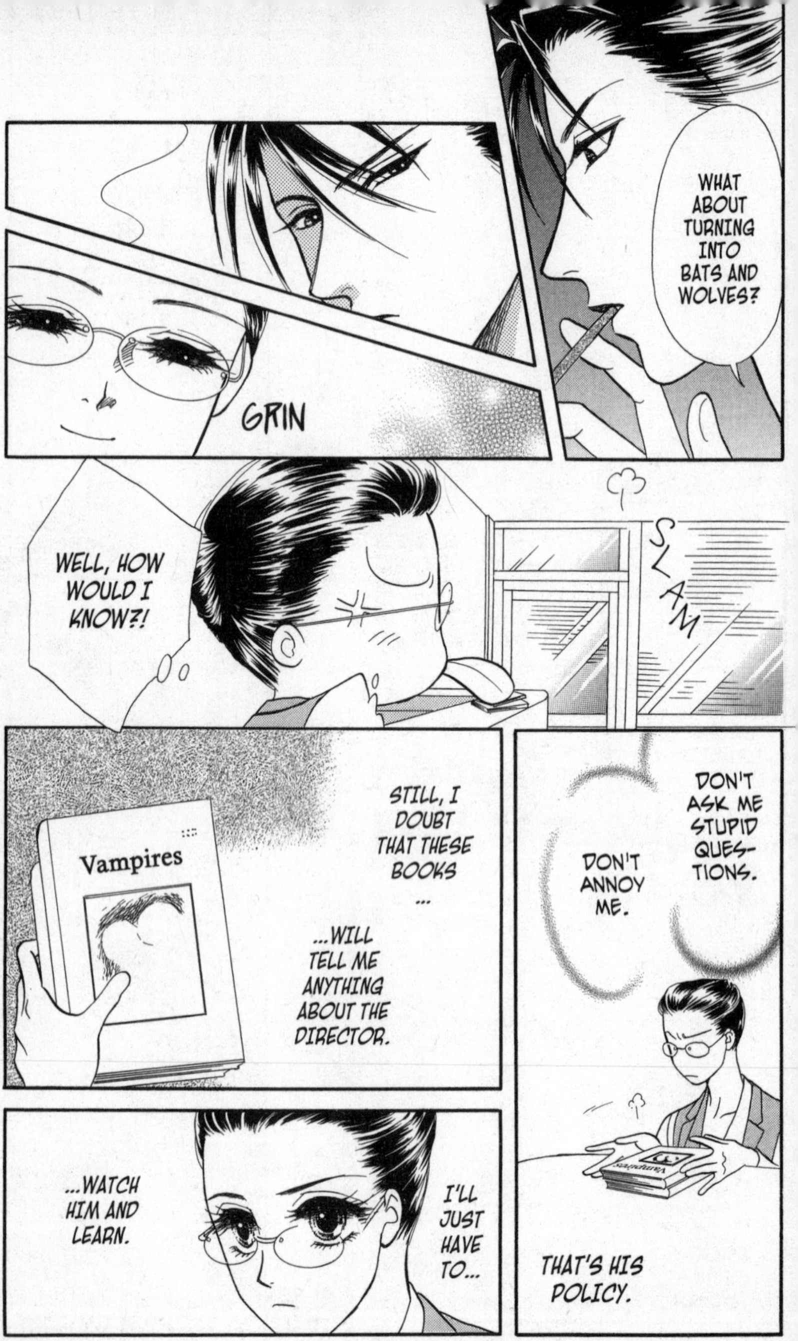
WHAT ABOUT TURNING INTO BATS AND WOLVES?
GRIN
SLAM
WELL, HOW WOULD I KNOW?!
DON'T ASK ME STUPID QUES-TIONS.
DON'T ANNOY ME.
THAT'S HIS POLICY.
STILL, I DOUBT THAT THESE BOOKS...
Vampires
...WILL TELL ME ANYTHING ABOUT THE DIRECTOR.
I'LL JUST HAVE TO...
...WATCH HIM AND LEARN.

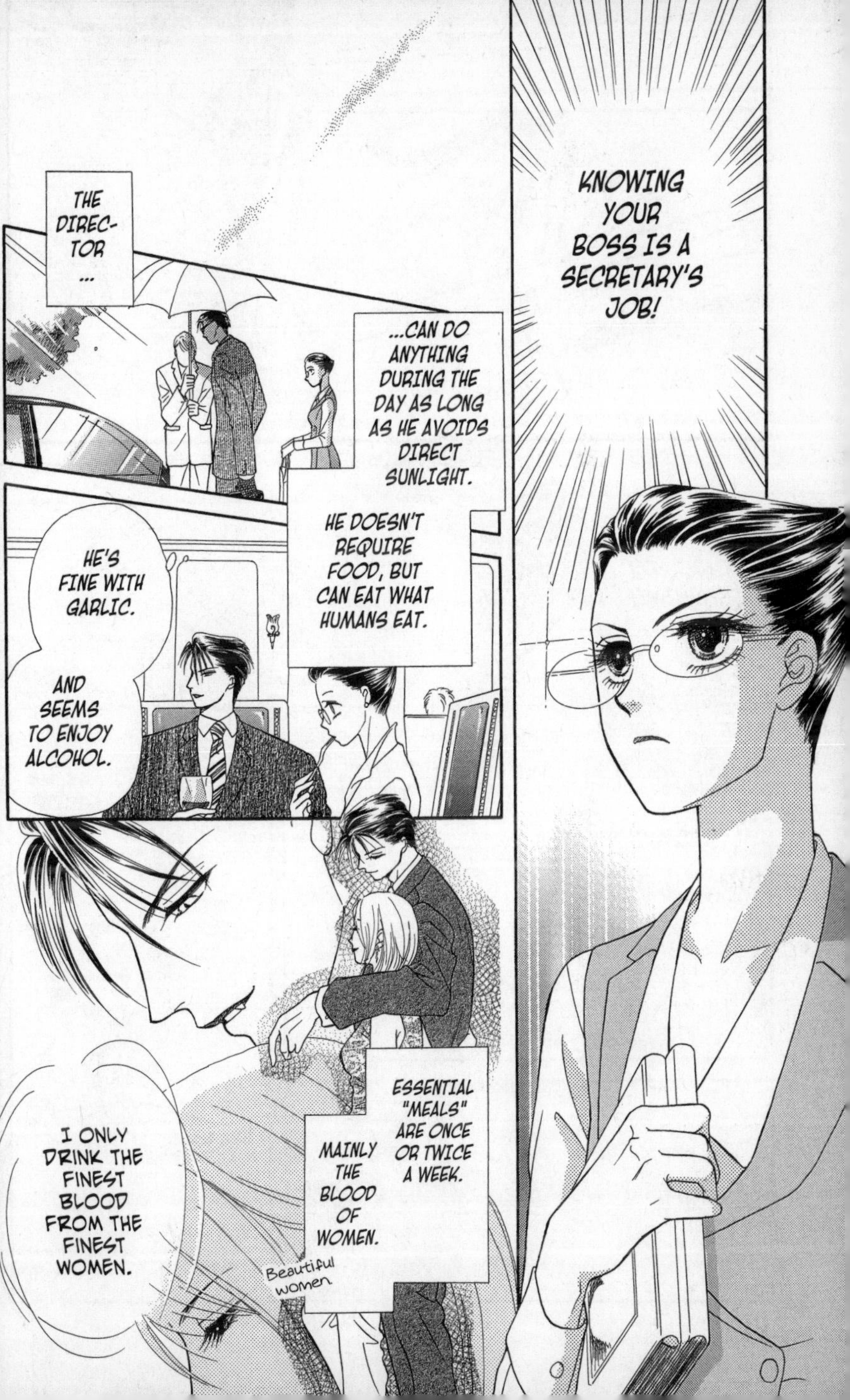
KNOWING YOUR BOSS IS A SECRETARY'S JOB!
THE DIRECTOR...
...CAN DO ANYTHING DURING THE DAY AS LONG AS HE AVOIDS DIRECT SUNLIGHT.
HE DOESN'T REQUIRE FOOD, BUT CAN EAT WHAT HUMANS EAT.
HE'S FINE WITH GARLIC.
AND SEEMS TO ENJOY ALCOHOL.
ESSENTIAL "MEALS" ARE ONCE OR TWICE A WEEK.
MAINLY THE BLOOD OF WOMEN.
Beautiful women.
I ONLY DRINK THE FINEST BLOOD FROM THE FINEST WOMEN.

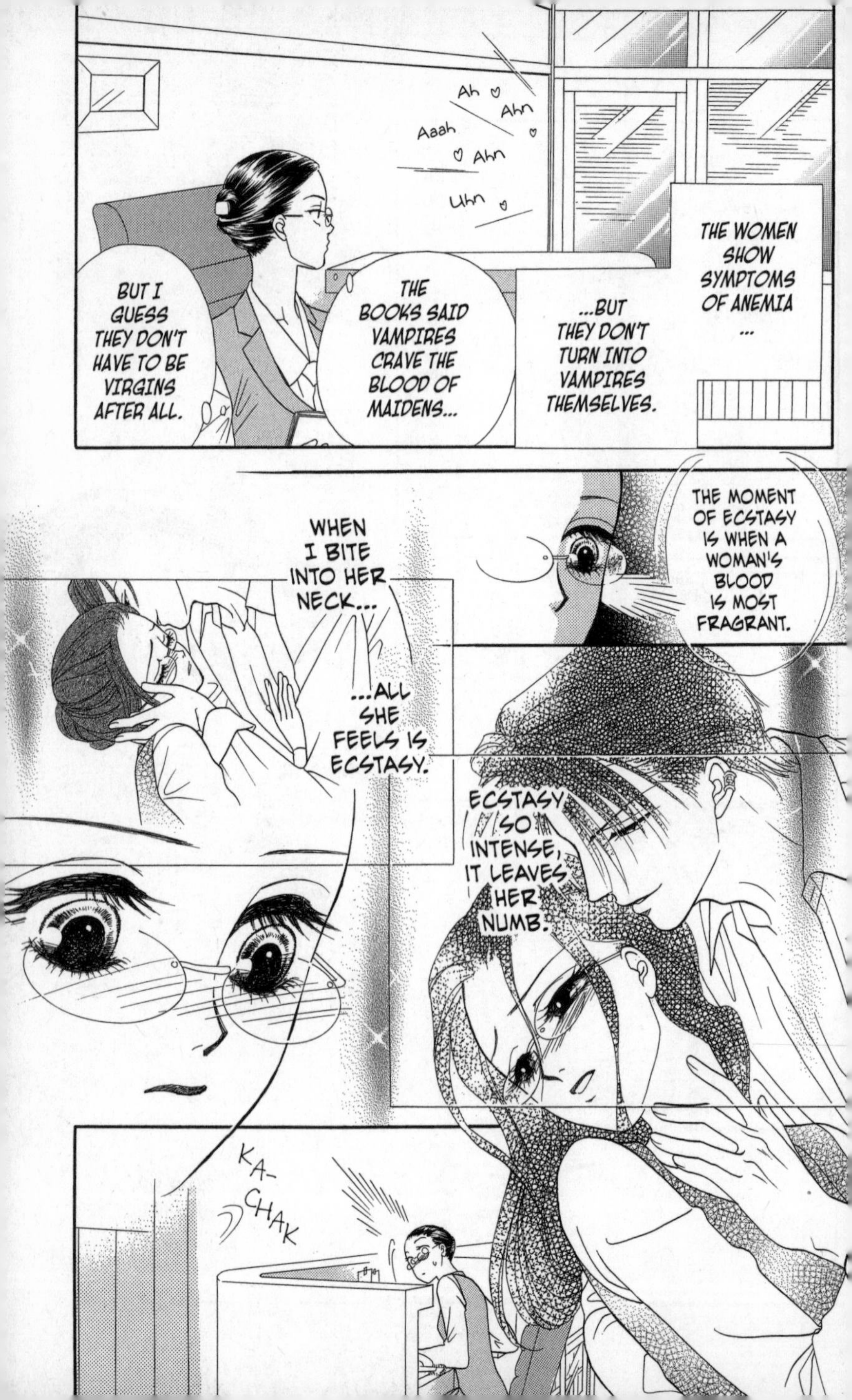
Ah Ahn Aaah Ahn Uhn
THE WOMEN SHOW SYMPTOMS OF ANEMIA ...
...BUT THEY DON'T TURN INTO VAMPIRES THEMSELVES.
THE BOOKS SAID VAMPIRES CRAVE THE BLOOD OF MAIDENS...
BUT I GUESS THEY DON'T HAVE TO BE VIRGINS AFTER ALL.
THE MOMENT OF ECSTASY IS WHEN A WOMAN'S BLOOD IS MOST FRAGRANT.
WHEN I BITE INTO HER NECK...
...ALL SHE FEELS IS ECSTASY.
ECSTASY SO INTENSE, IT LEAVES HER NUMB.
KA-CHAK

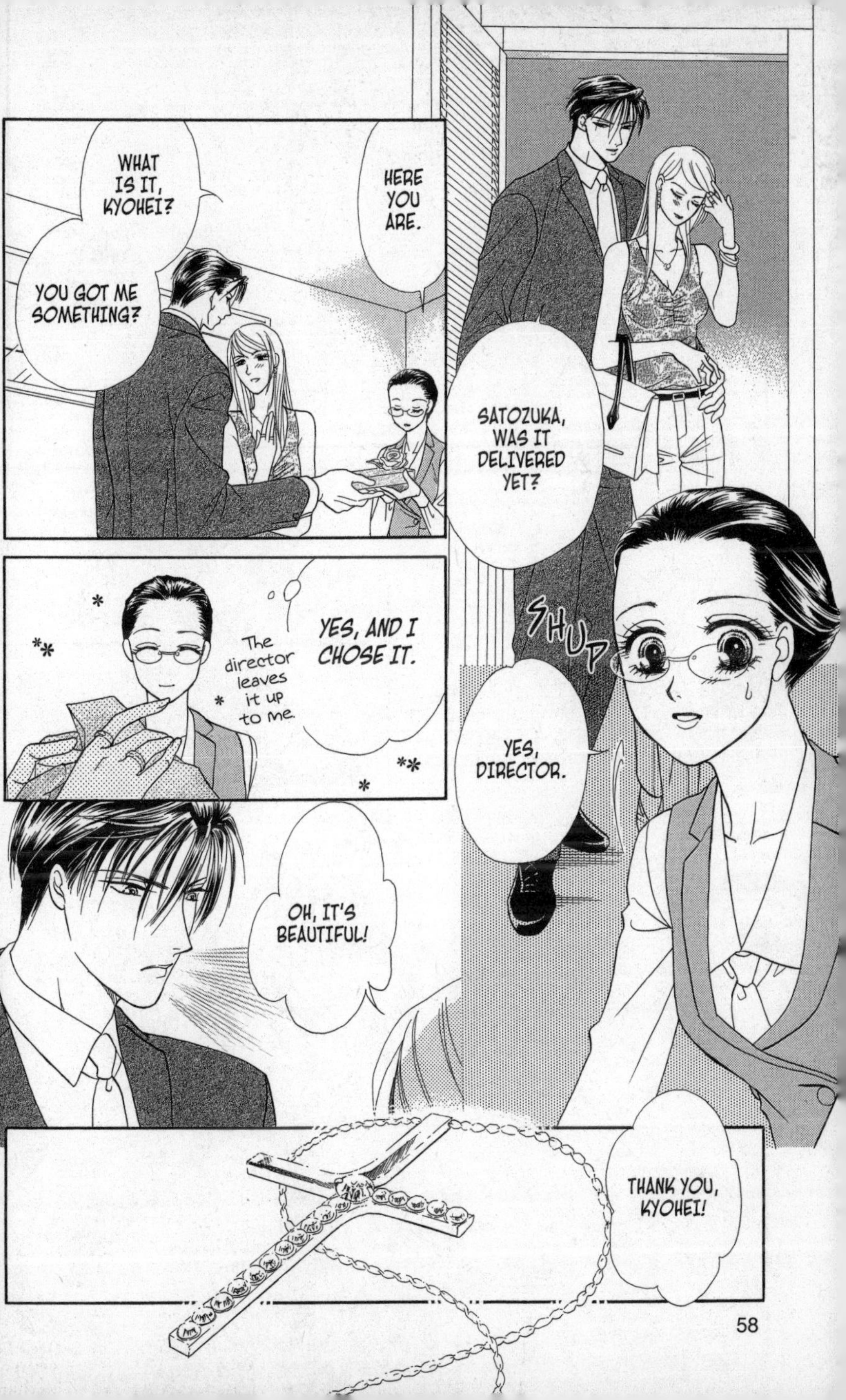
SATOZUKA, WAS IT DELIVERED YET?
SHUP
YES, DIRECTOR.
HERE YOU ARE.
WHAT IS IT, KYOHEI?
YOU GOT ME SOMETHING?
YES, AND I CHOSE IT.
The director leaves it up to me.
OH, IT'S BEAUTIFUL!
THANK YOU, KYOHEI!

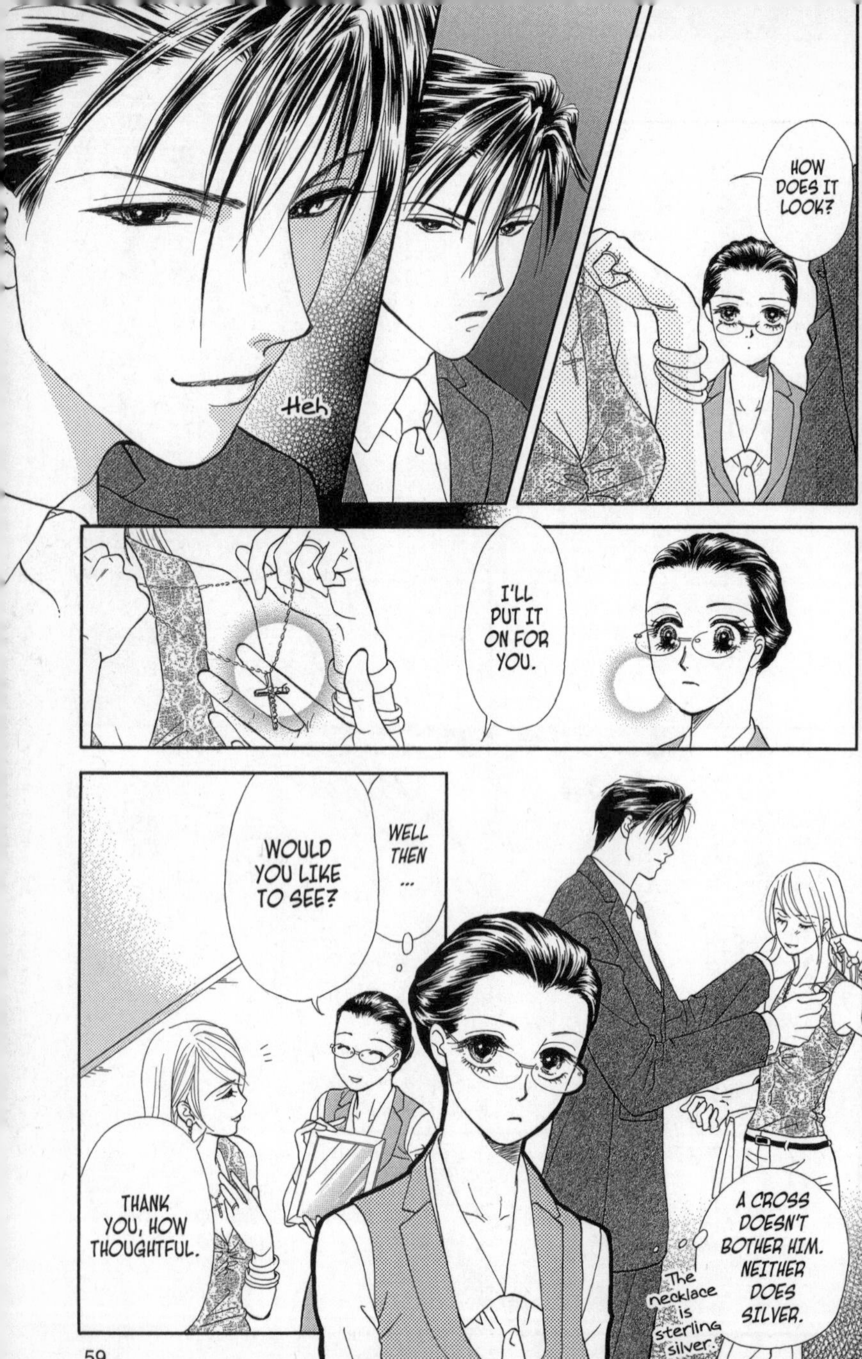
HOW DOES IT LOOK?
Heh
I'LL PUT IT ON FOR YOU.
A CROSS DOESN'T BOTHER HIM. NEITHER DOES SILVER.
The necklace is sterling silver.
WELL THEN ...
WOULD YOU LIKE TO SEE?
THANK YOU, HOW THOUGHTFUL.

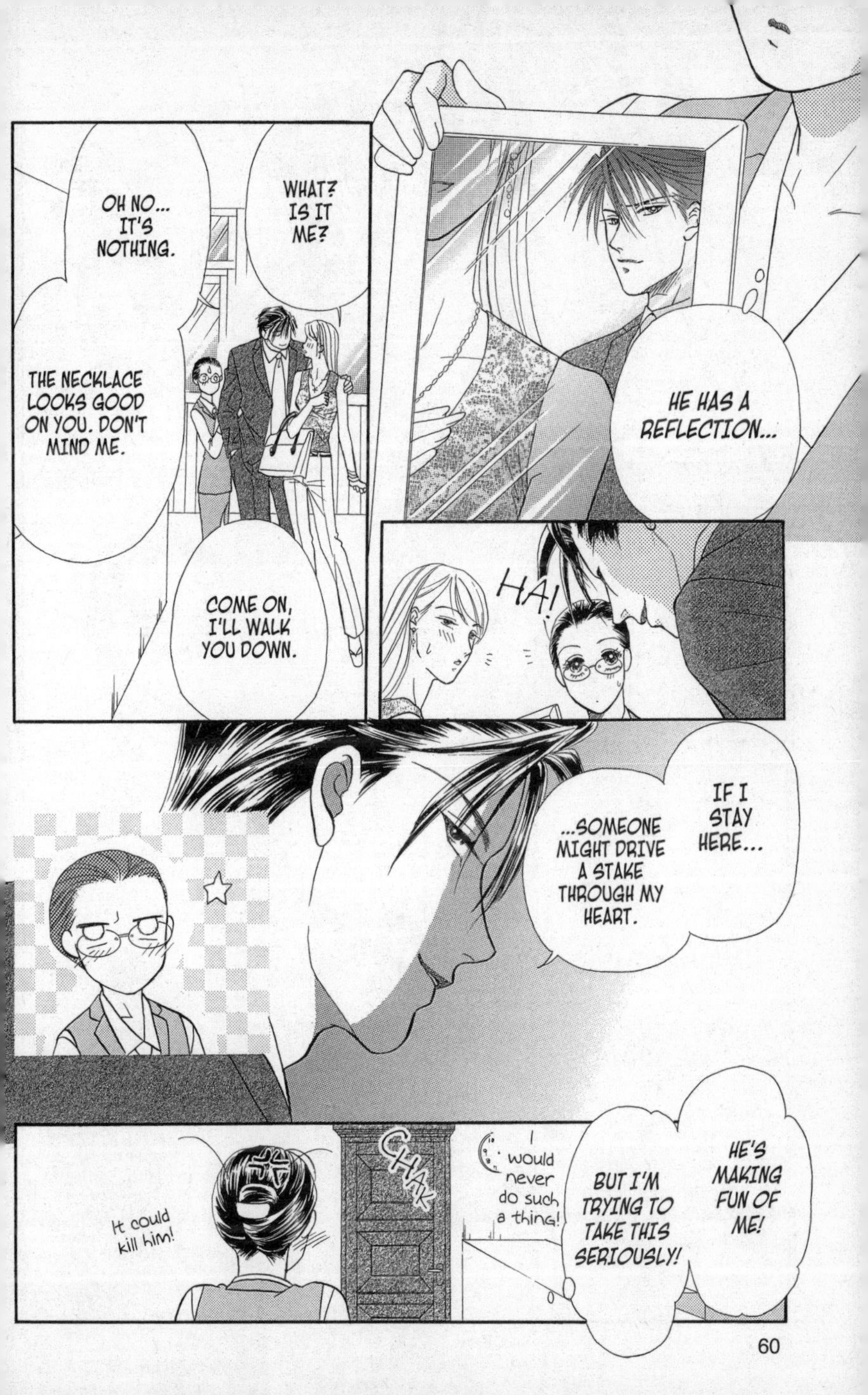
HE HAS A REFLECTION...
HA!
WHAT? IS IT ME?
OH NO... IT'S NOTHING.
THE NECKLACE LOOKS GOOD ON YOU. DON'T MIND ME.
COME ON, I'LL WALK YOU DOWN.
IF I STAY HERE...
...SOMEONE MIGHT DRIVE A STAKE THROUGH MY HEART.
HE'S MAKING FUN OF ME!
BUT I'M TRYING TO TAKE THIS SERIOUSLY!
I would never do such a thing!
CHAK
It could kill him!

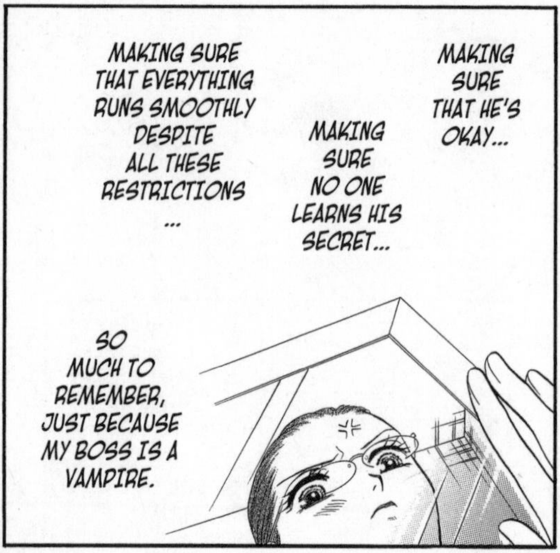
MAKING SURE THAT HE'S OKAY...
MAKING SURE NO ONE LEARNS HIS SECRET...
MAKING SURE THAT EVERYTHING RUNS SMOOTHLY DESPITE ALL THESE RESTRICTIONS ...
SO MUCH TO REMEMBER, JUST BECAUSE MY BOSS IS A VAMPIRE.

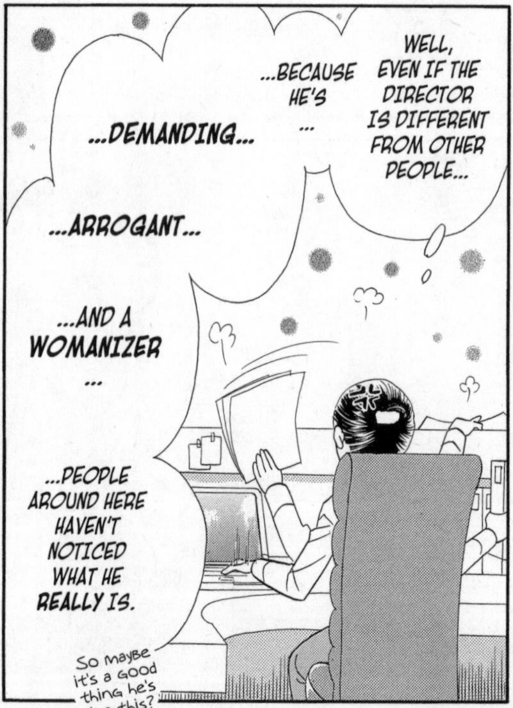
WELL, EVEN IF THE DIRECTOR IS DIFFERENT FROM OTHER PEOPLE...
...BECAUSE HE'S ...
...DEMANDING...
...ARROGANT...
...AND A WOMANIZER ...
...PEOPLE AROUND HERE HAVEN'T NOTICED WHAT HE REALLY IS.
So maybe it's a good thing he's like this?

- Bloody Night Office -

When drawing baby-faced Kaya, I visualize Hiromi Eisaku* and my sister-in-law.

Kaya is not based on them, but they're sorta the image I want her to convey.

*a singer/actress

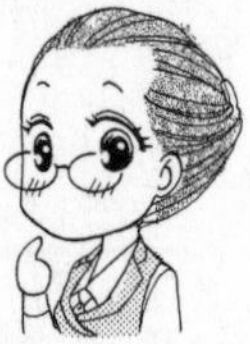

My sister-in-law is the mother of two children, but even now, when she's driving, people are shocked.

But she's very capable and smart. That's the kind of traits I'd like to give Kaya.

- Sweet Pain -

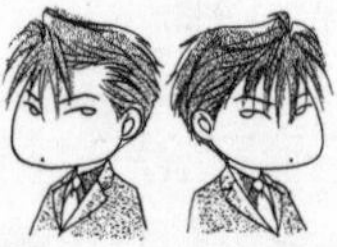

Kyohei being serious and Kyohei after a tryst. Getting the sweep of his bangs just right has been giving me lots of trouble.

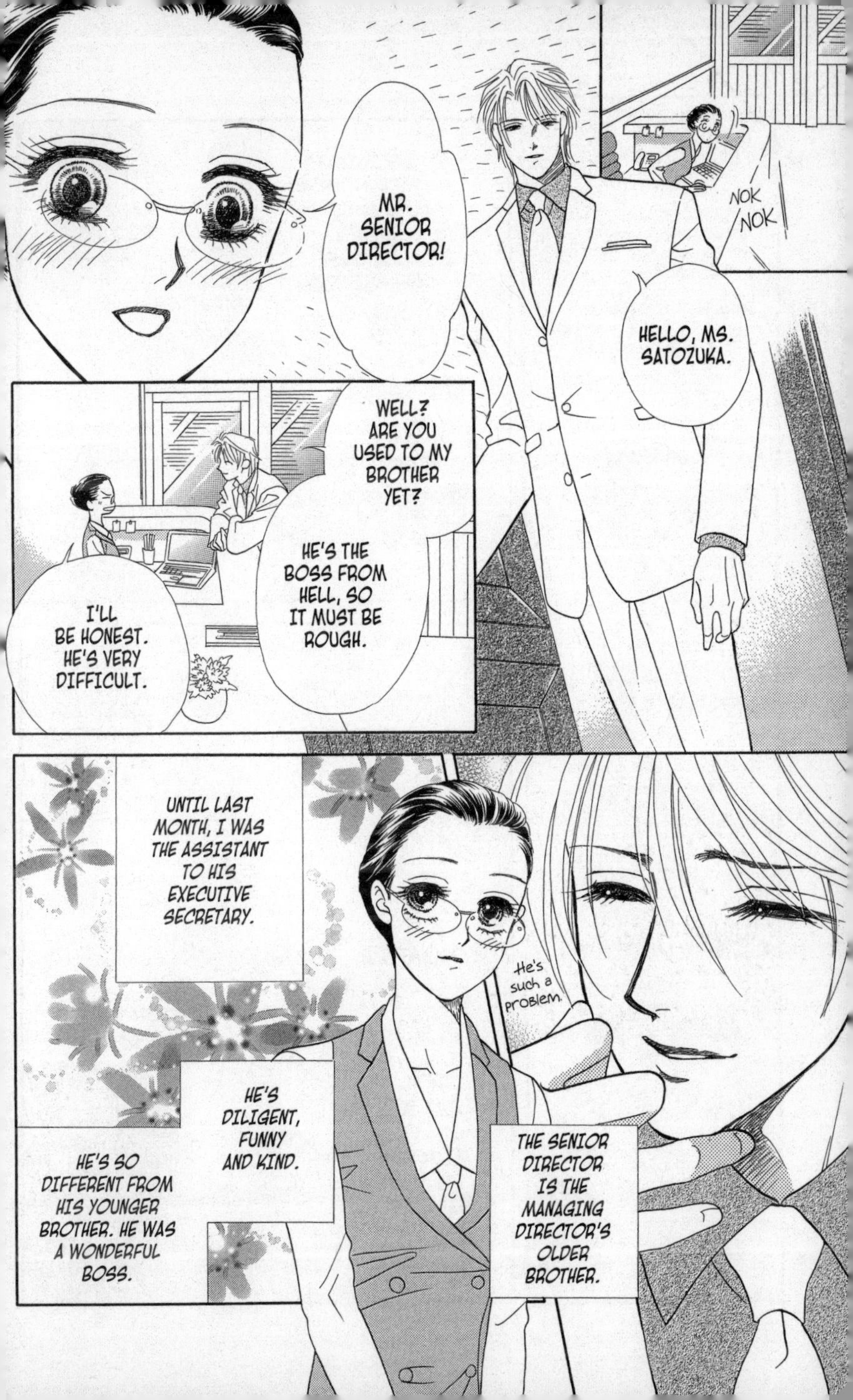
NOK NOK
HELLO, MS. SATOZUKA.
MR. SENIOR DIRECTOR!
WELL? ARE YOU USED TO MY BROTHER YET?
HE'S THE BOSS FROM HELL, SO IT MUST BE ROUGH.
I'LL BE HONEST. HE'S VERY DIFFICULT.
THE SENIOR DIRECTOR IS THE MANAGING DIRECTOR'S OLDER BROTHER.
He's such a problem.
UNTIL LAST MONTH, I WAS THE ASSISTANT TO HIS EXECUTIVE SECRETARY.
HE'S DILIGENT, FUNNY AND KIND.
HE'S SO DIFFERENT FROM HIS YOUNGER BROTHER. HE WAS A WONDERFUL BOSS.

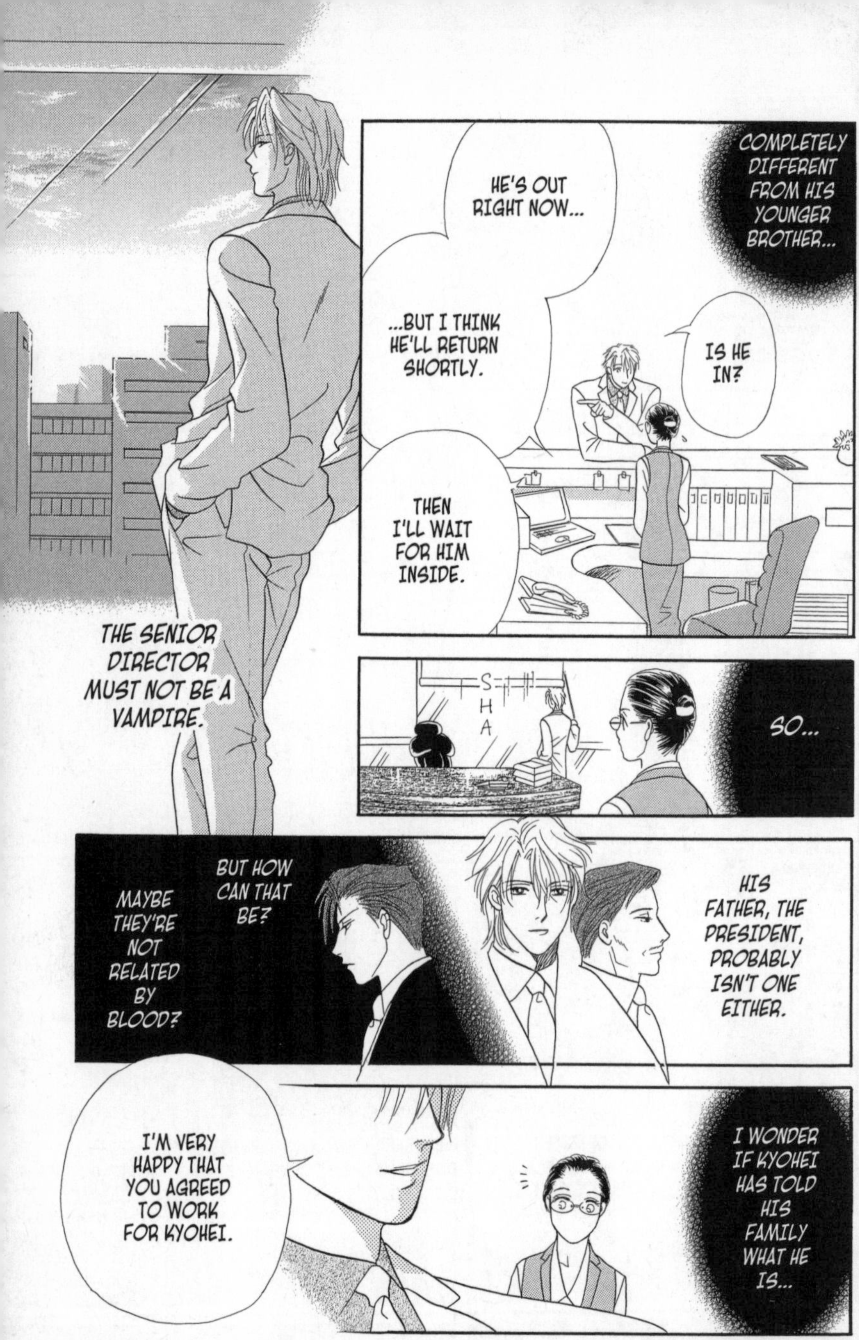
COMPLETELY DIFFERENT FROM HIS YOUNGER BROTHER...
IS HE IN?
HE'S OUT RIGHT NOW...
...BUT I THINK HE'LL RETURN SHORTLY.
THEN I'LL WAIT FOR HIM INSIDE.
SO...
S H A
THE SENIOR DIRECTOR MUST NOT BE A VAMPIRE.
HIS FATHER, THE PRESIDENT, PROBABLY ISN'T ONE EITHER.
BUT HOW CAN THAT BE?
MAYBE THEY'RE NOT RELATED BY BLOOD?
I WONDER IF KYOHEI HAS TOLD HIS FAMILY WHAT HE IS...
I'M VERY HAPPY THAT YOU AGREED TO WORK FOR KYOHEI.

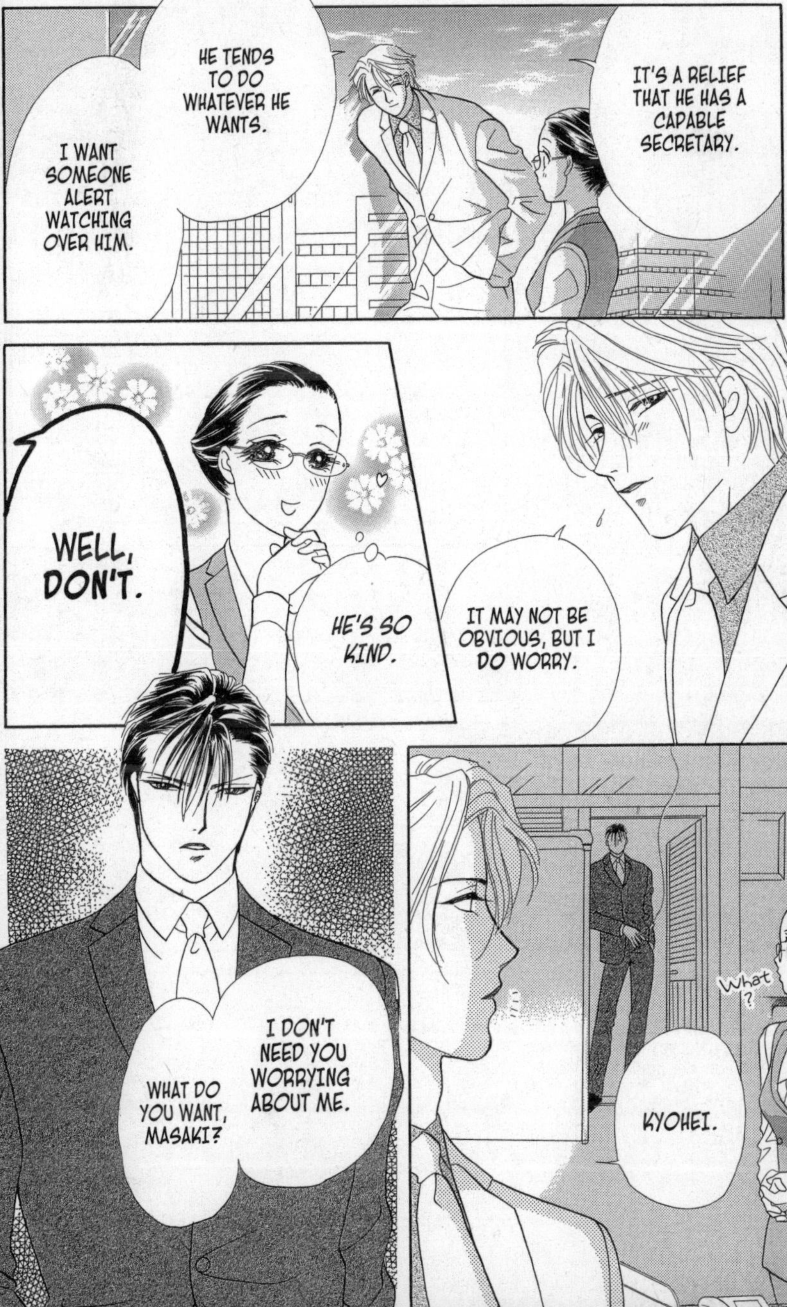
IT'S A RELIEF THAT HE HAS A CAPABLE SECRETARY.
HE TENDS TO DO WHATEVER HE WANTS.
I WANT SOMEONE ALERT WATCHING OVER HIM.
IT MAY NOT BE OBVIOUS, BUT I DO WORRY.
HE'S SO KIND.
WELL, DON'T.
What ?
KYOHEI.
I DON'T NEED YOU WORRYING ABOUT ME.
WHAT DO YOU WANT, MASAKI?

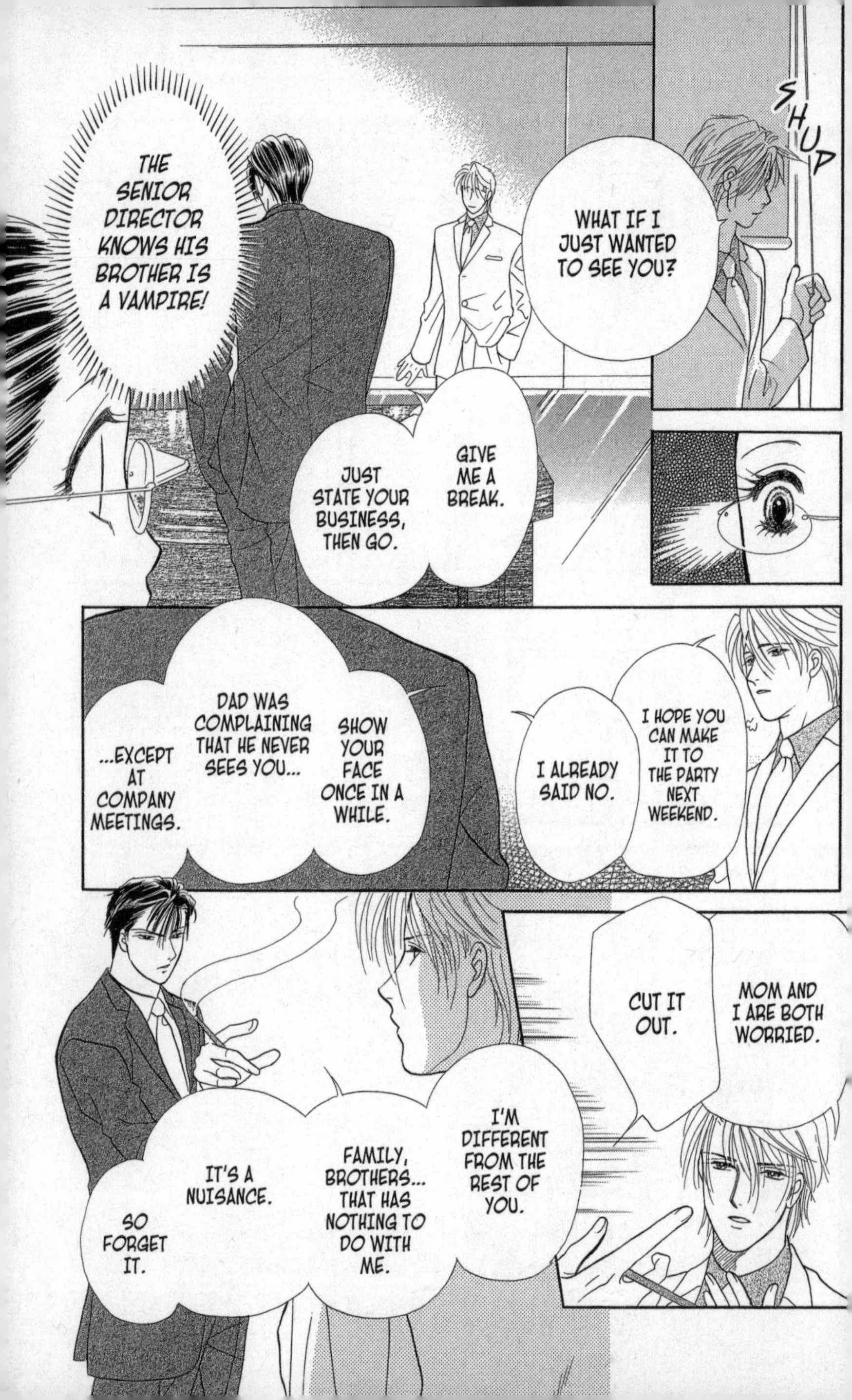
SHUP
WHAT IF I JUST WANTED TO SEE YOU?
GIVE ME A BREAK.
JUST STATE YOUR BUSINESS, THEN GO.
THE SENIOR DIRECTOR KNOWS HIS BROTHER IS A VAMPIRE!
I HOPE YOU CAN MAKE IT TO THE PARTY NEXT WEEKEND.
I ALREADY SAID NO.
SHOW YOUR FACE ONCE IN A WHILE.
DAD WAS COMPLAINING THAT HE NEVER SEES YOU...
...EXCEPT AT COMPANY MEETINGS.
MOM AND I ARE BOTH WORRIED.
CUT IT OUT.
I'M DIFFERENT FROM THE REST OF YOU.
FAMILY, BROTHERS... THAT HAS NOTHING TO DO WITH ME.
IT'S A NUISANCE.
SO FORGET IT.

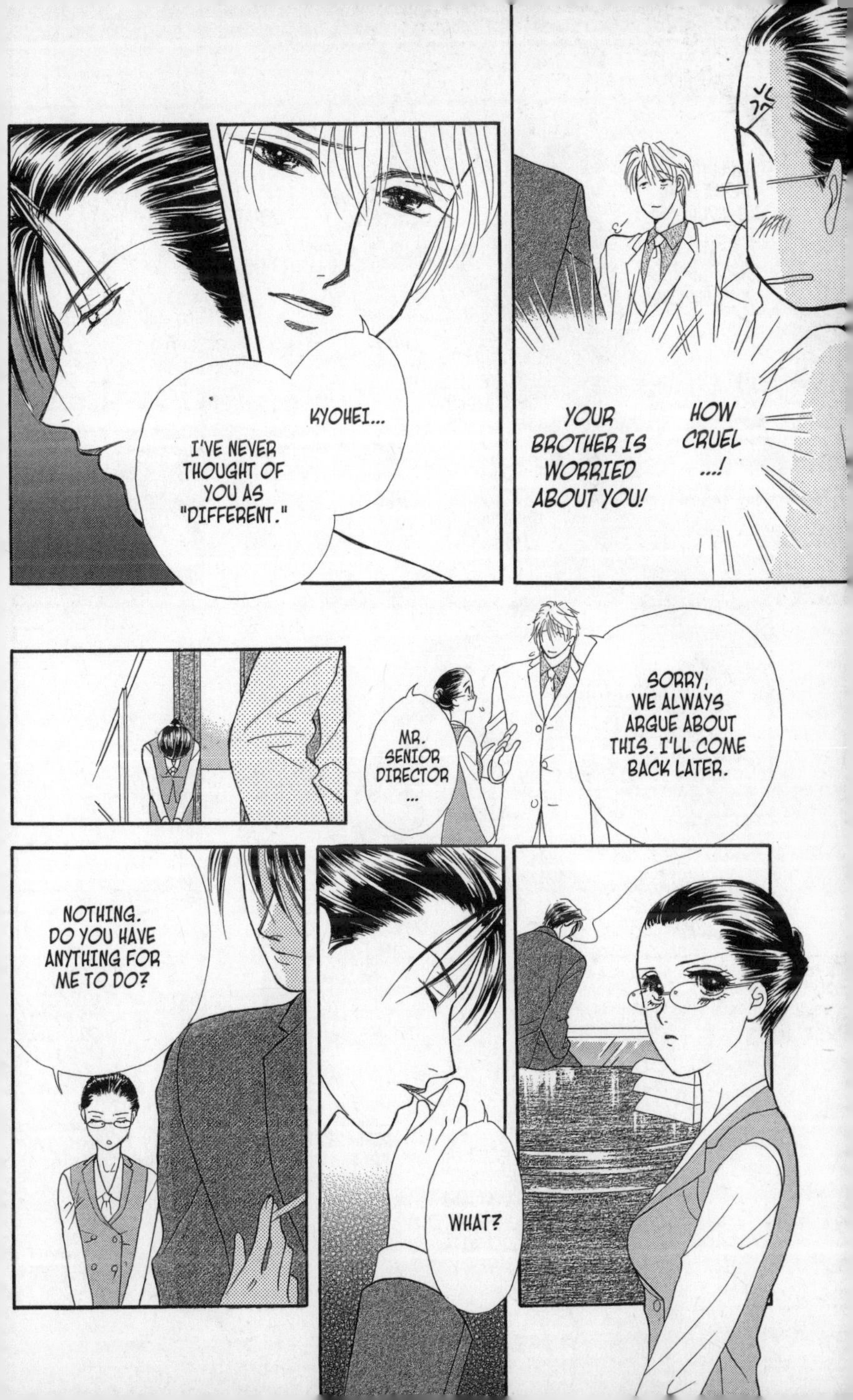
HOW CRUEL ...!
YOUR BROTHER IS WORRIED ABOUT YOU!
KYOHEI...
I'VE NEVER THOUGHT OF YOU AS "DIFFERENT."
SORRY, WE ALWAYS ARGUE ABOUT THIS. I'LL COME BACK LATER.
MR. SENIOR DIRECTOR ...
WHAT?
NOTHING. DO YOU HAVE ANYTHING FOR ME TO DO?

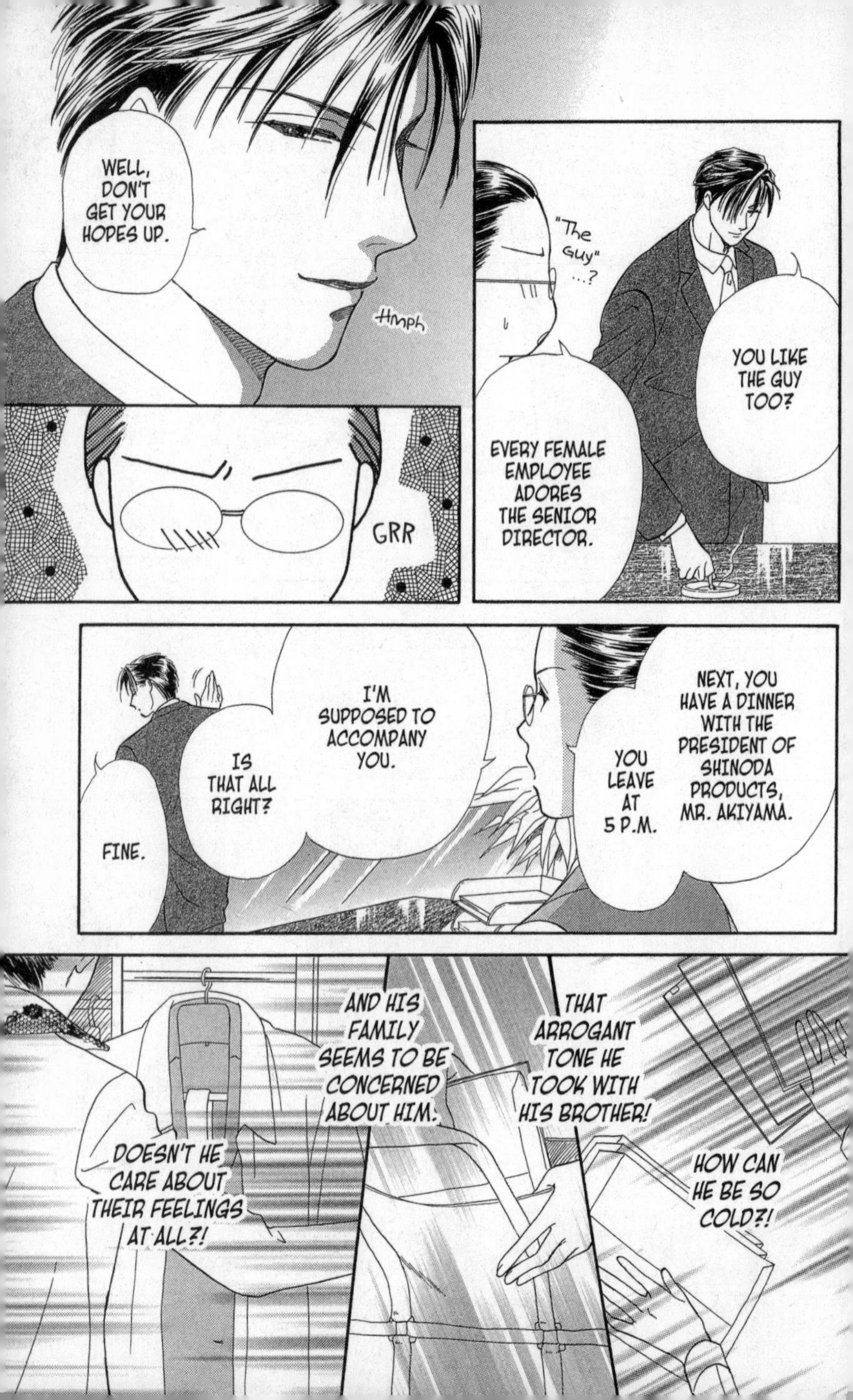

YOU LIKE THE GUY TOO?
"The Guy" ...?
EVERY FEMALE EMPLOYEE ADORES THE SENIOR DIRECTOR.
WELL, DON'T GET YOUR HOPES UP.
Hmph
GRR
NEXT, YOU HAVE A DINNER WITH THE PRESIDENT OF SHINODA PRODUCTS, MR. AKIYAMA.
YOU LEAVE AT 5 P.M.
I'M SUPPOSED TO ACCOMPANY YOU.
IS THAT ALL RIGHT?
FINE.
THAT ARROGANT TONE HE TOOK WITH HIS BROTHER!
AND HIS FAMILY SEEMS TO BE CONCERNED ABOUT HIM.
HOW CAN HE BE SO COLD?!
DOESN'T HE CARE ABOUT THEIR FEELINGS AT ALL?!

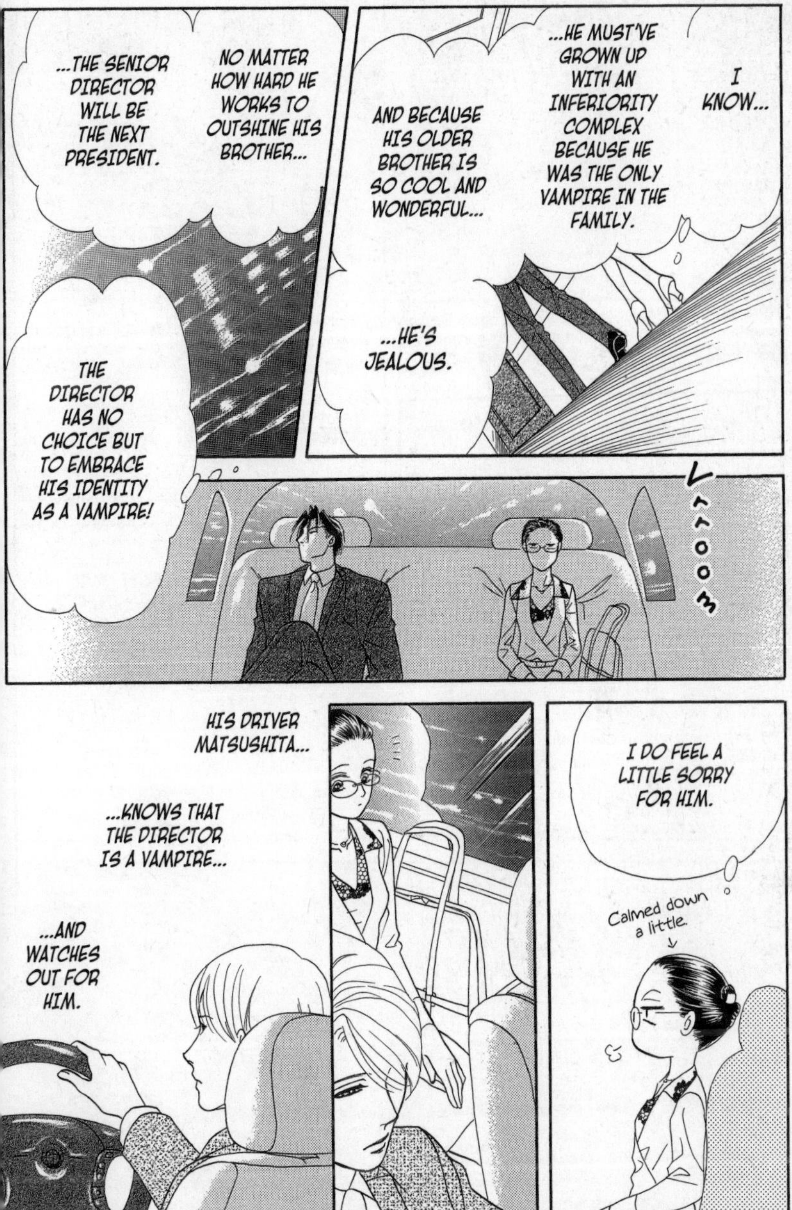
I KNOW...
...HE MUST'VE GROWN UP WITH AN INFERIORITY COMPLEX BECAUSE HE WAS THE ONLY VAMPIRE IN THE FAMILY.
AND BECAUSE HIS OLDER BROTHER IS SO COOL AND WONDERFUL...
...HE'S JEALOUS.
NO MATTER HOW HARD HE WORKS TO OUTSHINE HIS BROTHER...
...THE SENIOR DIRECTOR WILL BE THE NEXT PRESIDENT.
THE DIRECTOR HAS NO CHOICE BUT TO EMBRACE HIS IDENTITY AS A VAMPIRE!
Vrooom
I DO FEEL A LITTLE SORRY FOR HIM.
Calmed down a little.
HIS DRIVER MATSUSHITA...
...KNOWS THAT THE DIRECTOR IS A VAMPIRE...
...AND WATCHES OUT FOR HIM.

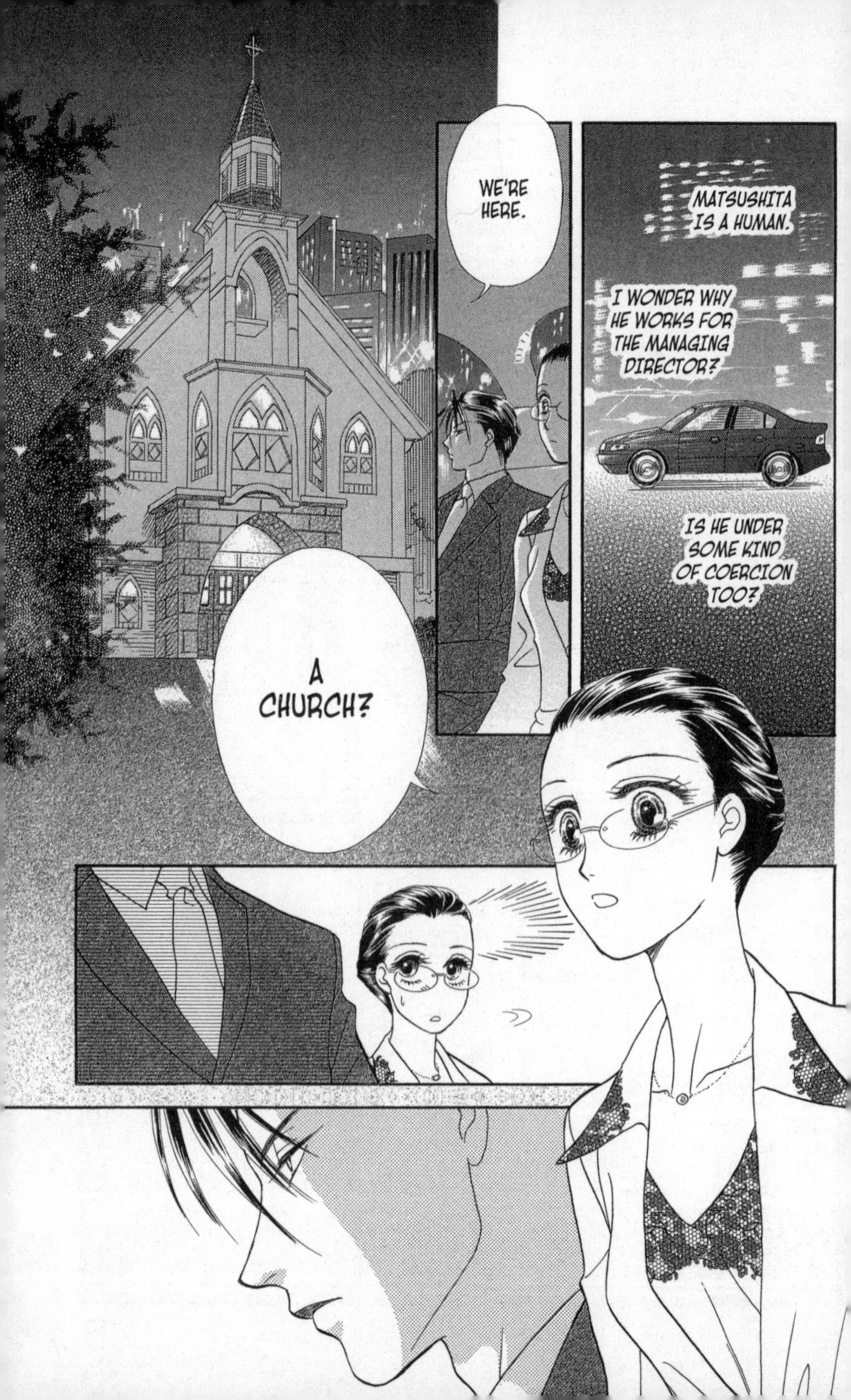
MATSUSHITA IS A HUMAN.
I WONDER WHY HE WORKS FOR THE MANAGING DIRECTOR?
IS HE UNDER SOME KIND OF COERCION TOO?
WE'RE HERE.
A CHURCH?

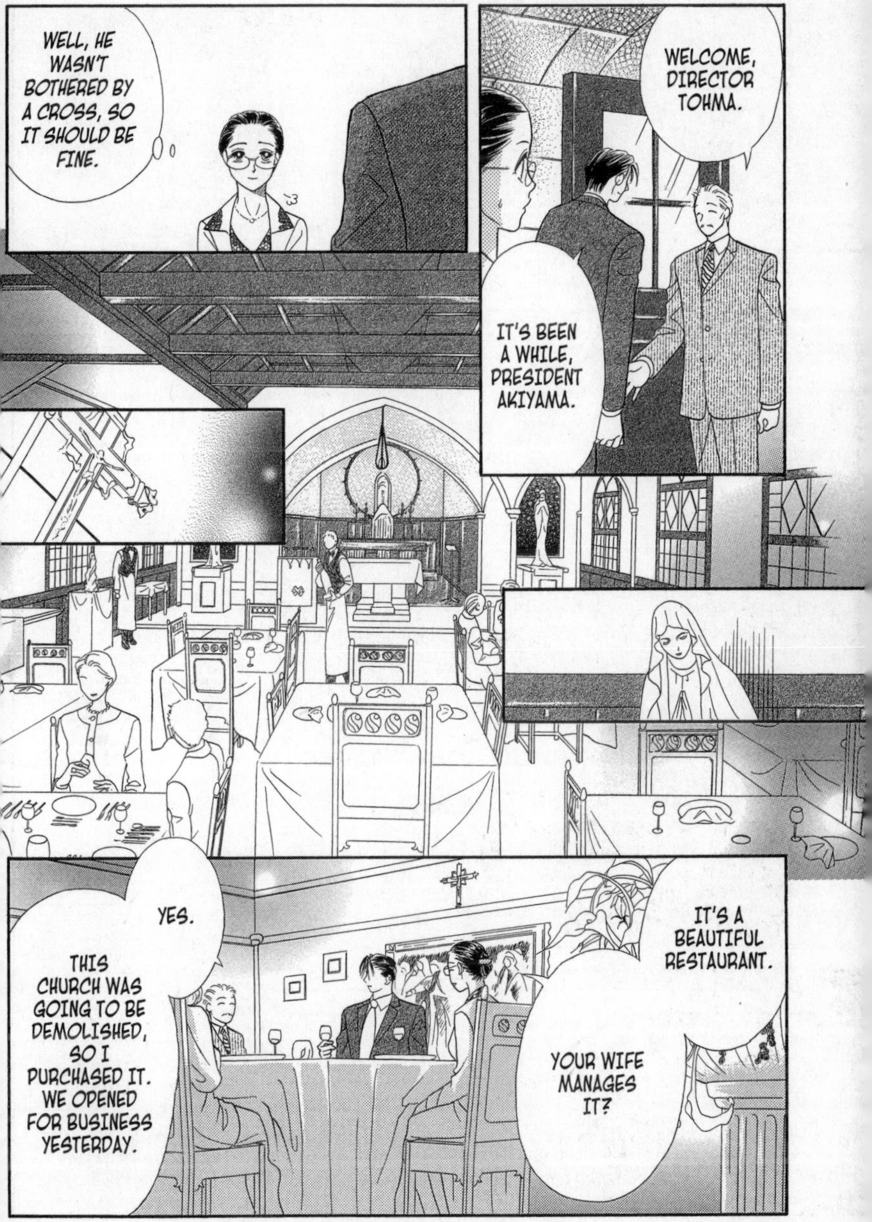
WELCOME, DIRECTOR TOHMA.
IT'S BEEN A WHILE, PRESIDENT AKIYAMA.
WELL, HE WASN'T BOTHERED BY A CROSS, SO IT SHOULD BE FINE.
IT'S A BEAUTIFUL RESTAURANT.
YOUR WIFE MANAGES IT?
YES.
THIS CHURCH WAS GOING TO BE DEMOLISHED, SO I PURCHASED IT. WE OPENED FOR BUSINESS YESTERDAY.

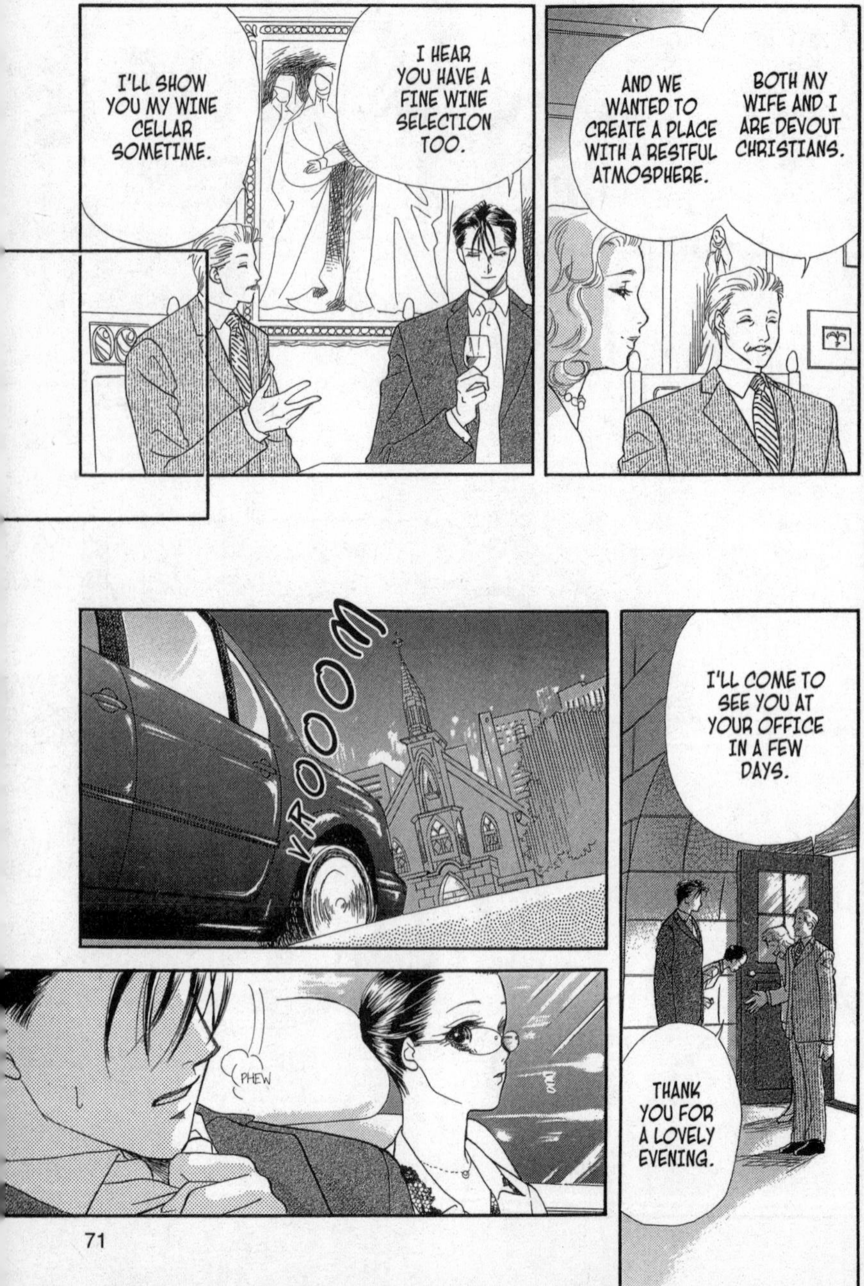
BOTH MY WIFE AND I ARE DEVOUT CHRISTIANS.
AND WE WANTED TO CREATE A PLACE WITH A RESTFUL ATMOSPHERE.
I HEAR YOU HAVE A FINE WINE SELECTION TOO.
I'LL SHOW YOU MY WINE CELLAR SOMETIME.
I'LL COME TO SEE YOU AT YOUR OFFICE IN A FEW DAYS.
THANK YOU FOR A LOVELY EVENING.
VROOOM
PHEW

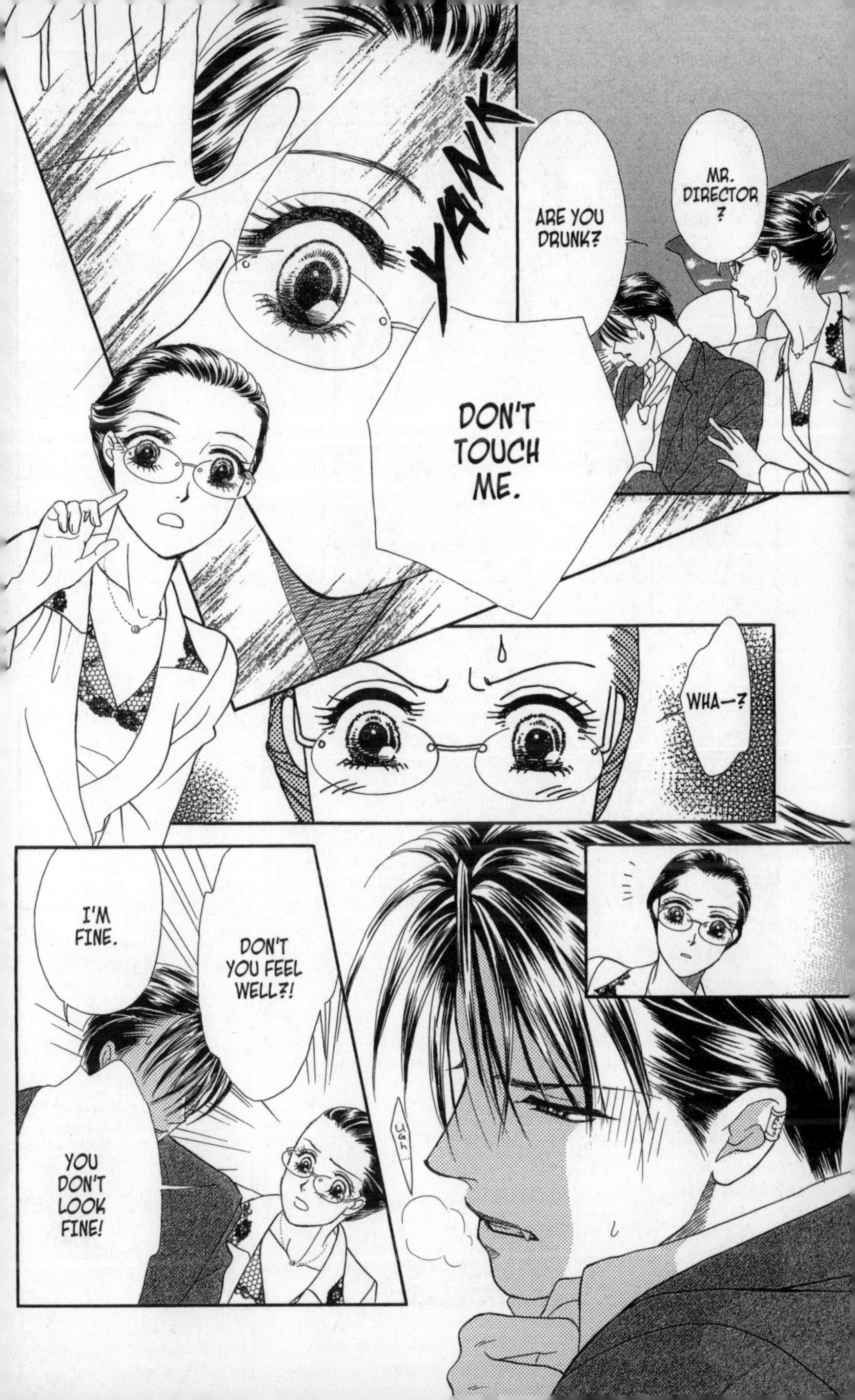
MR. DIRECTOR?
ARE YOU DRUNK?
YANK
DON'T TOUCH ME.
WHA—?
Ugh...
DON'T YOU FEEL WELL?!
I'M FINE.
YOU DON'T LOOK FINE!

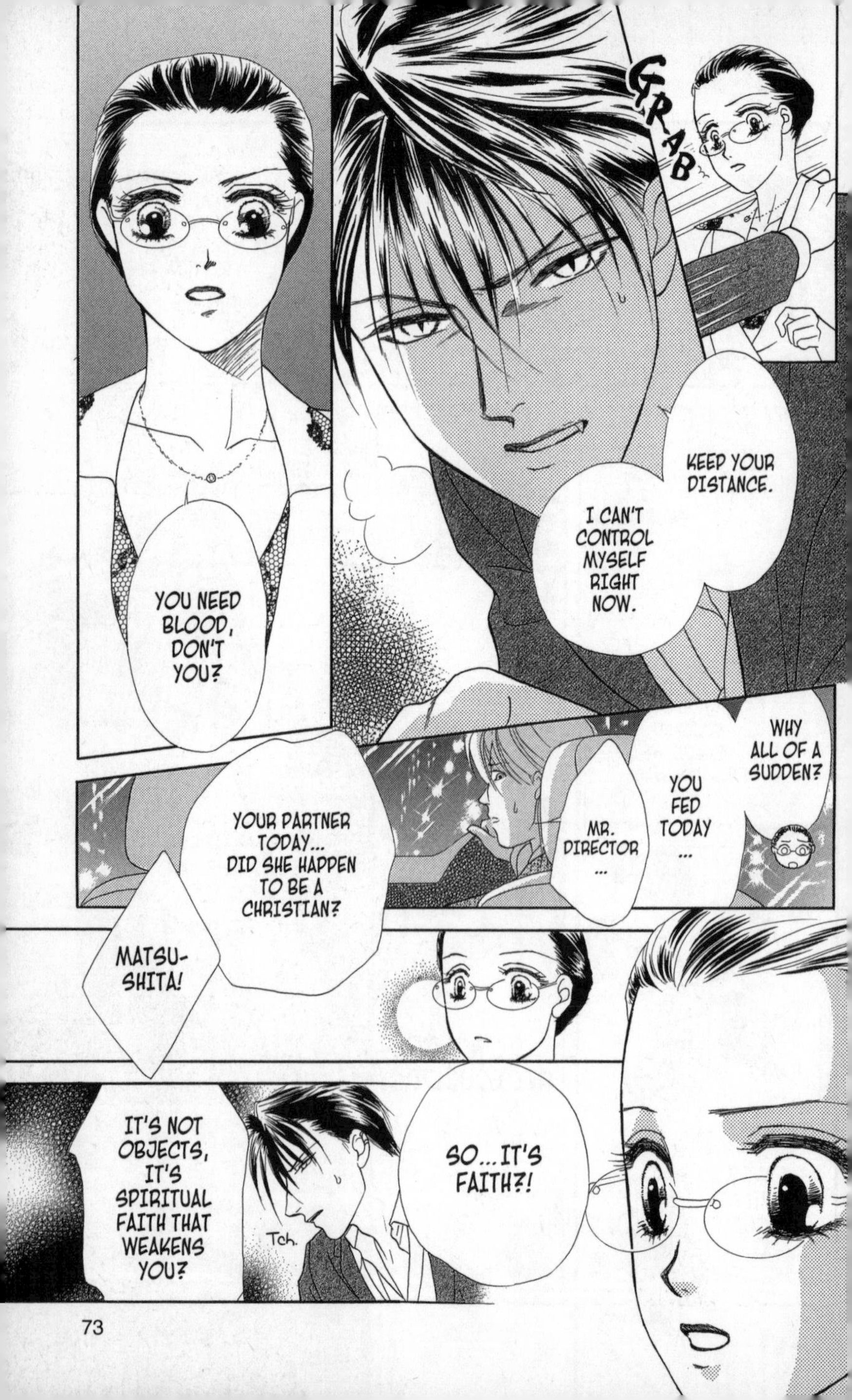
GRAB
KEEP YOUR DISTANCE.
I CAN'T CONTROL MYSELF RIGHT NOW.
YOU NEED BLOOD, DON'T YOU?
WHY ALL OF A SUDDEN?
YOU FED TODAY ...
MR. DIRECTOR ...
YOUR PARTNER TODAY... DID SHE HAPPEN TO BE A CHRISTIAN?
MATSU-SHITA!
SO...IT'S FAITH?!
Tch.
IT'S NOT OBJECTS, IT'S SPIRITUAL FAITH THAT WEAKENS YOU?

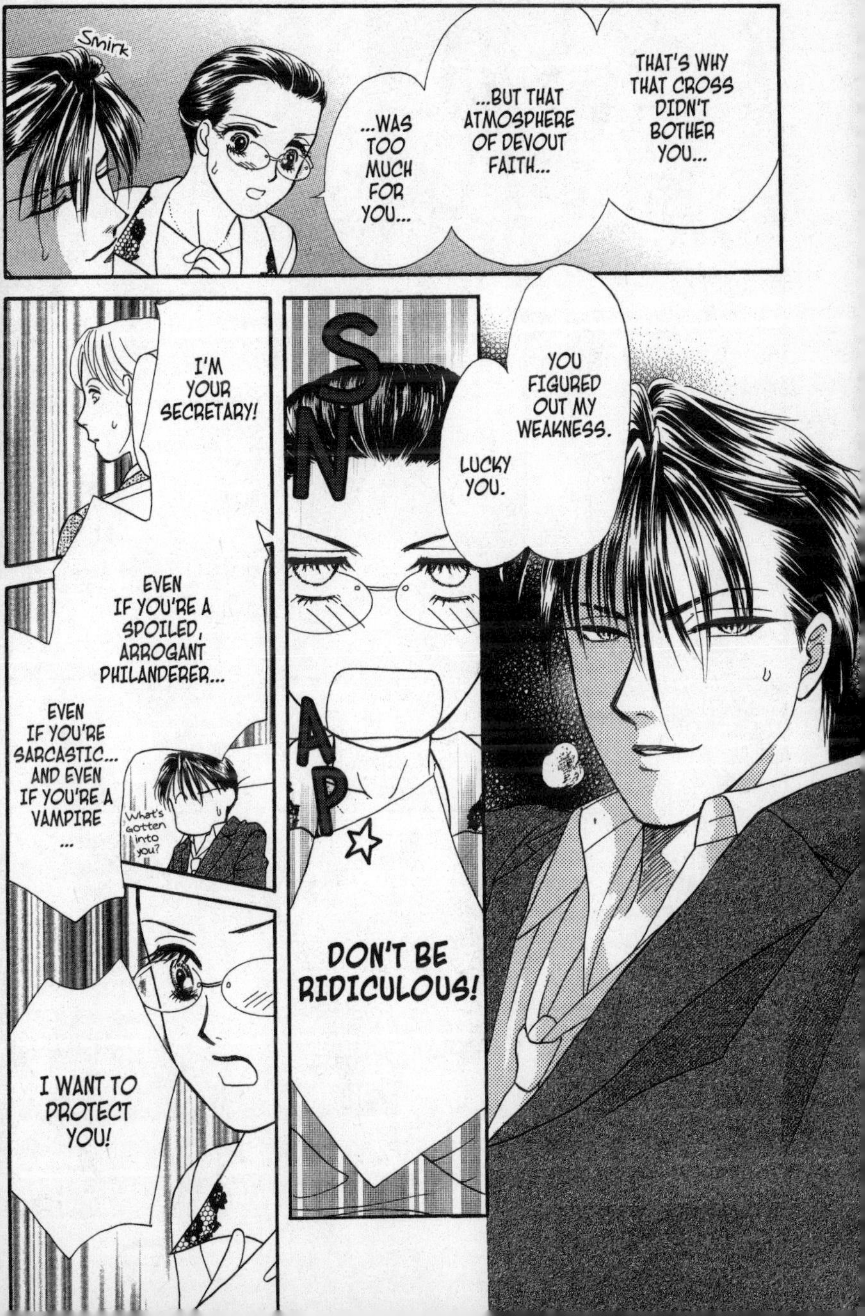
THAT'S WHY THAT CROSS DIDN'T BOTHER YOU...
...BUT THAT ATMOSPHERE OF DEVOUT FAITH...
...WAS TOO MUCH FOR YOU...
Smirk
YOU FIGURED OUT MY WEAKNESS.
LUCKY YOU.
SNAP☆
DON'T BE RIDICULOUS!
I'M YOUR SECRETARY!
EVEN IF YOU'RE A SPOILED, ARROGANT PHILANDERER...
EVEN IF YOU'RE SARCASTIC... AND EVEN IF YOU'RE A VAMPIRE ...
What's gotten into you?
I WANT TO PROTECT YOU!

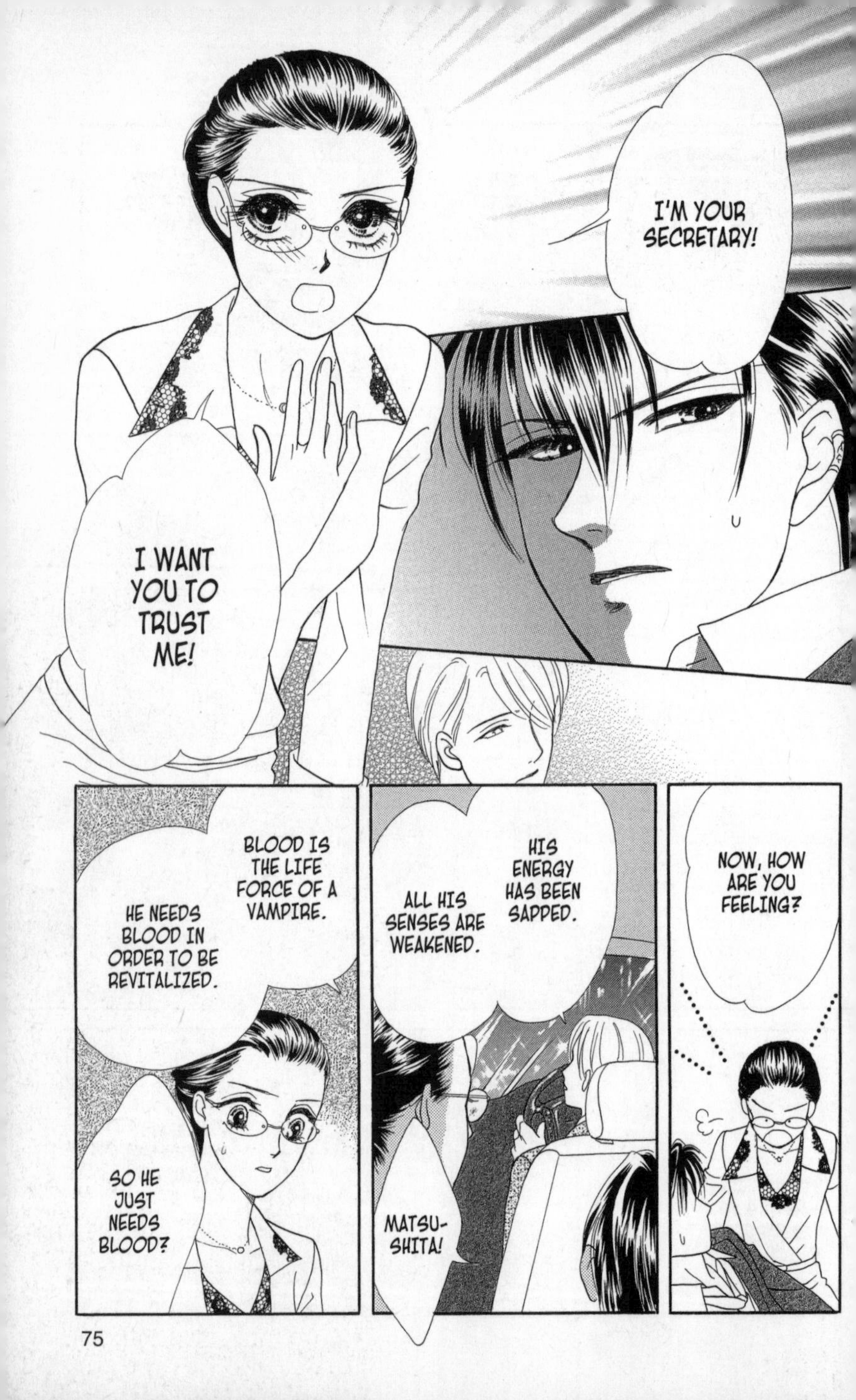
I'M YOUR SECRETARY!
I WANT YOU TO TRUST ME!
NOW, HOW ARE YOU FEELING?
HIS ENERGY HAS BEEN SAPPED.
ALL HIS SENSES ARE WEAKENED.
MATSU-SHITA!
BLOOD IS THE LIFE FORCE OF A VAMPIRE.
HE NEEDS BLOOD IN ORDER TO BE REVITALIZED.
SO HE JUST NEEDS BLOOD?

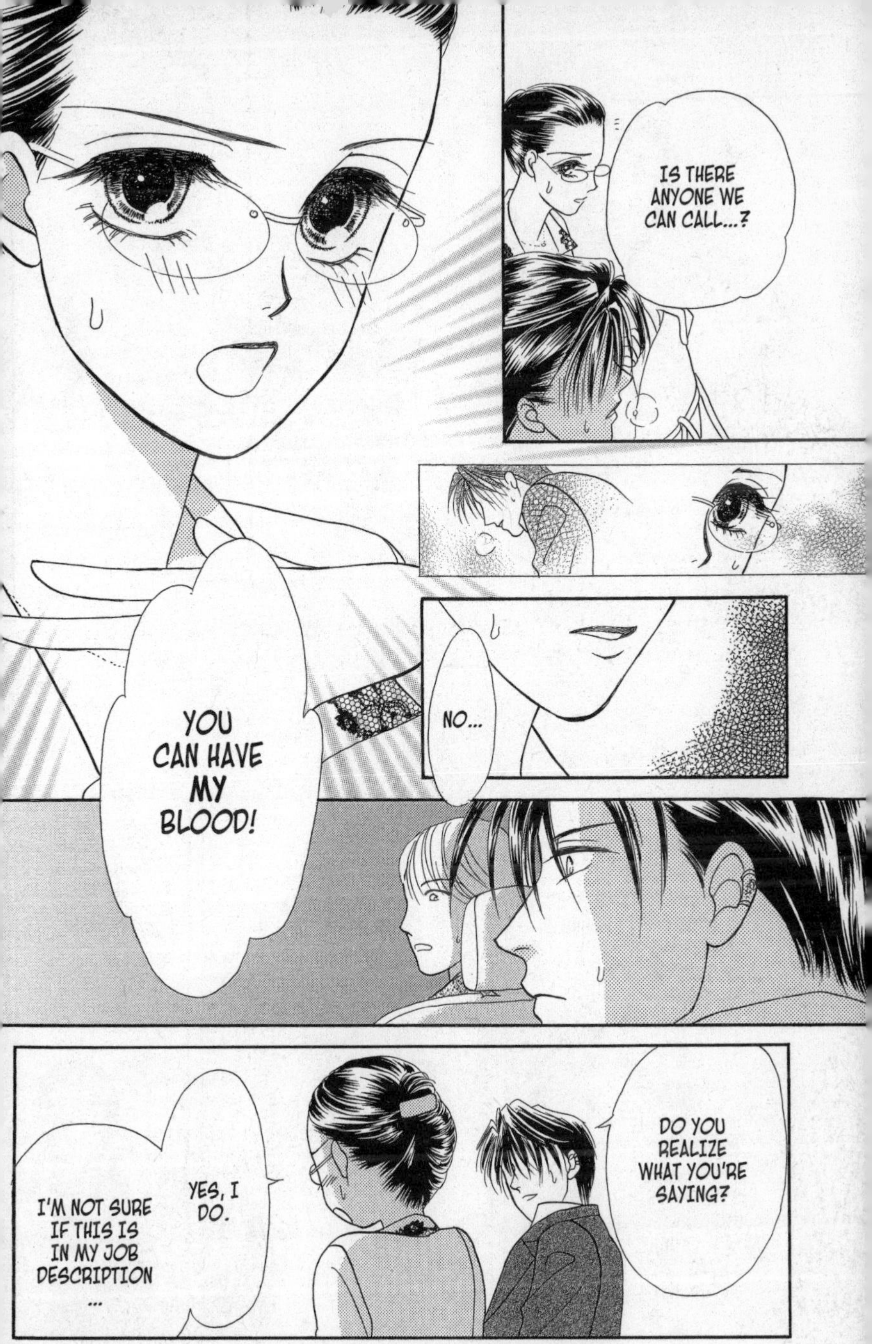
IS THERE ANYONE WE CAN CALL...?
NO...
YOU CAN HAVE MY BLOOD!
DO YOU REALIZE WHAT YOU'RE SAYING?
YES, I DO.
I'M NOT SURE IF THIS IS IN MY JOB DESCRIPTION ...

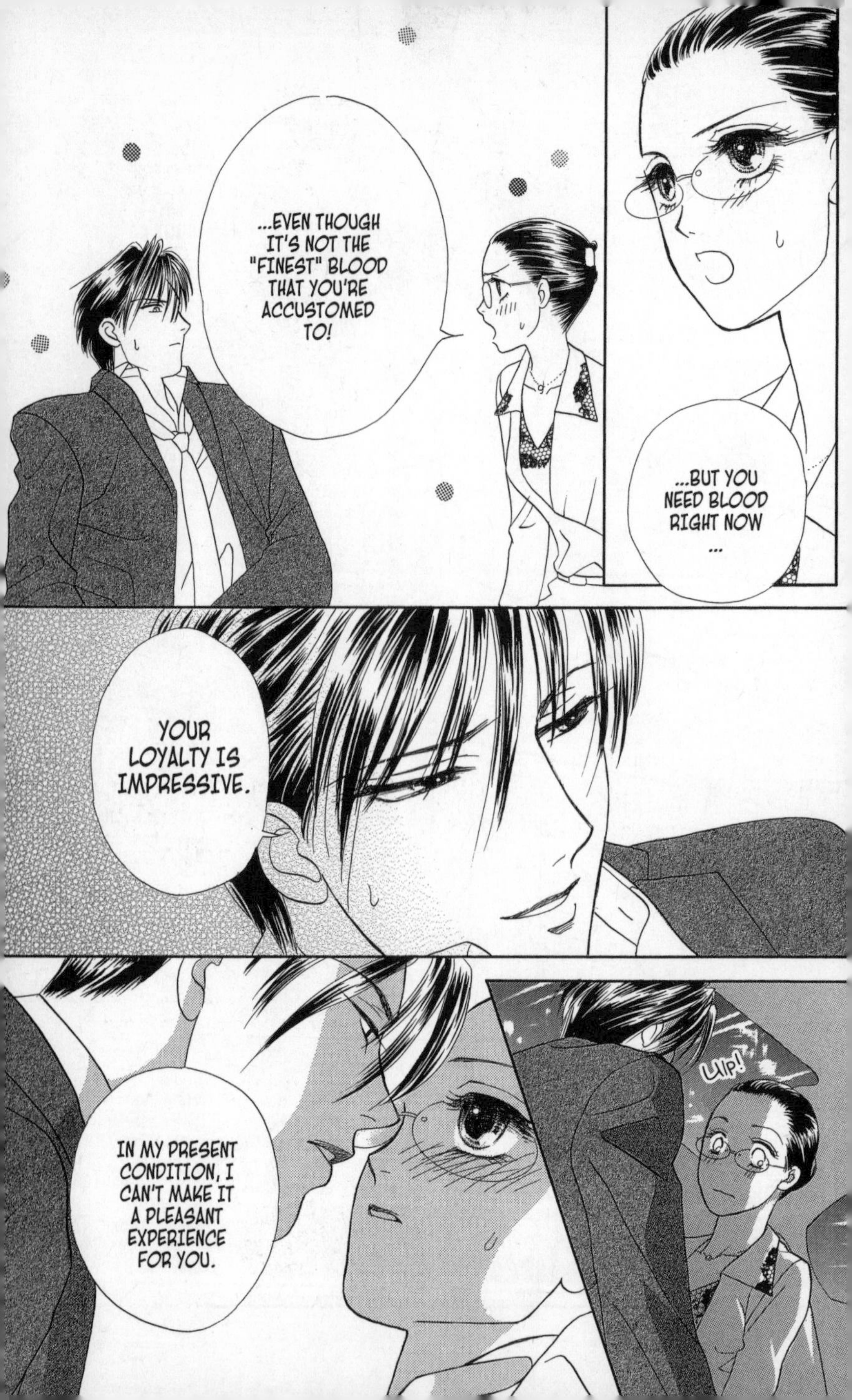
...BUT YOU NEED BLOOD RIGHT NOW ...
...EVEN THOUGH IT'S NOT THE "FINEST" BLOOD THAT YOU'RE ACCUSTOMED TO!
YOUR LOYALTY IS IMPRESSIVE.
UP!
IN MY PRESENT CONDITION, I CAN'T MAKE IT A PLEASANT EXPERIENCE FOR YOU.

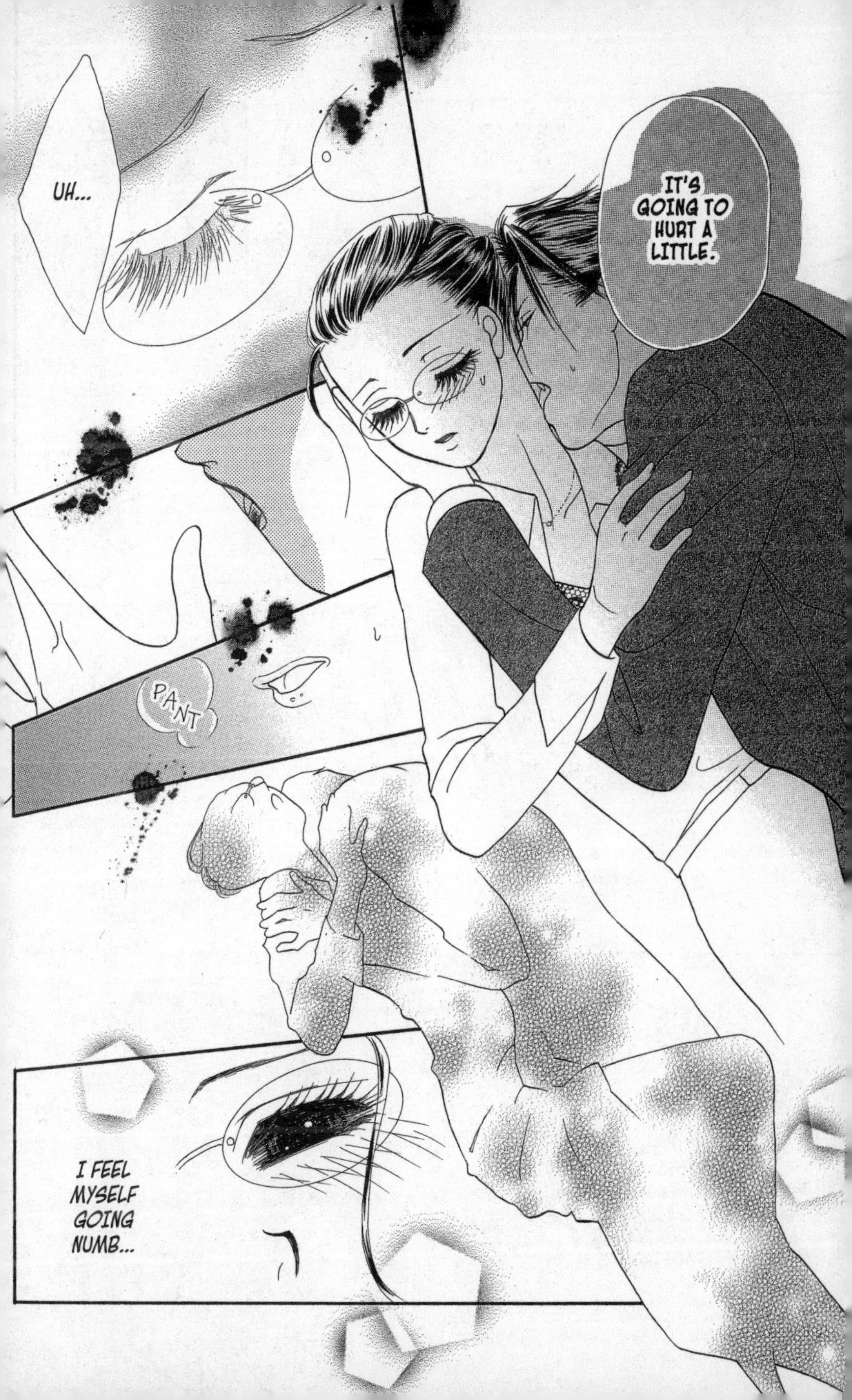
IT'S GOING TO HURT A LITTLE.
UH...
PANT
I FEEL MYSELF GOING NUMB...

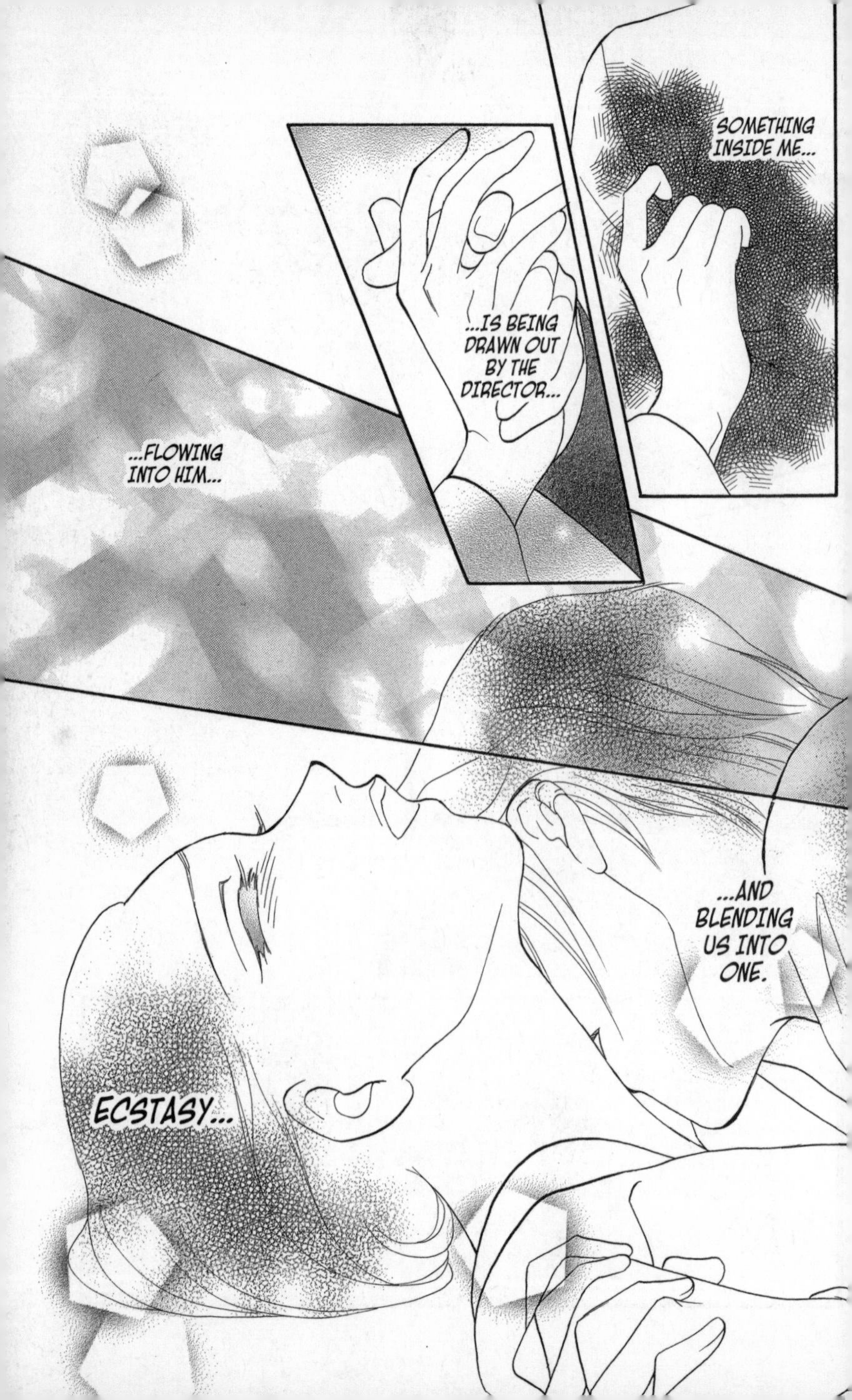
SOMETHING INSIDE ME...
...IS BEING DRAWN OUT BY THE DIRECTOR...
...FLOWING INTO HIM...
...AND BLENDING US INTO ONE.
ECSTASY...

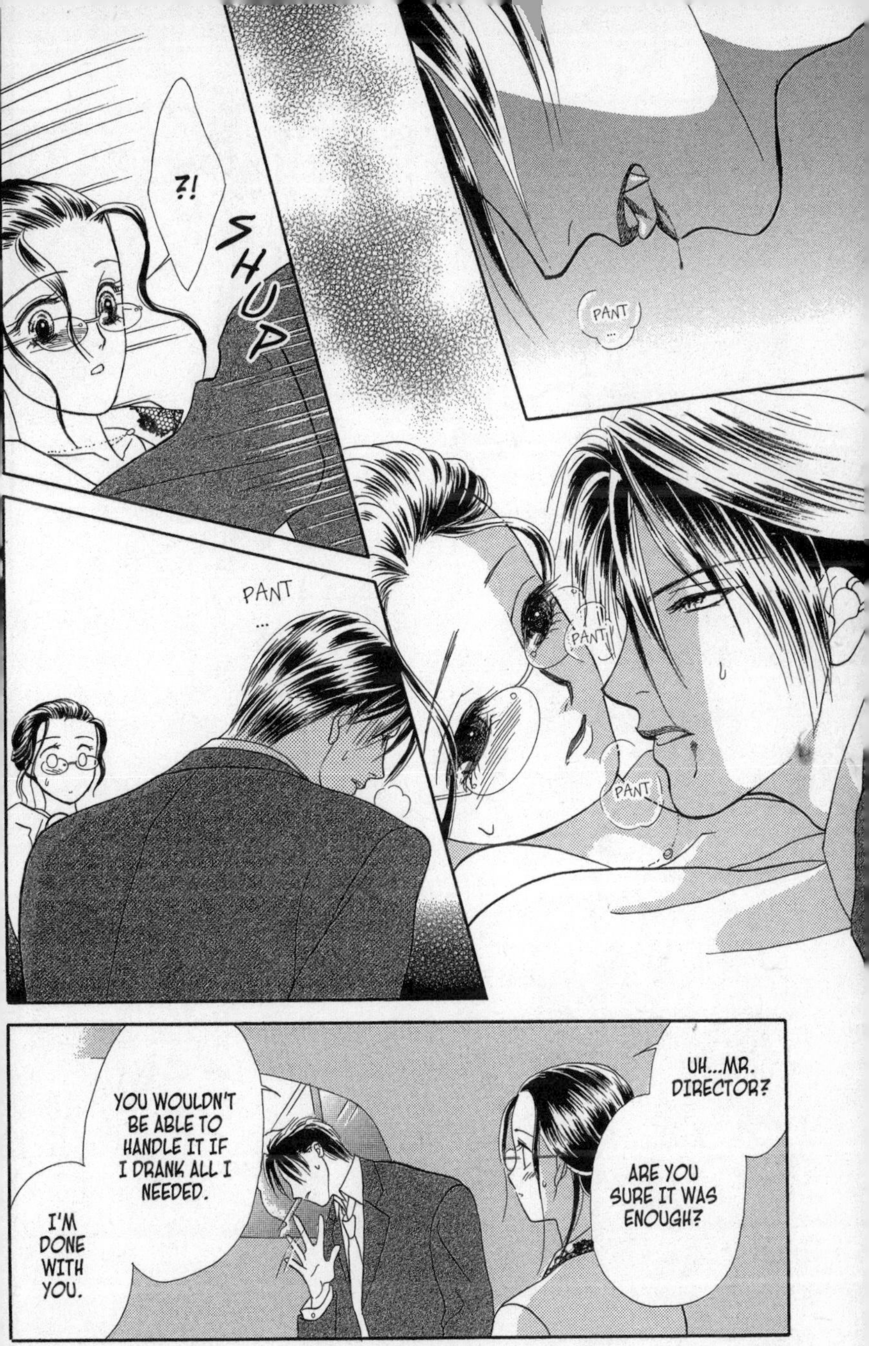
PANT ...
?!
SHUP
PANT!
PANT
PANT ...
UH...MR. DIRECTOR?
ARE YOU SURE IT WAS ENOUGH?
YOU WOULDN'T BE ABLE TO HANDLE IT IF I DRANK ALL I NEEDED.
I'M DONE WITH YOU.

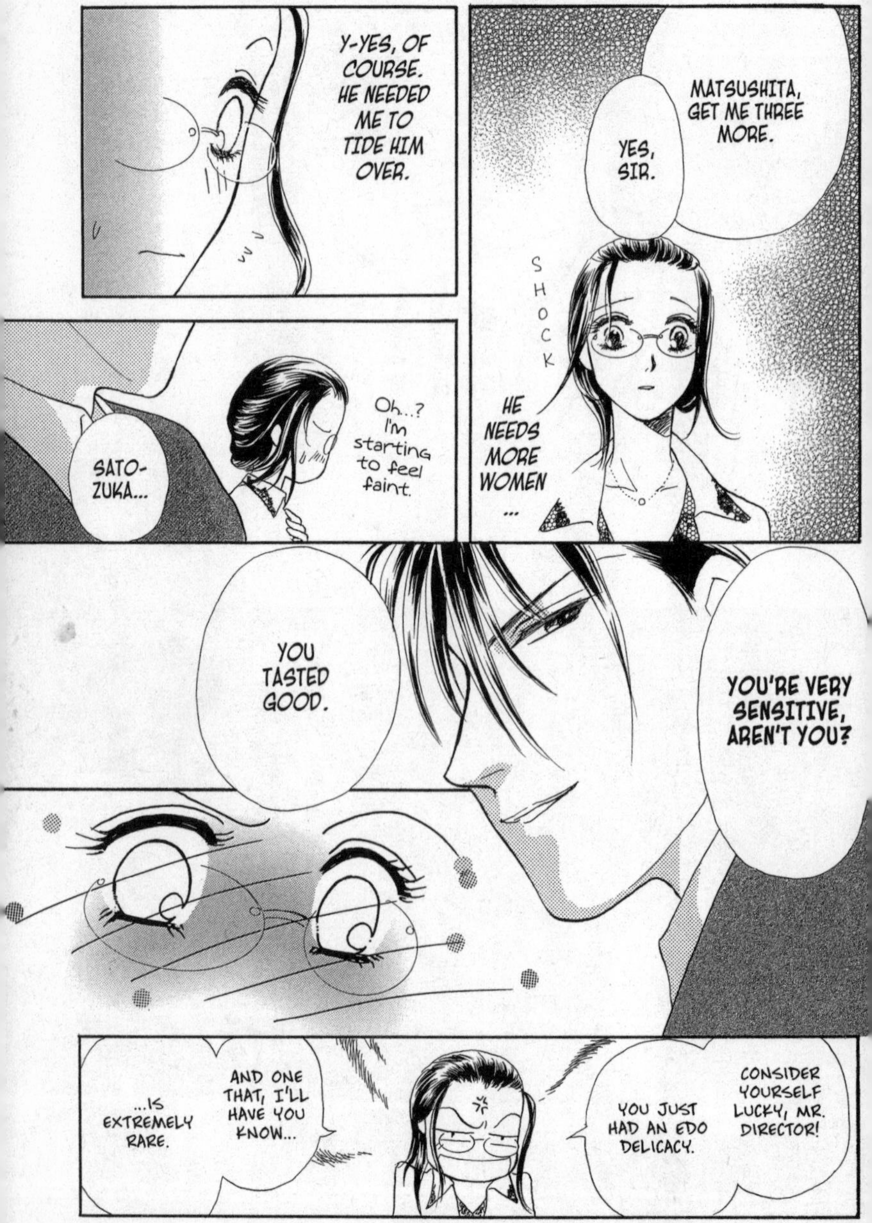
MATSUSHITA, GET ME THREE MORE.
YES, SIR.
SHOCK
HE NEEDS MORE WOMEN...
Y-YES, OF COURSE. HE NEEDED ME TO TIDE HIM OVER.
Oh...? I'm starting to feel faint.
SATO-ZUKA...
YOU'RE VERY SENSITIVE, AREN'T YOU?
YOU TASTED GOOD.
CONSIDER YOURSELF LUCKY, MR. DIRECTOR!
YOU JUST HAD AN EDO DELICACY.
AND ONE THAT, I'LL HAVE YOU KNOW...
...IS EXTREMELY RARE.

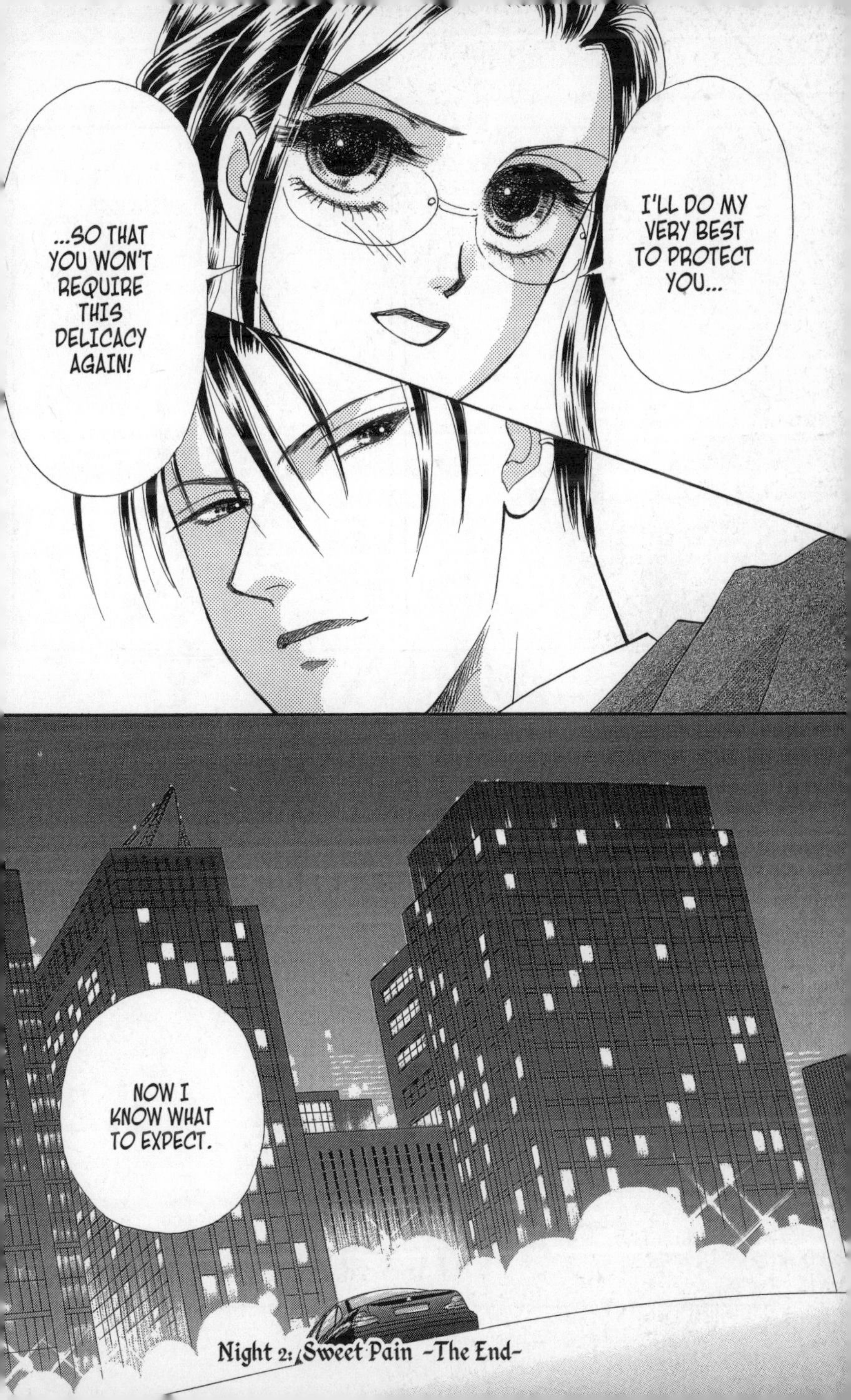
I'LL DO MY VERY BEST TO PROTECT YOU...
...SO THAT YOU WON'T REQUIRE THIS DELICACY AGAIN!
NOW I KNOW WHAT TO EXPECT.
Night 2: Sweet Pain -The End-

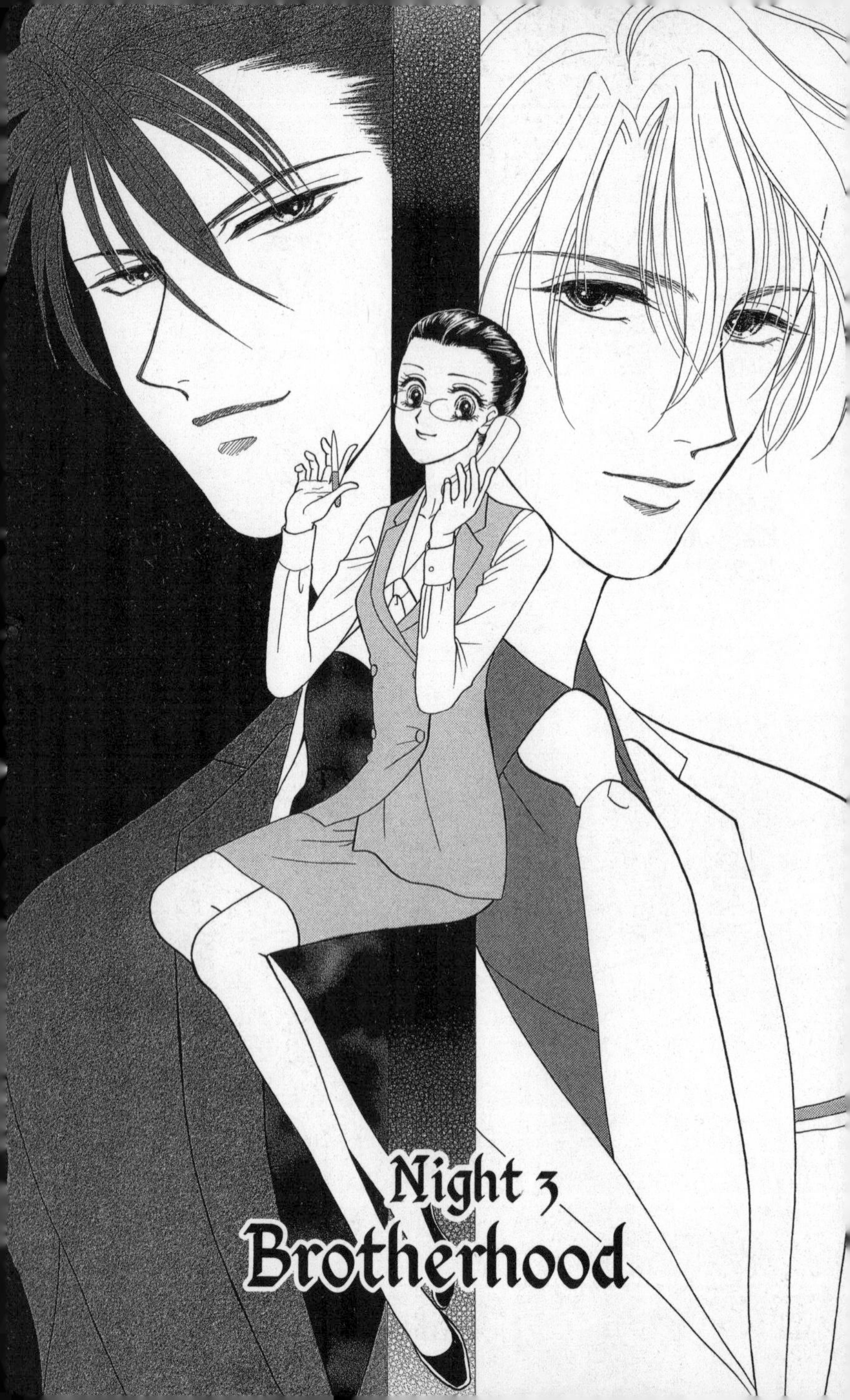
Night 3
Brotherhood

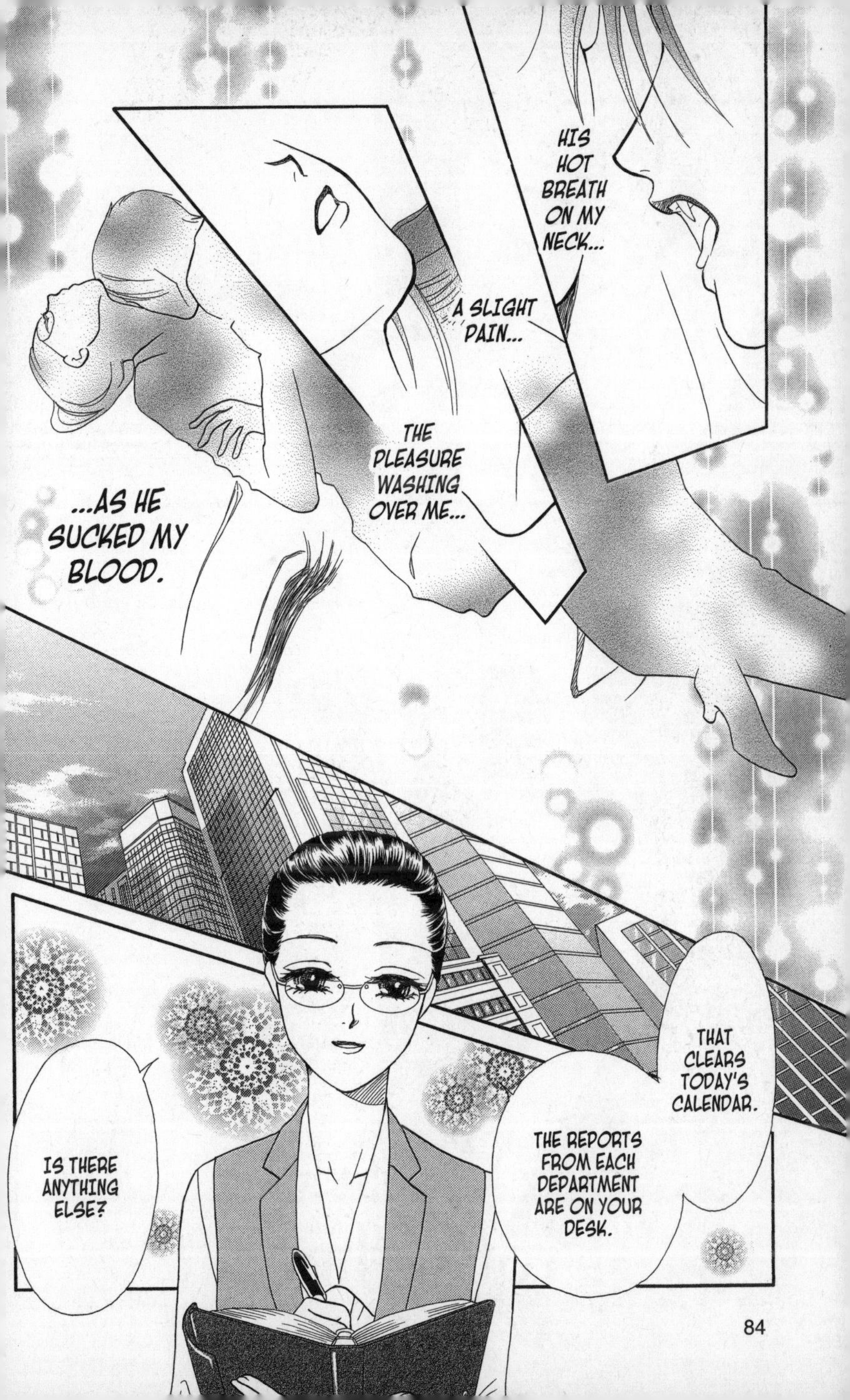
HIS HOT BREATH ON MY NECK...
A SLIGHT PAIN...
THE PLEASURE WASHING OVER ME...
...AS HE SUCKED MY BLOOD.
THAT CLEARS TODAY'S CALENDAR.
THE REPORTS FROM EACH DEPARTMENT ARE ON YOUR DESK.
IS THERE ANYTHING ELSE?

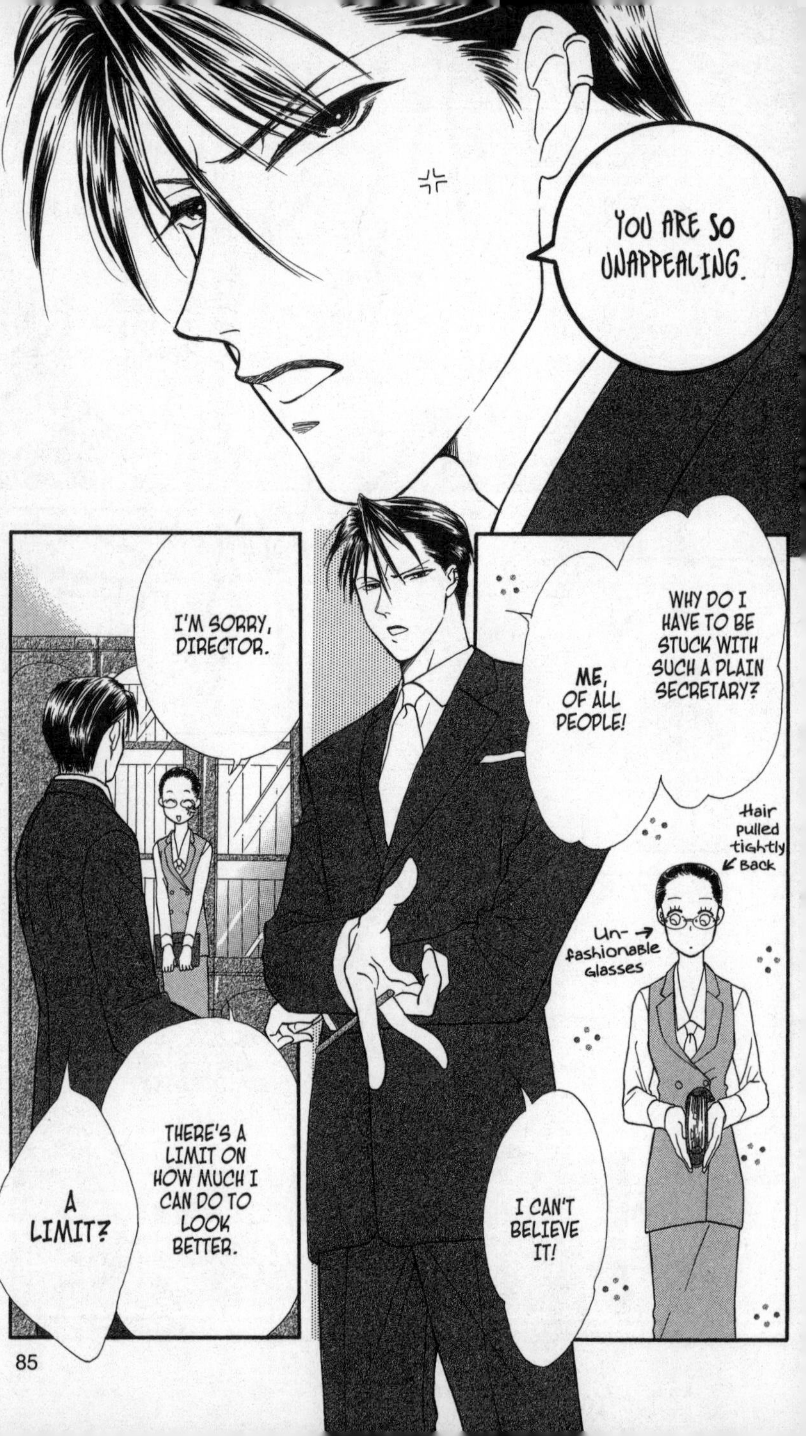
YOU ARE SO UNAPPEALING.
WHY DO I HAVE TO BE STUCK WITH SUCH A PLAIN SECRETARY?
ME, OF ALL PEOPLE!
Hair pulled tightly Back
Un-fashionable Glasses
I CAN'T BELIEVE IT!
I'M SORRY, DIRECTOR.
THERE'S A LIMIT ON HOW MUCH I CAN DO TO LOOK BETTER.
A LIMIT?

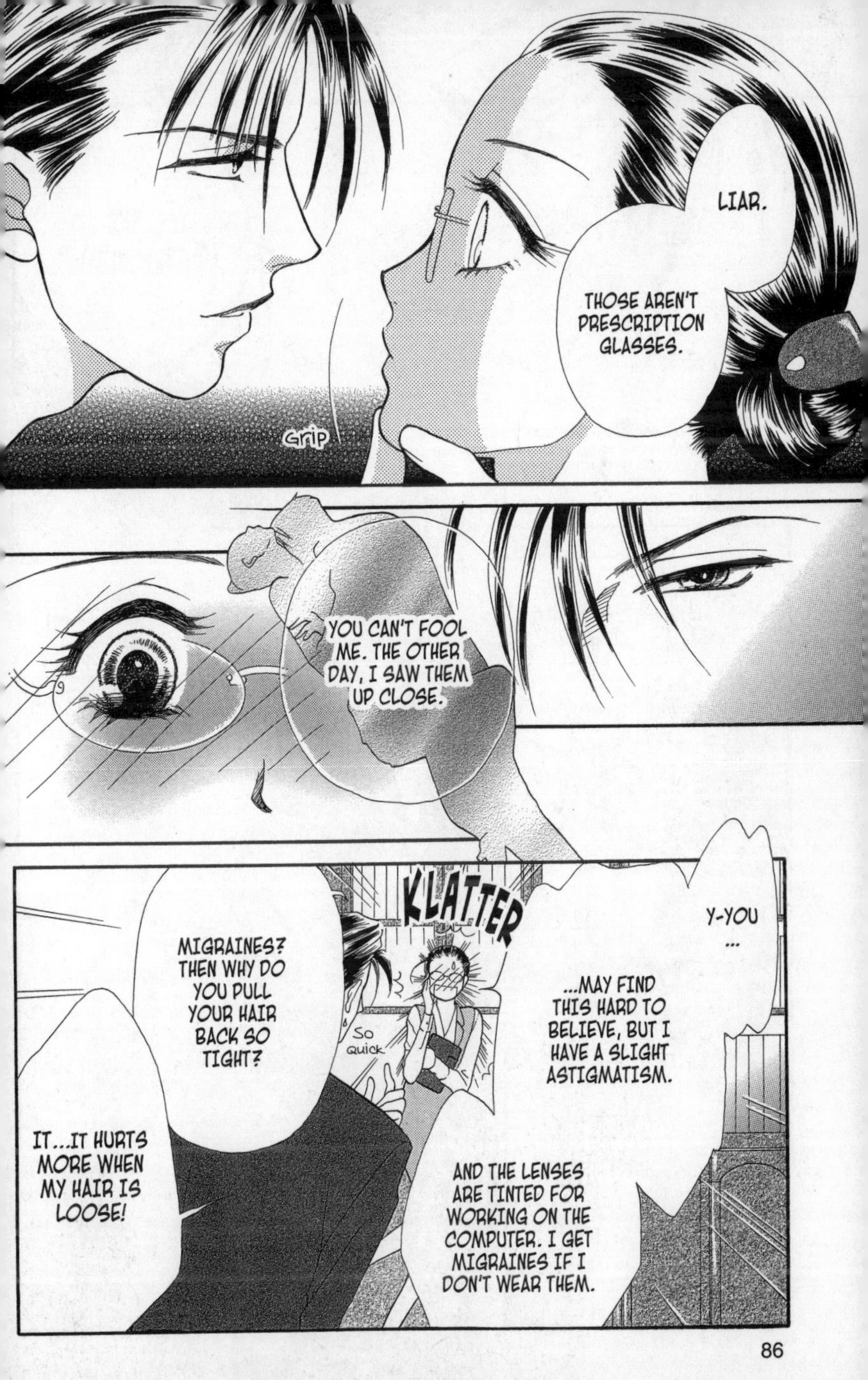
LIAR.
THOSE AREN'T PRESCRIPTION GLASSES.
Grip
YOU CAN'T FOOL ME. THE OTHER DAY, I SAW THEM UP CLOSE.
Y-YOU ...
...MAY FIND THIS HARD TO BELIEVE, BUT I HAVE A SLIGHT ASTIGMATISM.
AND THE LENSES ARE TINTED FOR WORKING ON THE COMPUTER. I GET MIGRAINES IF I DON'T WEAR THEM.
KLATTER
So quick
MIGRAINES? THEN WHY DO YOU PULL YOUR HAIR BACK SO TIGHT?
IT...IT HURTS MORE WHEN MY HAIR IS LOOSE!

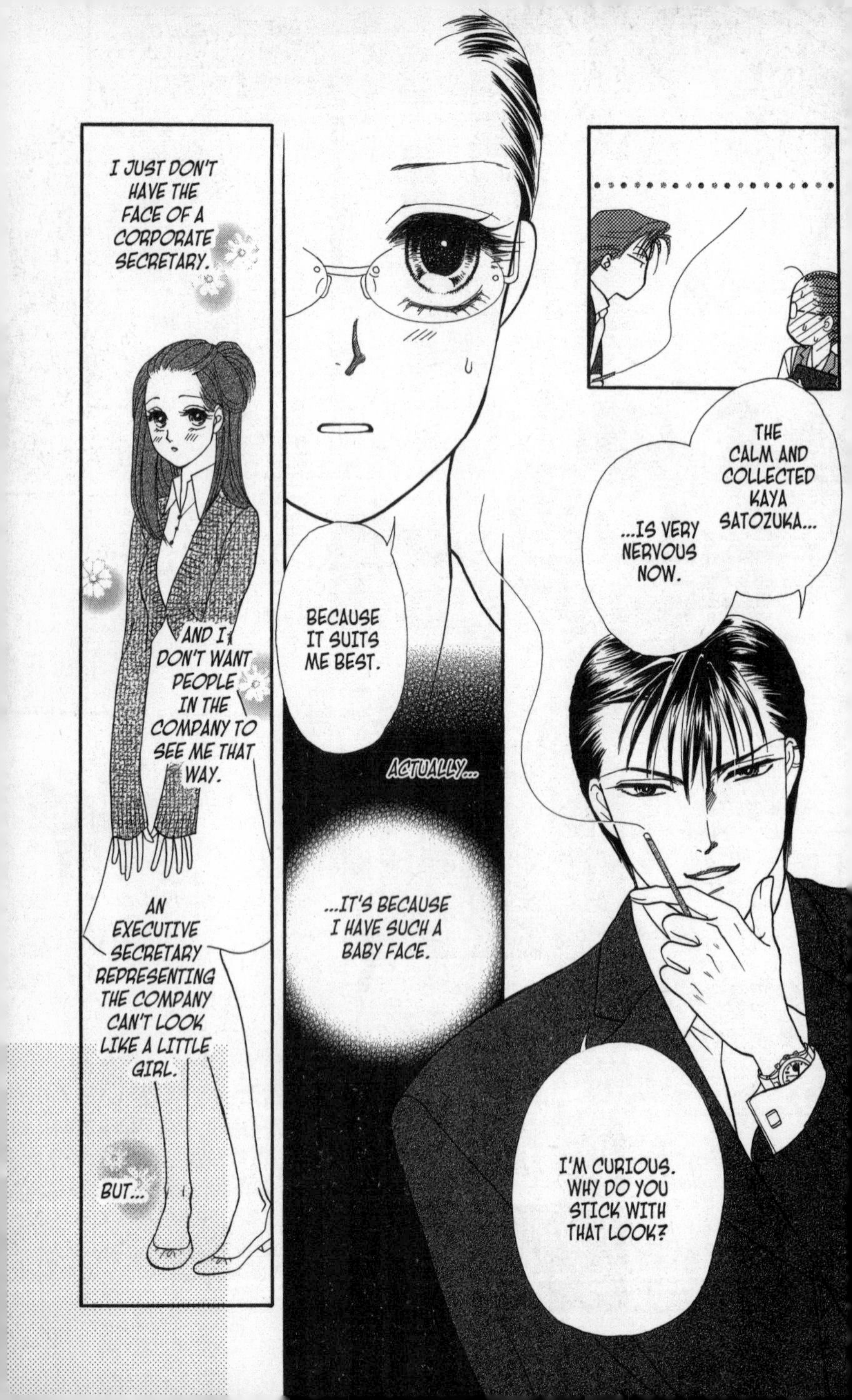
THE CALM AND COLLECTED KAYA SATOZUKA...
...IS VERY NERVOUS NOW.
I'M CURIOUS. WHY DO YOU STICK WITH THAT LOOK?
BECAUSE IT SUITS ME BEST.
ACTUALLY...
...IT'S BECAUSE I HAVE SUCH A BABY FACE.
I JUST DON'T HAVE THE FACE OF A CORPORATE SECRETARY.
AND I DON'T WANT PEOPLE IN THE COMPANY TO SEE ME THAT WAY.
AN EXECUTIVE SECRETARY REPRESENTING THE COMPANY CAN'T LOOK LIKE A LITTLE GIRL.
BUT...

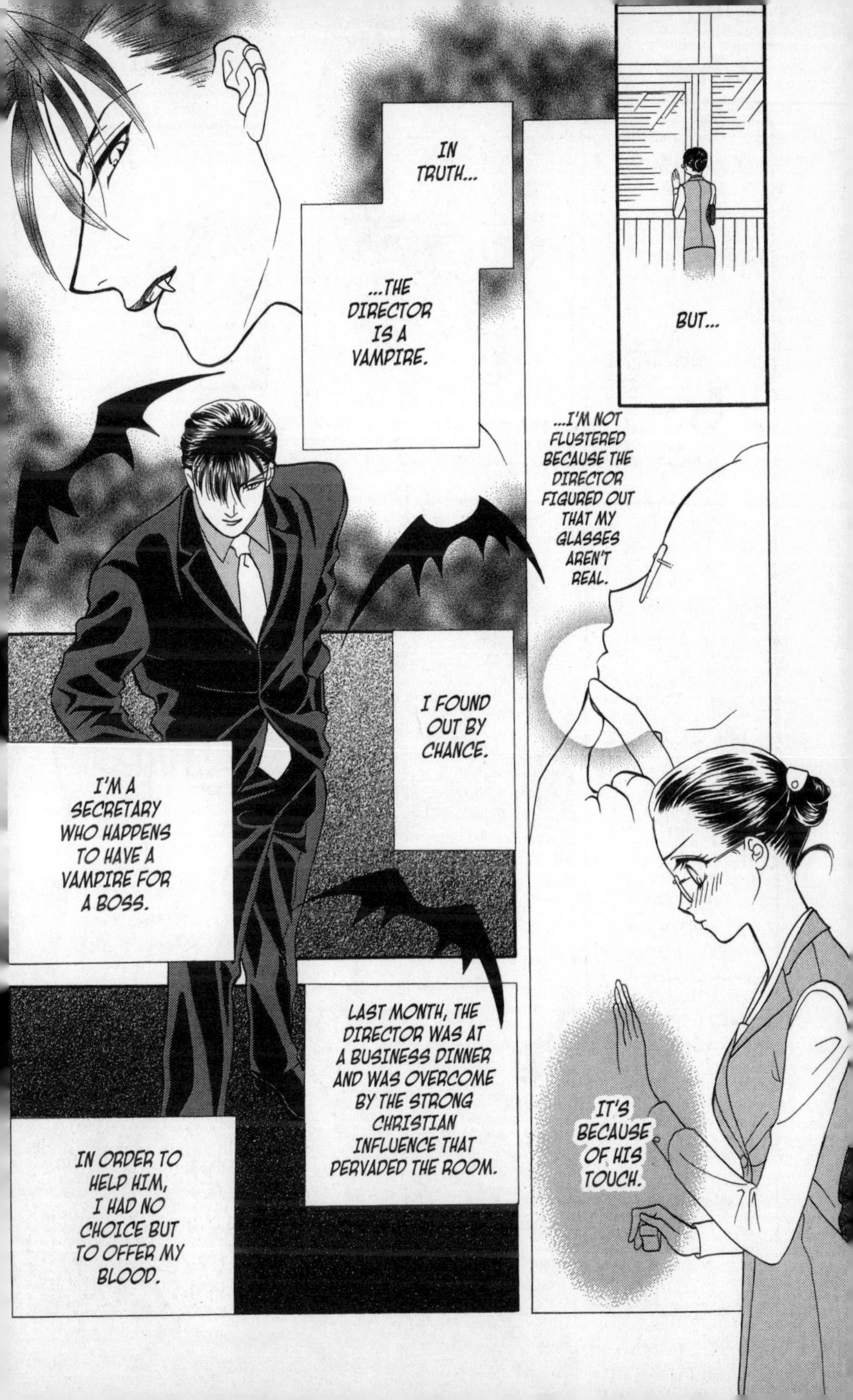
BUT...
...I'M NOT FLUSTERED BECAUSE THE DIRECTOR FIGURED OUT THAT MY GLASSES AREN'T REAL.
IT'S BECAUSE OF HIS TOUCH.
IN TRUTH...
...THE DIRECTOR IS A VAMPIRE.
I FOUND OUT BY CHANCE.
I'M A SECRETARY WHO HAPPENS TO HAVE A VAMPIRE FOR A BOSS.
LAST MONTH, THE DIRECTOR WAS AT A BUSINESS DINNER AND WAS OVERCOME BY THE STRONG CHRISTIAN INFLUENCE THAT PERVADED THE ROOM.
IN ORDER TO HELP HIM, I HAD NO CHOICE BUT TO OFFER MY BLOOD.

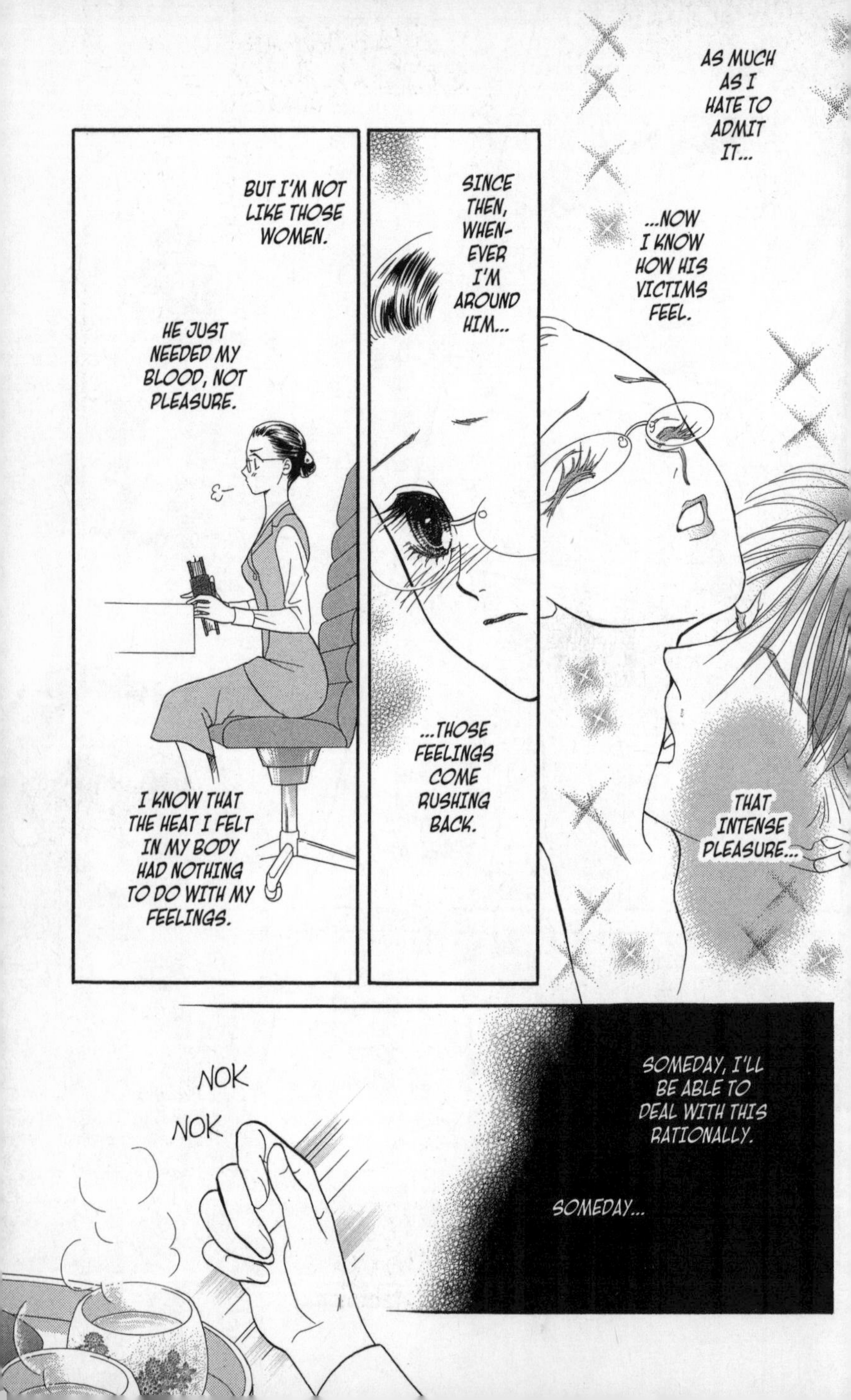
AS MUCH AS I HATE TO ADMIT IT...
...NOW I KNOW HOW HIS VICTIMS FEEL.
THAT INTENSE PLEASURE...
SINCE THEN, WHEN-EVER I'M AROUND HIM...
...THOSE FEELINGS COME RUSHING BACK.
BUT I'M NOT LIKE THOSE WOMEN.
HE JUST NEEDED MY BLOOD, NOT PLEASURE.
I KNOW THAT THE HEAT I FELT IN MY BODY HAD NOTHING TO DO WITH MY FEELINGS.
SOMEDAY, I'LL BE ABLE TO DEAL WITH THIS RATIONALLY.
SOMEDAY...
NOK
NOK

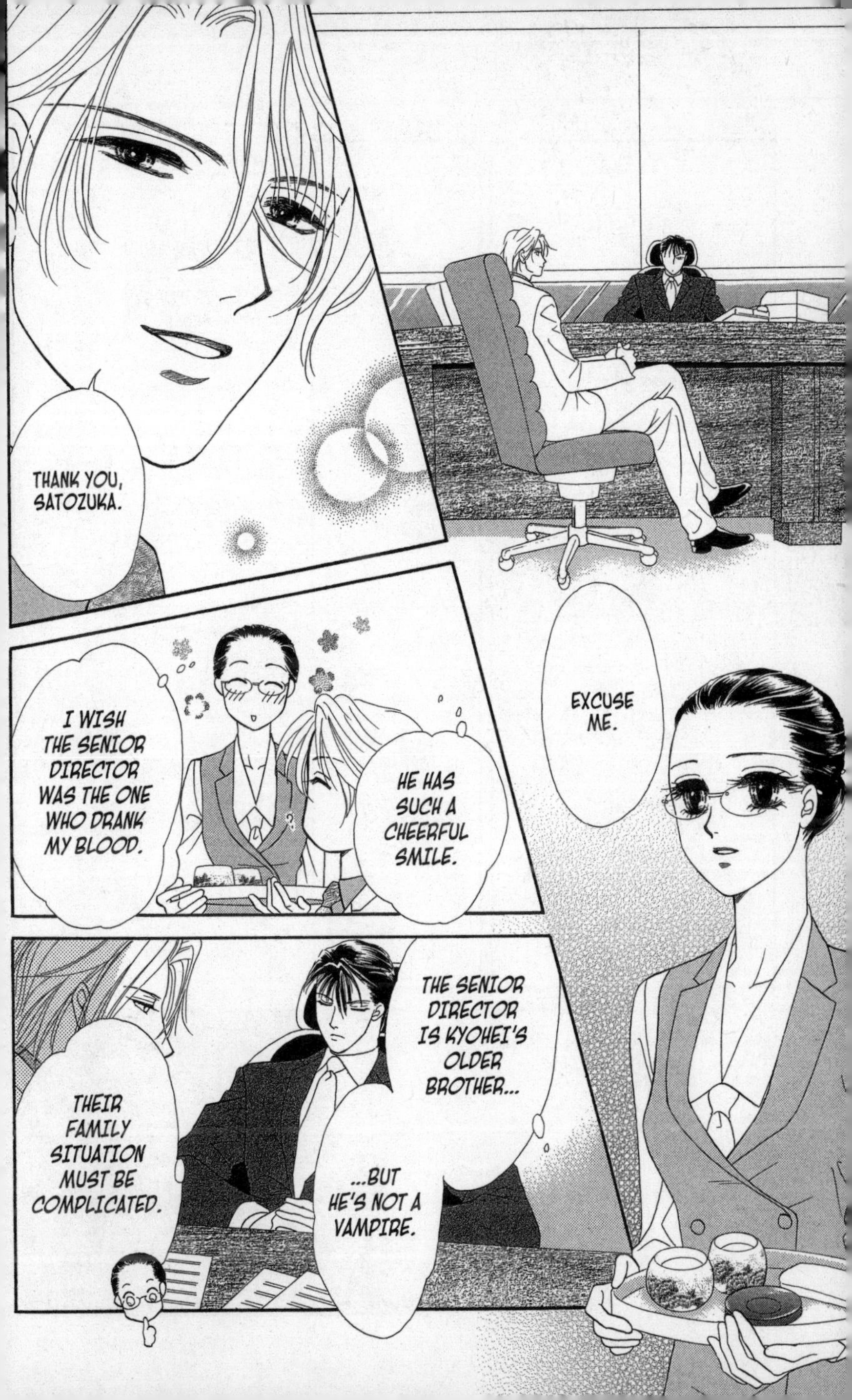
THANK YOU, SATOZUKA.
EXCUSE ME.
HE HAS SUCH A CHEERFUL SMILE.
I WISH THE SENIOR DIRECTOR WAS THE ONE WHO DRANK MY BLOOD.
THE SENIOR DIRECTOR IS KYOHEI'S OLDER BROTHER...
...BUT HE'S NOT A VAMPIRE.
THEIR FAMILY SITUATION MUST BE COMPLICATED.

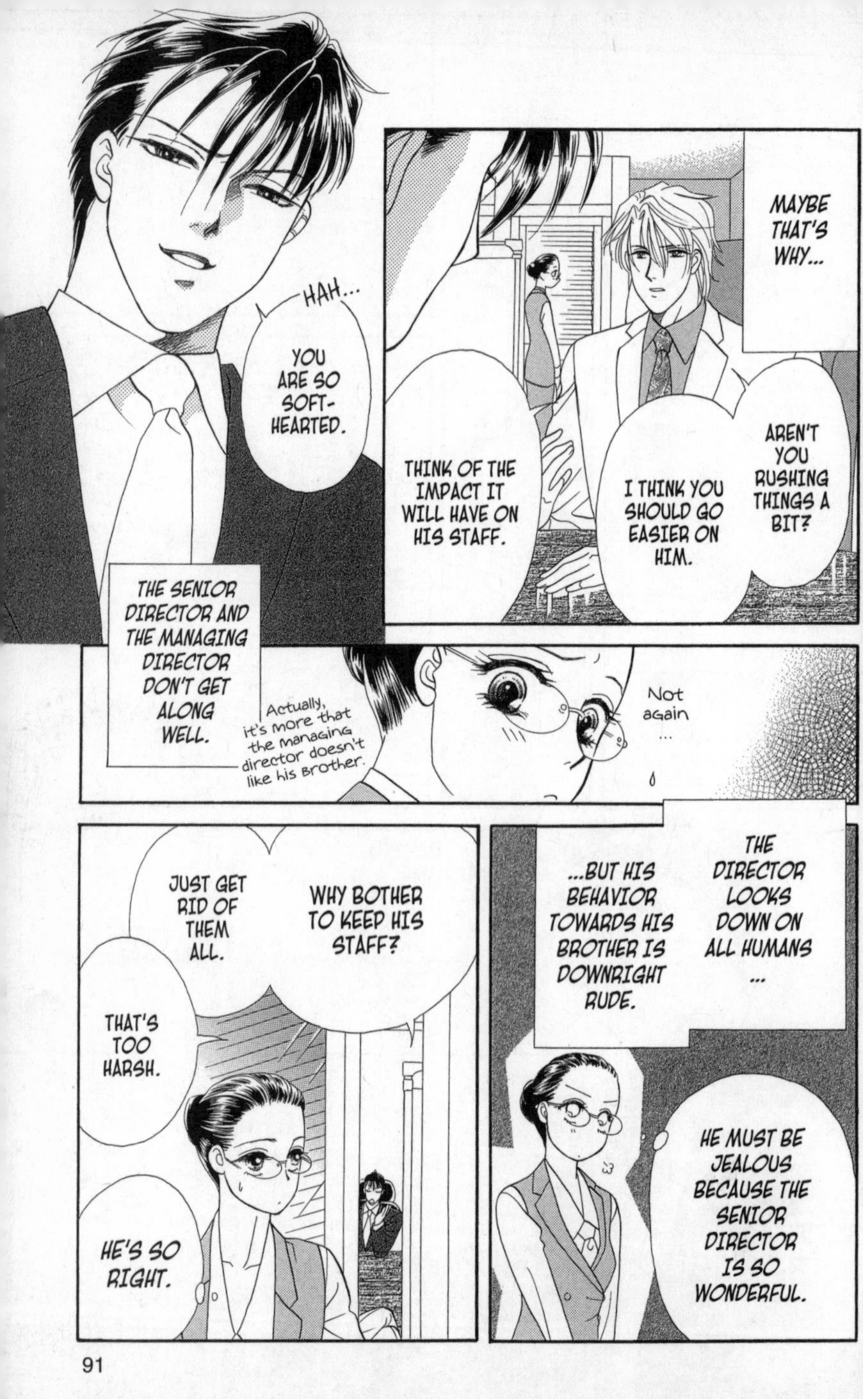
MAYBE THAT'S WHY...
AREN'T YOU RUSHING THINGS A BIT?
I THINK YOU SHOULD GO EASIER ON HIM.
THINK OF THE IMPACT IT WILL HAVE ON HIS STAFF.
HAH...
YOU ARE SO SOFT-HEARTED.
THE SENIOR DIRECTOR AND THE MANAGING DIRECTOR DON'T GET ALONG WELL.
Not again ...
Actually, it's more that the managing director doesn't like his brother.
THE DIRECTOR LOOKS DOWN ON ALL HUMANS ...
...BUT HIS BEHAVIOR TOWARDS HIS BROTHER IS DOWNRIGHT RUDE.
HE MUST BE JEALOUS BECAUSE THE SENIOR DIRECTOR IS SO WONDERFUL.
WHY BOTHER TO KEEP HIS STAFF?
JUST GET RID OF THEM ALL.
THAT'S TOO HARSH.
HE'S SO RIGHT.

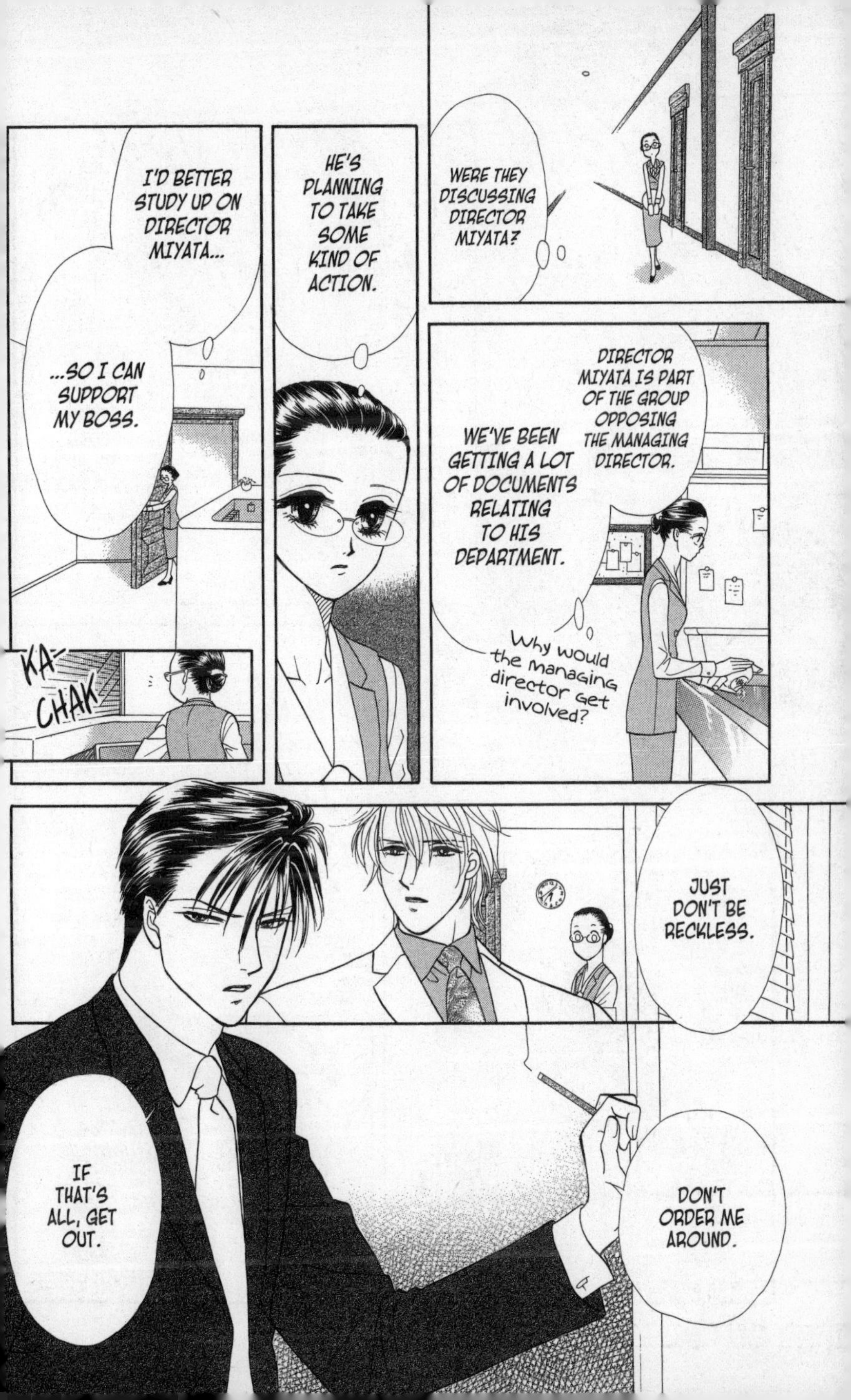
WERE THEY DISCUSSING DIRECTOR MIYATA?
DIRECTOR MIYATA IS PART OF THE GROUP OPPOSING THE MANAGING DIRECTOR.
WE'VE BEEN GETTING A LOT OF DOCUMENTS RELATING TO HIS DEPARTMENT.
Why would the managing director get involved?
HE'S PLANNING TO TAKE SOME KIND OF ACTION.
I'D BETTER STUDY UP ON DIRECTOR MIYATA...
...SO I CAN SUPPORT MY BOSS.
KA-CHAK
JUST DON'T BE RECKLESS.
DON'T ORDER ME AROUND.
IF THAT'S ALL, GET OUT.

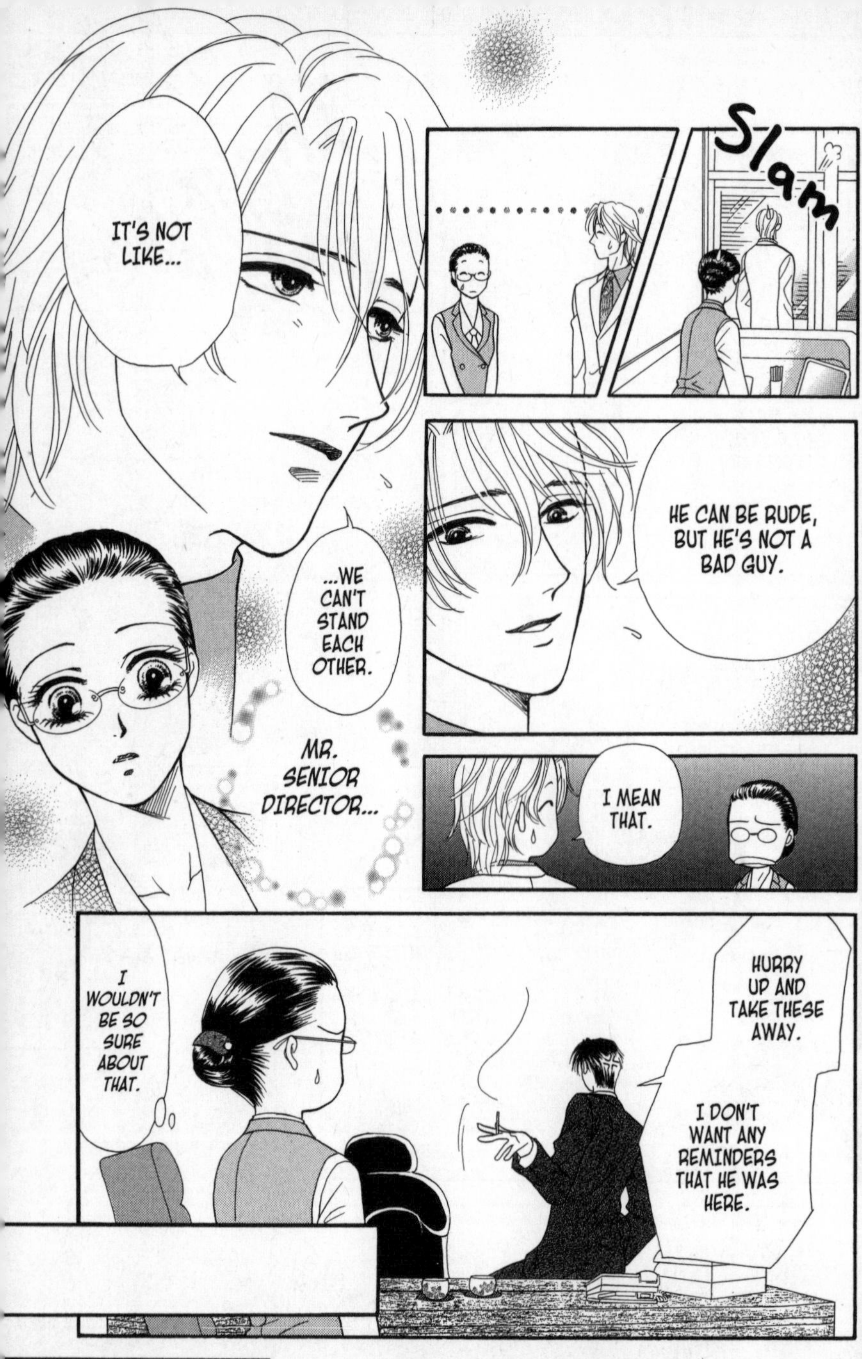
Slam
....
HE CAN BE RUDE, BUT HE'S NOT A BAD GUY.
I MEAN THAT.
IT'S NOT LIKE...
...WE CAN'T STAND EACH OTHER.
MR. SENIOR DIRECTOR...
HURRY UP AND TAKE THESE AWAY.
I DON'T WANT ANY REMINDERS THAT HE WAS HERE.
I WOULDN'T BE SO SURE ABOUT THAT.

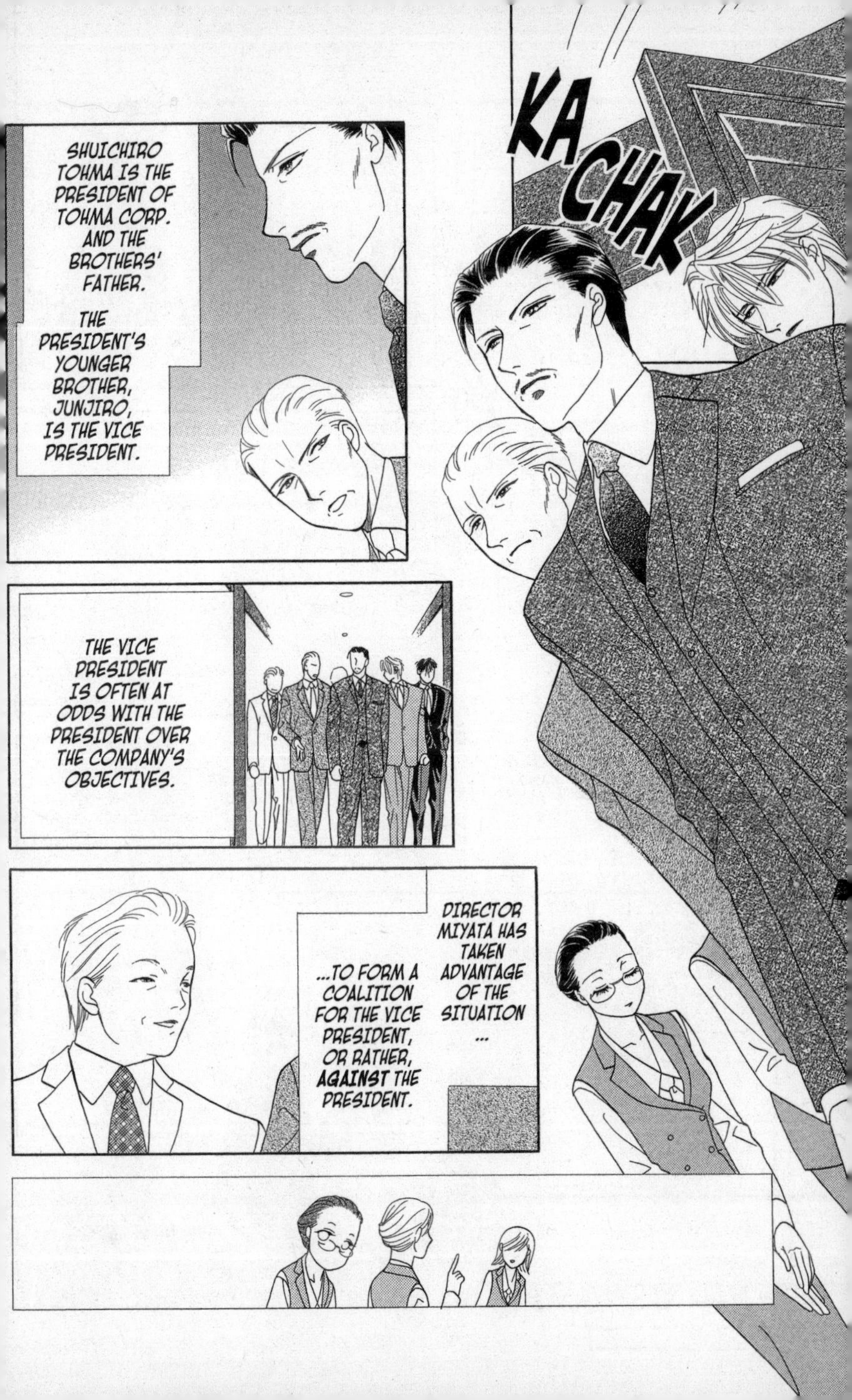
KA CHAK
SHUICHIRO TOHMA IS THE PRESIDENT OF TOHMA CORP. AND THE BROTHERS' FATHER.
THE PRESIDENT'S YOUNGER BROTHER, JUNJIRO, IS THE VICE PRESIDENT.
THE VICE PRESIDENT IS OFTEN AT ODDS WITH THE PRESIDENT OVER THE COMPANY'S OBJECTIVES.
DIRECTOR MIYATA HAS TAKEN ADVANTAGE OF THE SITUATION...
...TO FORM A COALITION FOR THE VICE PRESIDENT, OR RATHER, AGAINST THE PRESIDENT.

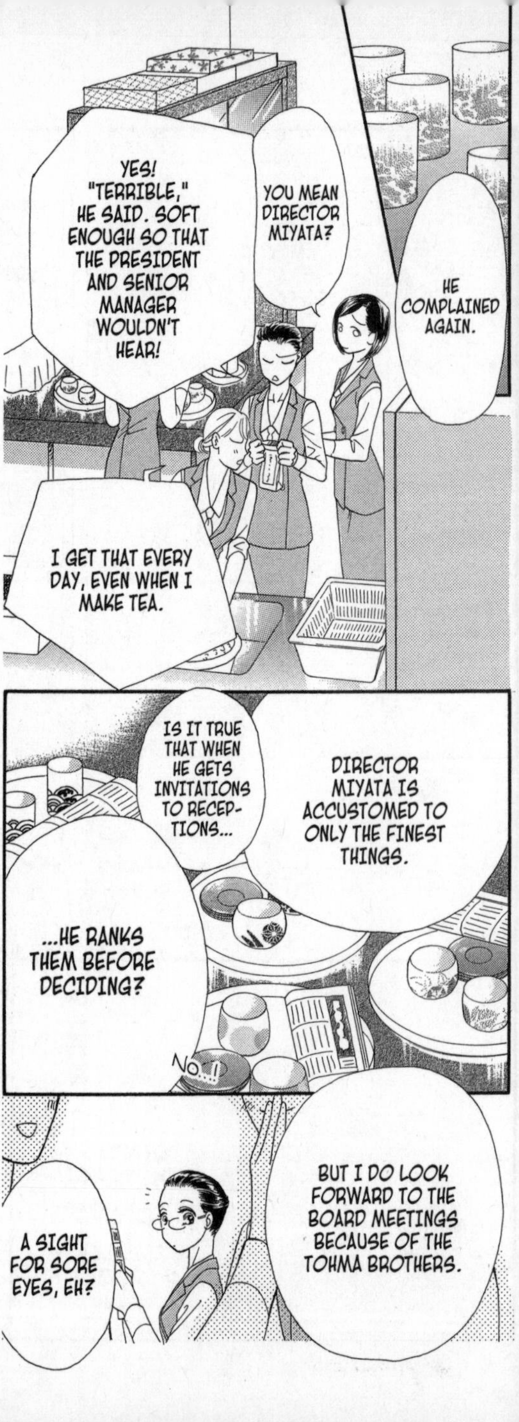
HE COMPLAINED AGAIN.
YOU MEAN DIRECTOR MIYATA?
YES! "TERRIBLE," HE SAID. SOFT ENOUGH SO THAT THE PRESIDENT AND SENIOR MANAGER WOULDN'T HEAR!
I GET THAT EVERY DAY, EVEN WHEN I MAKE TEA.
DIRECTOR MIYATA IS ACCUSTOMED TO ONLY THE FINEST THINGS.
IS IT TRUE THAT WHEN HE GETS INVITATIONS TO RECEPTIONS...
...HE RANKS THEM BEFORE DECIDING?
No...!
BUT I DO LOOK FORWARD TO THE BOARD MEETINGS BECAUSE OF THE TOHMA BROTHERS.
A SIGHT FOR SORE EYES, EH?

- Brotherhood -

Shuichiro Tohma, the Tohma brothers' father. I love drawing him. ♡ And drawing Junjiro, the Tohma brothers' uncle, is just as much fun... ♡

When I was working on a previous title, "Barairo My Honey," I looked forward to drawing the men at Yayoi Printing and Director Yamaguchi.

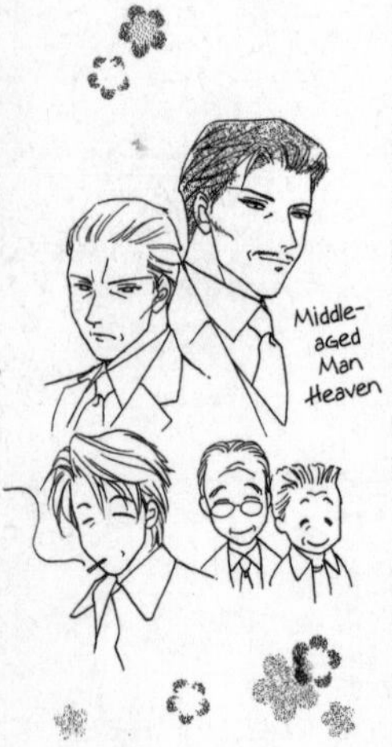
Middle-aged Man Heaven

I wish I could draw them much better. I'm going to keep trying.

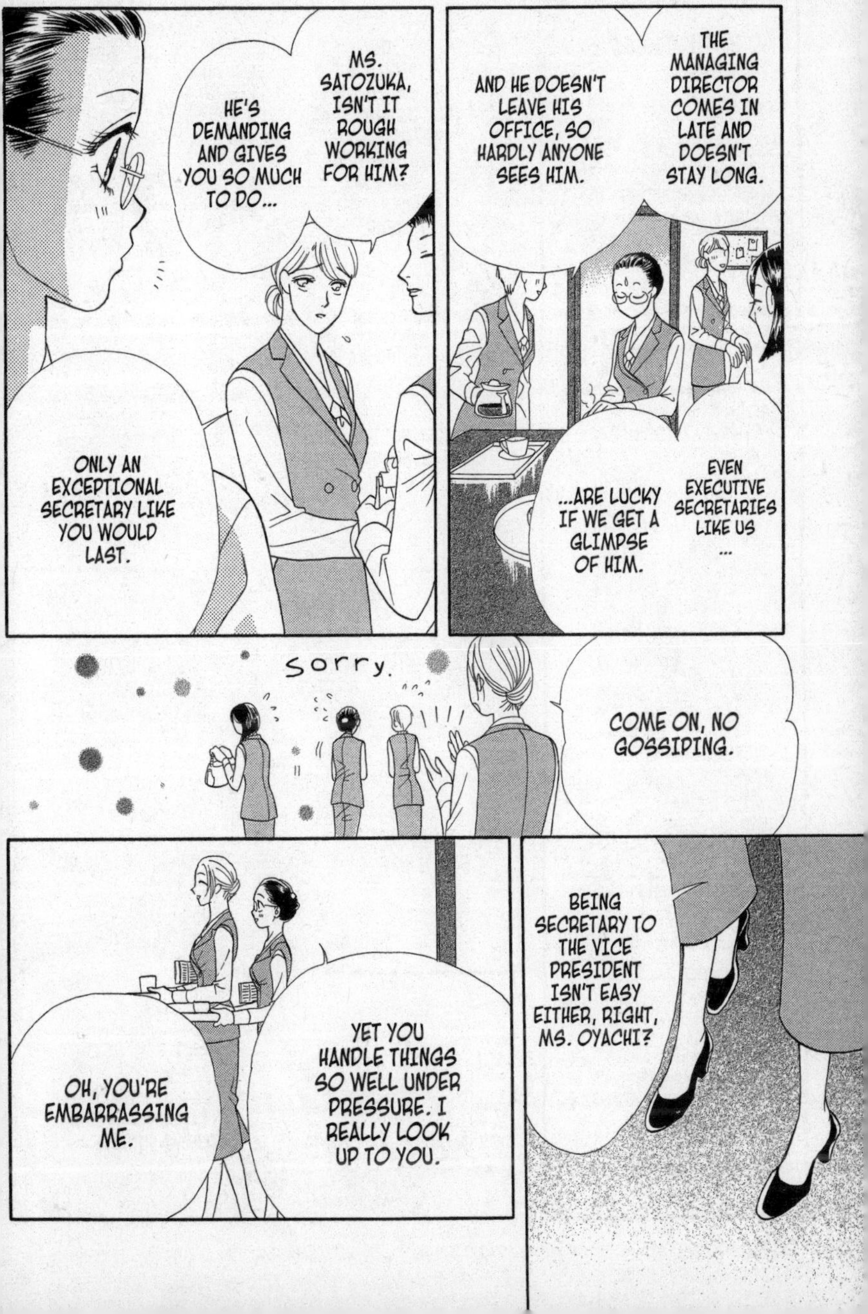
THE MANAGING DIRECTOR COMES IN LATE AND DOESN'T STAY LONG.
AND HE DOESN'T LEAVE HIS OFFICE, SO HARDLY ANYONE SEES HIM.
EVEN EXECUTIVE SECRETARIES LIKE US ...
...ARE LUCKY IF WE GET A GLIMPSE OF HIM.
MS. SATOZUKA, ISN'T IT ROUGH WORKING FOR HIM?
HE'S DEMANDING AND GIVES YOU SO MUCH TO DO...
ONLY AN EXCEPTIONAL SECRETARY LIKE YOU WOULD LAST.
COME ON, NO GOSSIPING.
Sorry.
BEING SECRETARY TO THE VICE PRESIDENT ISN'T EASY EITHER, RIGHT, MS. OYACHI?
YET YOU HANDLE THINGS SO WELL UNDER PRESSURE. I REALLY LOOK UP TO YOU.
OH, YOU'RE EMBARRASSING ME.

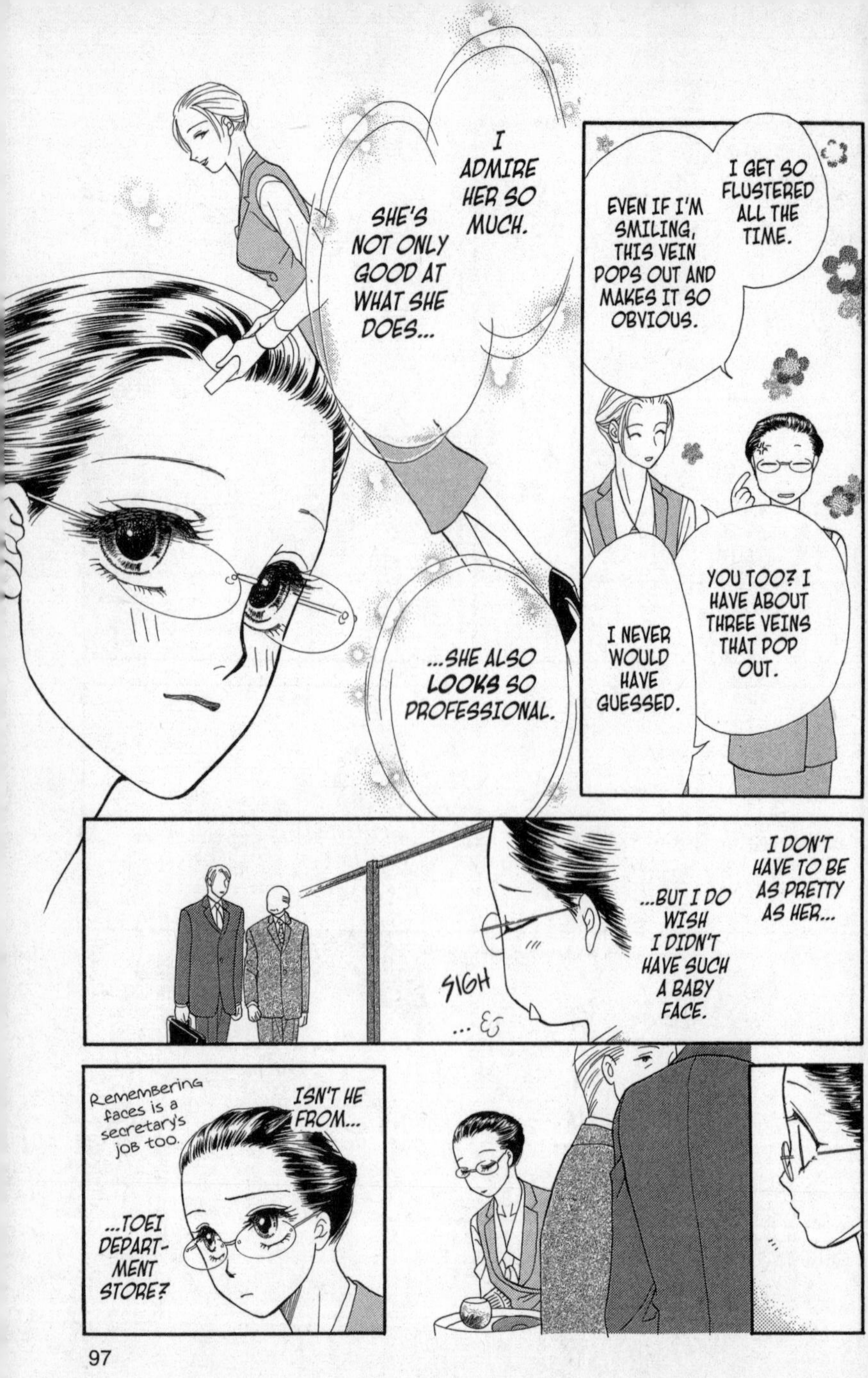
I GET SO FLUSTERED ALL THE TIME.
EVEN IF I'M SMILING, THIS VEIN POPS OUT AND MAKES IT SO OBVIOUS.
YOU TOO? I HAVE ABOUT THREE VEINS THAT POP OUT.
I NEVER WOULD HAVE GUESSED.
I ADMIRE HER SO MUCH.
SHE'S NOT ONLY GOOD AT WHAT SHE DOES...
...SHE ALSO LOOKS SO PROFESSIONAL.
I DON'T HAVE TO BE AS PRETTY AS HER...
...BUT I DO WISH I DIDN'T HAVE SUCH A BABY FACE.
SIGH
...
ISN'T HE FROM...
...TOEI DEPARTMENT STORE?
Remembering faces is a secretary's job too.

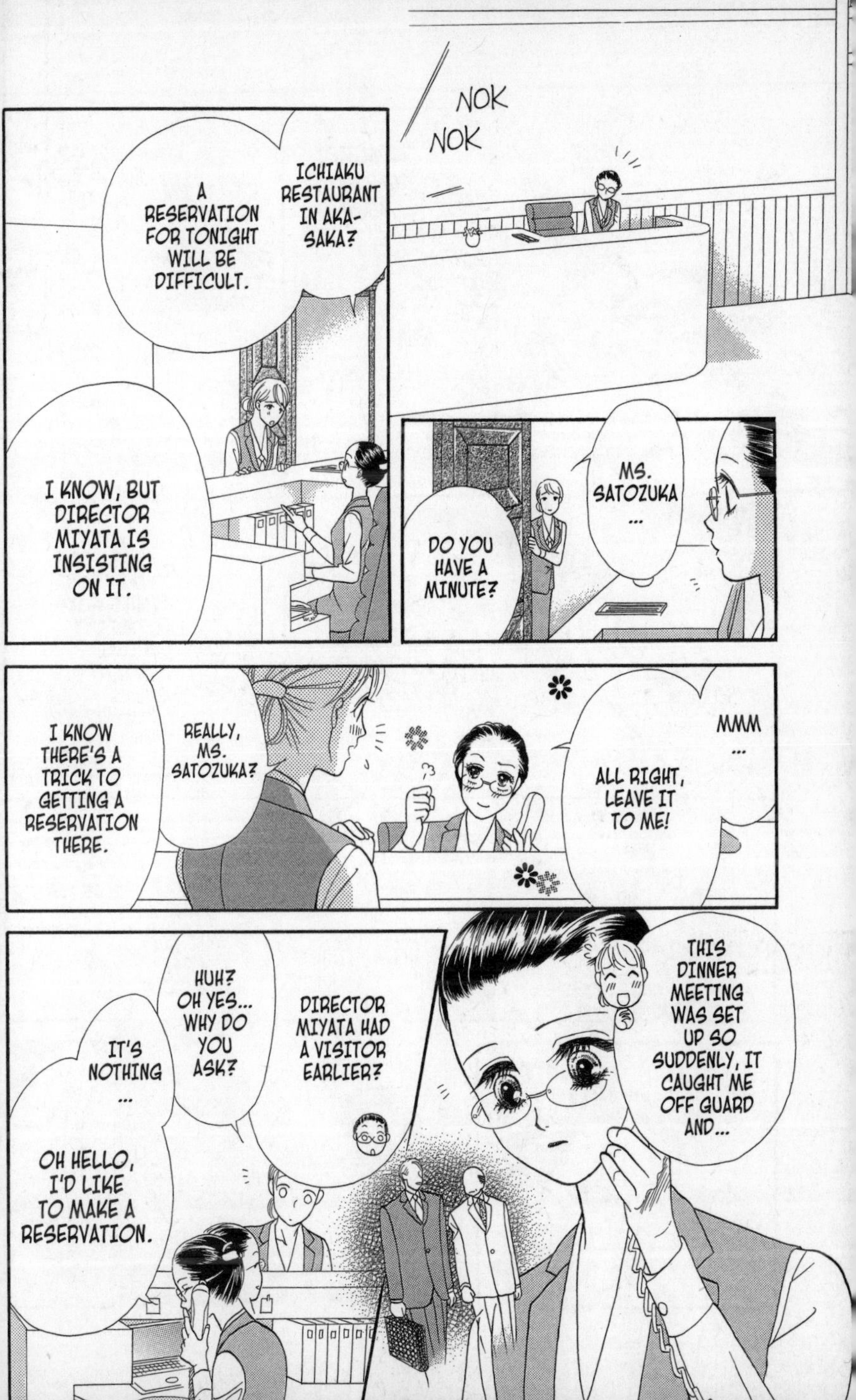
NOK NOK
ICHIAKU RESTAURANT IN AKA-SAKA?
A RESERVATION FOR TONIGHT WILL BE DIFFICULT.
I KNOW, BUT DIRECTOR MIYATA IS INSISTING ON IT.
MS. SATOZUKA ...
DO YOU HAVE A MINUTE?
MMM ...
ALL RIGHT, LEAVE IT TO ME!
REALLY, MS. SATOZUKA?
I KNOW THERE'S A TRICK TO GETTING A RESERVATION THERE.
THIS DINNER MEETING WAS SET UP SO SUDDENLY, IT CAUGHT ME OFF GUARD AND...
DIRECTOR MIYATA HAD A VISITOR EARLIER?
HUH? OH YES... WHY DO YOU ASK?
IT'S NOTHING ...
OH HELLO, I'D LIKE TO MAKE A RESERVATION.

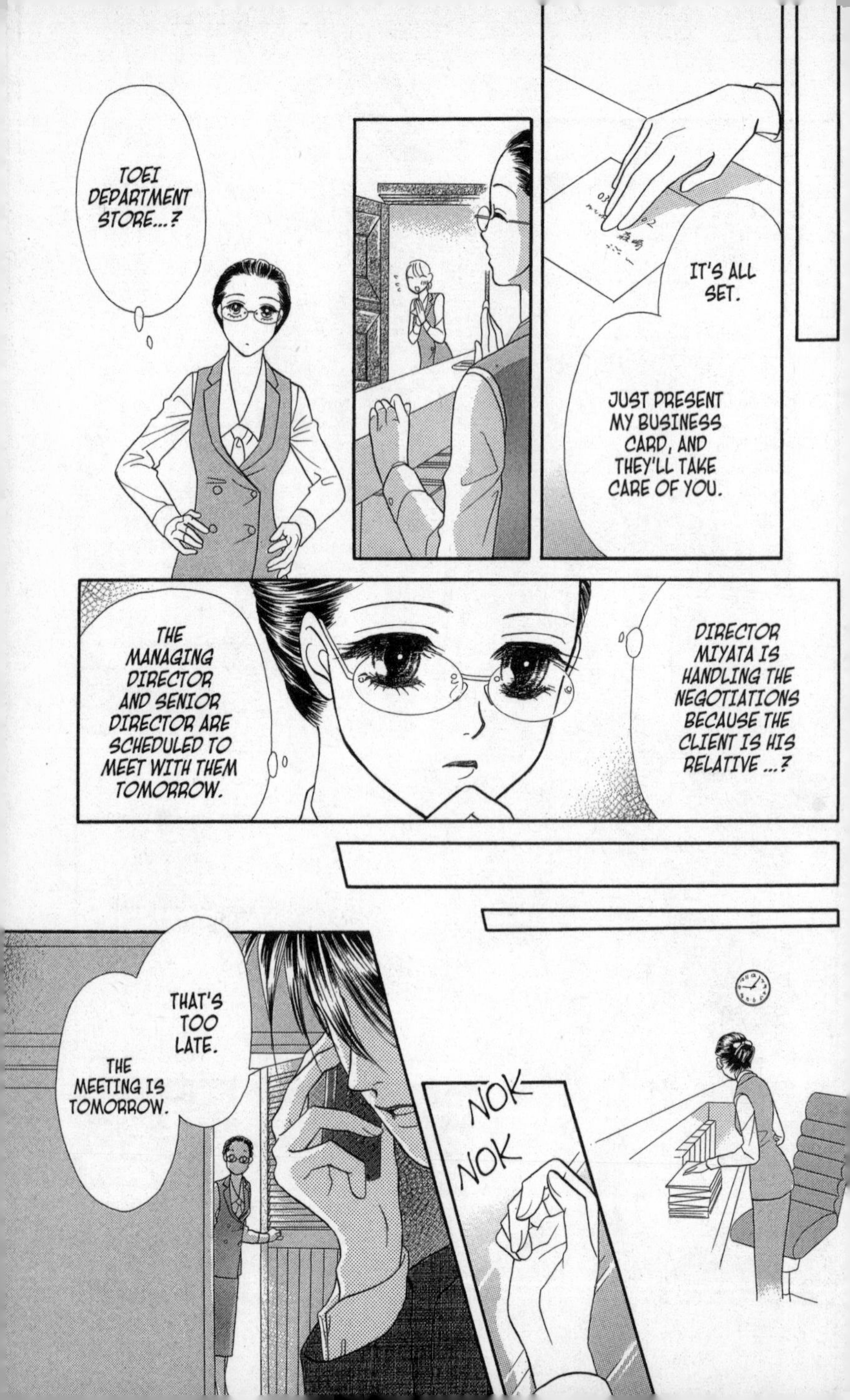
IT'S ALL SET.
JUST PRESENT MY BUSINESS CARD, AND THEY'LL TAKE CARE OF YOU.
TOEI DEPARTMENT STORE...?
DIRECTOR MIYATA IS HANDLING THE NEGOTIATIONS BECAUSE THE CLIENT IS HIS RELATIVE ...?
THE MANAGING DIRECTOR AND SENIOR DIRECTOR ARE SCHEDULED TO MEET WITH THEM TOMORROW.
NOK NOK
THAT'S TOO LATE.
THE MEETING IS TOMORROW.

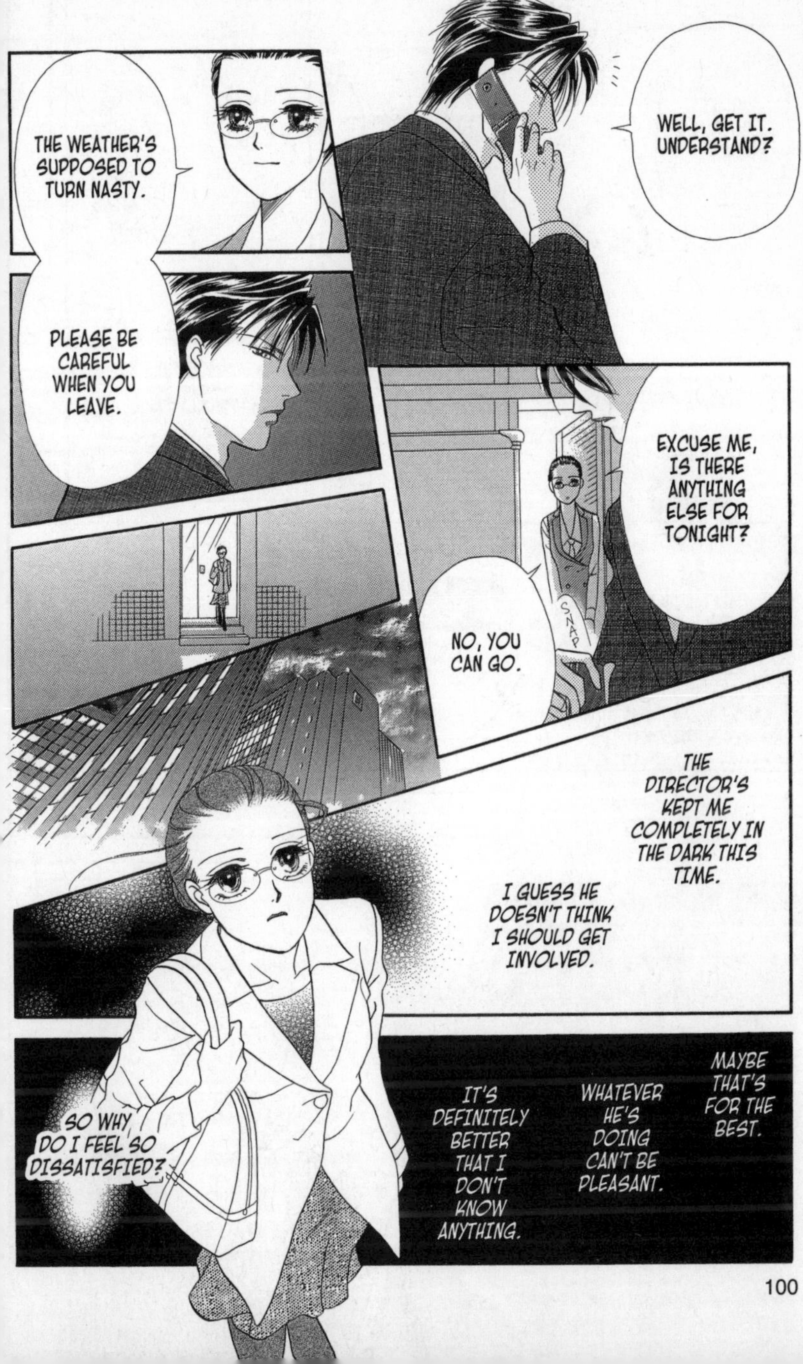
WELL, GET IT. UNDERSTAND?
THE WEATHER'S SUPPOSED TO TURN NASTY.
EXCUSE ME, IS THERE ANYTHING ELSE FOR TONIGHT?
SNAP
NO, YOU CAN GO.
PLEASE BE CAREFUL WHEN YOU LEAVE.
THE DIRECTOR'S KEPT ME COMPLETELY IN THE DARK THIS TIME.
I GUESS HE DOESN'T THINK I SHOULD GET INVOLVED.
MAYBE THAT'S FOR THE BEST.
WHATEVER HE'S DOING CAN'T BE PLEASANT.
IT'S DEFINITELY BETTER THAT I DON'T KNOW ANYTHING.
SO WHY DO I FEEL SO DISSATISFIED?

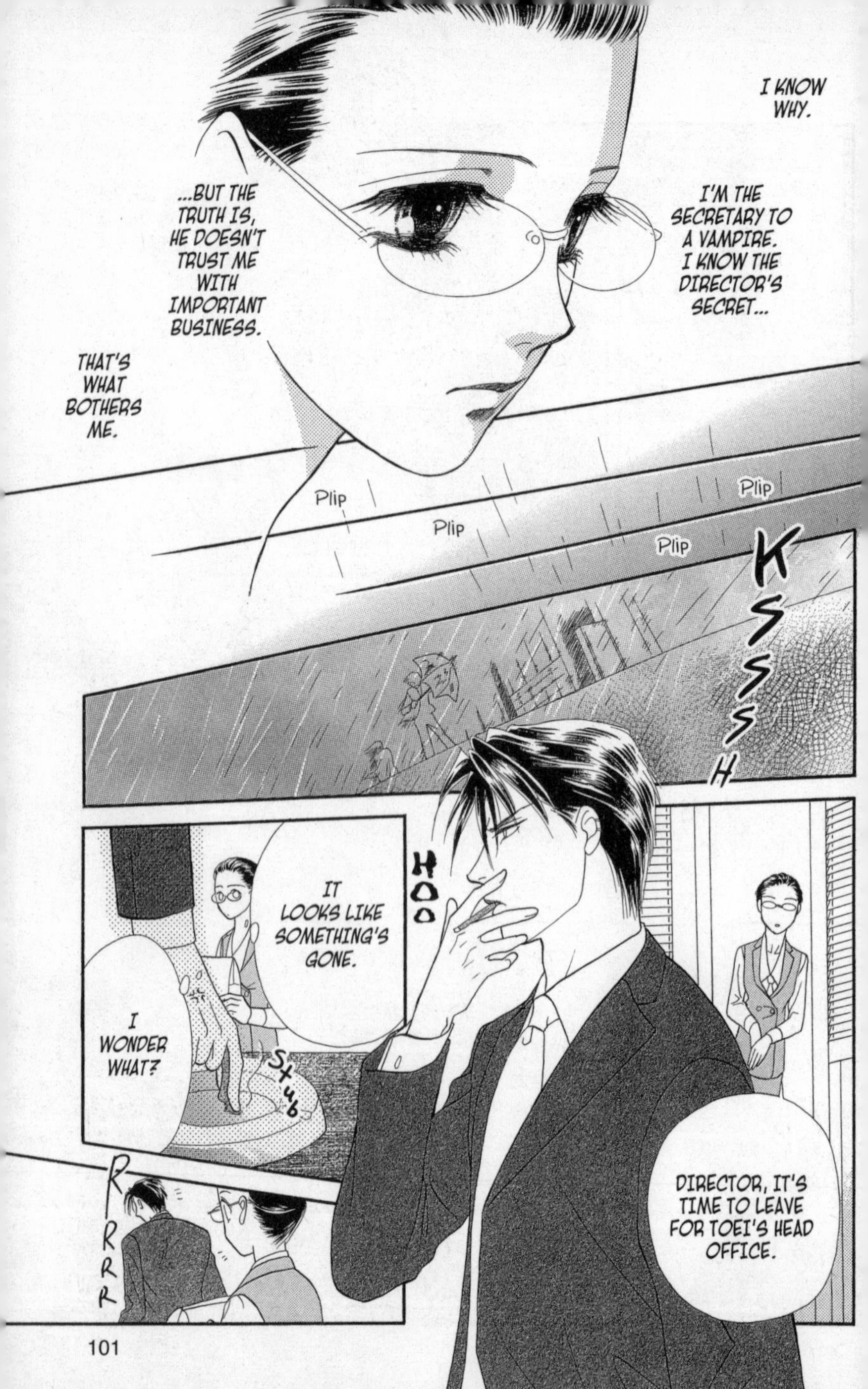
I KNOW WHY.
I'M THE SECRETARY TO A VAMPIRE. I KNOW THE DIRECTOR'S SECRET...
...BUT THE TRUTH IS, HE DOESN'T TRUST ME WITH IMPORTANT BUSINESS.
THAT'S WHAT BOTHERS ME.
Plip
Plip
Plip
Plip
KSSSSH
HOO
DIRECTOR, IT'S TIME TO LEAVE FOR TOEI'S HEAD OFFICE.
IT LOOKS LIKE SOMETHING'S GONE.
I WONDER WHAT?
Stub
RRRR

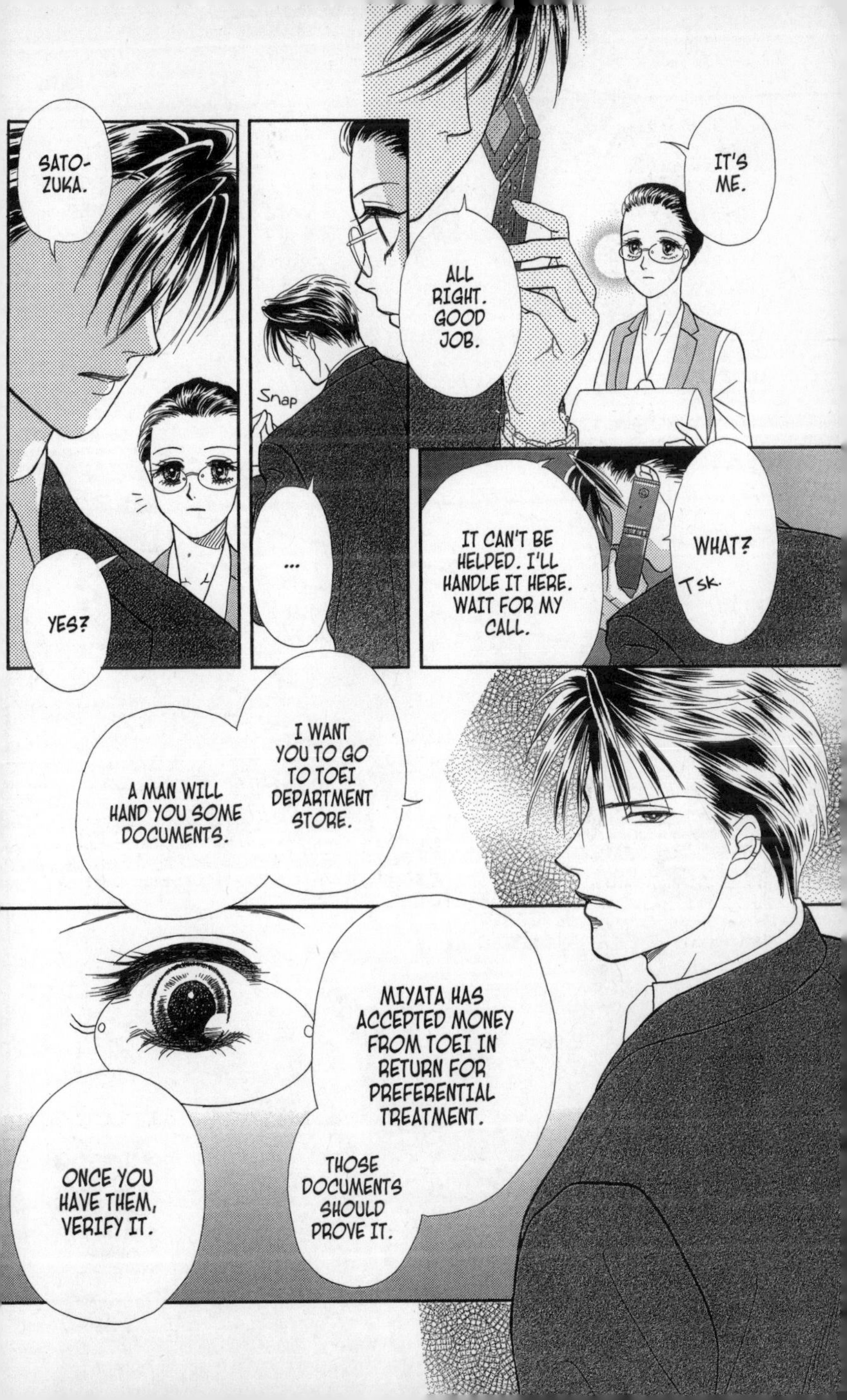
IT'S ME.
ALL RIGHT. GOOD JOB.
WHAT?
Tsk.
IT CAN'T BE HELPED. I'LL HANDLE IT HERE. WAIT FOR MY CALL.
Snap
...
SATO-ZUKA.
YES?
I WANT YOU TO GO TO TOEI DEPARTMENT STORE.
A MAN WILL HAND YOU SOME DOCUMENTS.
MIYATA HAS ACCEPTED MONEY FROM TOEI IN RETURN FOR PREFERENTIAL TREATMENT.
THOSE DOCUMENTS SHOULD PROVE IT.
ONCE YOU HAVE THEM, VERIFY IT.

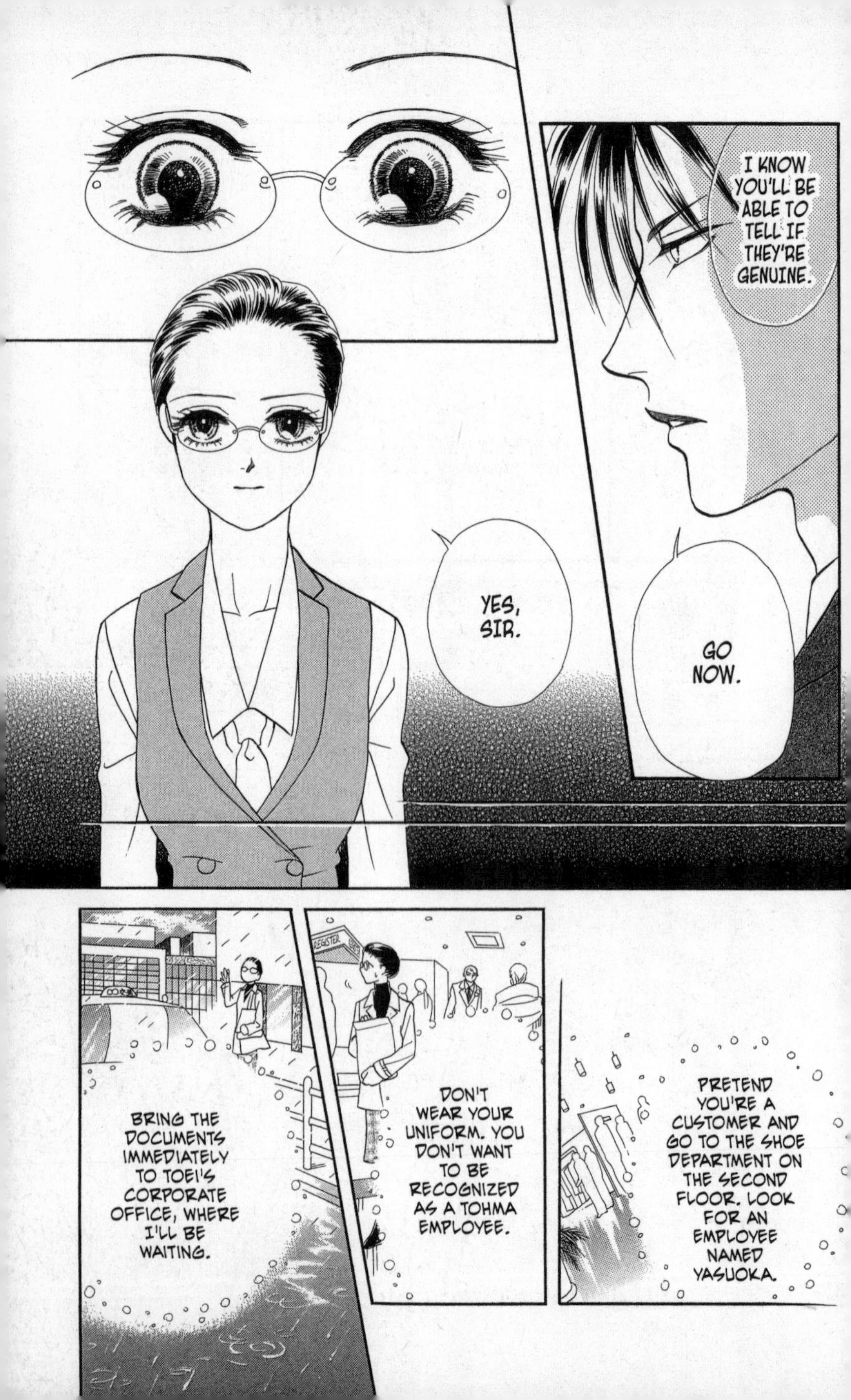
I KNOW YOU'LL BE ABLE TO TELL IF THEY'RE GENUINE.
GO NOW.
YES, SIR.
PRETEND YOU'RE A CUSTOMER AND GO TO THE SHOE DEPARTMENT ON THE SECOND FLOOR. LOOK FOR AN EMPLOYEE NAMED YASUOKA.
DON'T WEAR YOUR UNIFORM. YOU DON'T WANT TO BE RECOGNIZED AS A TOHMA EMPLOYEE.
BRING THE DOCUMENTS IMMEDIATELY TO TOEI'S CORPORATE OFFICE, WHERE I'LL BE WAITING.

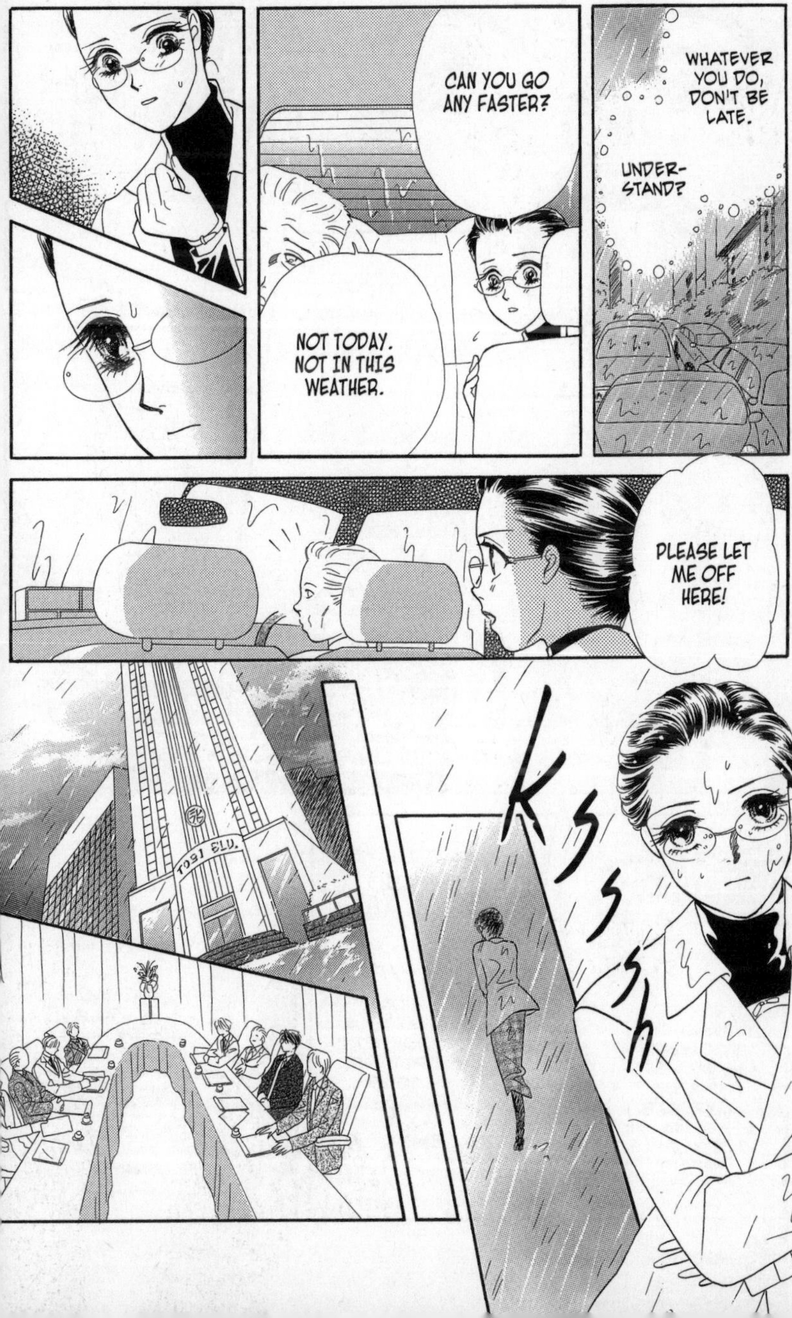

WHATEVER YOU DO, DON'T BE LATE.
UNDER-STAND?
CAN YOU GO ANY FASTER?
NOT TODAY. NOT IN THIS WEATHER.
PLEASE LET ME OFF HERE!
KSSSH
TOSI BLD.

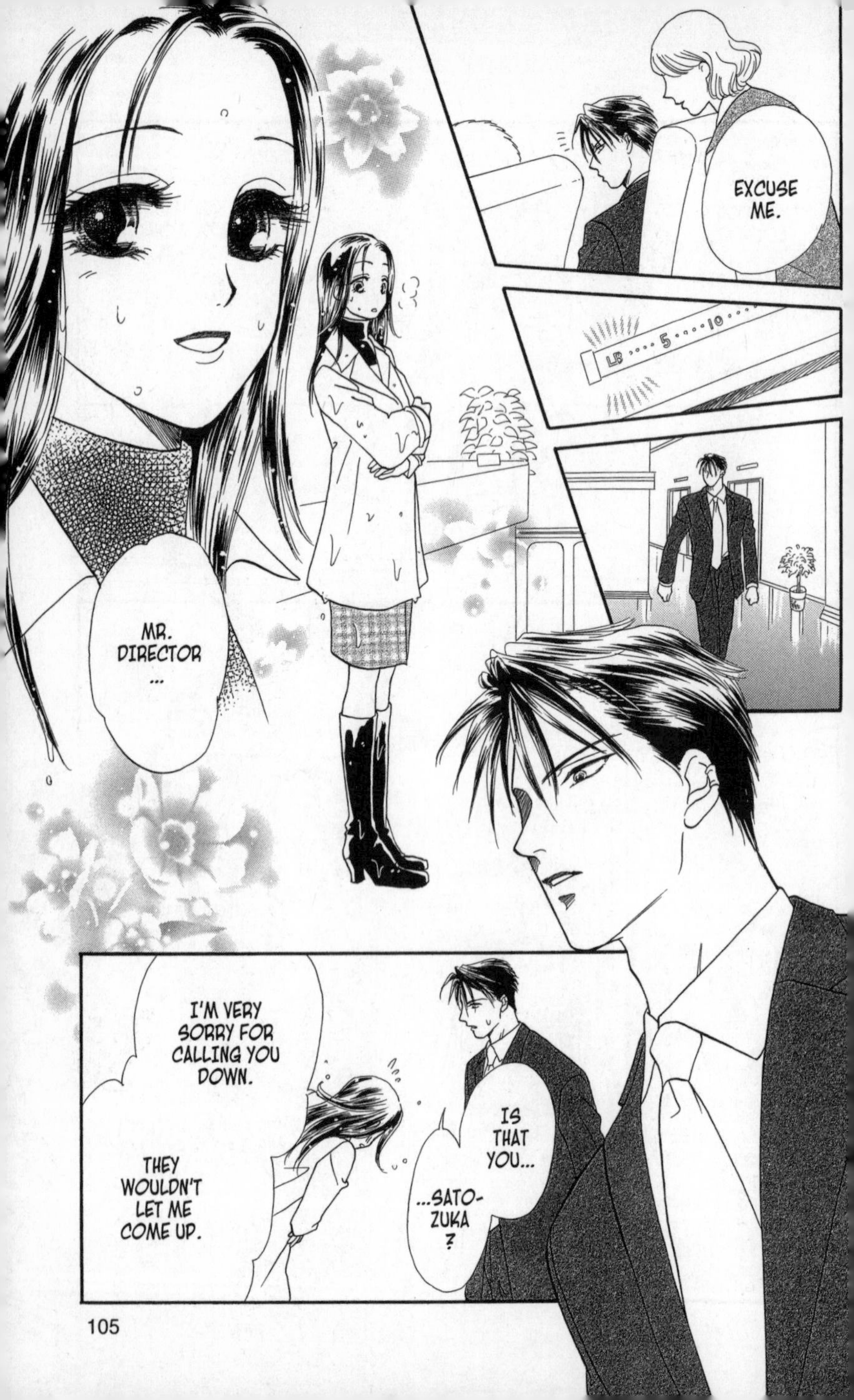
EXCUSE ME.
MR. DIRECTOR ...
IS THAT YOU...
...SATO-ZUKA?
I'M VERY SORRY FOR CALLING YOU DOWN.
THEY WOULDN'T LET ME COME UP.

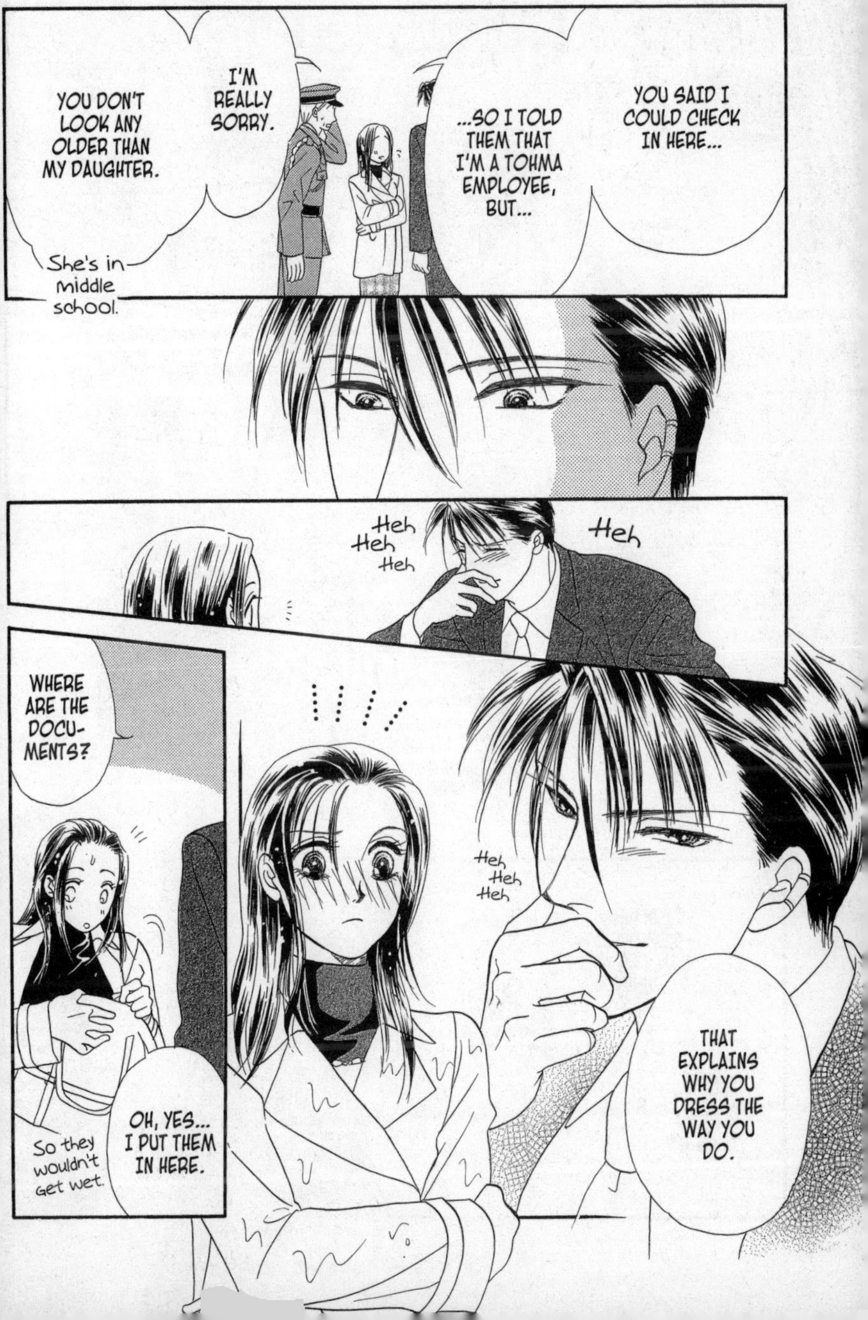
YOU SAID I COULD CHECK IN HERE...
...SO I TOLD THEM THAT I'M A TOHMA EMPLOYEE, BUT...
I'M REALLY SORRY.
YOU DON'T LOOK ANY OLDER THAN MY DAUGHTER.
She's in middle school.
Heh
Heh Heh Heh
Heh Heh Heh
THAT EXPLAINS WHY YOU DRESS THE WAY YOU DO.
WHERE ARE THE DOCU-MENTS?
OH, YES... I PUT THEM IN HERE.
So they wouldn't get wet.

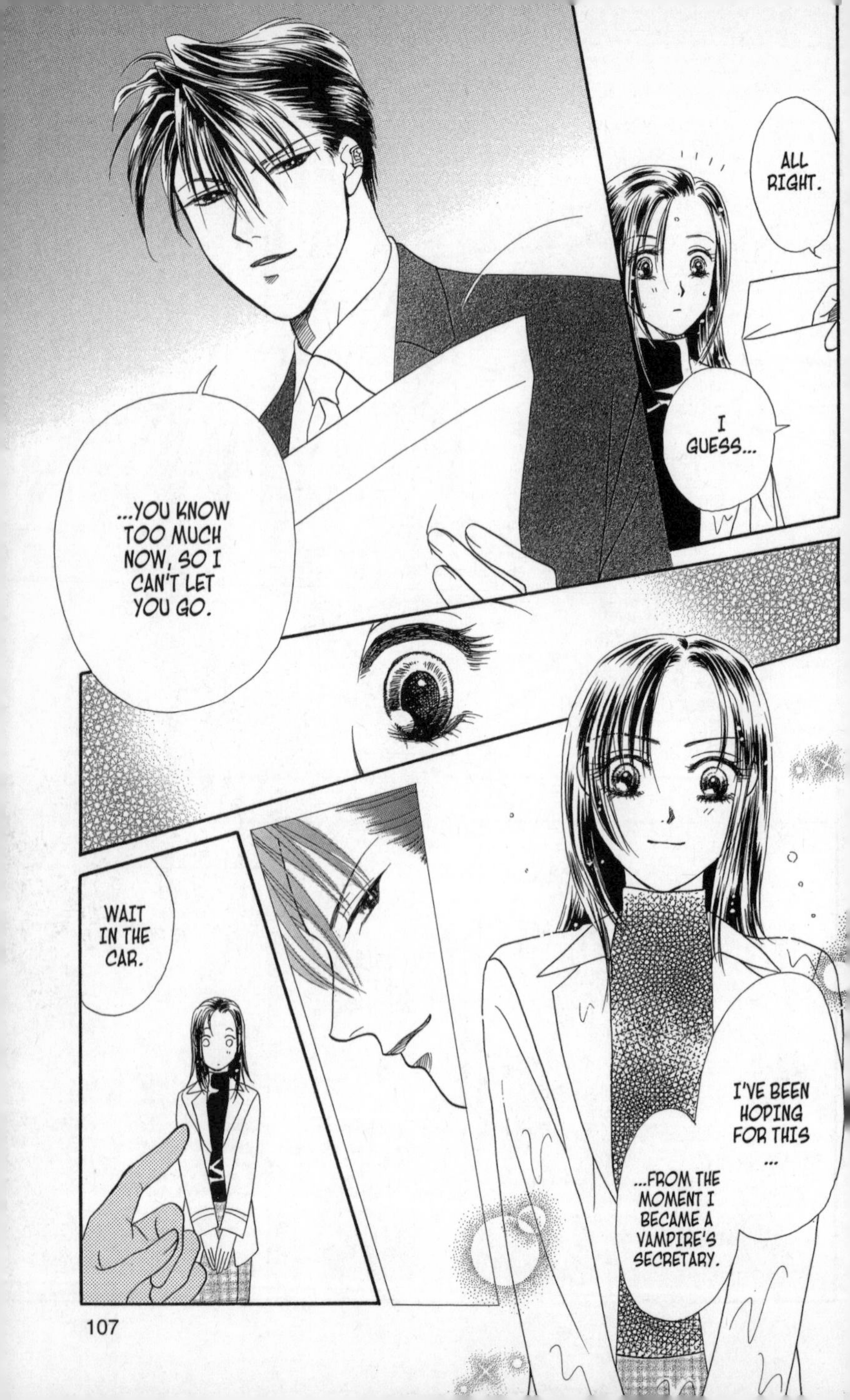
ALL RIGHT.
I GUESS...
...YOU KNOW TOO MUCH NOW, SO I CAN'T LET YOU GO.
I'VE BEEN HOPING FOR THIS ...
...FROM THE MOMENT I BECAME A VAMPIRE'S SECRETARY.
WAIT IN THE CAR.

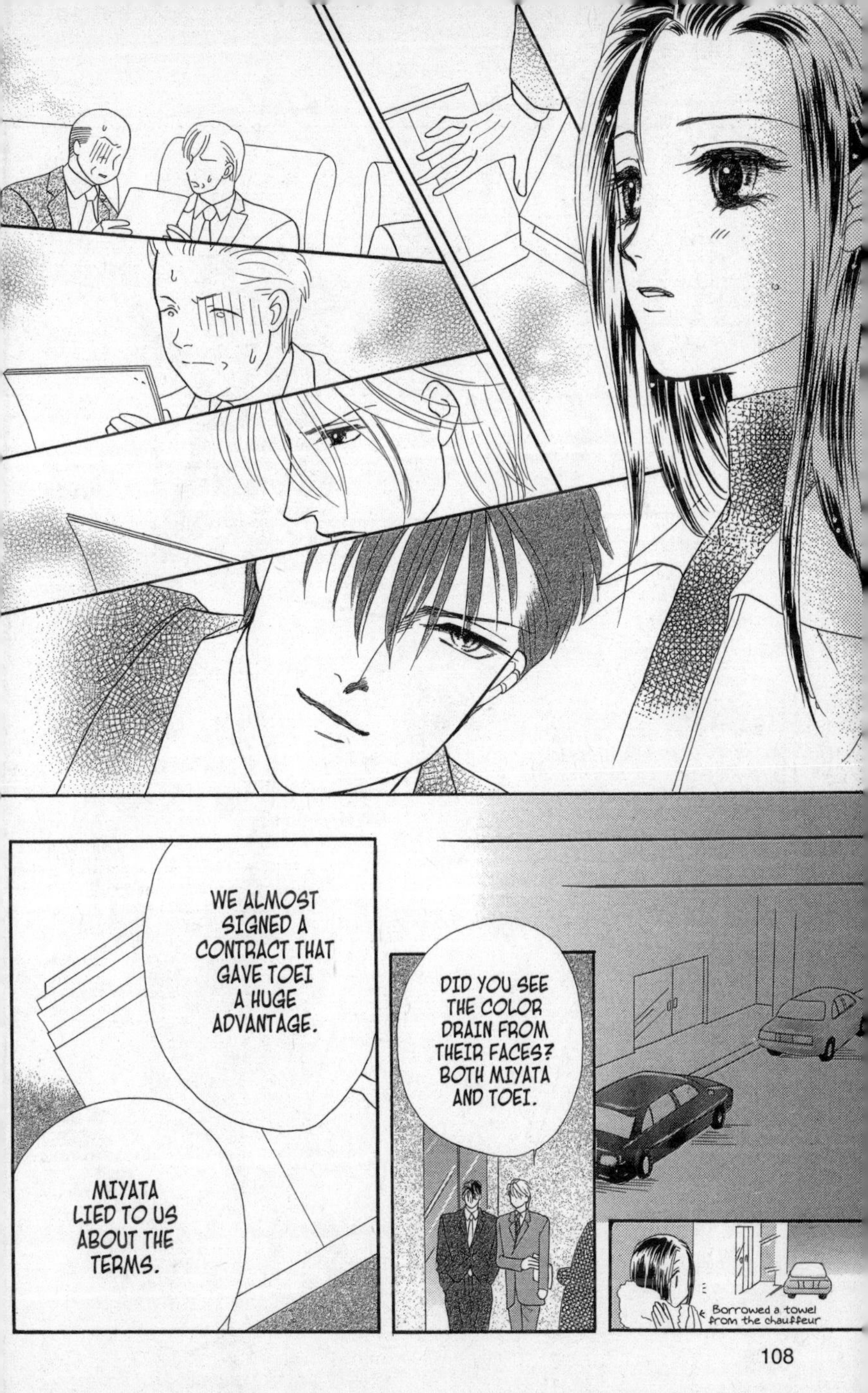
Borrowed a towel from the chauffeur
DID YOU SEE THE COLOR DRAIN FROM THEIR FACES? BOTH MIYATA AND TOEI.
WE ALMOST SIGNED A CONTRACT THAT GAVE TOEI A HUGE ADVANTAGE.
MIYATA LIED TO US ABOUT THE TERMS.

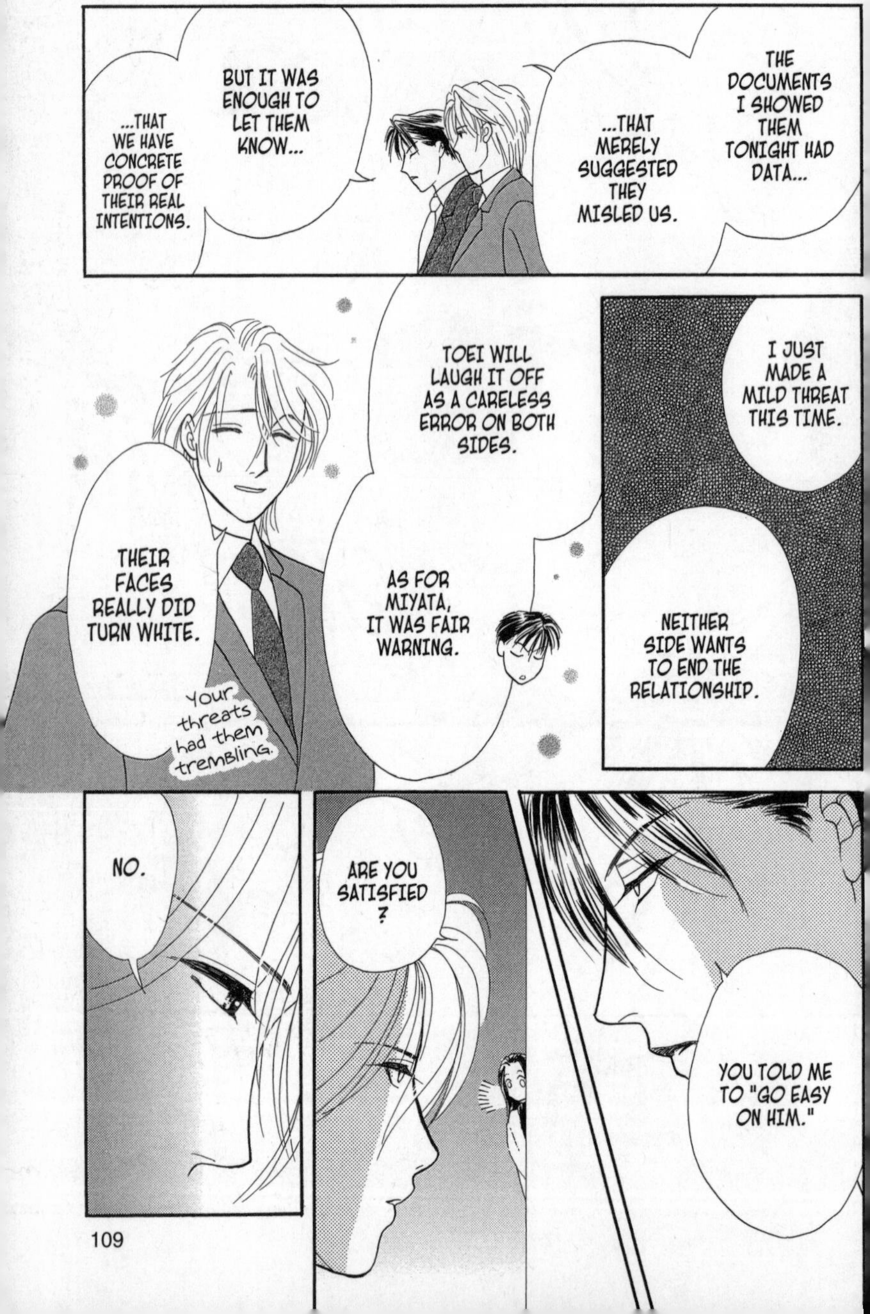
THE DOCUMENTS I SHOWED THEM TONIGHT HAD DATA...
...THAT MERELY SUGGESTED THEY MISLED US.
BUT IT WAS ENOUGH TO LET THEM KNOW...
...THAT WE HAVE CONCRETE PROOF OF THEIR REAL INTENTIONS.
I JUST MADE A MILD THREAT THIS TIME.
NEITHER SIDE WANTS TO END THE RELATIONSHIP.
TOEI WILL LAUGH IT OFF AS A CARELESS ERROR ON BOTH SIDES.
AS FOR MIYATA, IT WAS FAIR WARNING.
THEIR FACES REALLY DID TURN WHITE.
Your threats had them trembling.
YOU TOLD ME TO "GO EASY ON HIM."
ARE YOU SATISFIED?
NO.

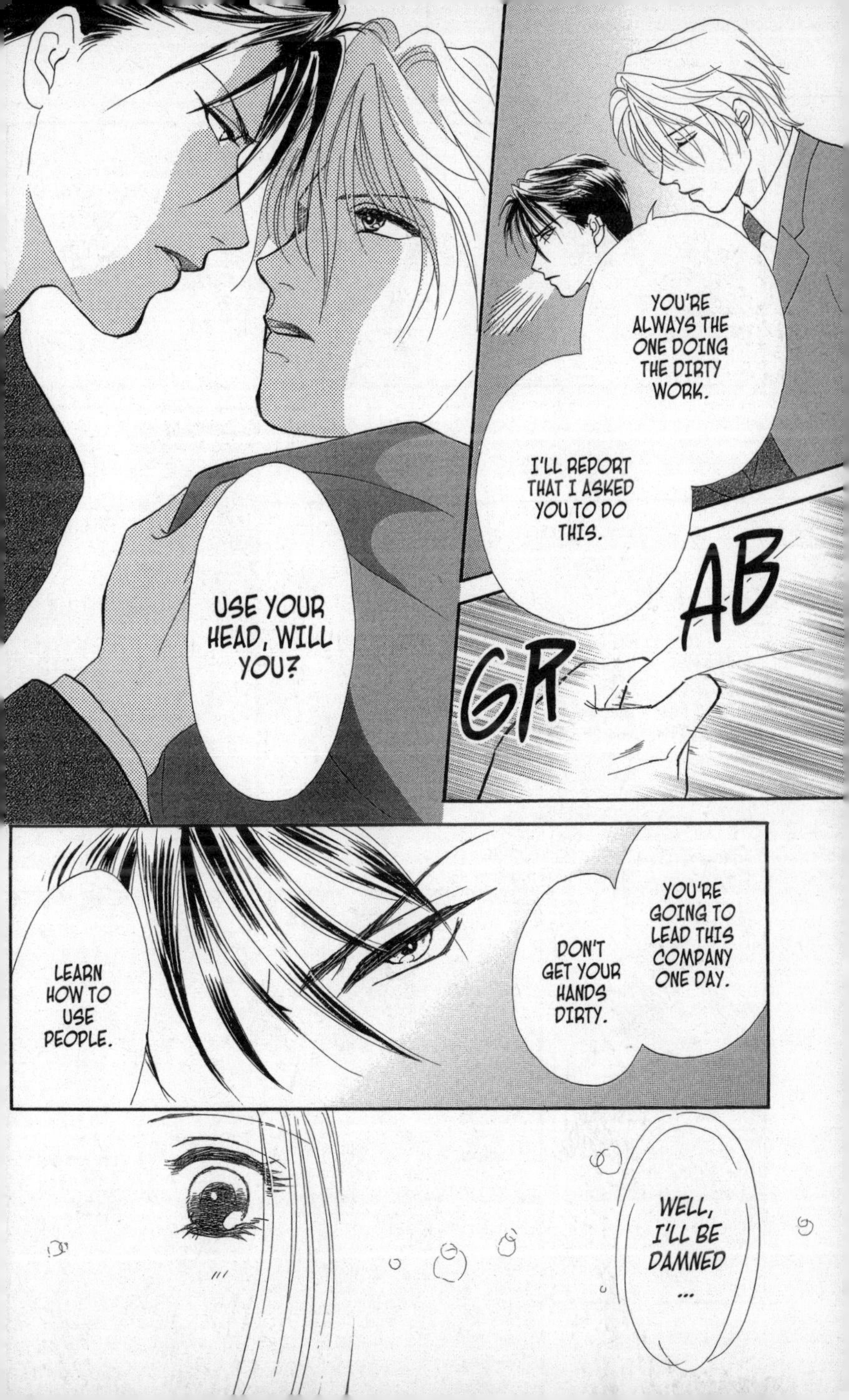
YOU'RE ALWAYS THE ONE DOING THE DIRTY WORK.
I'LL REPORT THAT I ASKED YOU TO DO THIS.
GRAB
USE YOUR HEAD, WILL YOU?
YOU'RE GOING TO LEAD THIS COMPANY ONE DAY.
DON'T GET YOUR HANDS DIRTY.
LEARN HOW TO USE PEOPLE.
WELL, I'LL BE DAMNED ...

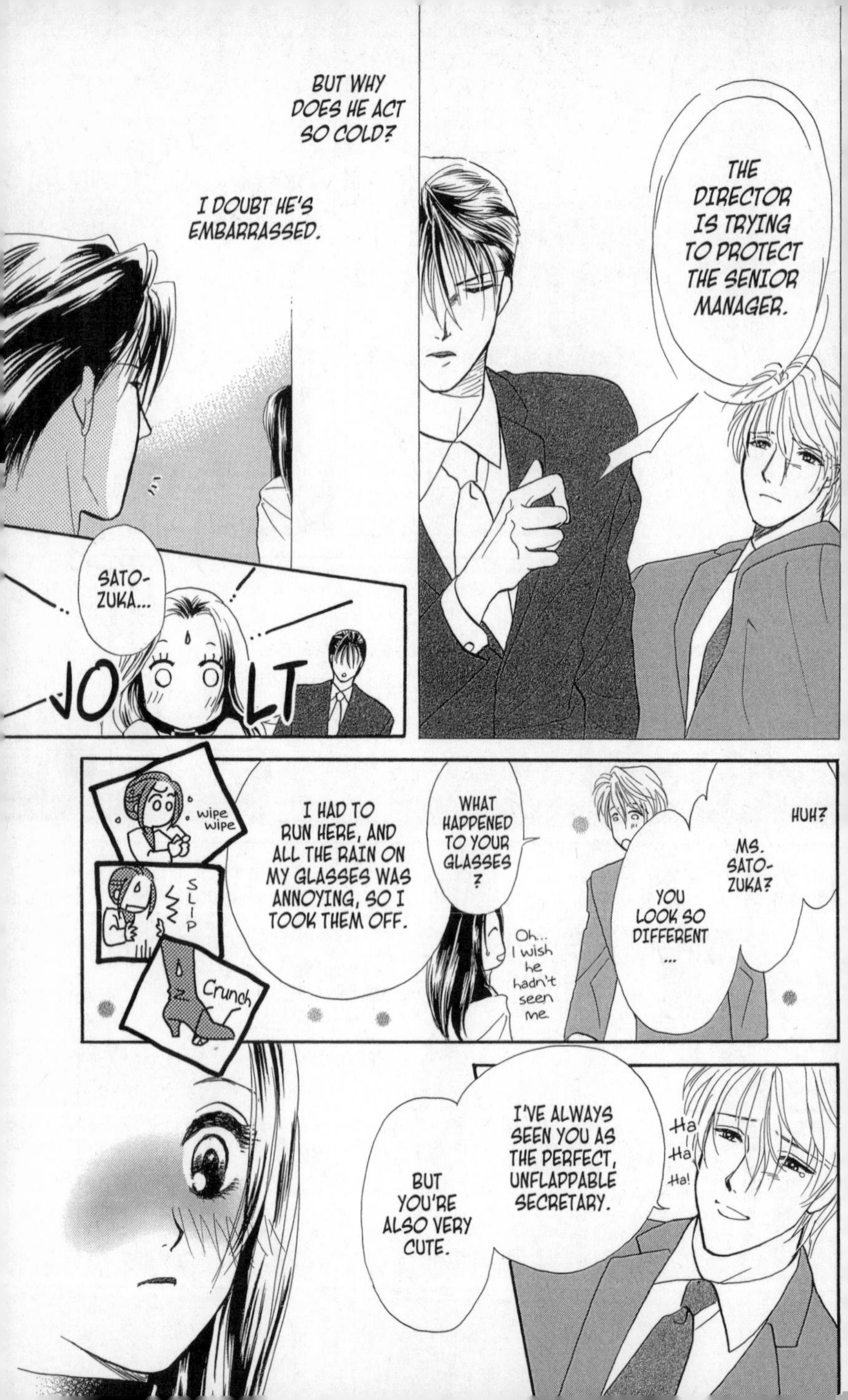
THE DIRECTOR IS TRYING TO PROTECT THE SENIOR MANAGER.
BUT WHY DOES HE ACT SO COLD?
I DOUBT HE'S EMBARRASSED.
SATO-ZUKA...
JOLT
HUH?
MS. SATO-ZUKA?
YOU LOOK SO DIFFERENT...
WHAT HAPPENED TO YOUR GLASSES?
Oh... I wish he hadn't seen me.
I HAD TO RUN HERE, AND ALL THE RAIN ON MY GLASSES WAS ANNOYING, SO I TOOK THEM OFF.
wipe wipe
SLIP
Crunch
Ha Ha Ha!
I'VE ALWAYS SEEN YOU AS THE PERFECT, UNFLAPPABLE SECRETARY.
BUT YOU'RE ALSO VERY CUTE.

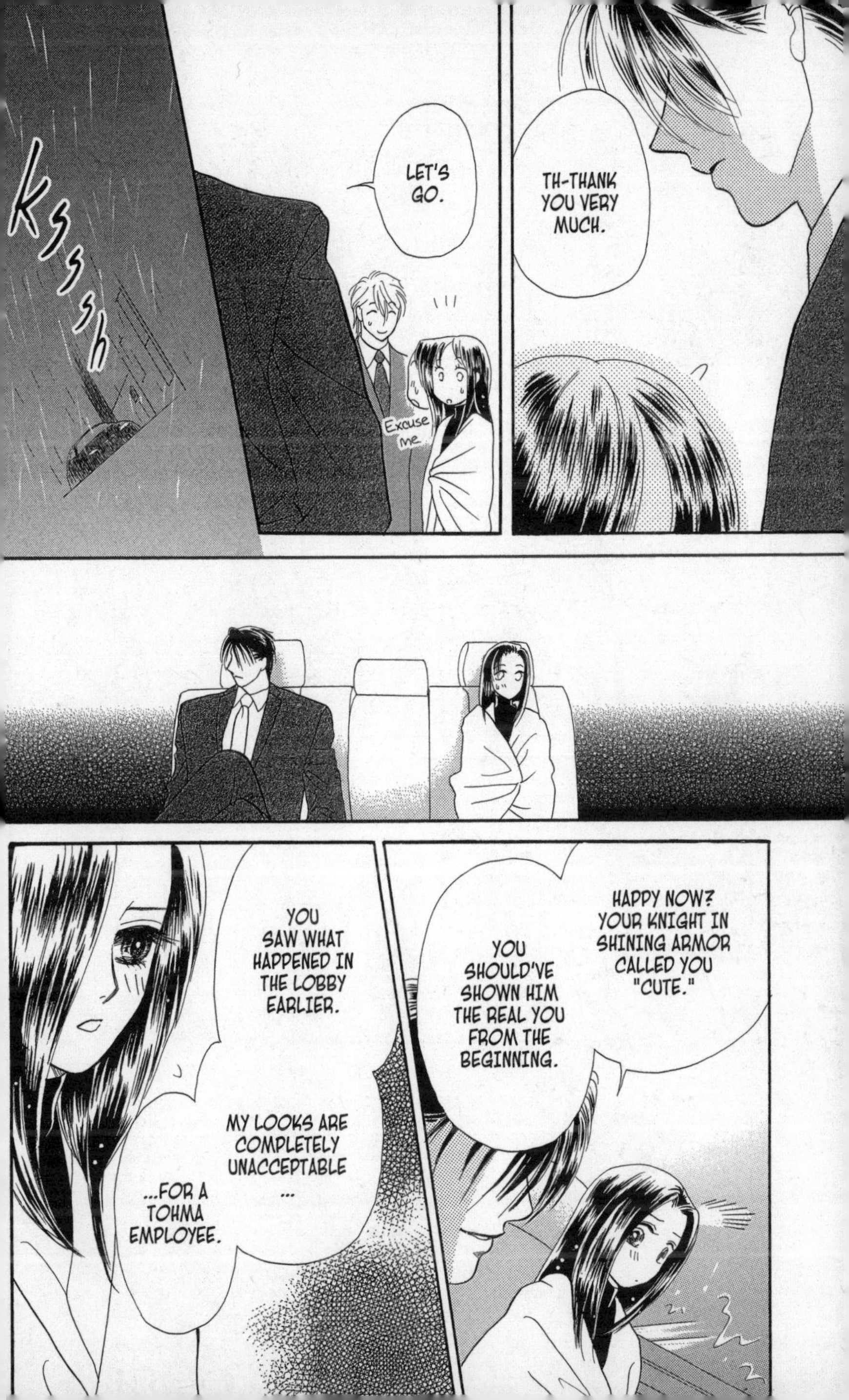
TH-THANK YOU VERY MUCH.
LET'S GO.
Excuse me.
Ksssh
HAPPY NOW? YOUR KNIGHT IN SHINING ARMOR CALLED YOU "CUTE."
YOU SHOULD'VE SHOWN HIM THE REAL YOU FROM THE BEGINNING.
YOU SAW WHAT HAPPENED IN THE LOBBY EARLIER.
MY LOOKS ARE COMPLETELY UNACCEPTABLE ...
...FOR A TOHMA EMPLOYEE.

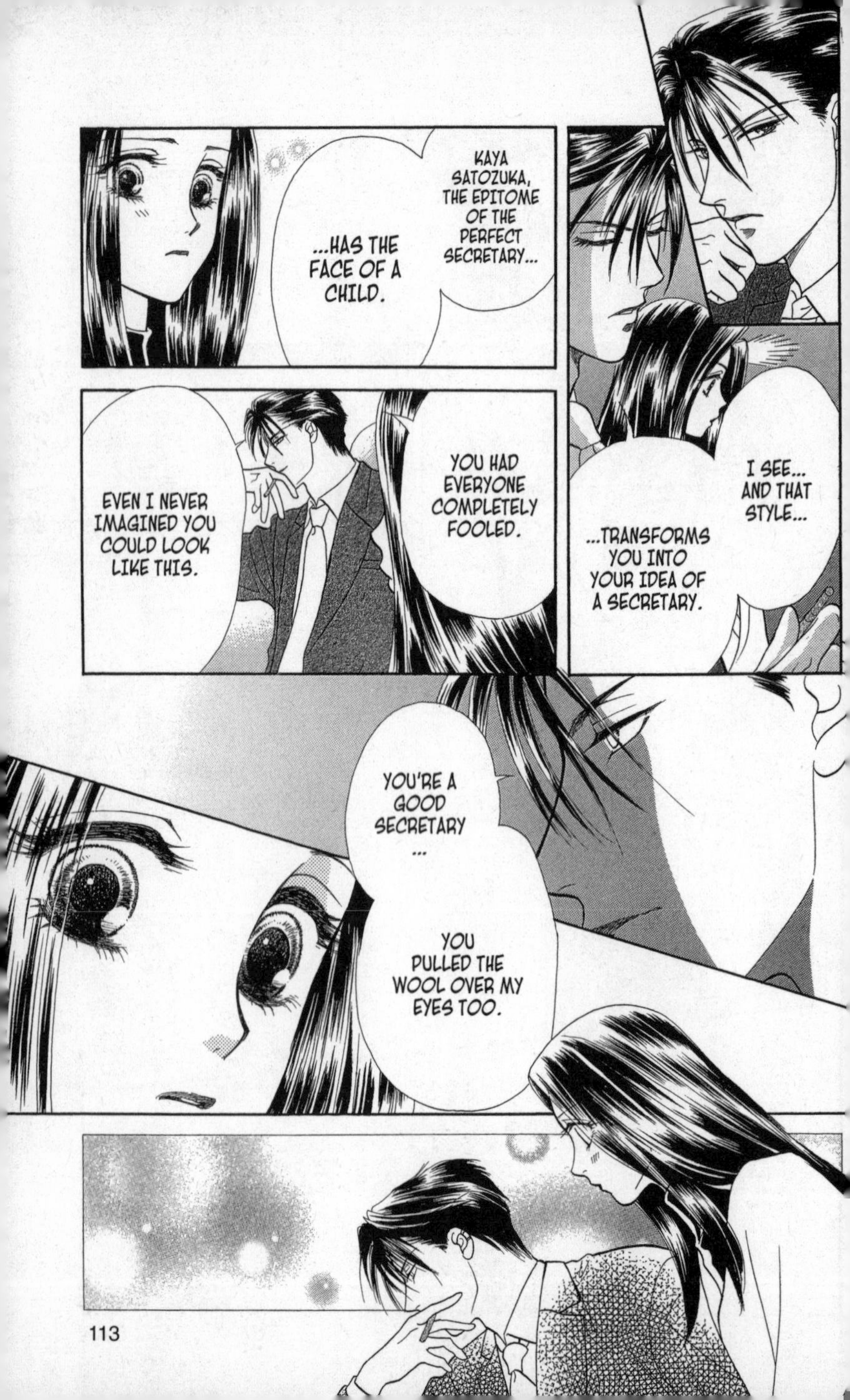
I SEE... AND THAT STYLE...
...TRANSFORMS YOU INTO YOUR IDEA OF A SECRETARY.
KAYA SATOZUKA, THE EPITOME OF THE PERFECT SECRETARY...
...HAS THE FACE OF A CHILD.
YOU HAD EVERYONE COMPLETELY FOOLED.
EVEN I NEVER IMAGINED YOU COULD LOOK LIKE THIS.
YOU'RE A GOOD SECRETARY ...
YOU PULLED THE WOOL OVER MY EYES TOO.

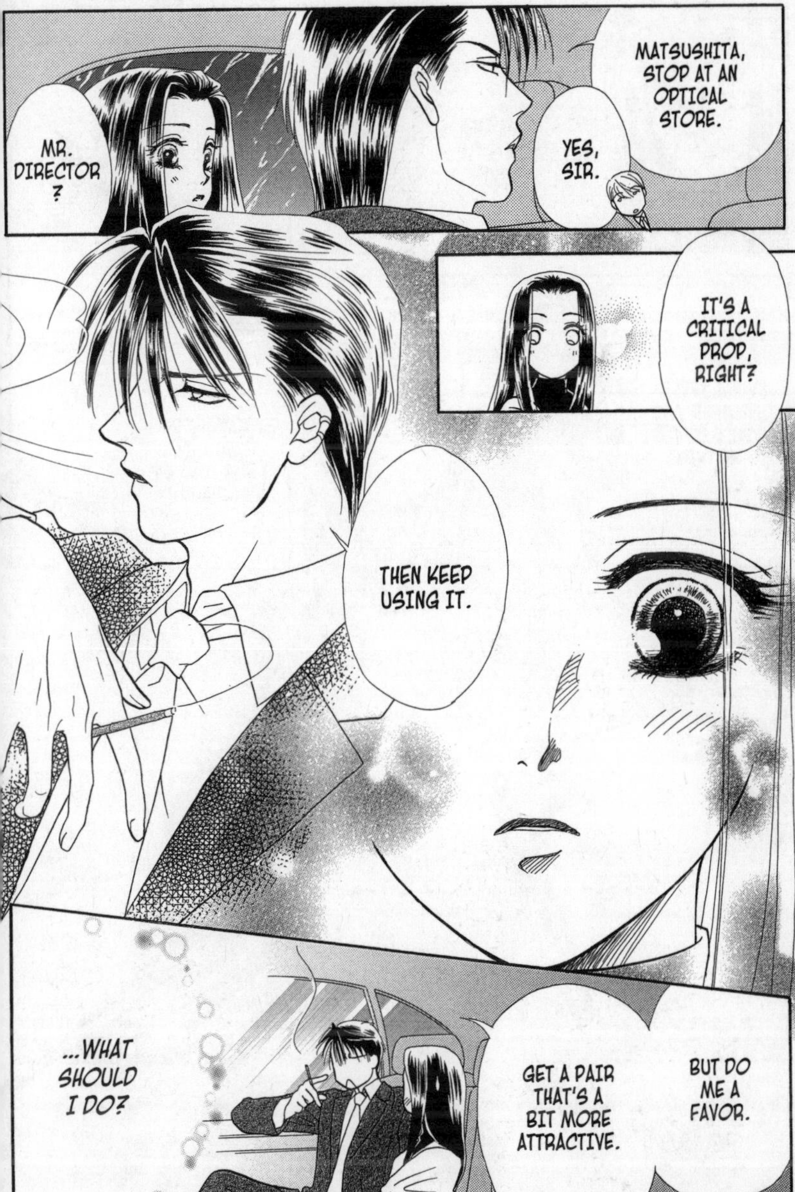
MATSUSHITA, STOP AT AN OPTICAL STORE.
YES, SIR.
MR. DIRECTOR?
IT'S A CRITICAL PROP, RIGHT?
THEN KEEP USING IT.
BUT DO ME A FAVOR.
GET A PAIR THAT'S A BIT MORE ATTRACTIVE.
...WHAT SHOULD I DO?

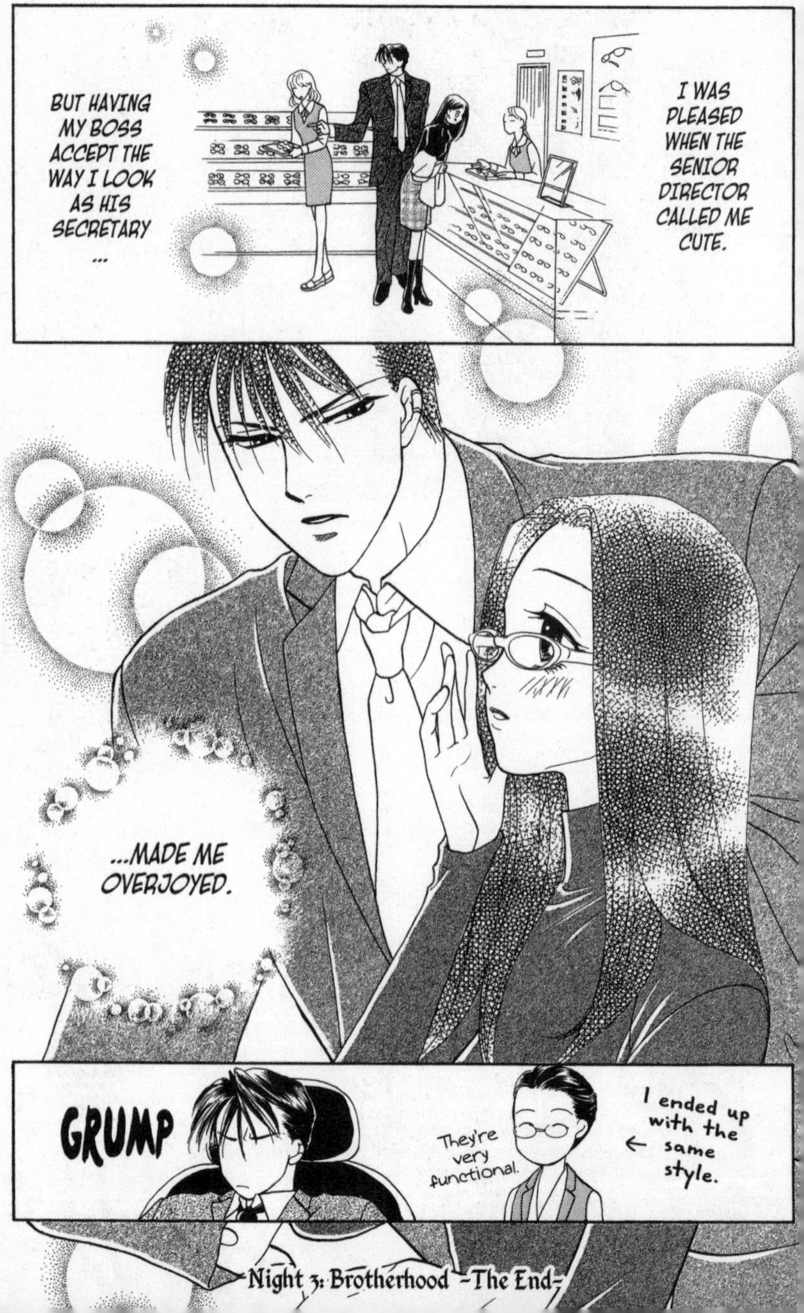
I WAS PLEASED WHEN THE SENIOR DIRECTOR CALLED ME CUTE.
BUT HAVING MY BOSS ACCEPT THE WAY I LOOK AS HIS SECRETARY ...
...MADE ME OVERJOYED.
I ended up with the same style.
They're very functional.
GRUMP
Night 3: Brotherhood -The End-

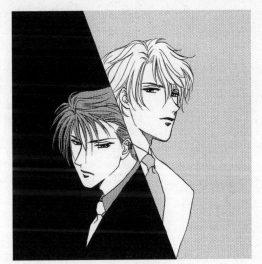

▲ Night 4: Workaholic Girl preview

When I draw the Tohma Brothers, I'm told that somehow Masaki, the older one, looks shadier. Nah, he's a very nice person. Really.

↑ Sounds awfully forced. (strained laugh)

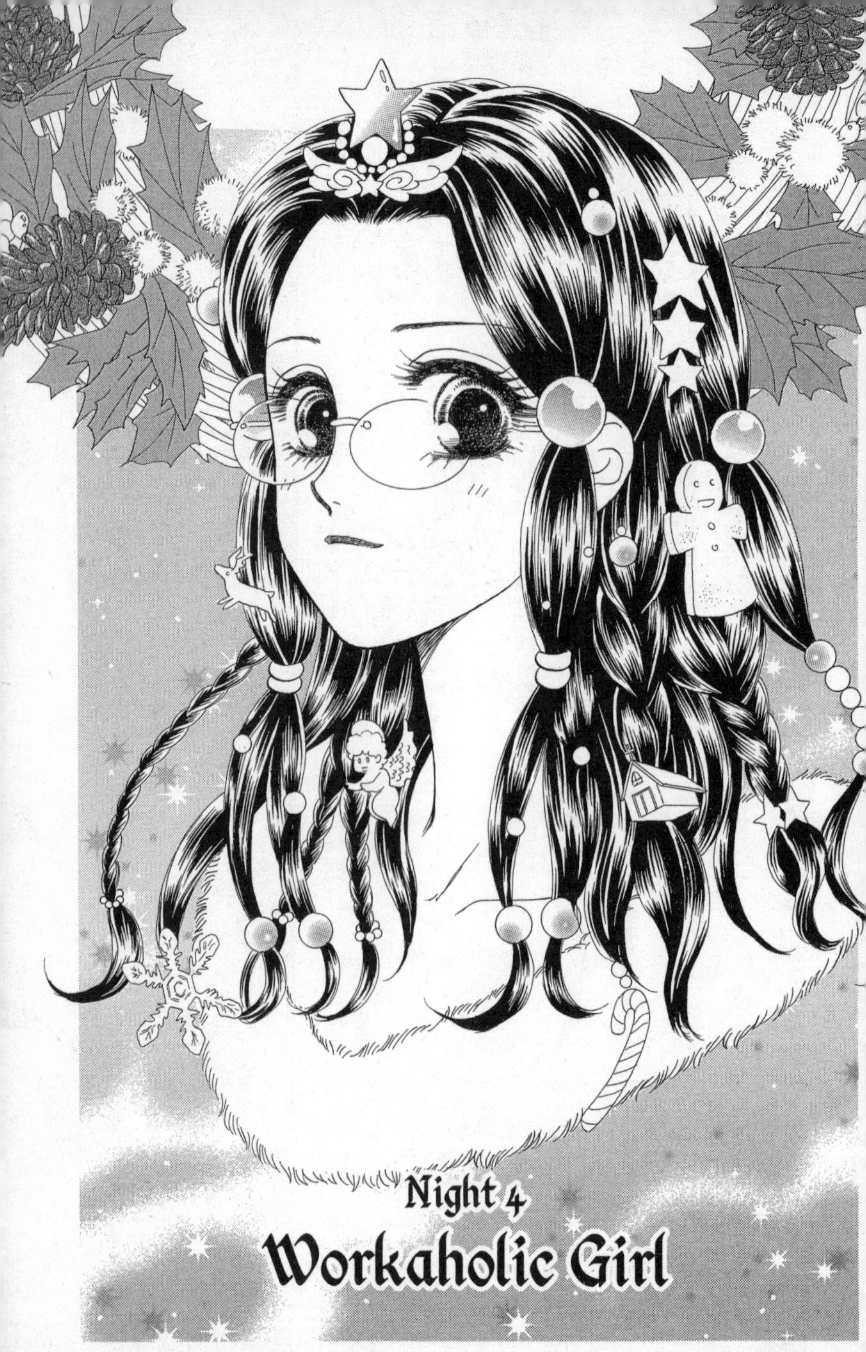
Night 4
Workaholic Girl

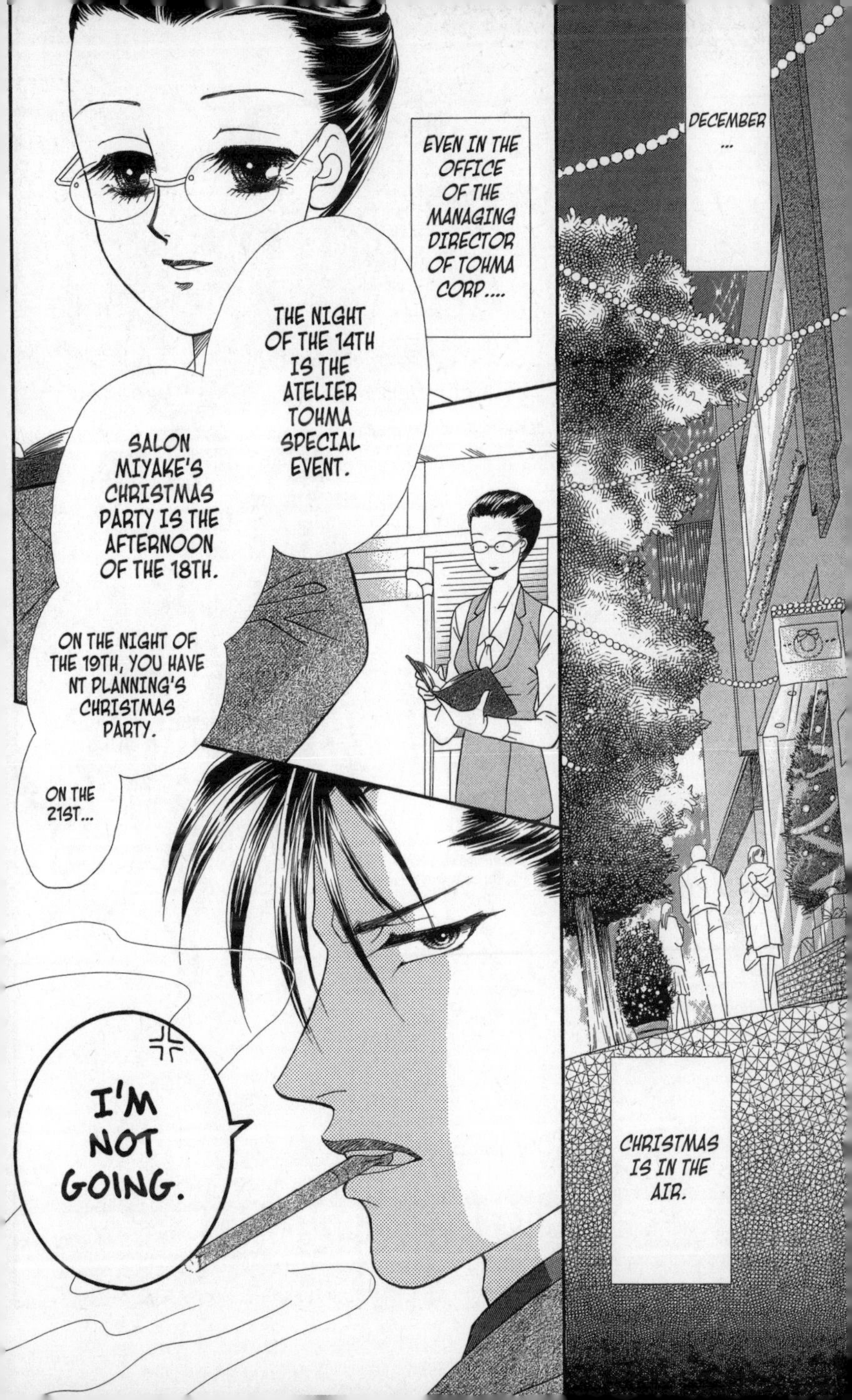
DECEMBER ...
CHRISTMAS IS IN THE AIR.
EVEN IN THE OFFICE OF THE MANAGING DIRECTOR OF TOHMA CORP....
THE NIGHT OF THE 14TH IS THE ATELIER TOHMA SPECIAL EVENT.
SALON MIYAKE'S CHRISTMAS PARTY IS THE AFTERNOON OF THE 18TH.
ON THE NIGHT OF THE 19TH, YOU HAVE NT PLANNING'S CHRISTMAS PARTY.
ON THE 21ST...
I'M NOT GOING.

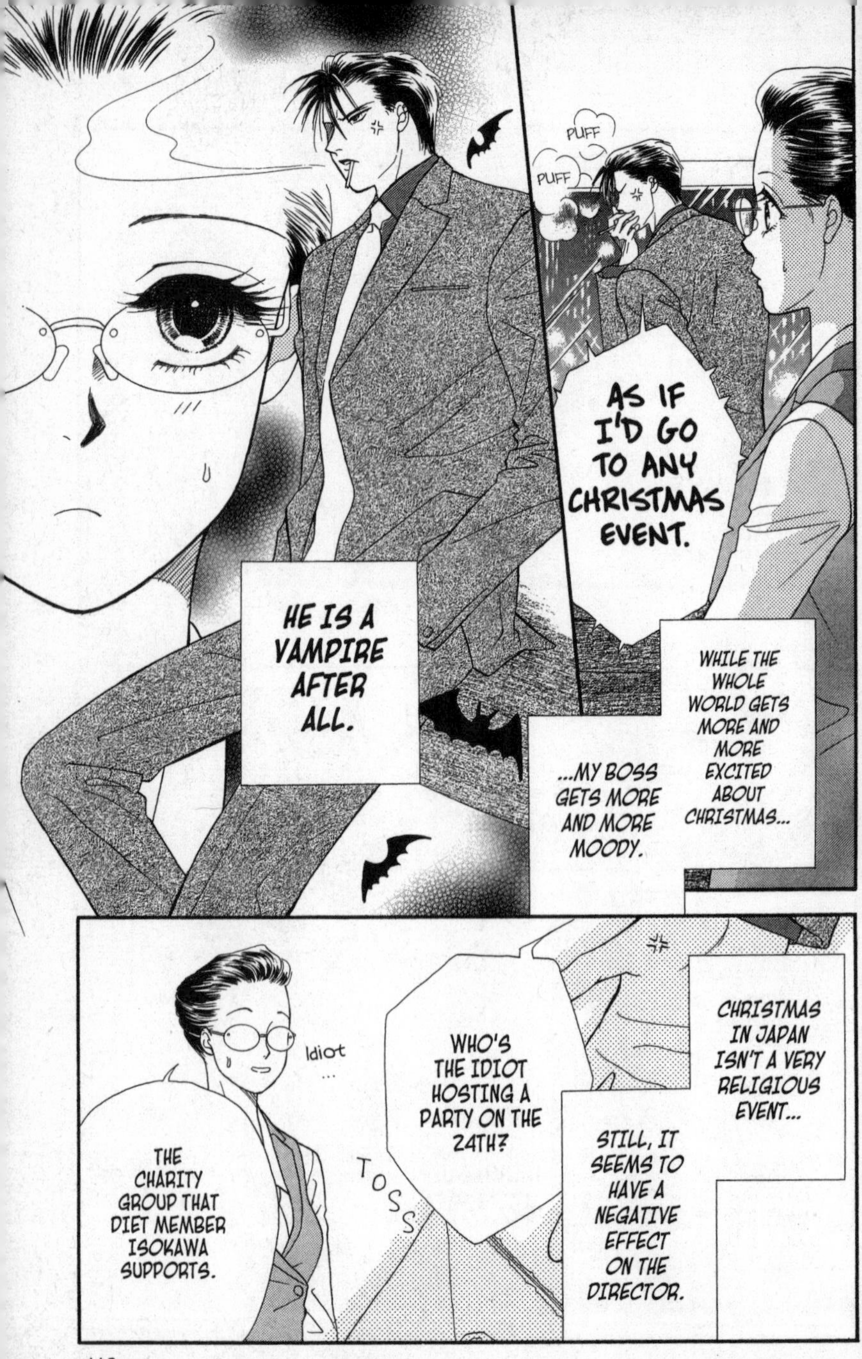
PUFF
PUFF
AS IF I'D GO TO ANY CHRISTMAS EVENT.
WHILE THE WHOLE WORLD GETS MORE AND MORE EXCITED ABOUT CHRISTMAS...
...MY BOSS GETS MORE AND MORE MOODY.
HE IS A VAMPIRE AFTER ALL.
CHRISTMAS IN JAPAN ISN'T A VERY RELIGIOUS EVENT...
STILL, IT SEEMS TO HAVE A NEGATIVE EFFECT ON THE DIRECTOR.
WHO'S THE IDIOT HOSTING A PARTY ON THE 24TH?
TOSS
Idiot ...
THE CHARITY GROUP THAT DIET MEMBER ISOKAWA SUPPORTS.

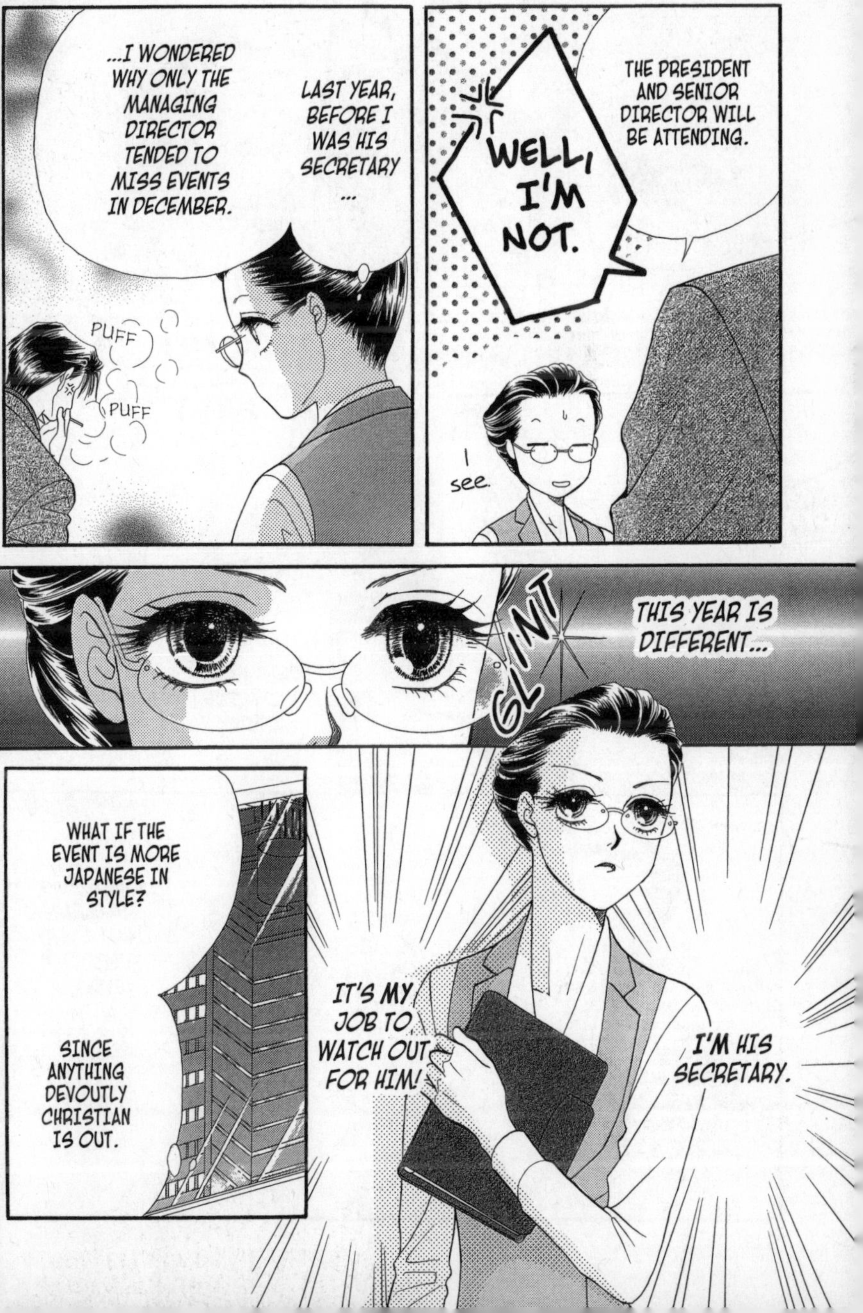
THE PRESIDENT AND SENIOR DIRECTOR WILL BE ATTENDING.
WELL, I'M NOT.
I see.
LAST YEAR, BEFORE I WAS HIS SECRETARY ...
...I WONDERED WHY ONLY THE MANAGING DIRECTOR TENDED TO MISS EVENTS IN DECEMBER.
PUFF
PUFF
THIS YEAR IS DIFFERENT...
GLINT
I'M HIS SECRETARY.
IT'S MY JOB TO WATCH OUT FOR HIM!
WHAT IF THE EVENT IS MORE JAPANESE IN STYLE?
SINCE ANYTHING DEVOUTLY CHRISTIAN IS OUT.

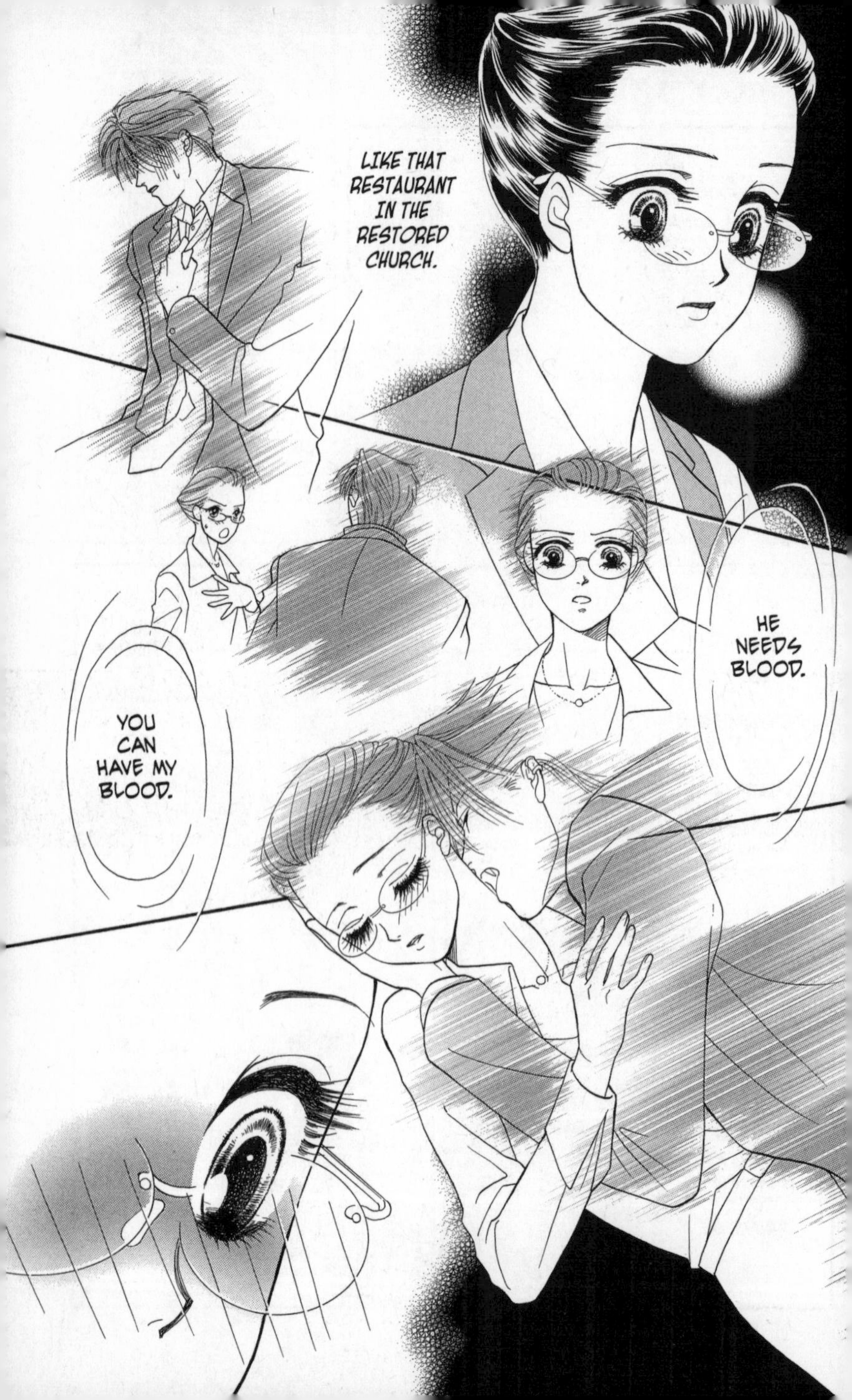
LIKE THAT RESTAURANT IN THE RESTORED CHURCH.
HE NEEDS BLOOD.
YOU CAN HAVE MY BLOOD.

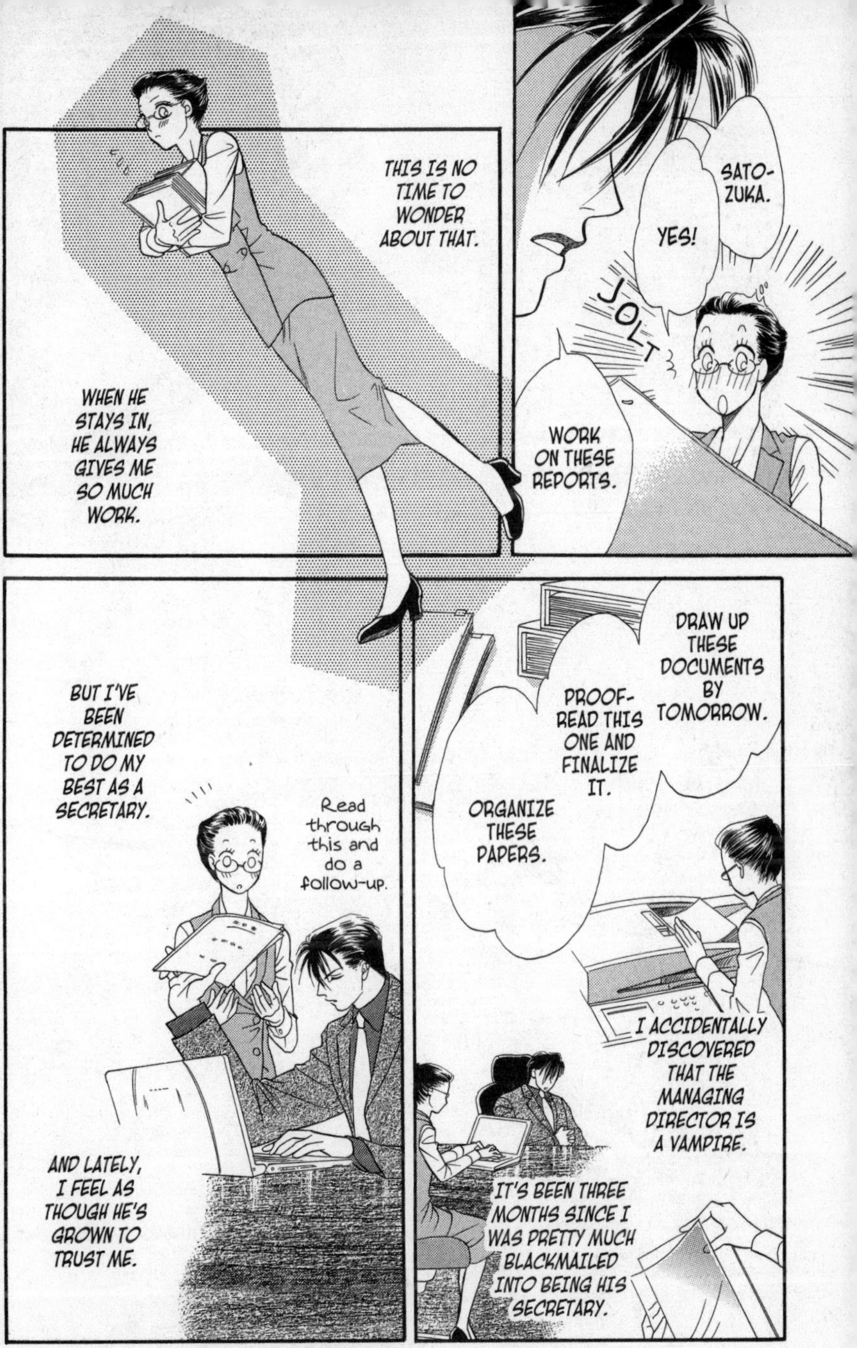
SATO-ZUKA.
YES!
JOLT
WORK ON THESE REPORTS.
THIS IS NO TIME TO WONDER ABOUT THAT.
WHEN HE STAYS IN, HE ALWAYS GIVES ME SO MUCH WORK.
DRAW UP THESE DOCUMENTS BY TOMORROW.
PROOF-READ THIS ONE AND FINALIZE IT.
ORGANIZE THESE PAPERS.
I ACCIDENTALLY DISCOVERED THAT THE MANAGING DIRECTOR IS A VAMPIRE.
IT'S BEEN THREE MONTHS SINCE I WAS PRETTY MUCH BLACKMAILED INTO BEING HIS SECRETARY.
BUT I'VE BEEN DETERMINED TO DO MY BEST AS A SECRETARY.
Read through this and do a follow-up.
AND LATELY, I FEEL AS THOUGH HE'S GROWN TO TRUST ME.

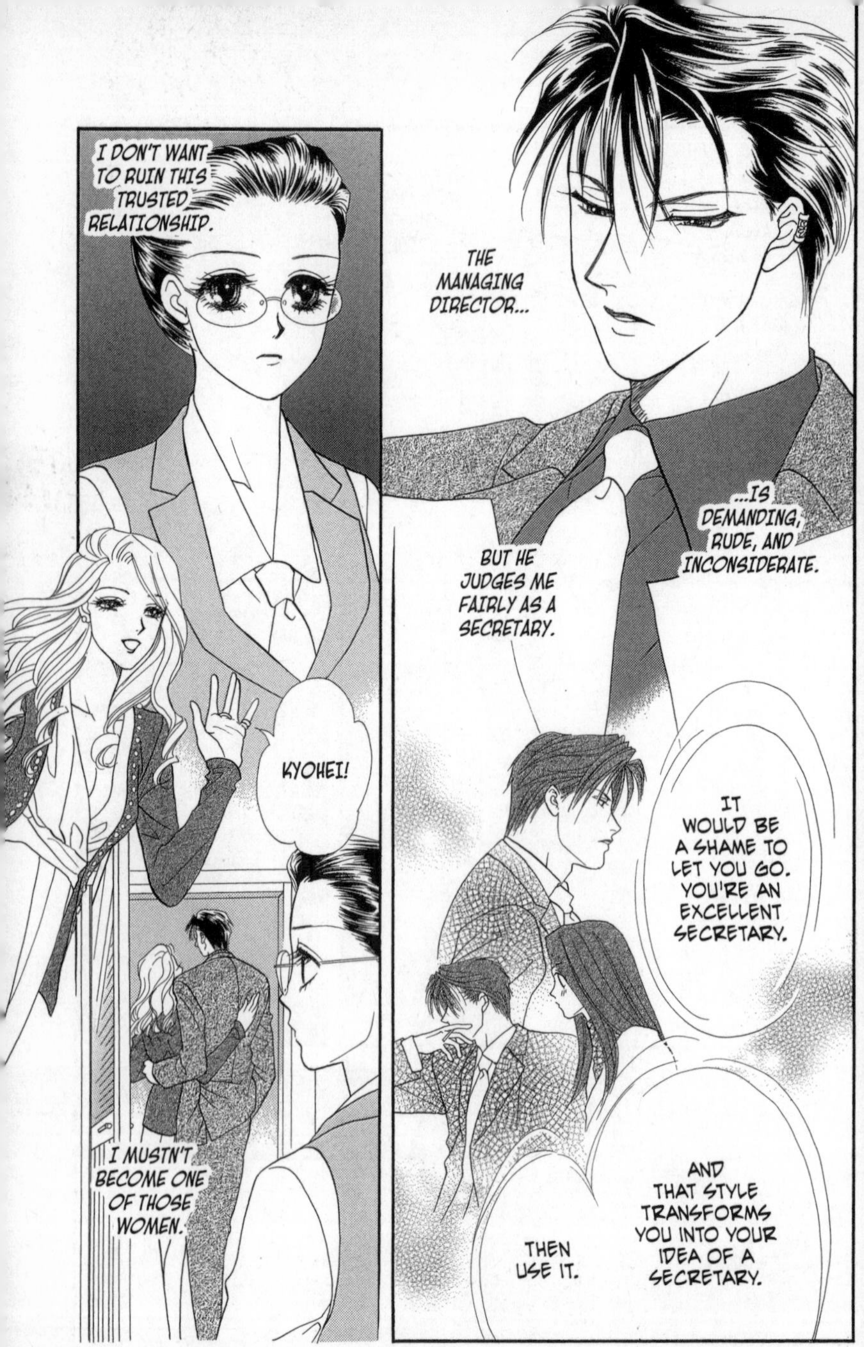
THE MANAGING DIRECTOR...
...IS DEMANDING, RUDE, AND INCONSIDERATE.
BUT HE JUDGES ME FAIRLY AS A SECRETARY.
IT WOULD BE A SHAME TO LET YOU GO. YOU'RE AN EXCELLENT SECRETARY.
AND THAT STYLE TRANSFORMS YOU INTO YOUR IDEA OF A SECRETARY.
THEN USE IT.
I DON'T WANT TO RUIN THIS TRUSTED RELATIONSHIP.
KYOHEI!
I MUSTN'T BECOME ONE OF THOSE WOMEN.

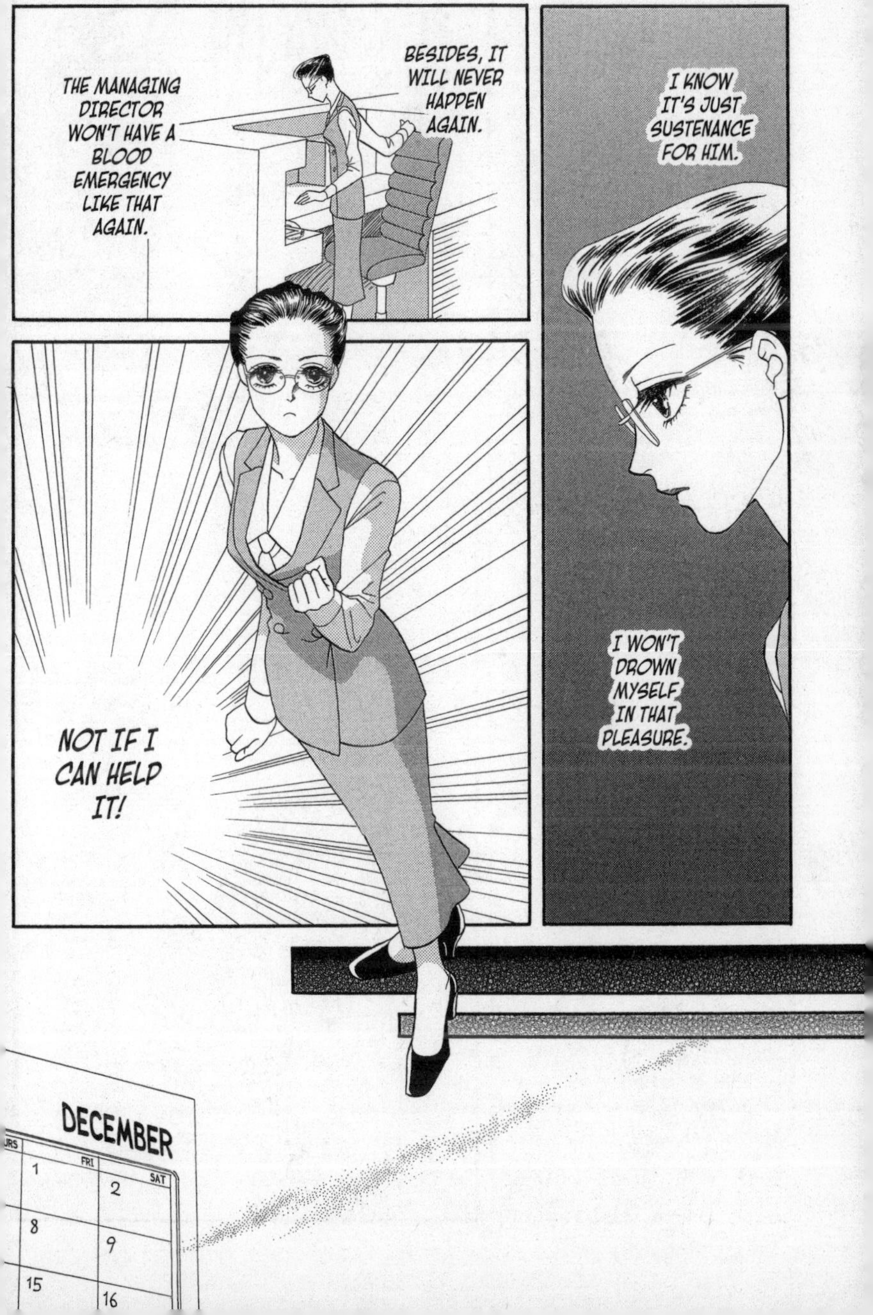
I KNOW IT'S JUST SUSTENANCE FOR HIM.
I WON'T DROWN MYSELF IN THAT PLEASURE.
BESIDES, IT WILL NEVER HAPPEN AGAIN.
THE MANAGING DIRECTOR WON'T HAVE A BLOOD EMERGENCY LIKE THAT AGAIN.
NOT IF I CAN HELP IT!
DECEMBER
FRI
SAT
1
2
8
9
15
16

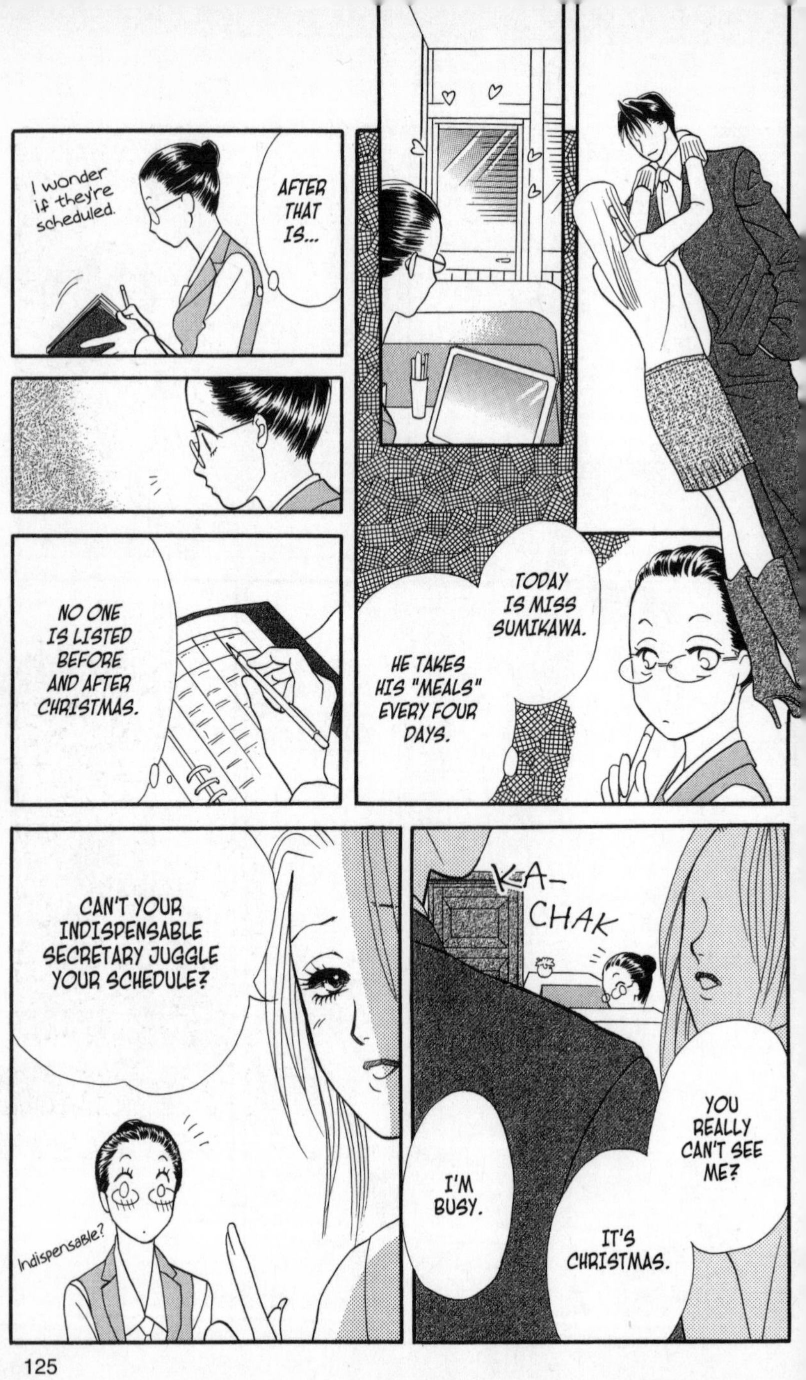
TODAY IS MISS SUMIKAWA.
HE TAKES HIS "MEALS" EVERY FOUR DAYS.
AFTER THAT IS...
I wonder if they're scheduled.
NO ONE IS LISTED BEFORE AND AFTER CHRISTMAS.
KA-CHAK
YOU REALLY CAN'T SEE ME?
IT'S CHRISTMAS.
I'M BUSY.
CAN'T YOUR INDISPENSABLE SECRETARY JUGGLE YOUR SCHEDULE?
Indispensable?

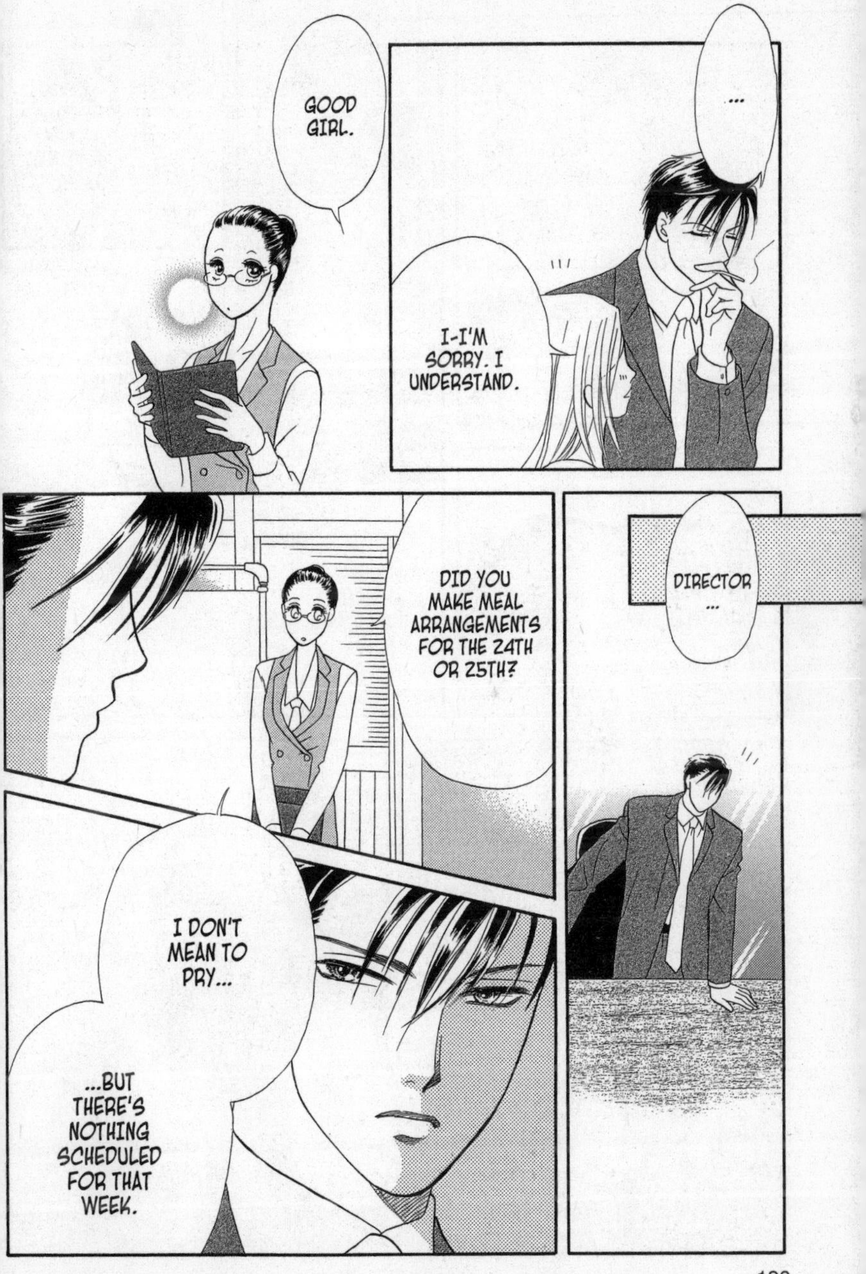
...
I-I'M SORRY. I UNDERSTAND.
GOOD GIRL.
DIRECTOR ...
DID YOU MAKE MEAL ARRANGEMENTS FOR THE 24TH OR 25TH?
I DON'T MEAN TO PRY...
...BUT THERE'S NOTHING SCHEDULED FOR THAT WEEK.

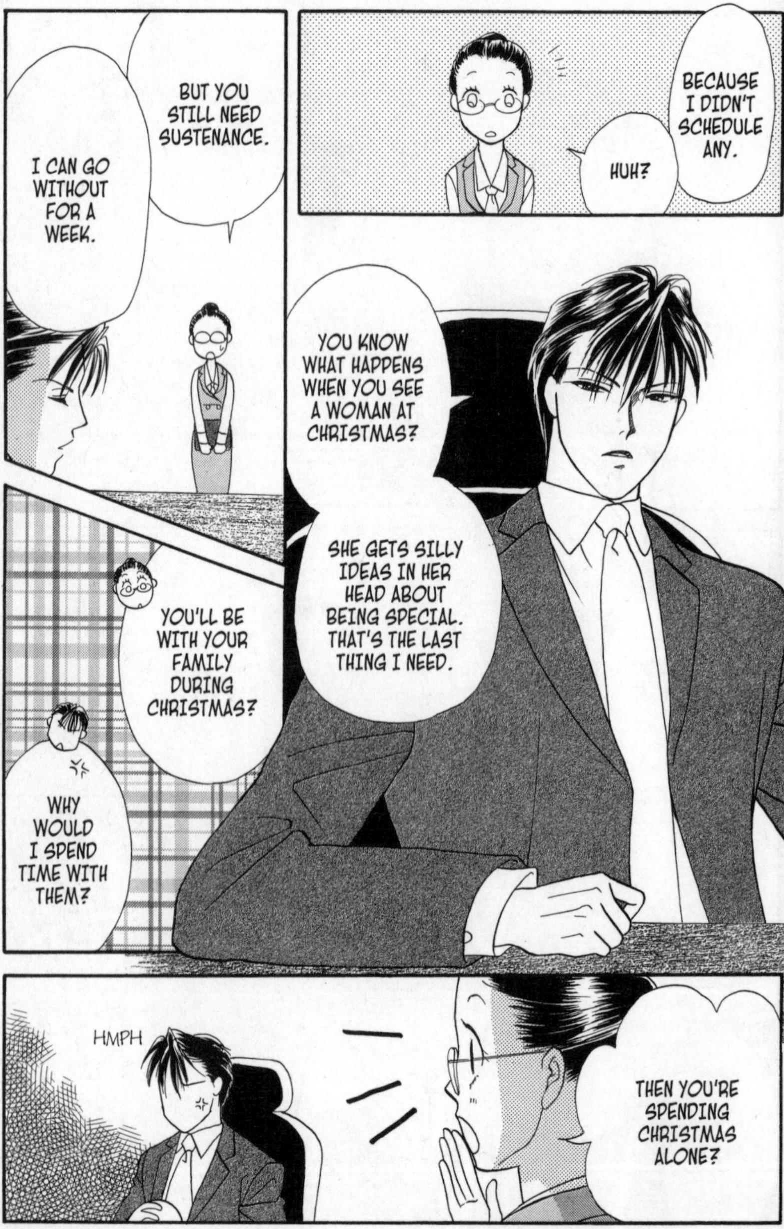
BECAUSE I DIDN'T SCHEDULE ANY.
HUH?
BUT YOU STILL NEED SUSTENANCE.
I CAN GO WITHOUT FOR A WEEK.
YOU KNOW WHAT HAPPENS WHEN YOU SEE A WOMAN AT CHRISTMAS?
SHE GETS SILLY IDEAS IN HER HEAD ABOUT BEING SPECIAL. THAT'S THE LAST THING I NEED.
YOU'LL BE WITH YOUR FAMILY DURING CHRISTMAS?
WHY WOULD I SPEND TIME WITH THEM?
THEN YOU'RE SPENDING CHRISTMAS ALONE?
HMPH

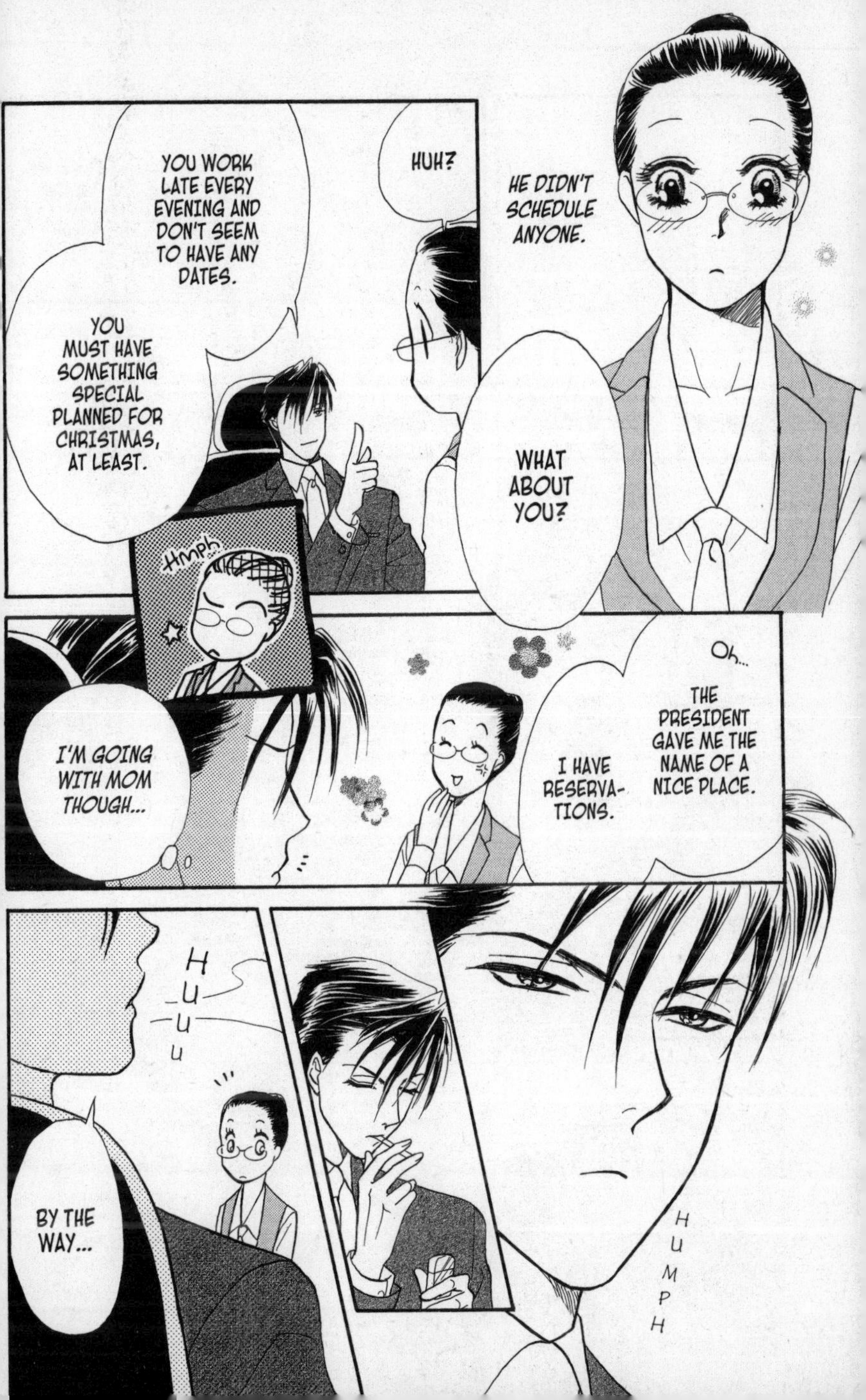
HE DIDN'T SCHEDULE ANYONE.
WHAT ABOUT YOU?
HUH?
YOU WORK LATE EVERY EVENING AND DON'T SEEM TO HAVE ANY DATES.
YOU MUST HAVE SOMETHING SPECIAL PLANNED FOR CHRISTMAS, AT LEAST.
Hmph
Oh...
THE PRESIDENT GAVE ME THE NAME OF A NICE PLACE.
I HAVE RESERVATIONS.
I'M GOING WITH MOM THOUGH...
HUMPH
Huuu
BY THE WAY...

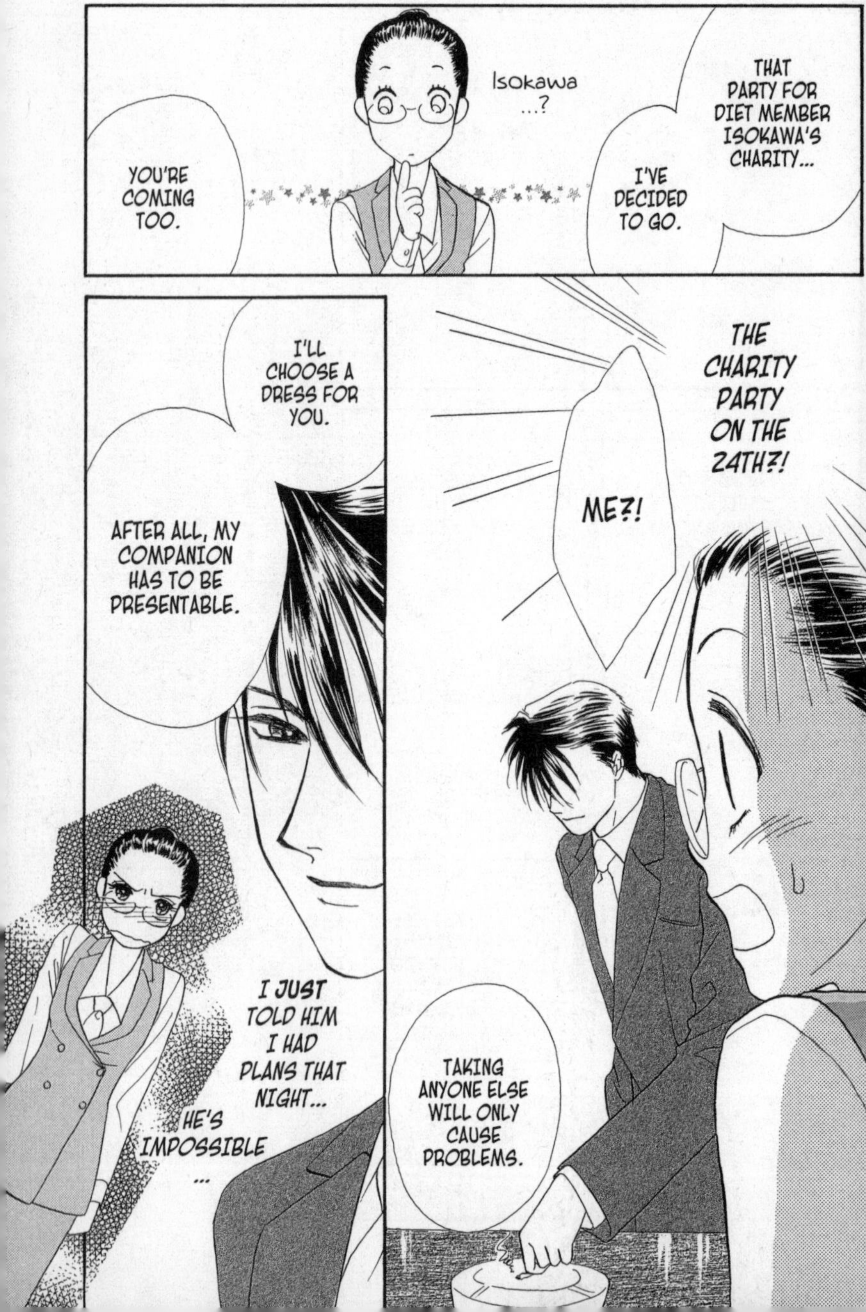
THAT PARTY FOR DIET MEMBER ISOKAWA'S CHARITY...
I'VE DECIDED TO GO.
Isokawa ...?
YOU'RE COMING TOO.
THE CHARITY PARTY ON THE 24TH?!
ME?!
TAKING ANYONE ELSE WILL ONLY CAUSE PROBLEMS.
I'LL CHOOSE A DRESS FOR YOU.
AFTER ALL, MY COMPANION HAS TO BE PRESENTABLE.
I JUST TOLD HIM I HAD PLANS THAT NIGHT...
HE'S IMPOSSIBLE ...

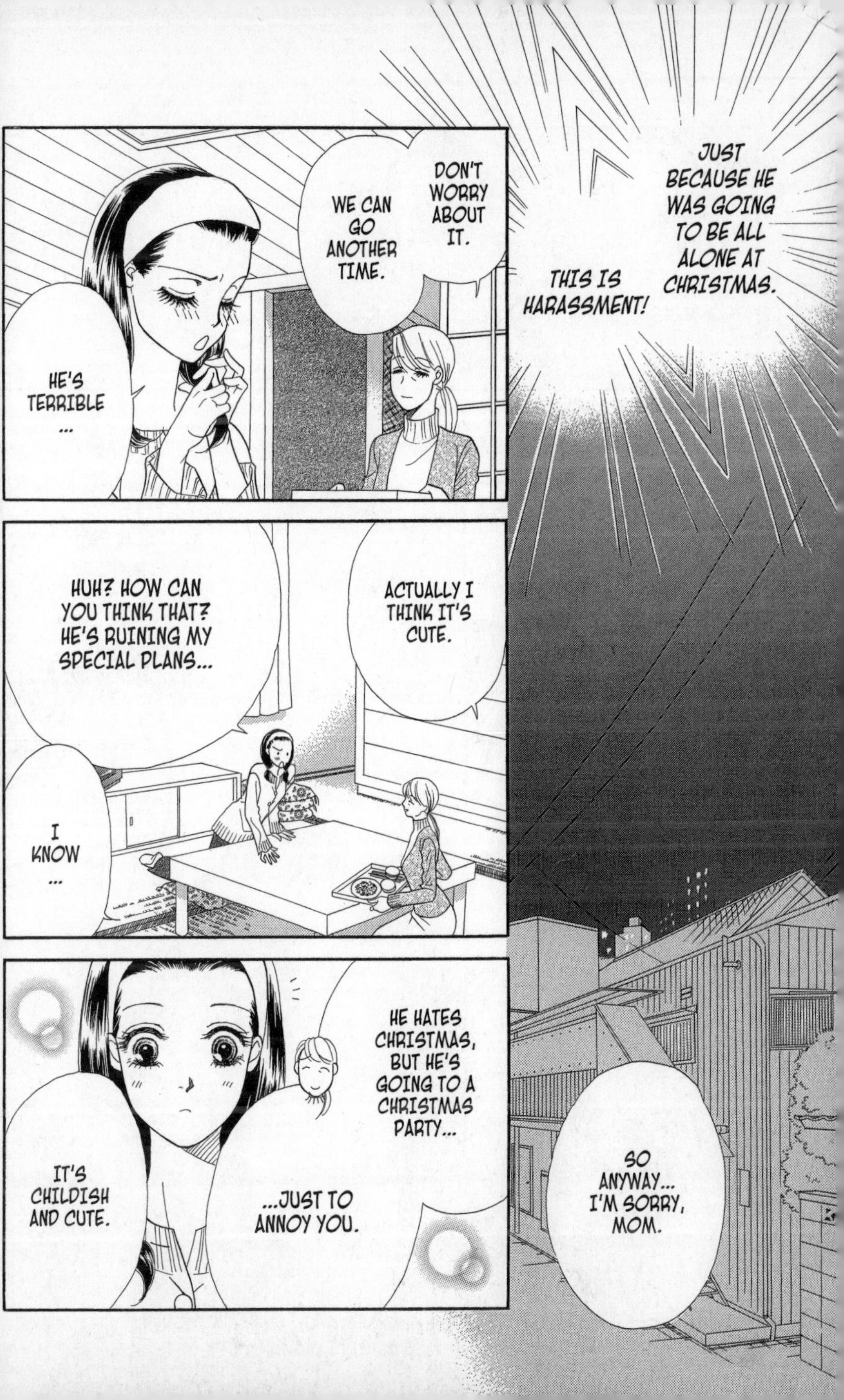
JUST BECAUSE HE WAS GOING TO BE ALL ALONE AT CHRISTMAS.
THIS IS HARASSMENT!
SO ANYWAY... I'M SORRY, MOM.
DON'T WORRY ABOUT IT.
WE CAN GO ANOTHER TIME.
HE'S TERRIBLE...
ACTUALLY I THINK IT'S CUTE.
HUH? HOW CAN YOU THINK THAT? HE'S RUINING MY SPECIAL PLANS...
I KNOW...
HE HATES CHRISTMAS, BUT HE'S GOING TO A CHRISTMAS PARTY...
...JUST TO ANNOY YOU.
IT'S CHILDISH AND CUTE.

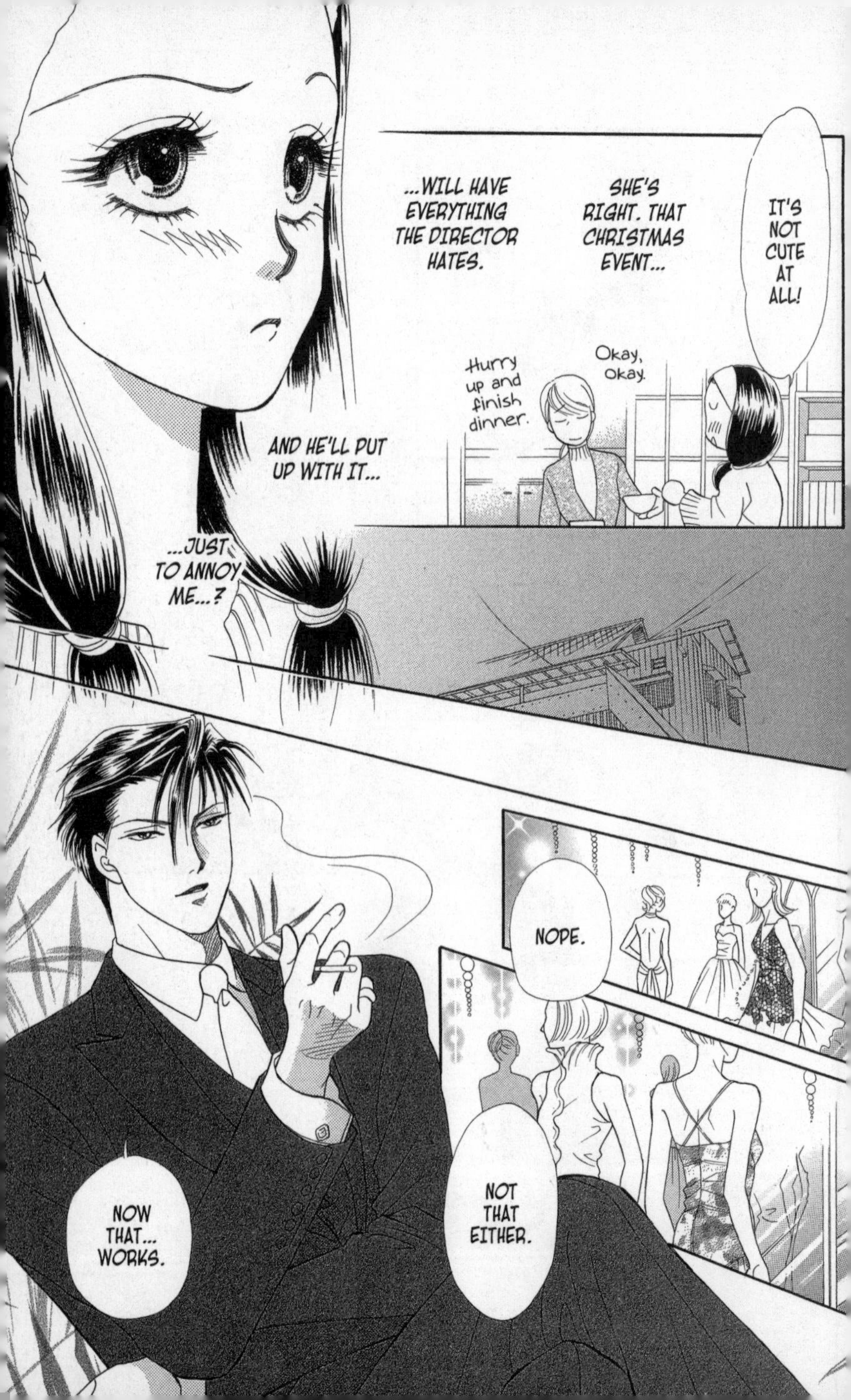
IT'S NOT CUTE AT ALL!
SHE'S RIGHT. THAT CHRISTMAS EVENT...
...WILL HAVE EVERYTHING THE DIRECTOR HATES.
Okay, okay.
Hurry up and finish dinner.
AND HE'LL PUT UP WITH IT...
...JUST TO ANNOY ME...?
NOPE.
NOT THAT EITHER.
NOW THAT... WORKS.

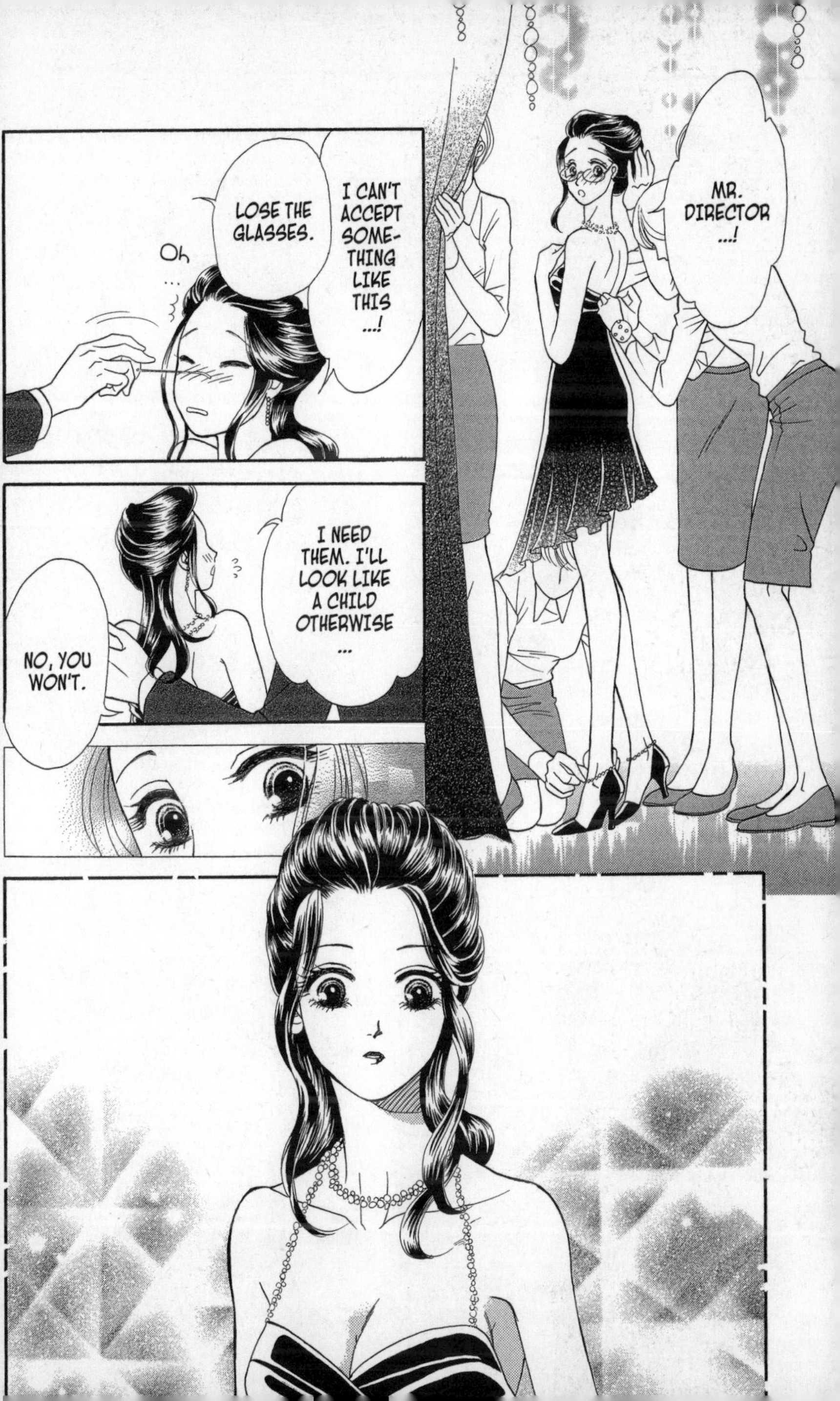
MR. DIRECTOR ...!
I CAN'T ACCEPT SOME-THING LIKE THIS ...!
LOSE THE GLASSES.
Oh ...
I NEED THEM. I'LL LOOK LIKE A CHILD OTHERWISE ...
NO, YOU WON'T.

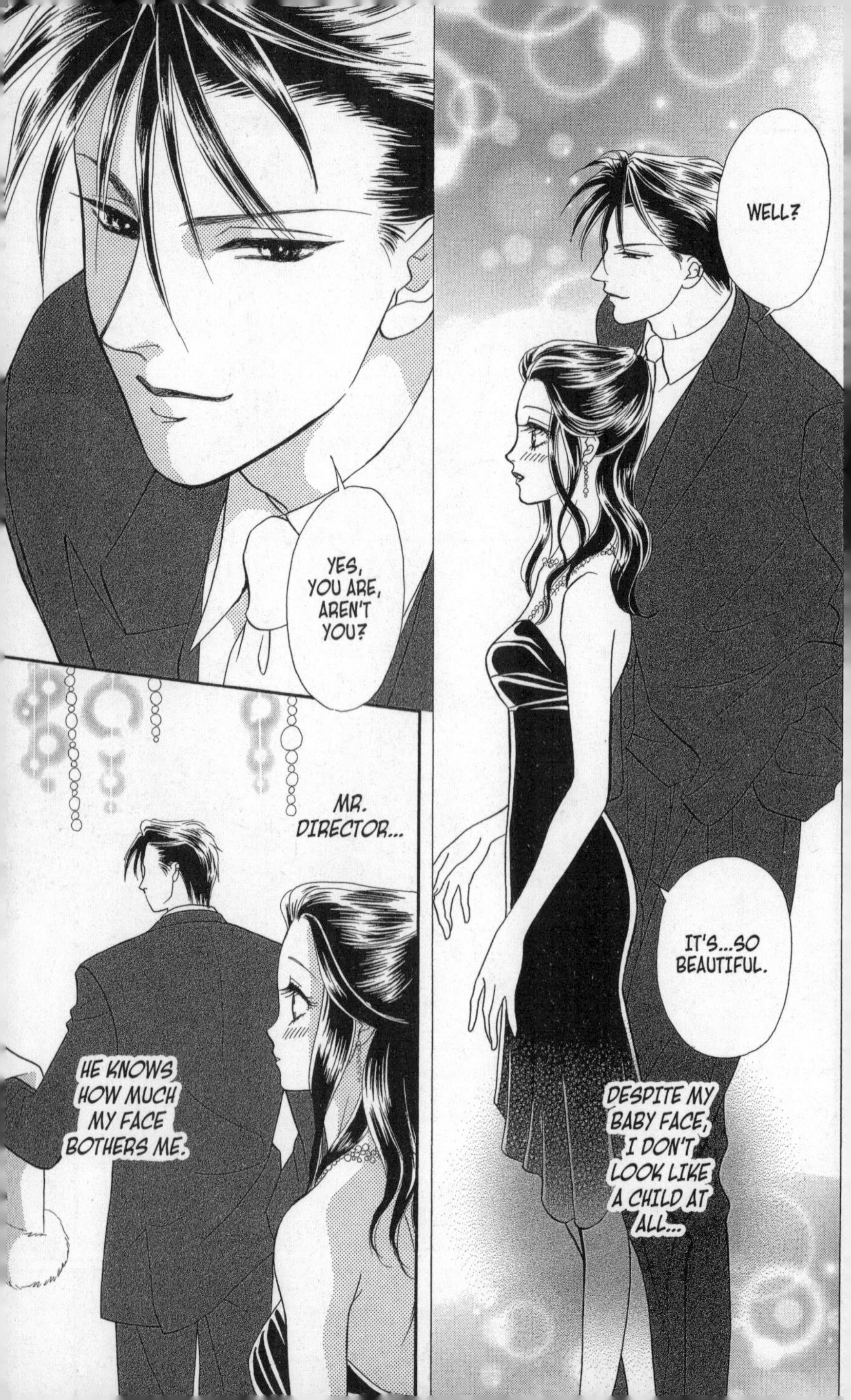
WELL?
IT'S...SO BEAUTIFUL.
DESPITE MY BABY FACE, I DON'T LOOK LIKE A CHILD AT ALL...
YES, YOU ARE, AREN'T YOU?
MR. DIRECTOR...
HE KNOWS HOW MUCH MY FACE BOTHERS ME.

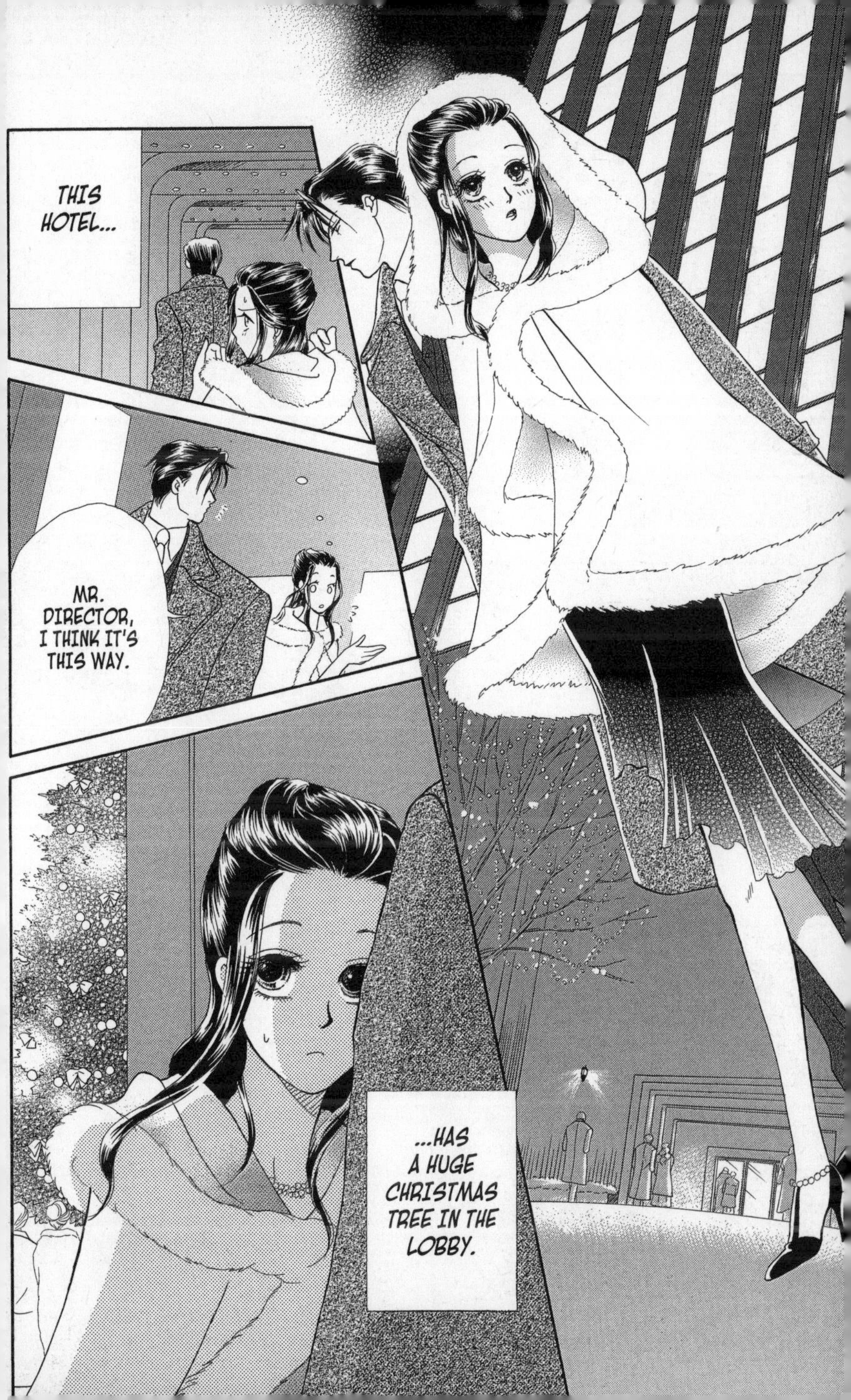
THIS HOTEL...
MR. DIRECTOR, I THINK IT'S THIS WAY.
...HAS A HUGE CHRISTMAS TREE IN THE LOBBY.

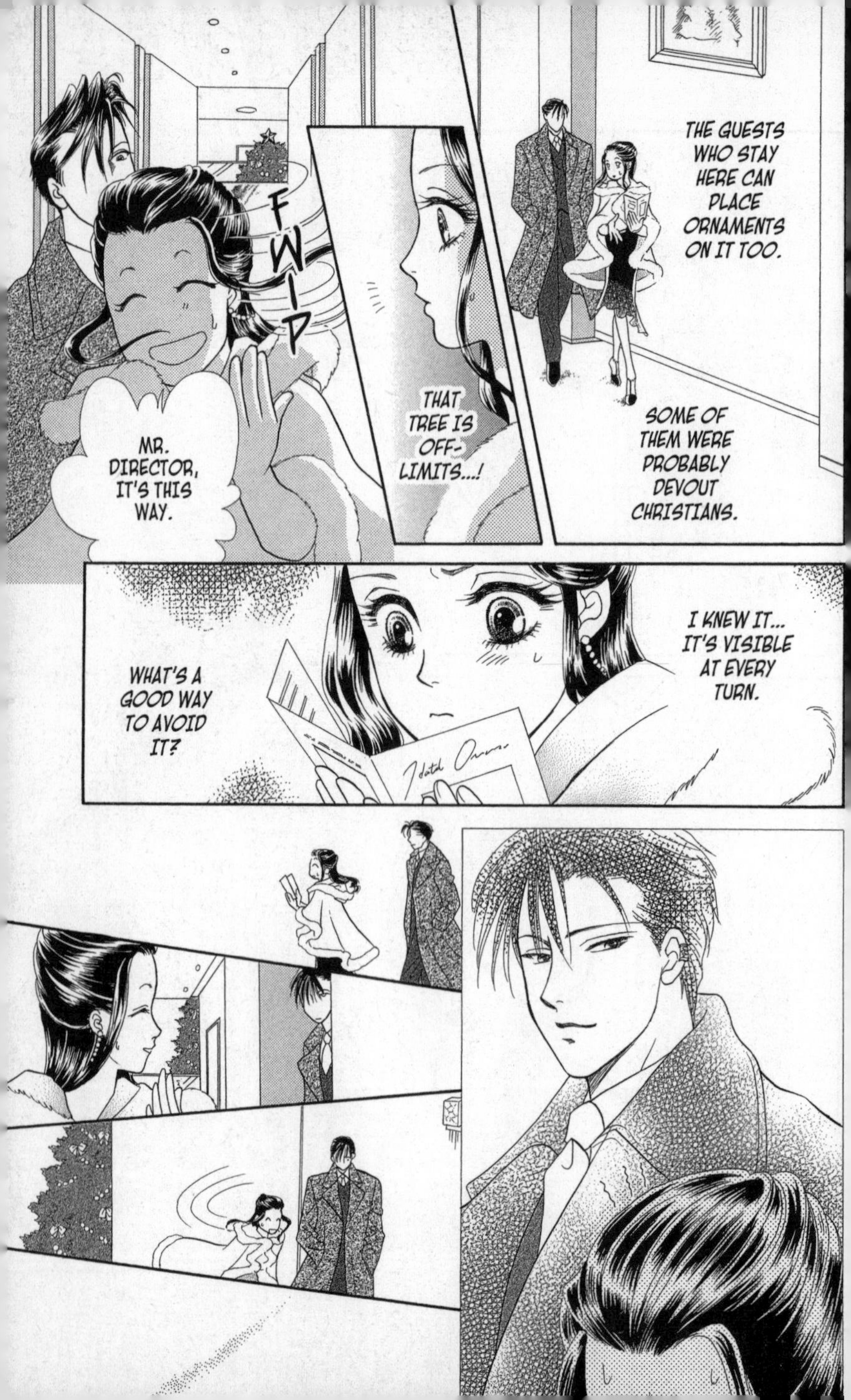
THE GUESTS WHO STAY HERE CAN PLACE ORNAMENTS ON IT TOO.
SOME OF THEM WERE PROBABLY DEVOUT CHRISTIANS.
THAT TREE IS OFF-LIMITS...!
FWIP
MR. DIRECTOR, IT'S THIS WAY.
I KNEW IT... IT'S VISIBLE AT EVERY TURN.
WHAT'S A GOOD WAY TO AVOID IT?

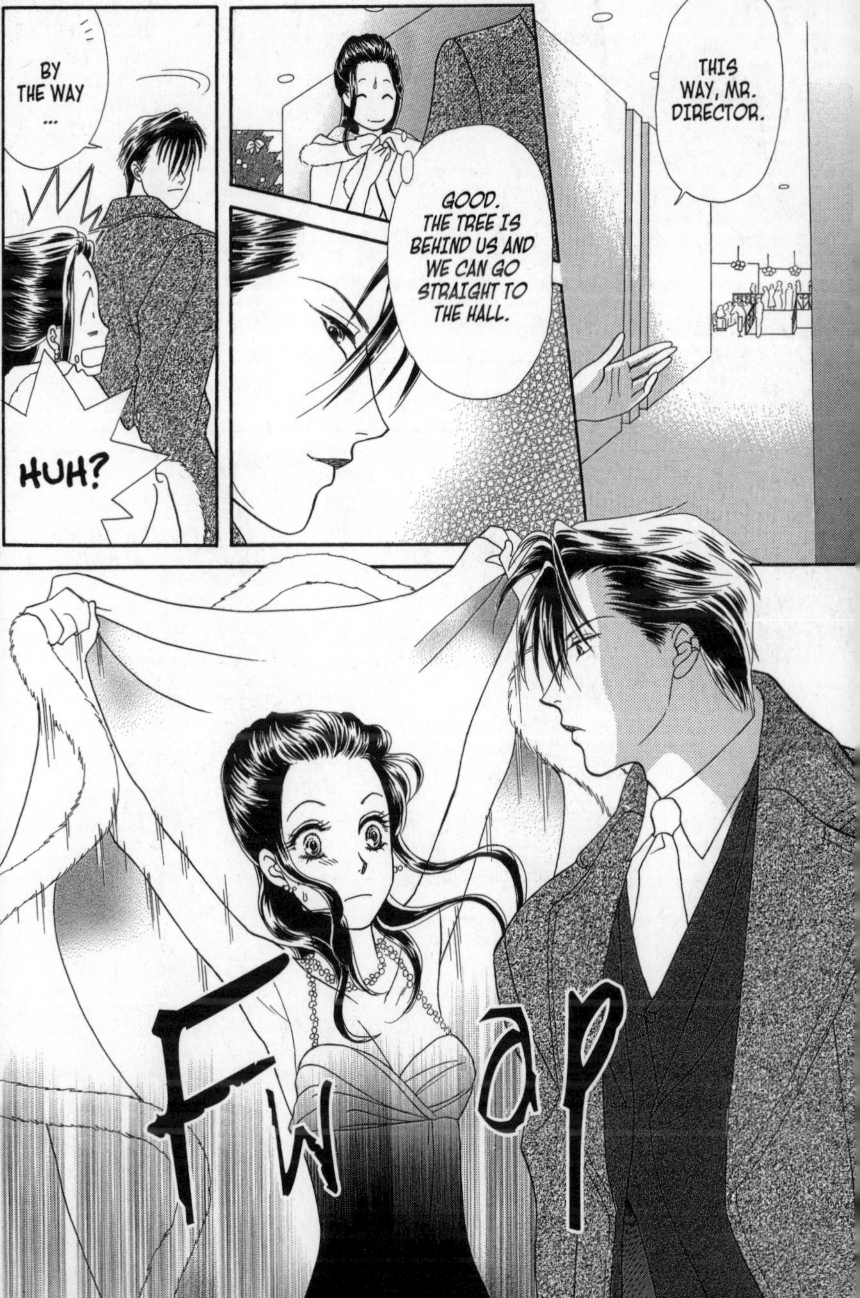
THIS WAY, MR. DIRECTOR.
GOOD. THE TREE IS BEHIND US AND WE CAN GO STRAIGHT TO THE HALL.
BY THE WAY ...
HUH?
Fwap

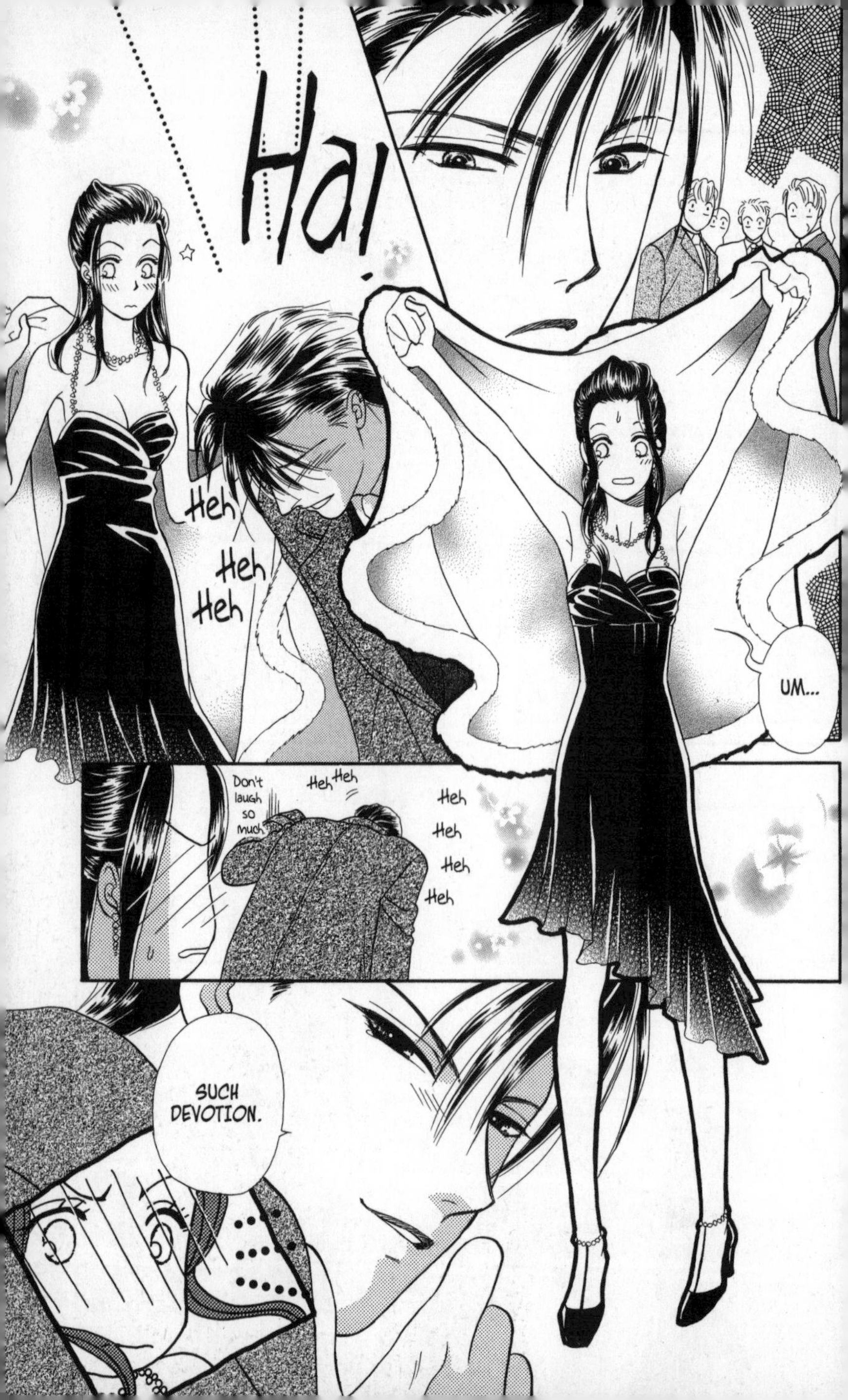
Ha!
Heh Heh Heh
UM...
Heh Heh Heh Heh
Heh Heh
Don't laugh so much
SUCH DEVOTION.
......

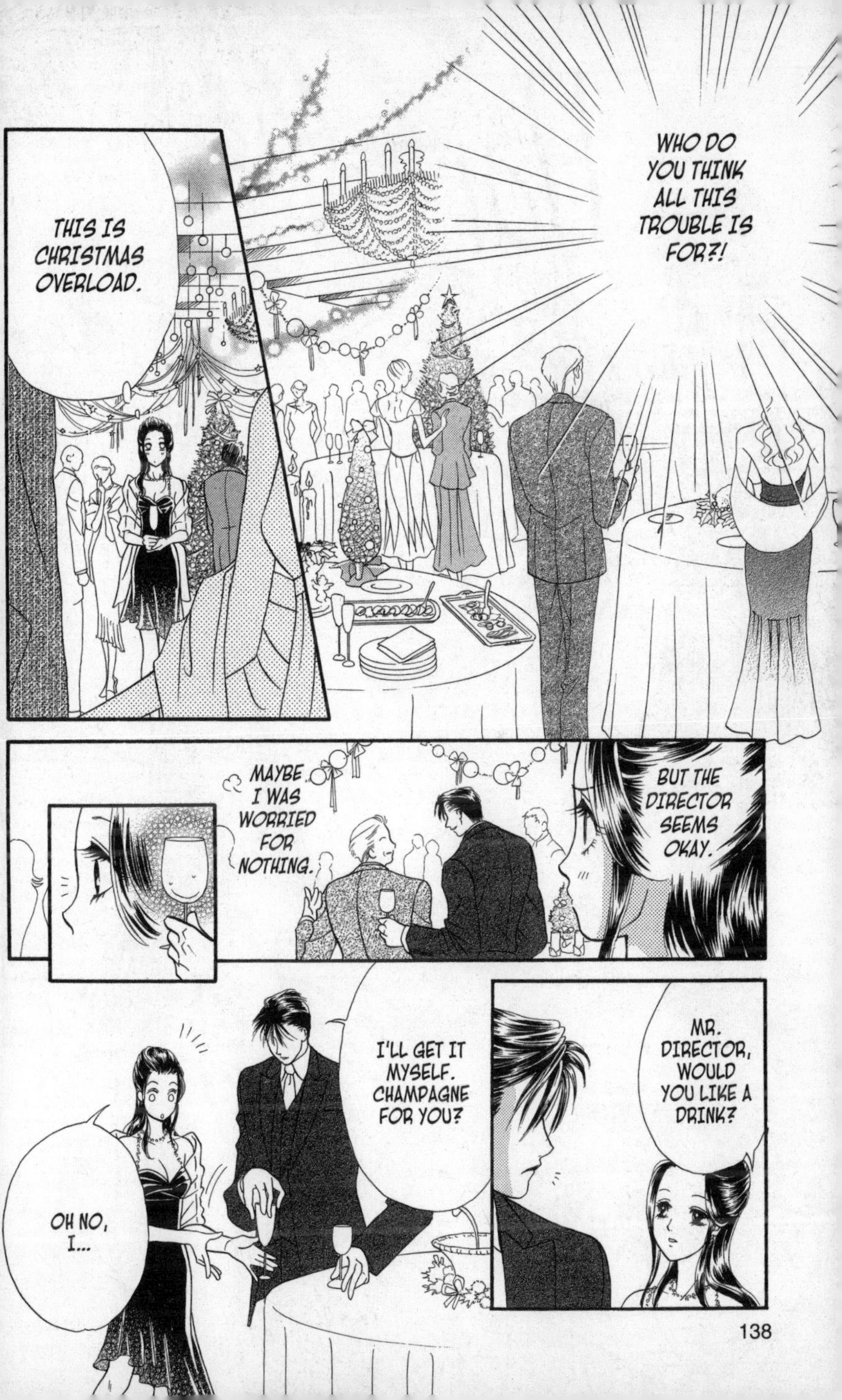
WHO DO YOU THINK ALL THIS TROUBLE IS FOR?!
THIS IS CHRISTMAS OVERLOAD.
BUT THE DIRECTOR SEEMS OKAY.
MAYBE I WAS WORRIED FOR NOTHING.
MR. DIRECTOR, WOULD YOU LIKE A DRINK?
I'LL GET IT MYSELF. CHAMPAGNE FOR YOU?
OH NO, I...

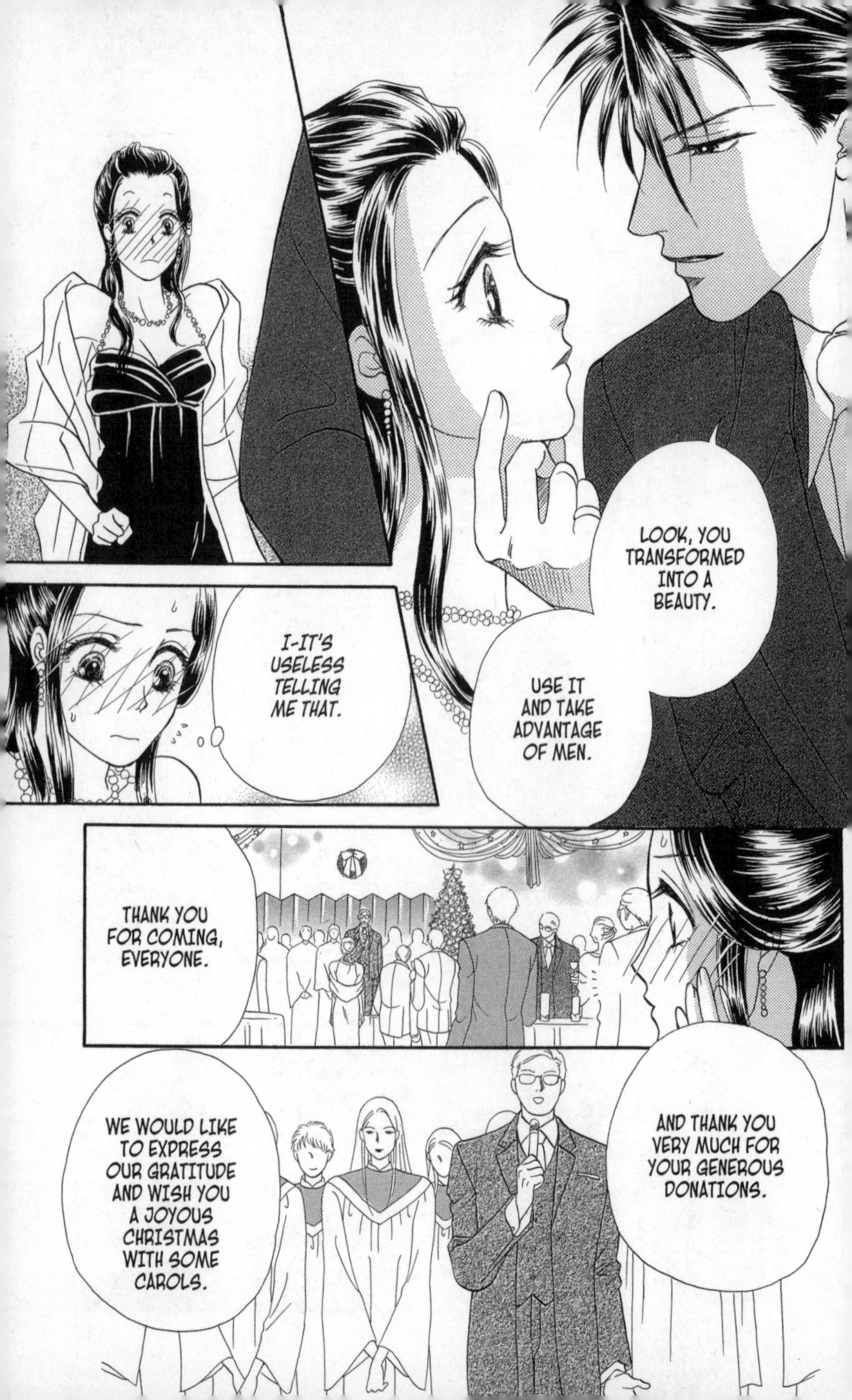
LOOK, YOU TRANSFORMED INTO A BEAUTY.
USE IT AND TAKE ADVANTAGE OF MEN.
I-IT'S USELESS TELLING ME THAT.
THANK YOU FOR COMING, EVERYONE.
AND THANK YOU VERY MUCH FOR YOUR GENEROUS DONATIONS.
WE WOULD LIKE TO EXPRESS OUR GRATITUDE AND WISH YOU A JOYOUS CHRISTMAS WITH SOME CAROLS.

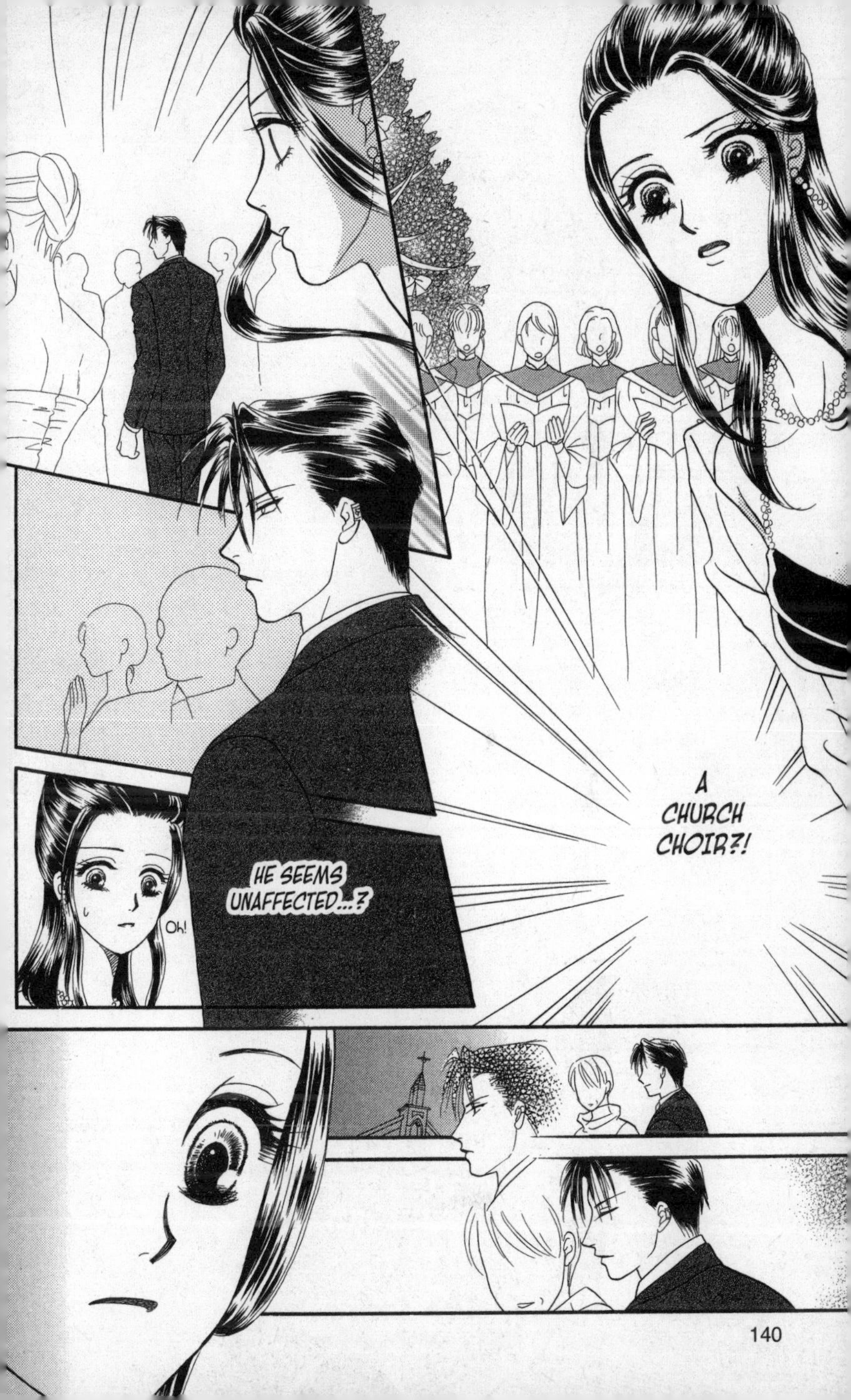
A CHURCH CHOIR?!
HE SEEMS UNAFFECTED...?
Oh!

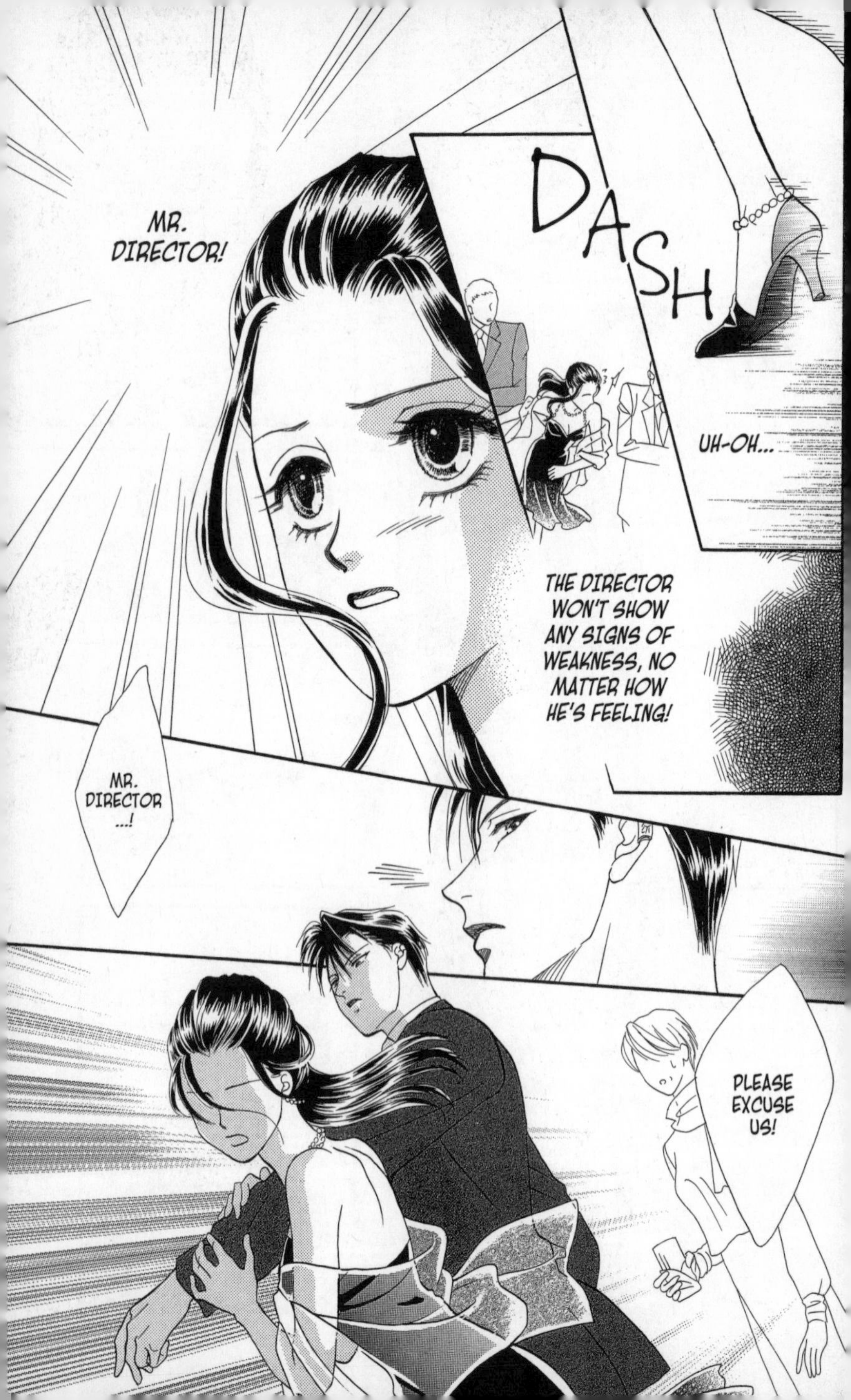
DASH
UH-OH...
MR. DIRECTOR!
THE DIRECTOR WON'T SHOW ANY SIGNS OF WEAKNESS, NO MATTER HOW HE'S FEELING!
MR. DIRECTOR ...!
PLEASE EXCUSE US!

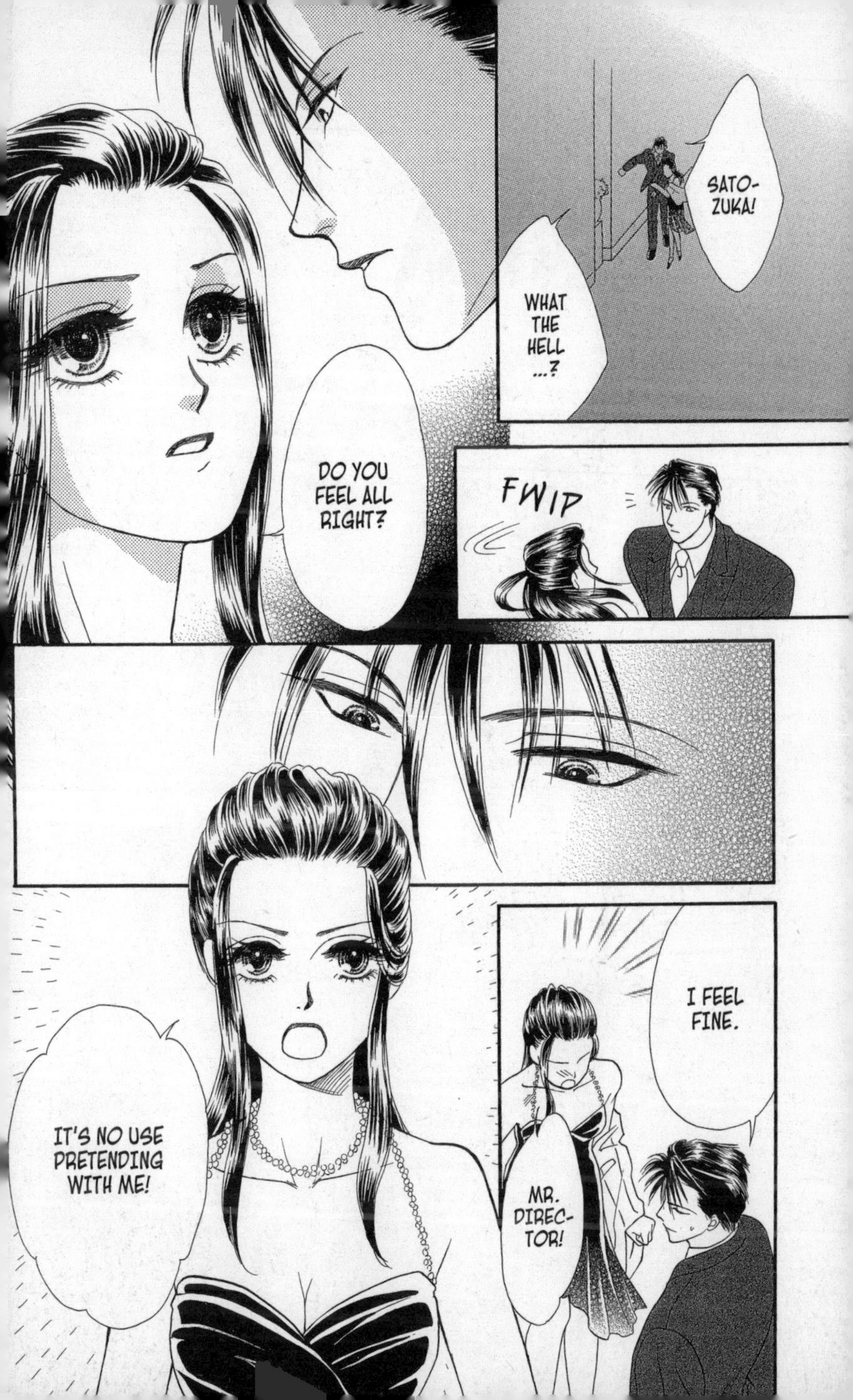
SATO-ZUKA!
WHAT THE HELL ...?
FWIP
DO YOU FEEL ALL RIGHT?
I FEEL FINE.
MR. DIRECTOR!
IT'S NO USE PRETENDING WITH ME!

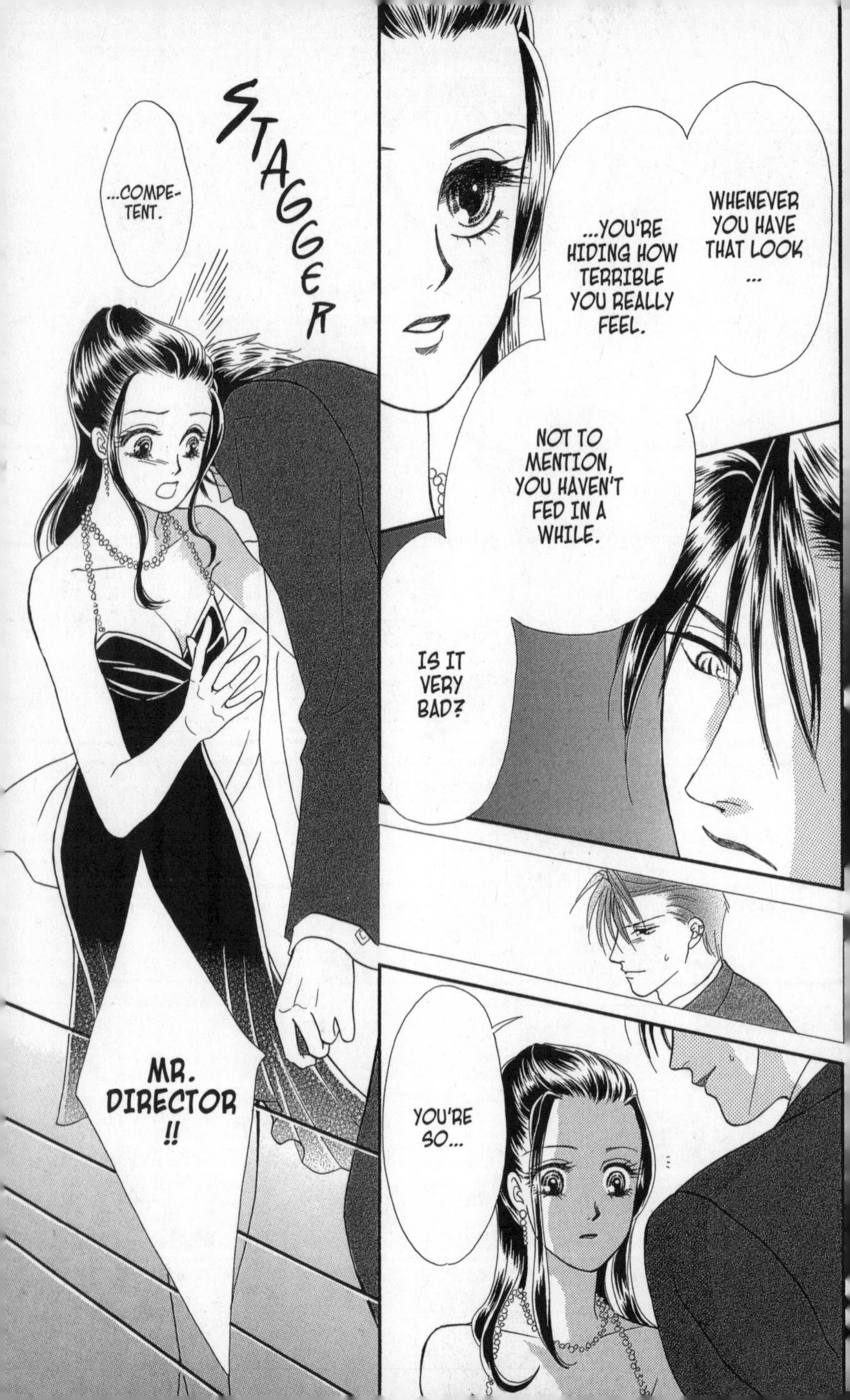
WHENEVER YOU HAVE THAT LOOK ...
...YOU'RE HIDING HOW TERRIBLE YOU REALLY FEEL.
NOT TO MENTION, YOU HAVEN'T FED IN A WHILE.
IS IT VERY BAD?
YOU'RE SO...
...COMPE-TENT.
STAGGER
MR. DIRECTOR !!

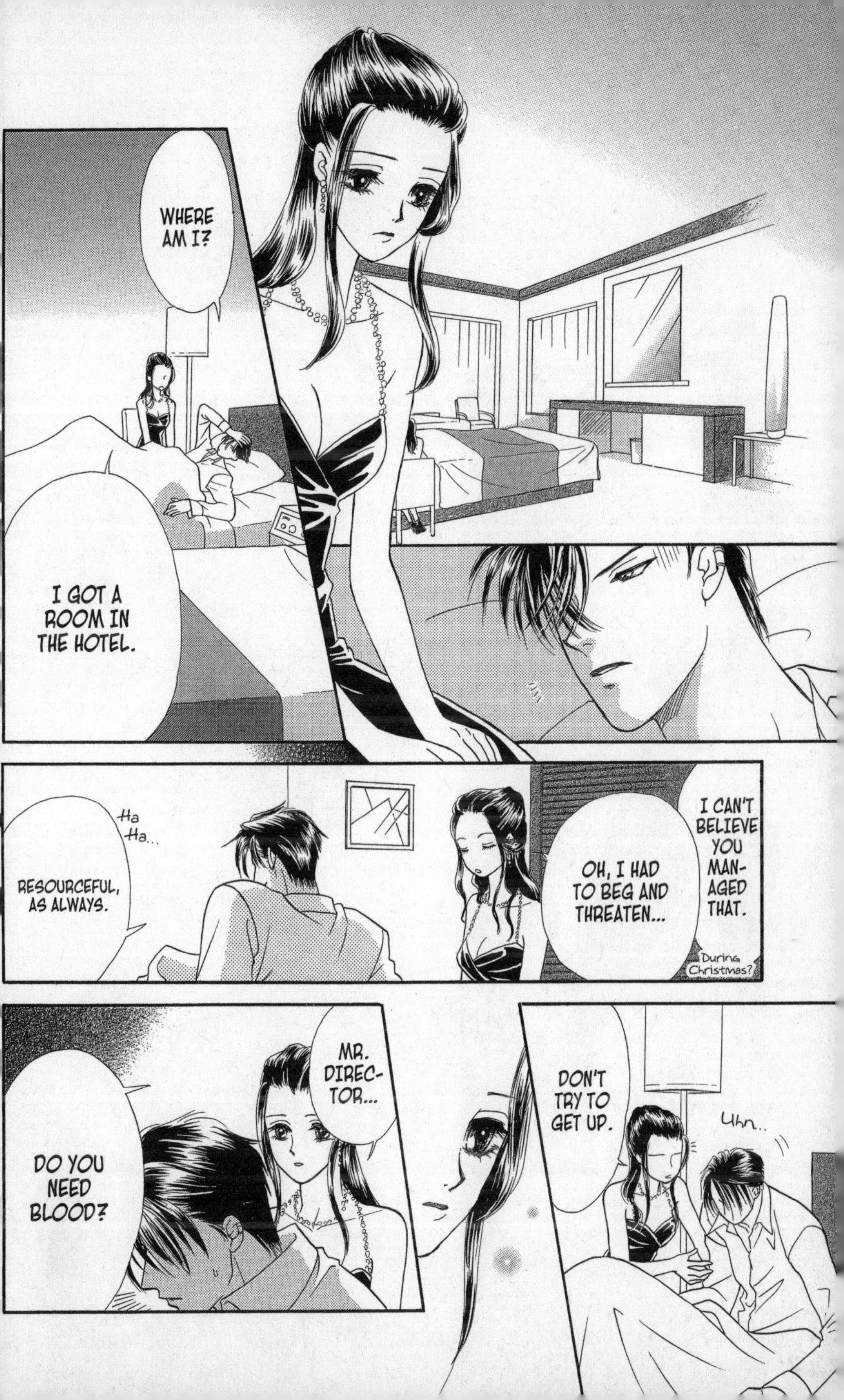
WHERE AM I?
I GOT A ROOM IN THE HOTEL.
I CAN'T BELIEVE YOU MAN-AGED THAT.
During Christmas?
OH, I HAD TO BEG AND THREATEN...
Ha Ha...
RESOURCEFUL, AS ALWAYS.
DON'T TRY TO GET UP.
Uhn..
MR. DIREC-TOR...
DO YOU NEED BLOOD?

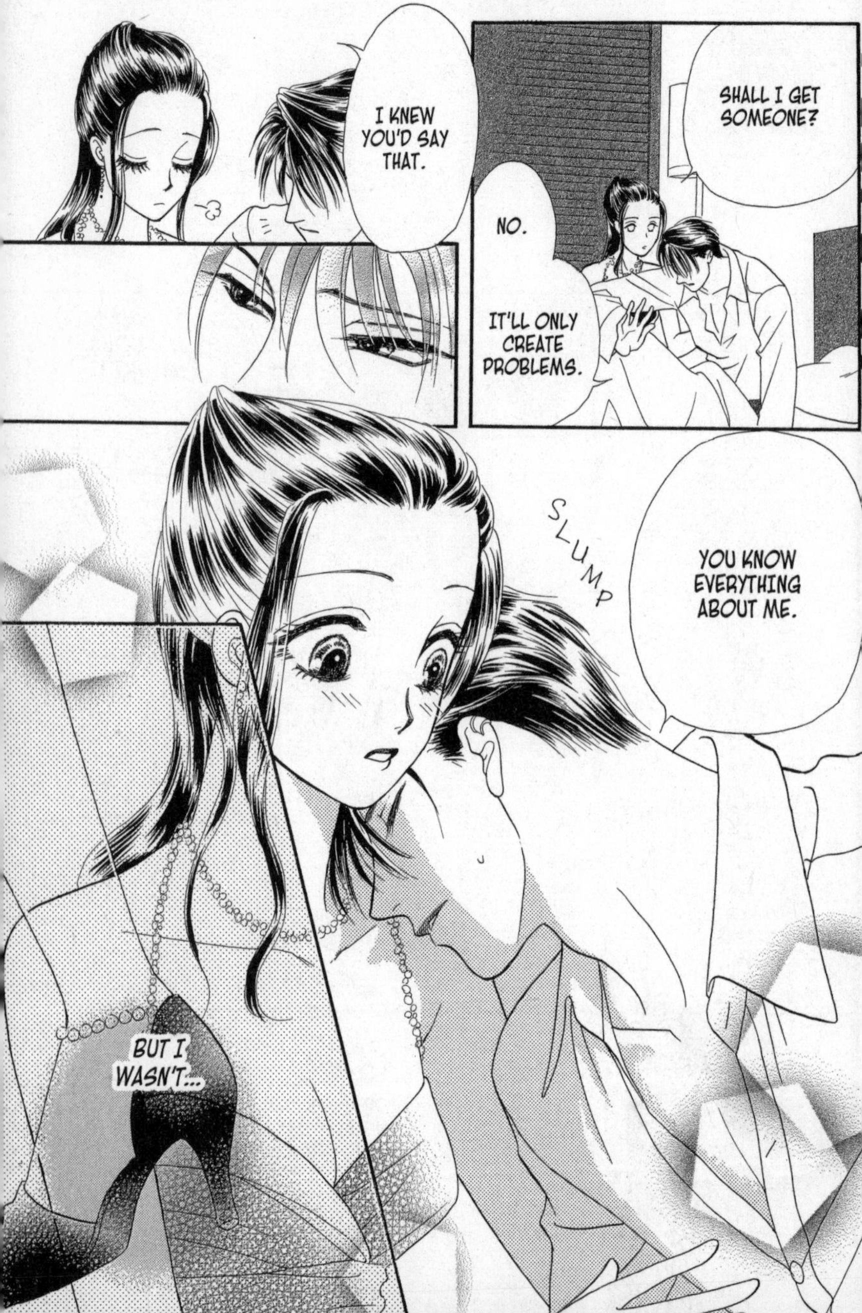
SHALL I GET SOMEONE?
NO.
IT'LL ONLY CREATE PROBLEMS.
I KNEW YOU'D SAY THAT.
YOU KNOW EVERYTHING ABOUT ME.
SLUMP
BUT I WASN'T...

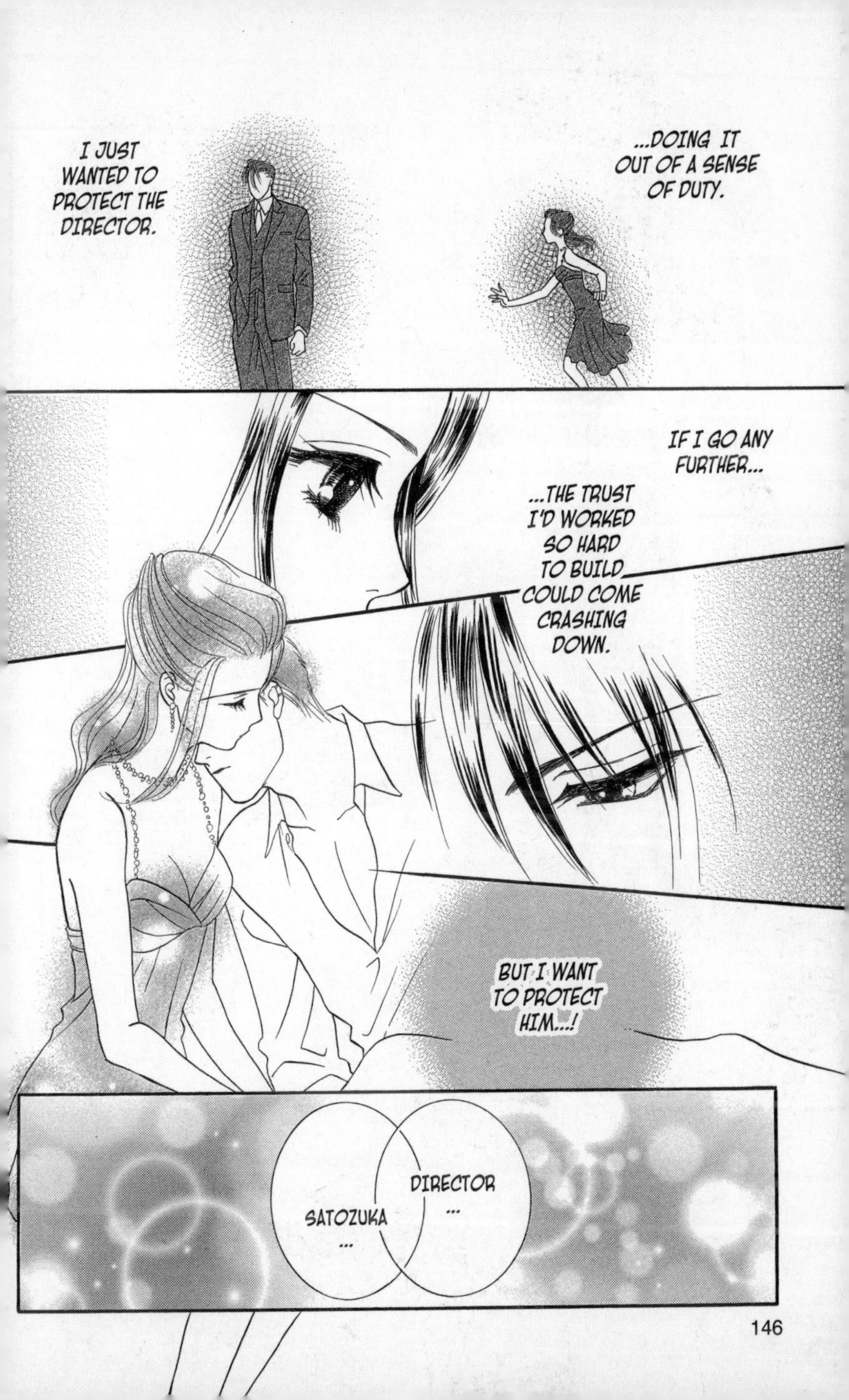
...DOING IT OUT OF A SENSE OF DUTY.
I JUST WANTED TO PROTECT THE DIRECTOR.
IF I GO ANY FURTHER...
...THE TRUST I'D WORKED SO HARD TO BUILD COULD COME CRASHING DOWN.
BUT I WANT TO PROTECT HIM...!
DIRECTOR ...
SATOZUKA ...

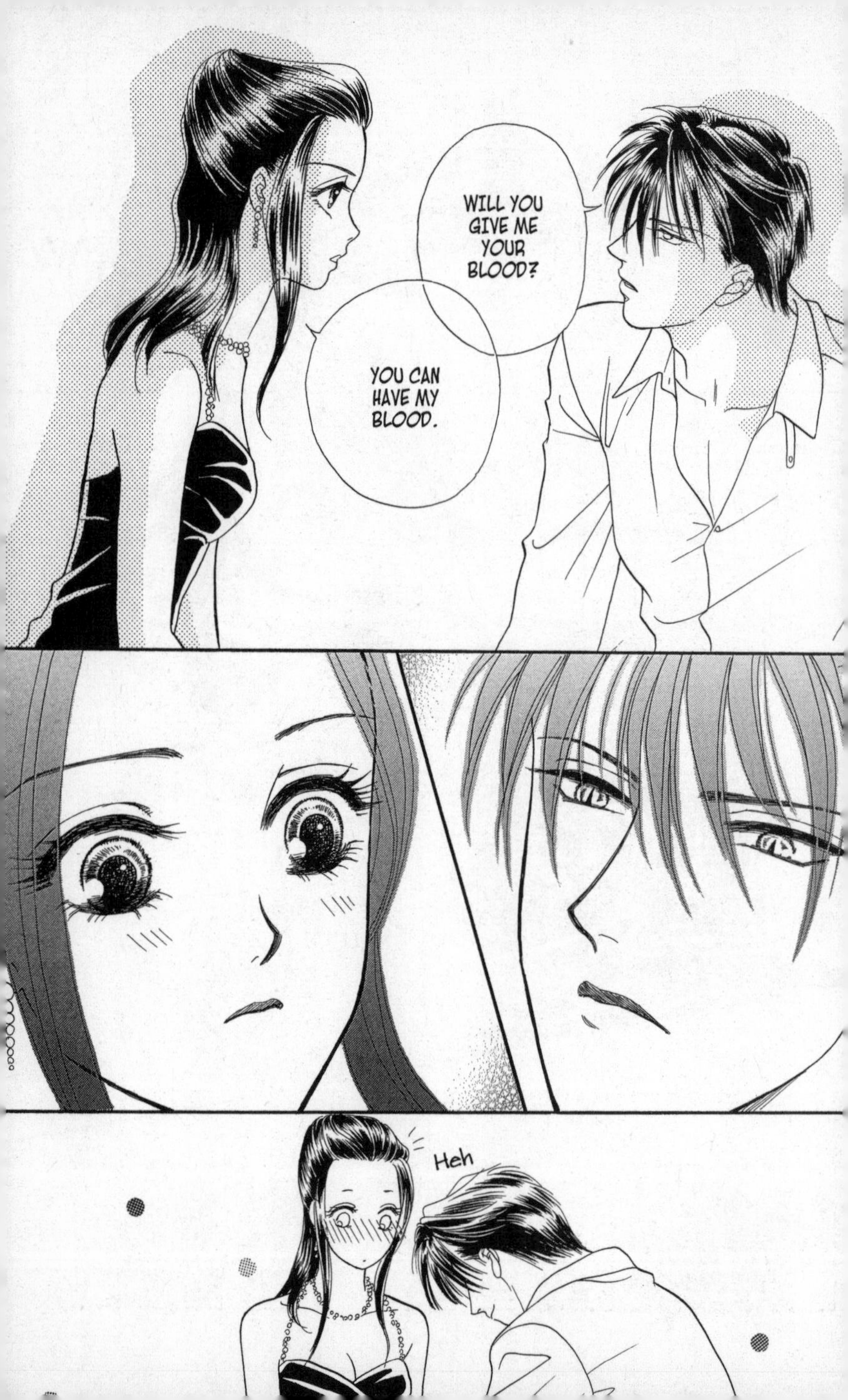
WILL YOU GIVE ME YOUR BLOOD?
YOU CAN HAVE MY BLOOD.
Heh

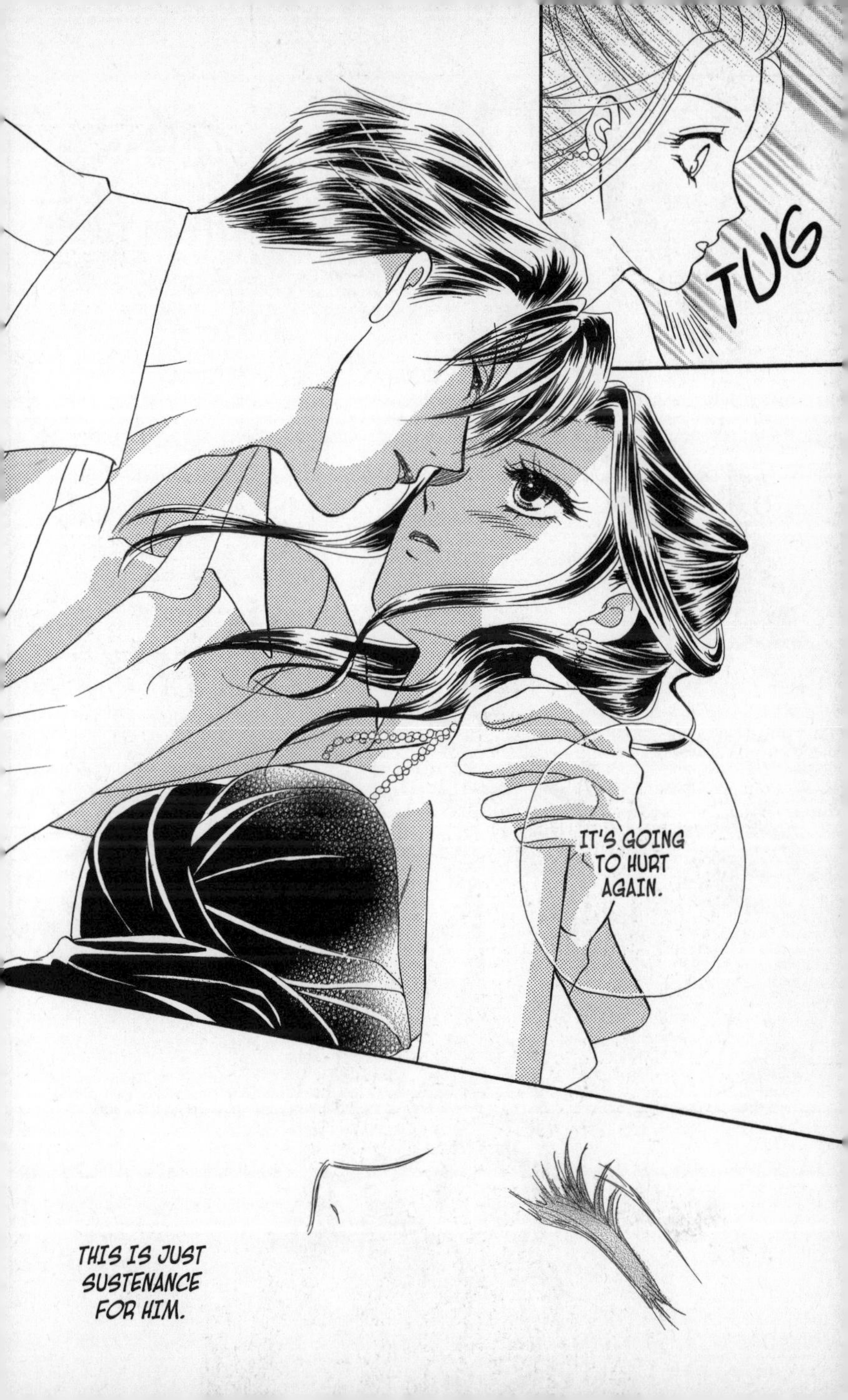
TUG
IT'S GOING TO HURT AGAIN.
THIS IS JUST SUSTENANCE FOR HIM.

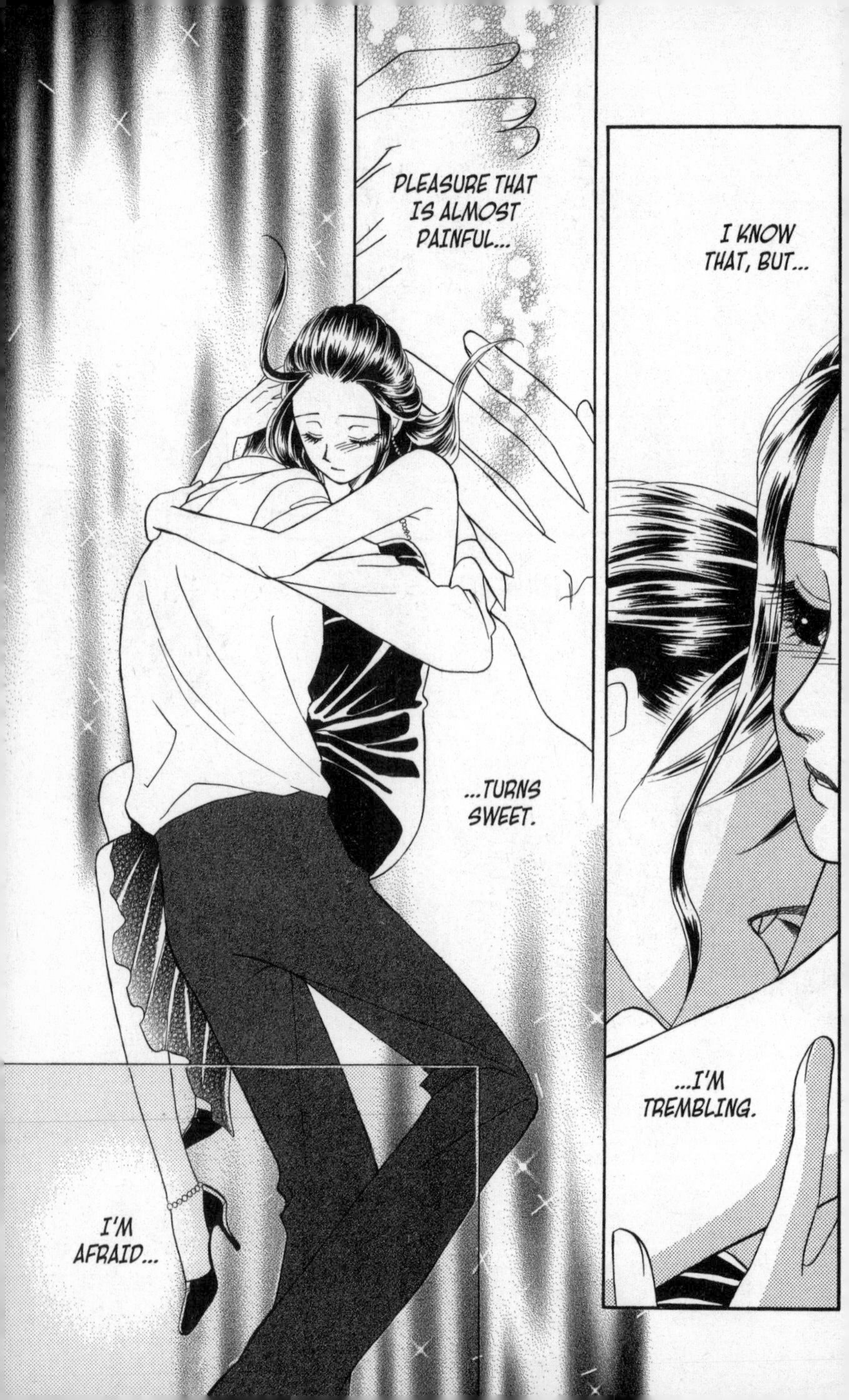
I KNOW THAT, BUT...
...I'M TREMBLING.
PLEASURE THAT IS ALMOST PAINFUL...
...TURNS SWEET.
I'M AFRAID...

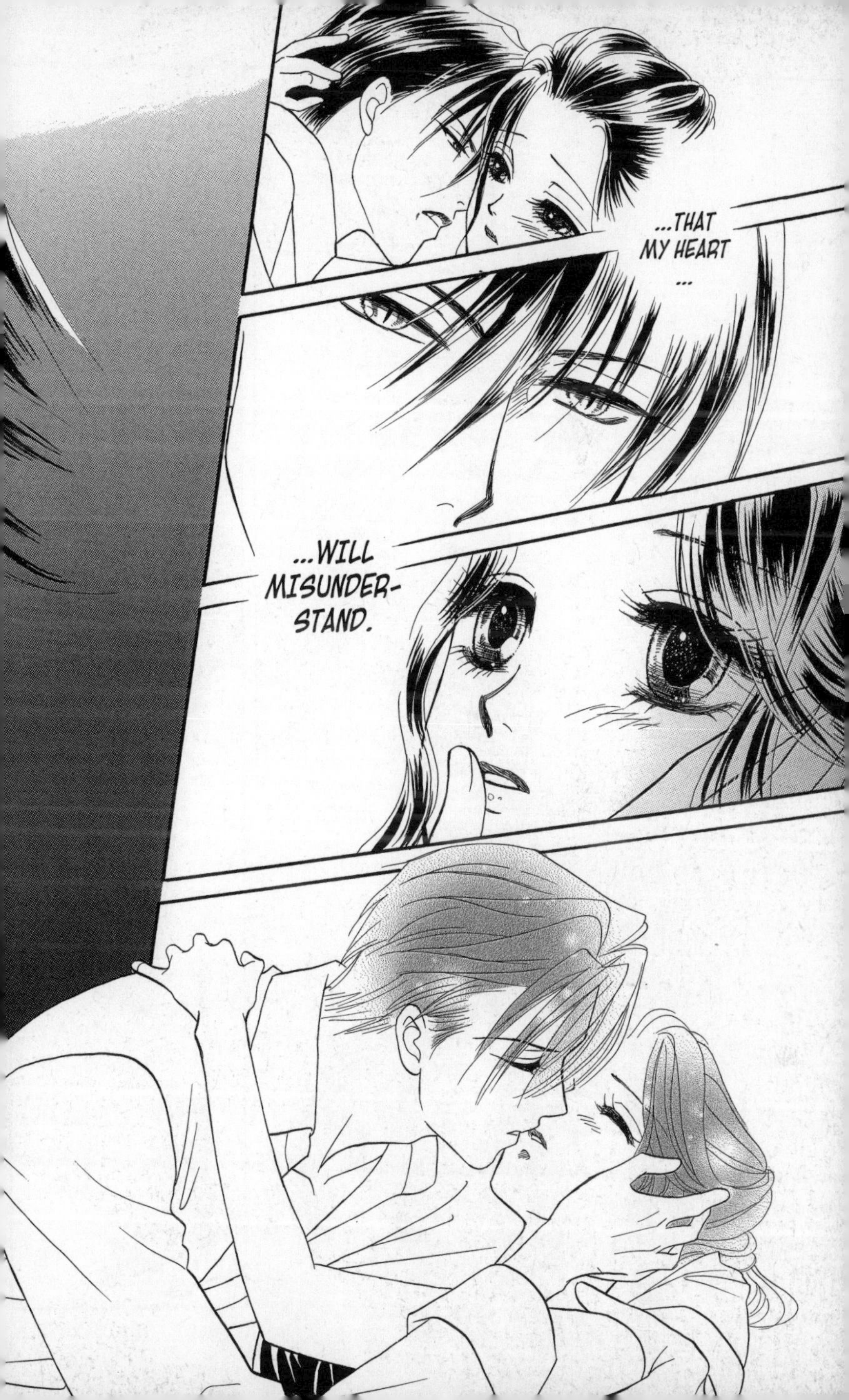
...THAT MY HEART ...
...WILL MISUNDER-STAND.

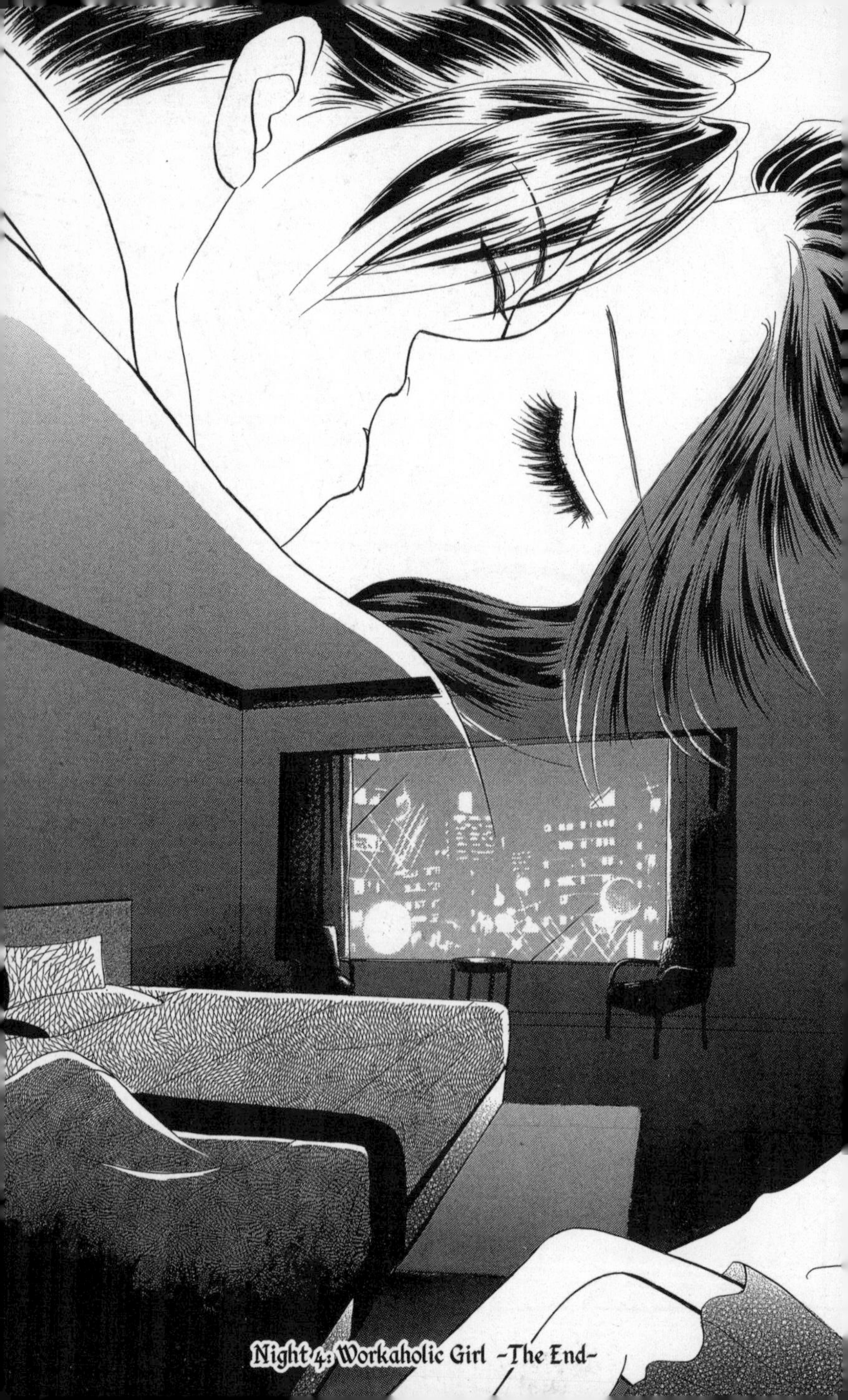
Night 4: Workaholic Girl -The End-

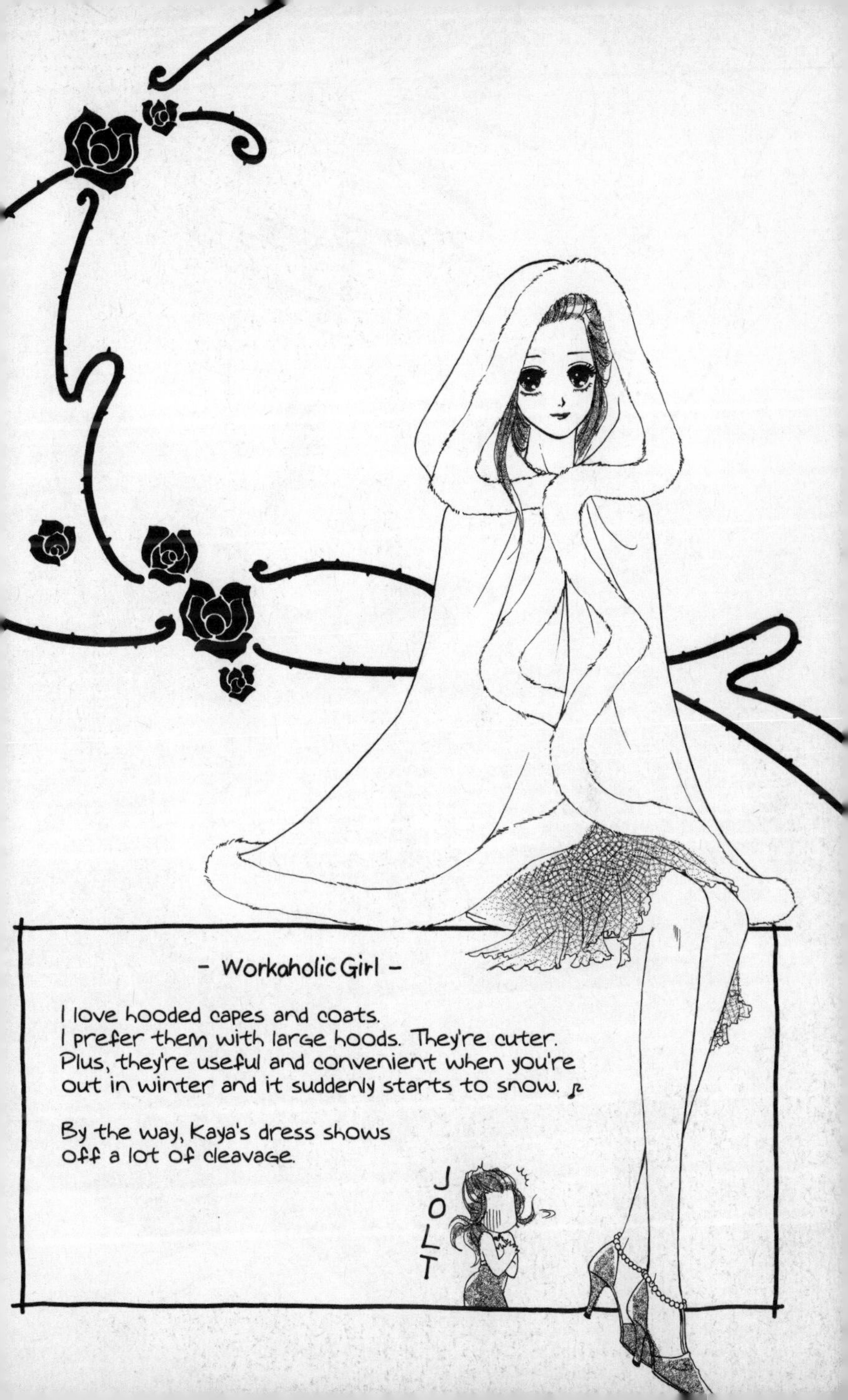
- Workaholic Girl -
I love hooded capes and coats.
I prefer them with large hoods. They're cuter.
Plus, they're useful and convenient when you're
out in winter and it suddenly starts to snow. ♪
By the way, Kaya's dress shows
off a lot of cleavage.
JOLT

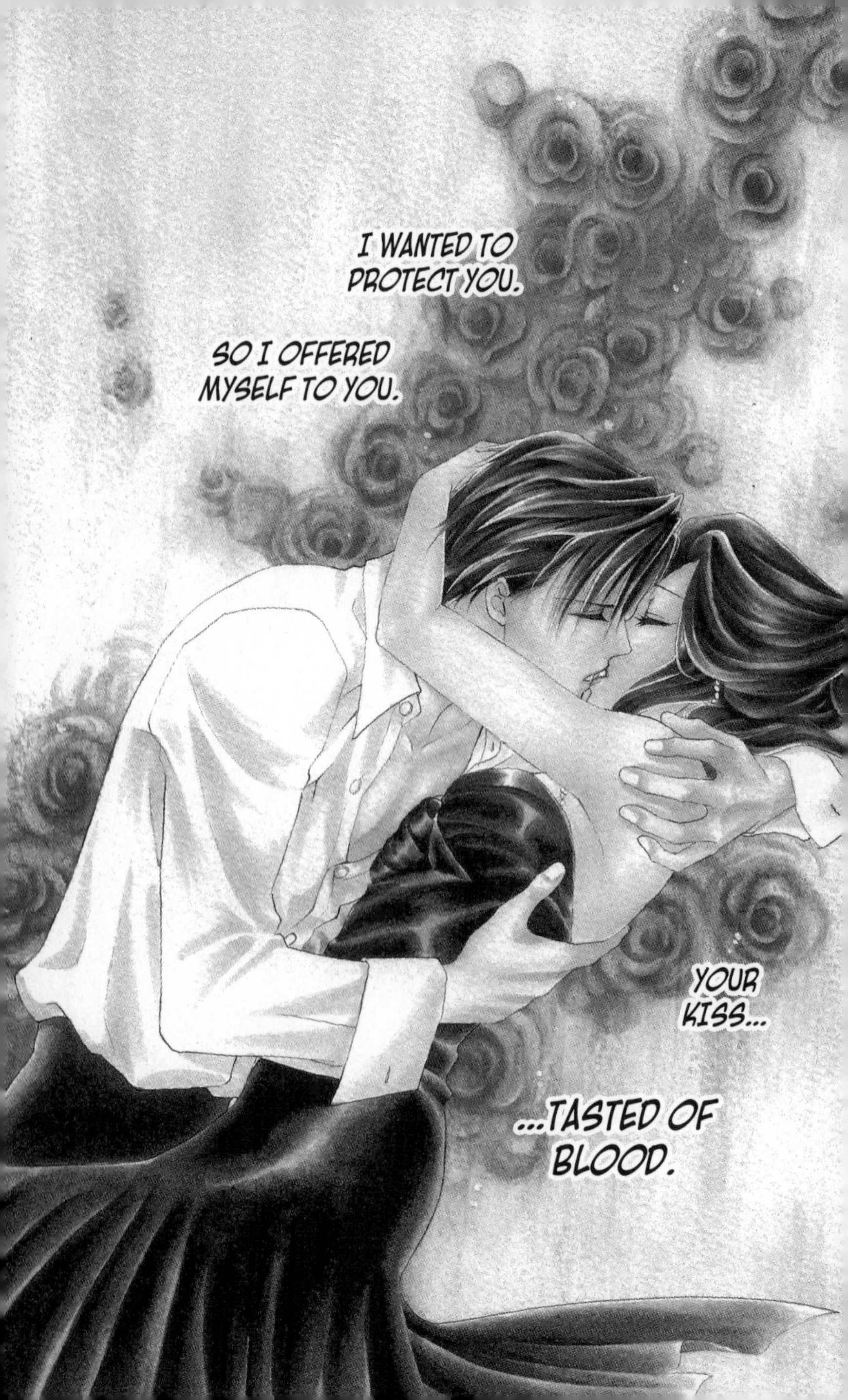
I WANTED TO PROTECT YOU.
SO I OFFERED MYSELF TO YOU.
YOUR KISS...
...TASTED OF BLOOD.

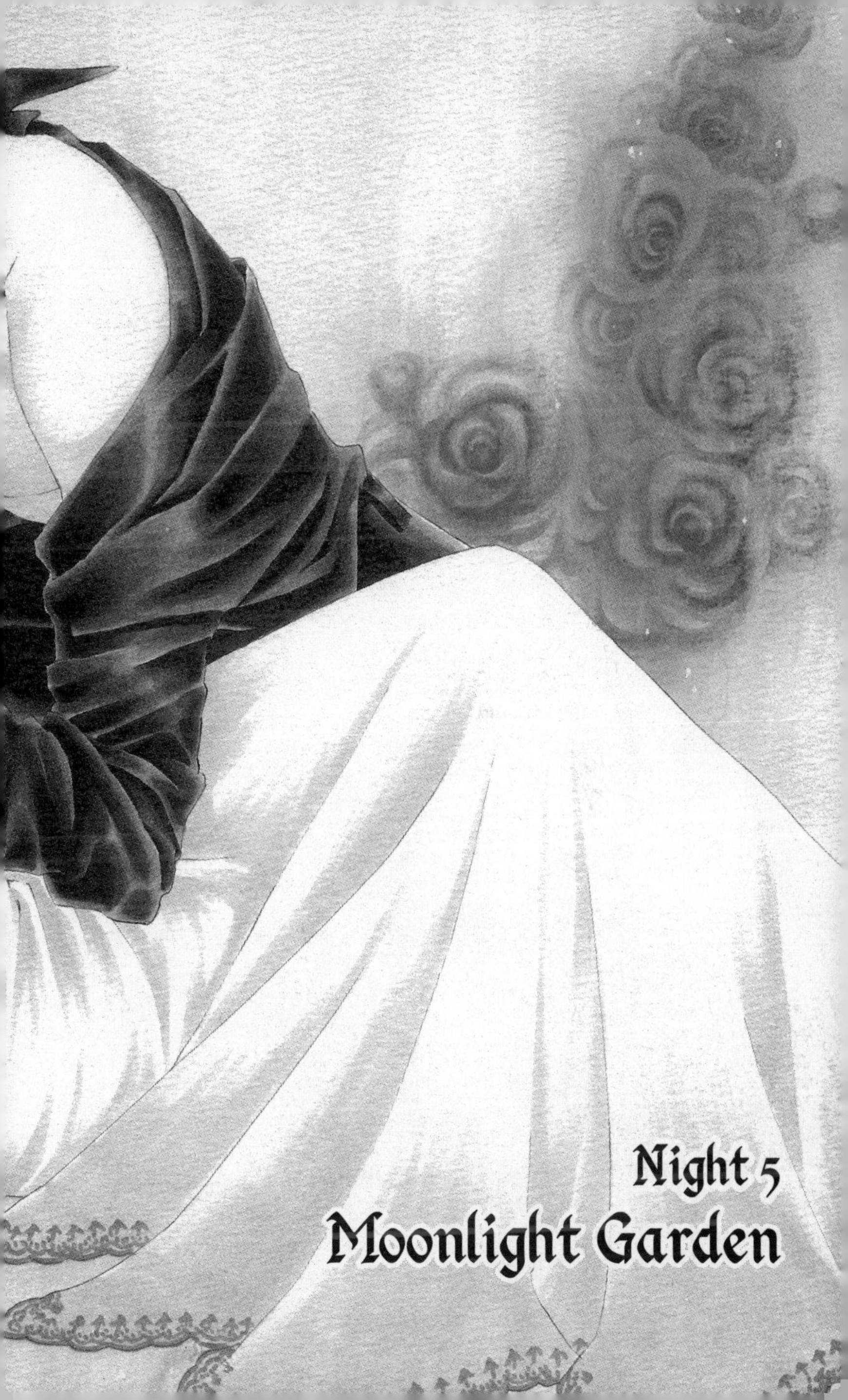
Night 5
Moonlight Garden

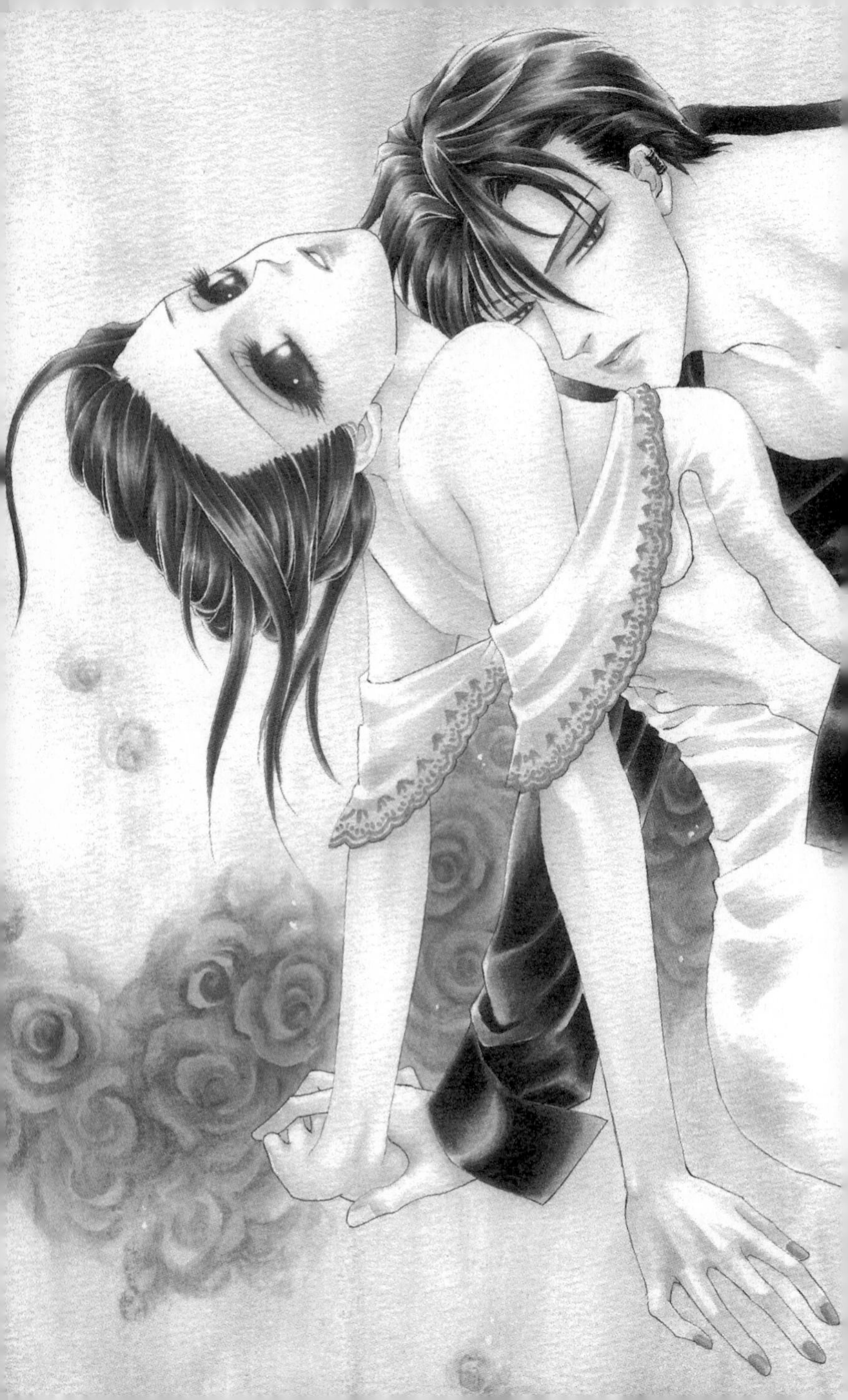

This story is about a vampire, but there are no bats in it.

Still, I end up using bats in my motifs. I love the bat marks that the designer wove into the design, for example, in the title of each chapter for the magazine publication. Please look at them, since they're very decorative.

They're really cute. ♡

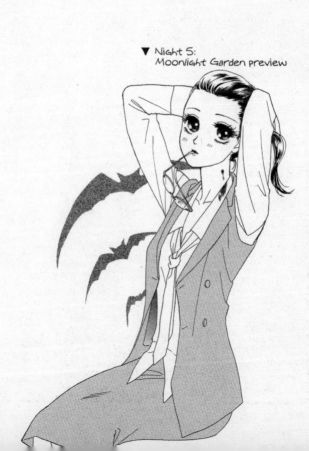

▼ Night 5:
Moonlight Garden preview

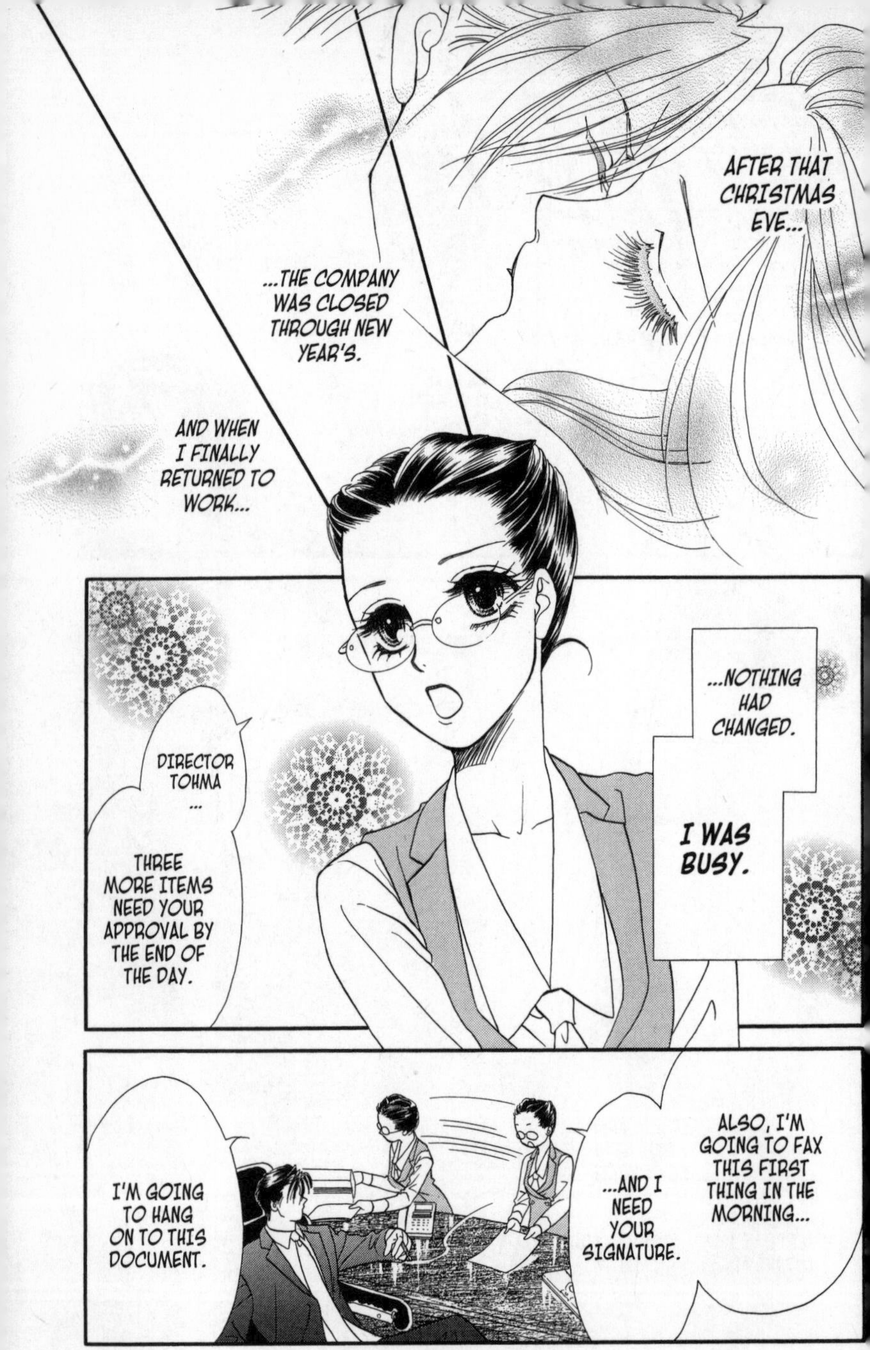
AFTER THAT CHRISTMAS EVE...
...THE COMPANY WAS CLOSED THROUGH NEW YEAR'S.
AND WHEN I FINALLY RETURNED TO WORK...
...NOTHING HAD CHANGED.
I WAS BUSY.
DIRECTOR TOHMA ...
THREE MORE ITEMS NEED YOUR APPROVAL BY THE END OF THE DAY.
ALSO, I'M GOING TO FAX THIS FIRST THING IN THE MORNING...
...AND I NEED YOUR SIGNATURE.
I'M GOING TO HANG ON TO THIS DOCUMENT.

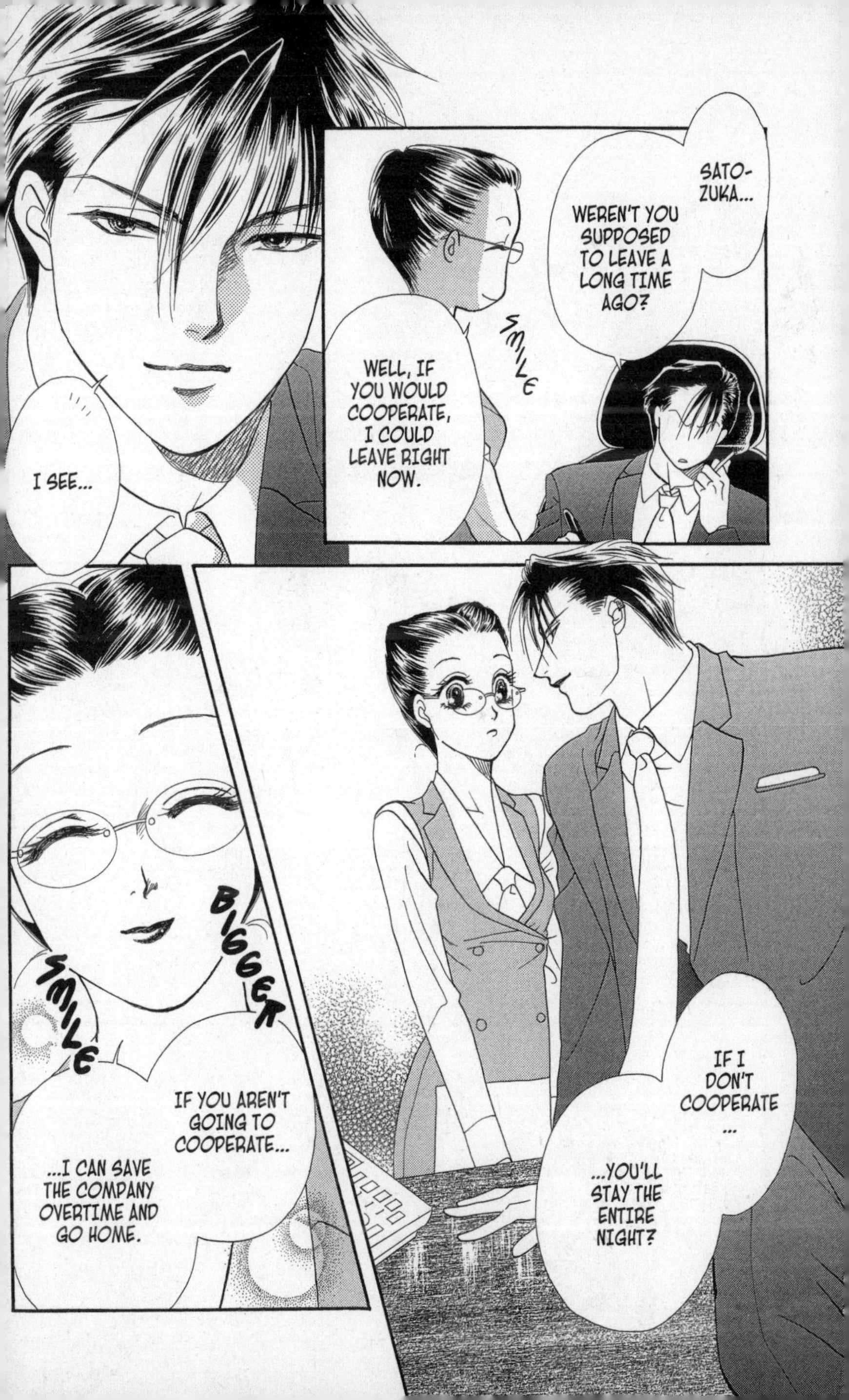
SATO-ZUKA...
WEREN'T YOU SUPPOSED TO LEAVE A LONG TIME AGO?
SMILE
WELL, IF YOU WOULD COOPERATE, I COULD LEAVE RIGHT NOW.
I SEE...
IF I DON'T COOPERATE ...
...YOU'LL STAY THE ENTIRE NIGHT?
BIGGER SMILE
IF YOU AREN'T GOING TO COOPERATE...
...I CAN SAVE THE COMPANY OVERTIME AND GO HOME.

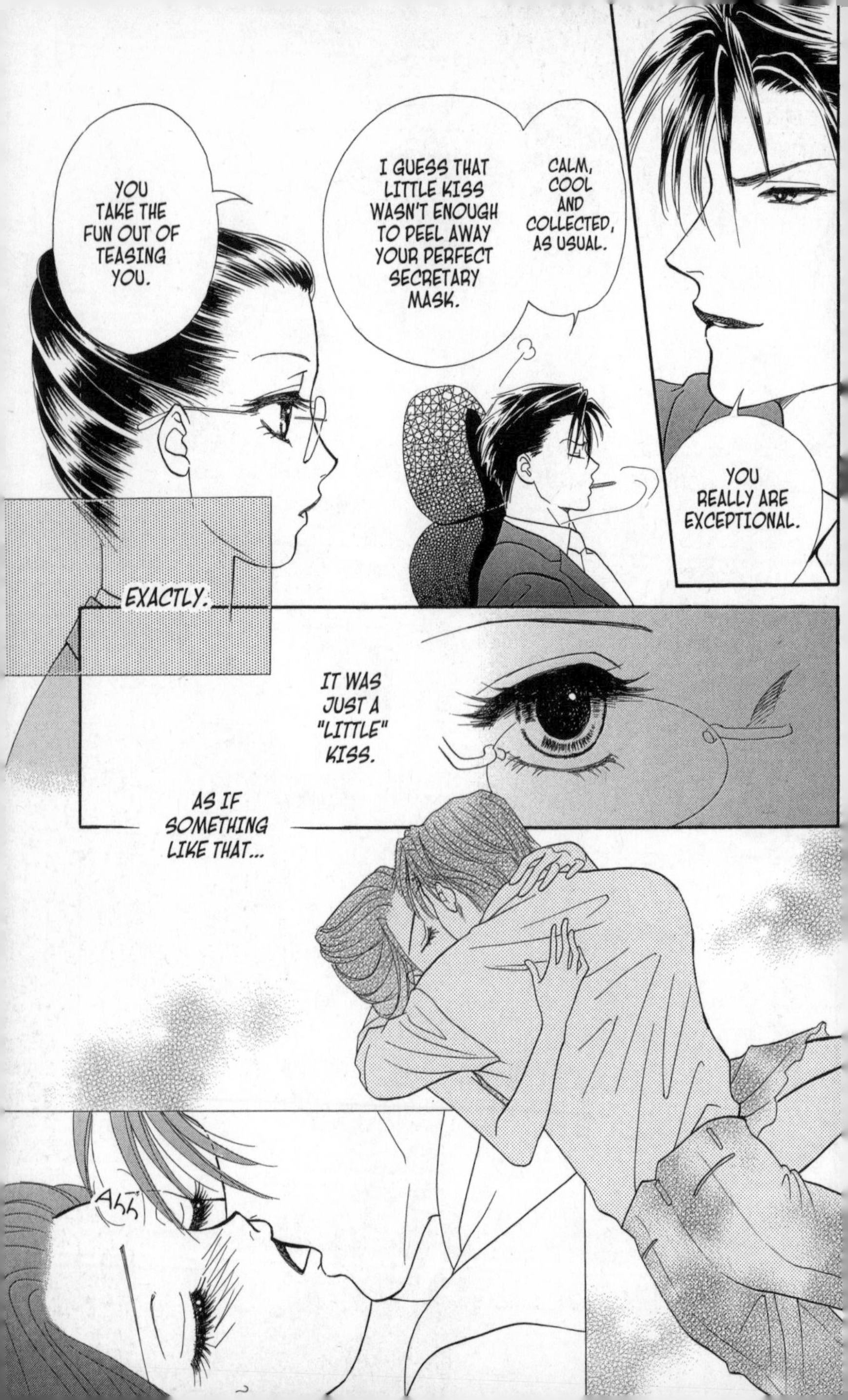
YOU REALLY ARE EXCEPTIONAL.
CALM, COOL AND COLLECTED, AS USUAL.
I GUESS THAT LITTLE KISS WASN'T ENOUGH TO PEEL AWAY YOUR PERFECT SECRETARY MASK.
YOU TAKE THE FUN OUT OF TEASING YOU.
EXACTLY.
IT WAS JUST A "LITTLE" KISS.
AS IF SOMETHING LIKE THAT...
Ahh

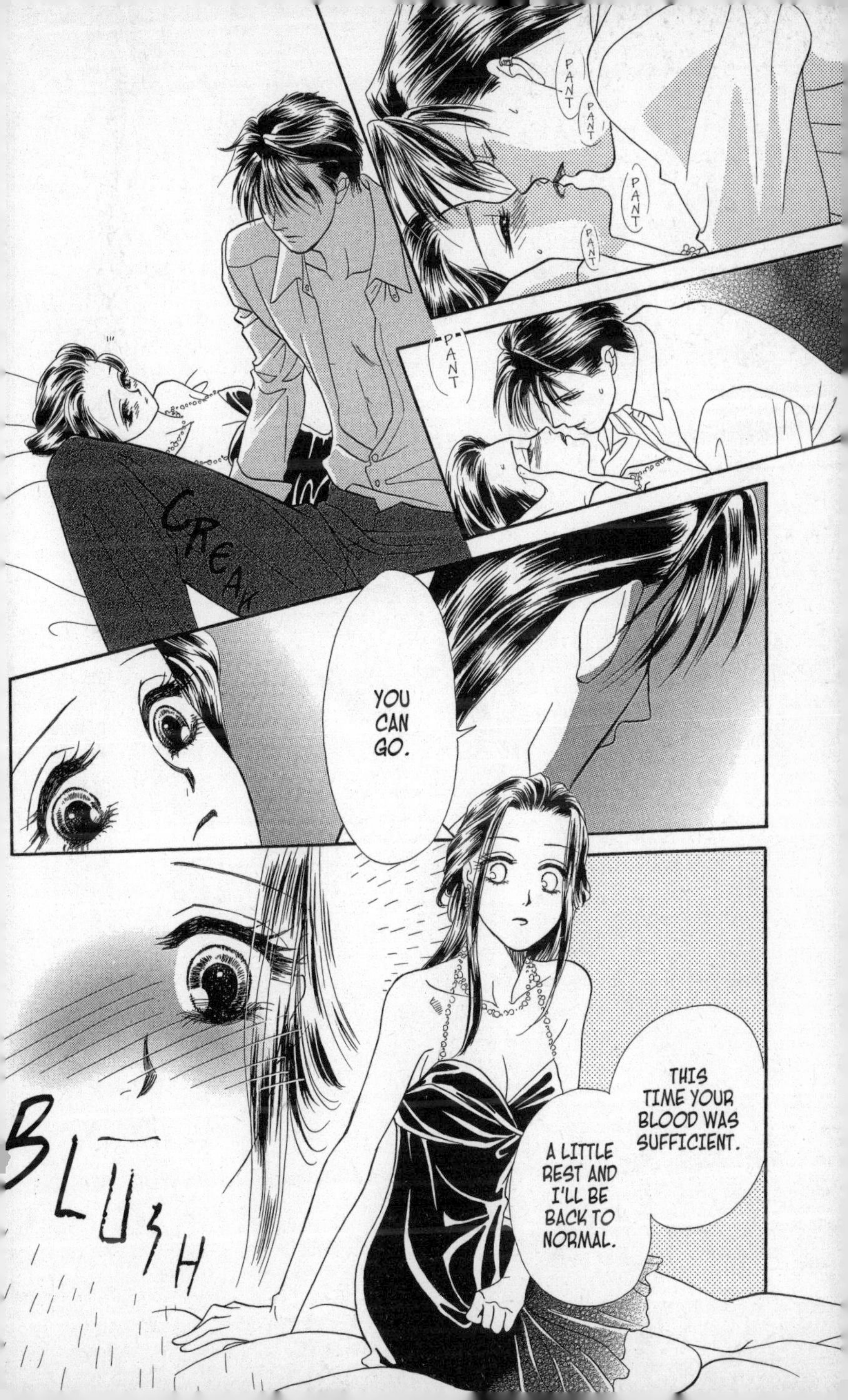
PANT
PANT
PANT
PANT
PANT
CREAK
YOU CAN GO.
THIS TIME YOUR BLOOD WAS SUFFICIENT.
A LITTLE REST AND I'LL BE BACK TO NORMAL.
BLUSH

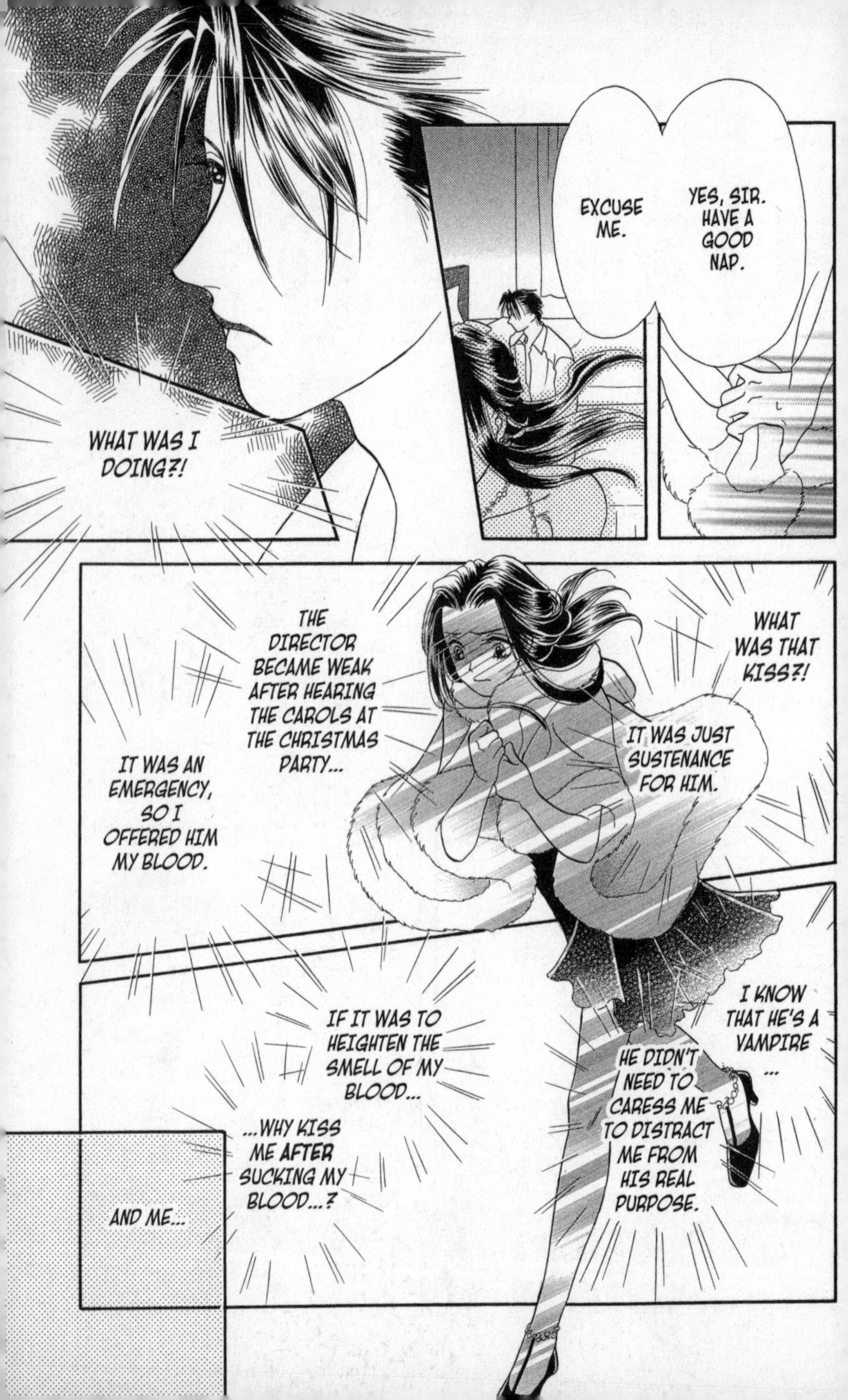

YES, SIR. HAVE A GOOD NAP.
EXCUSE ME.
WHAT WAS I DOING?!
WHAT WAS THAT KISS?!
IT WAS JUST SUSTENANCE FOR HIM.
THE DIRECTOR BECAME WEAK AFTER HEARING THE CAROLS AT THE CHRISTMAS PARTY...
IT WAS AN EMERGENCY, SO I OFFERED HIM MY BLOOD.
I KNOW THAT HE'S A VAMPIRE ...
HE DIDN'T NEED TO CARESS ME TO DISTRACT ME FROM HIS REAL PURPOSE.
IF IT WAS TO HEIGHTEN THE SMELL OF MY BLOOD...
...WHY KISS ME AFTER SUCKING MY BLOOD...?
AND ME...

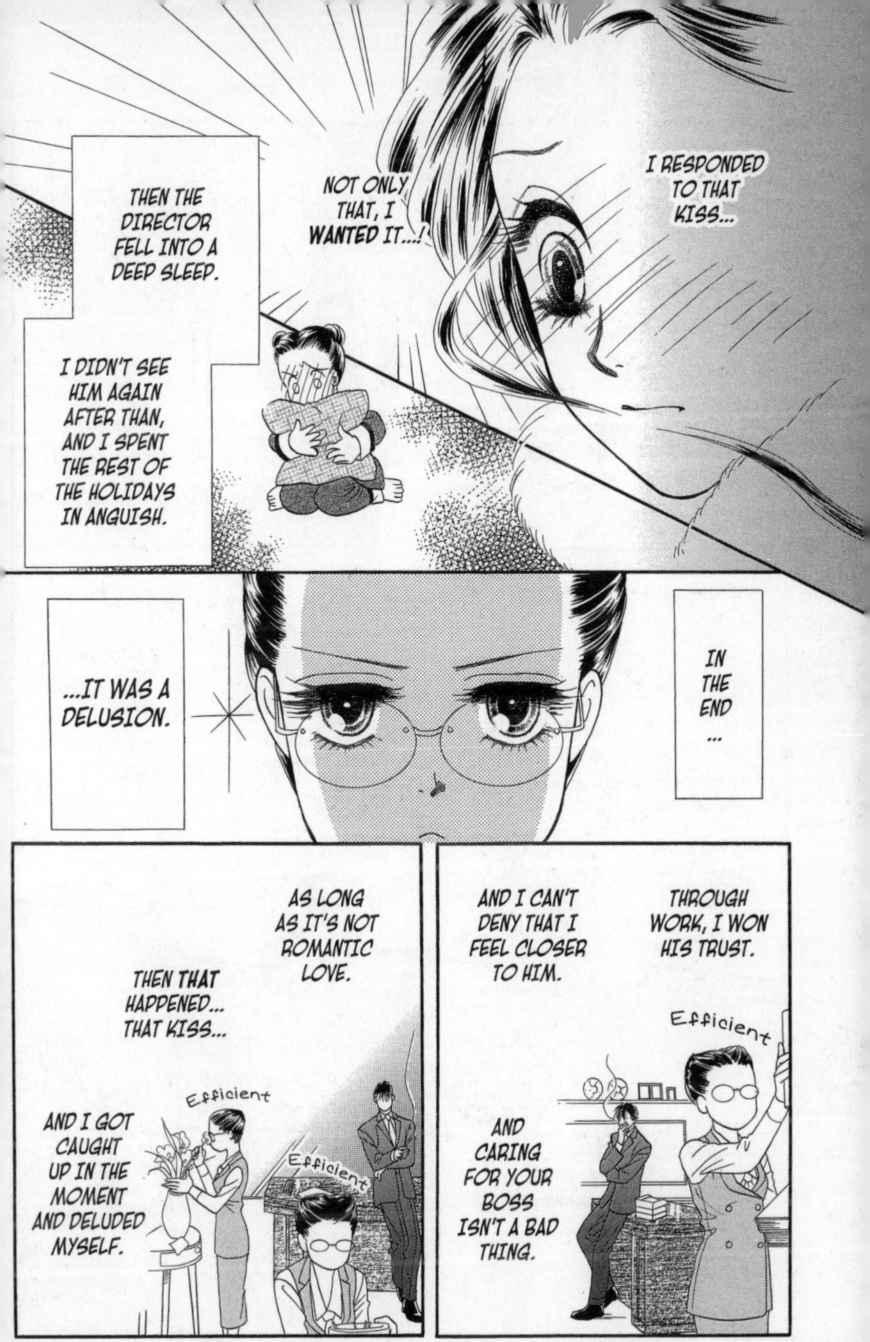
I RESPONDED TO THAT KISS...
NOT ONLY THAT, I WANTED IT...!
THEN THE DIRECTOR FELL INTO A DEEP SLEEP.
I DIDN'T SEE HIM AGAIN AFTER THAN, AND I SPENT THE REST OF THE HOLIDAYS IN ANGUISH.
IN THE END ...
...IT WAS A DELUSION.
THROUGH WORK, I WON HIS TRUST.
AND I CAN'T DENY THAT I FEEL CLOSER TO HIM.
Efficient
AND CARING FOR YOUR BOSS ISN'T A BAD THING.
AS LONG AS IT'S NOT ROMANTIC LOVE.
THEN THAT HAPPENED... THAT KISS...
Efficient
Efficient
AND I GOT CAUGHT UP IN THE MOMENT AND DELUDED MYSELF.

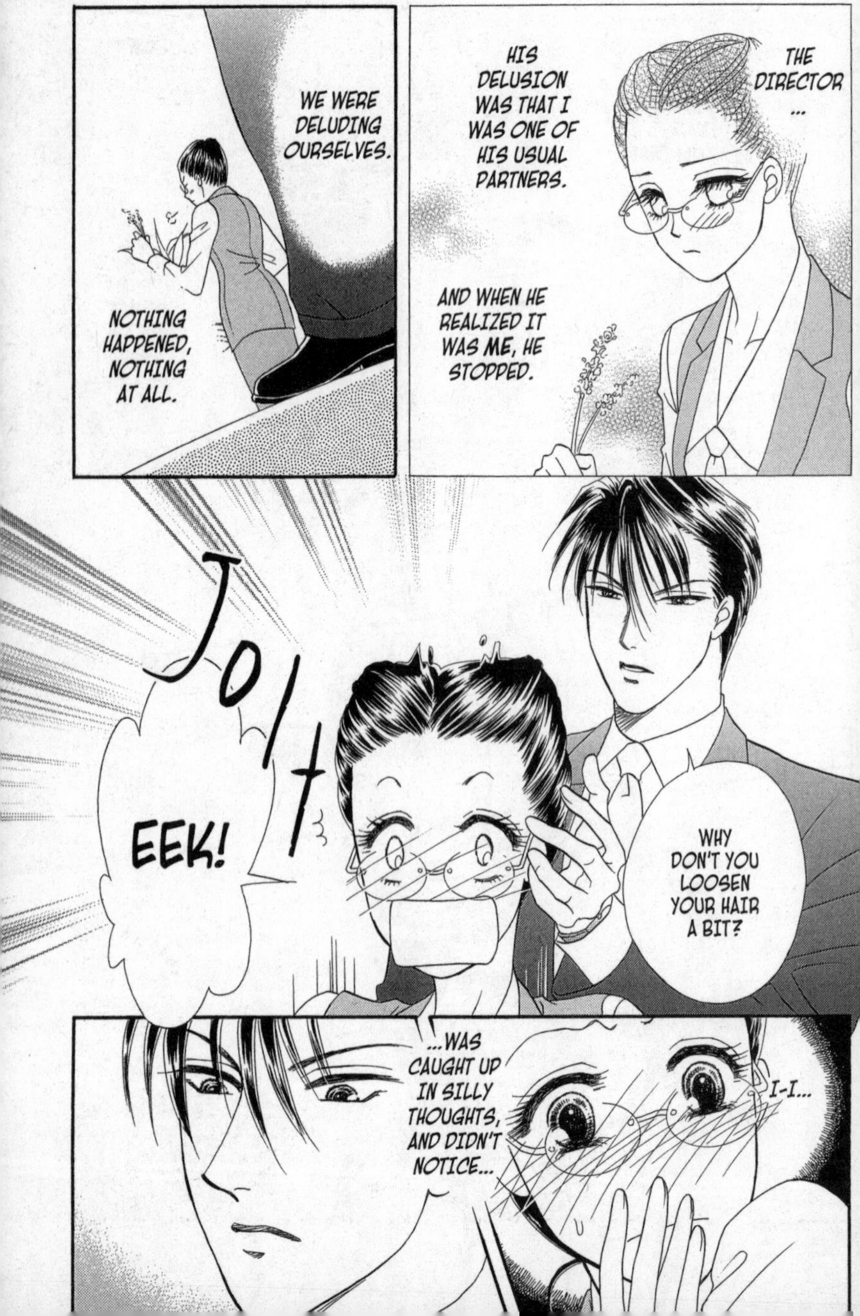
THE DIRECTOR ...
HIS DELUSION WAS THAT I WAS ONE OF HIS USUAL PARTNERS.
AND WHEN HE REALIZED IT WAS ME, HE STOPPED.
WE WERE DELUDING OURSELVES.
NOTHING HAPPENED, NOTHING AT ALL.
WHY DON'T YOU LOOSEN YOUR HAIR A BIT?
JOLT
EEK!
I-I...
...WAS CAUGHT UP IN SILLY THOUGHTS, AND DIDN'T NOTICE...

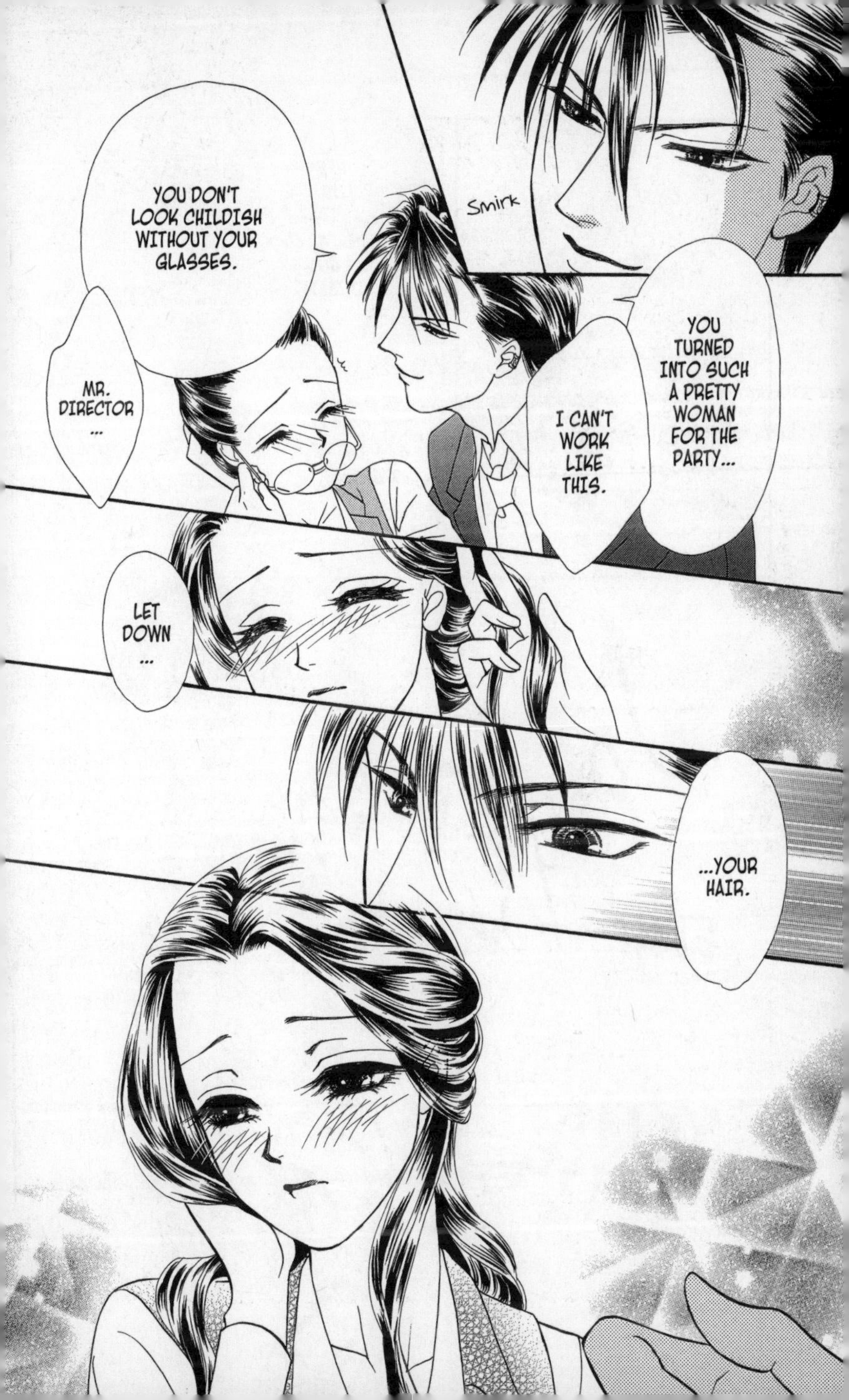
Smirk
YOU DON'T LOOK CHILDISH WITHOUT YOUR GLASSES.
YOU TURNED INTO SUCH A PRETTY WOMAN FOR THE PARTY...
I CAN'T WORK LIKE THIS.
MR. DIRECTOR...
LET DOWN...
...YOUR HAIR.

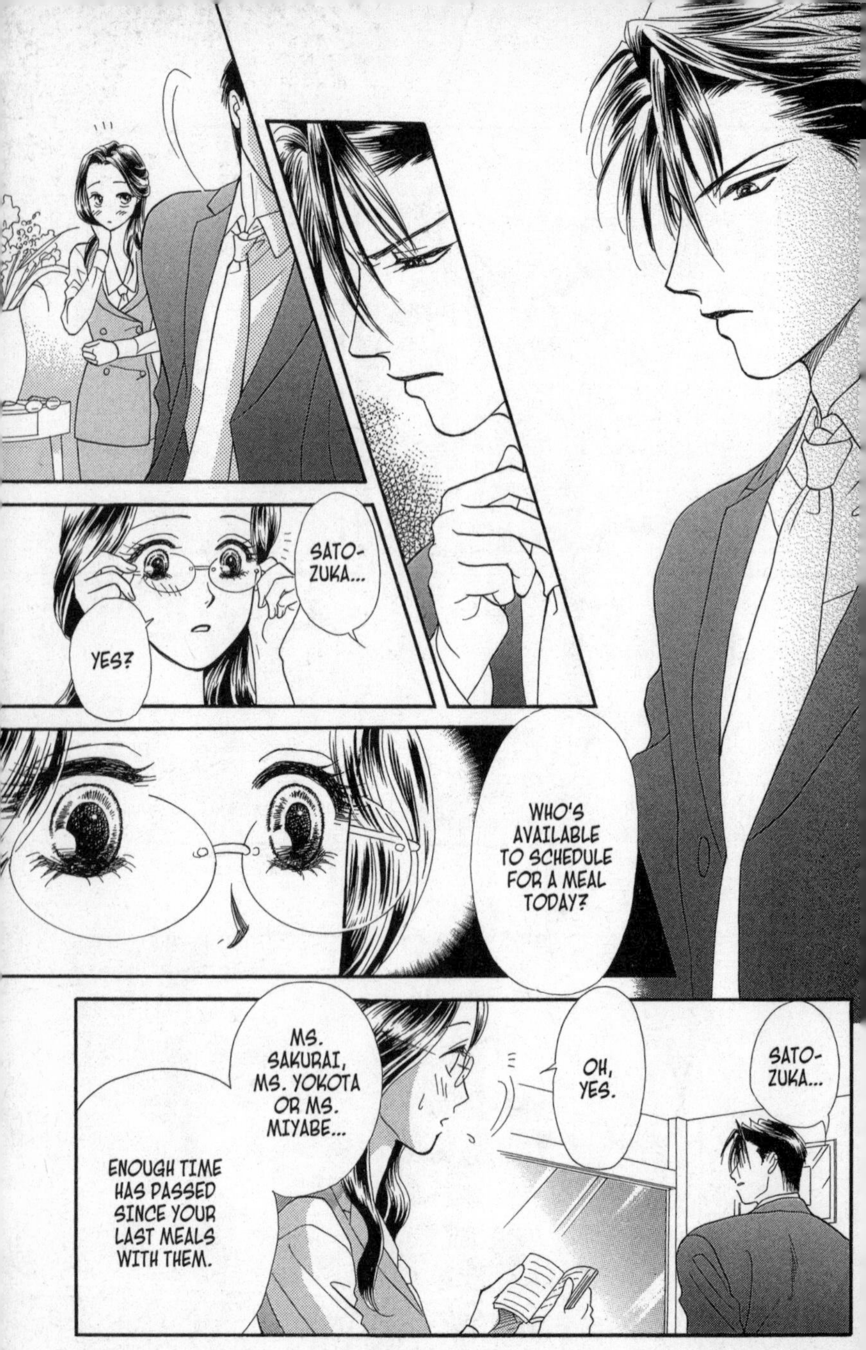
SATO-ZUKA...
YES?
WHO'S AVAILABLE TO SCHEDULE FOR A MEAL TODAY?
SATO-ZUKA...
OH, YES.
MS. SAKURAI, MS. YOKOTA OR MS. MIYABE...
ENOUGH TIME HAS PASSED SINCE YOUR LAST MEALS WITH THEM.

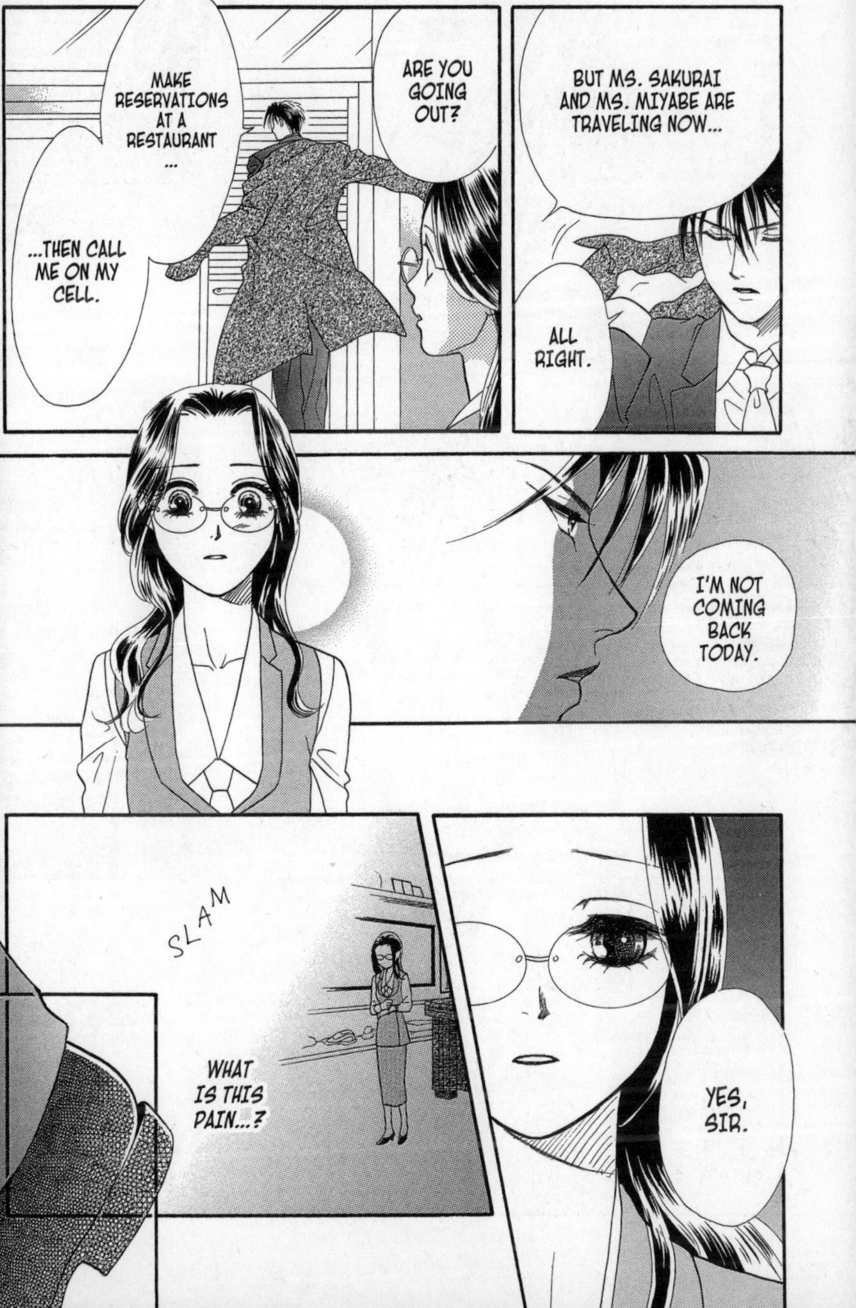

BUT MS. SAKURAI AND MS. MIYABE ARE TRAVELING NOW...
ALL RIGHT.
ARE YOU GOING OUT?
MAKE RESERVATIONS AT A RESTAURANT ...
...THEN CALL ME ON MY CELL.
I'M NOT COMING BACK TODAY.
YES, SIR.
SLAM
WHAT IS THIS PAIN...?

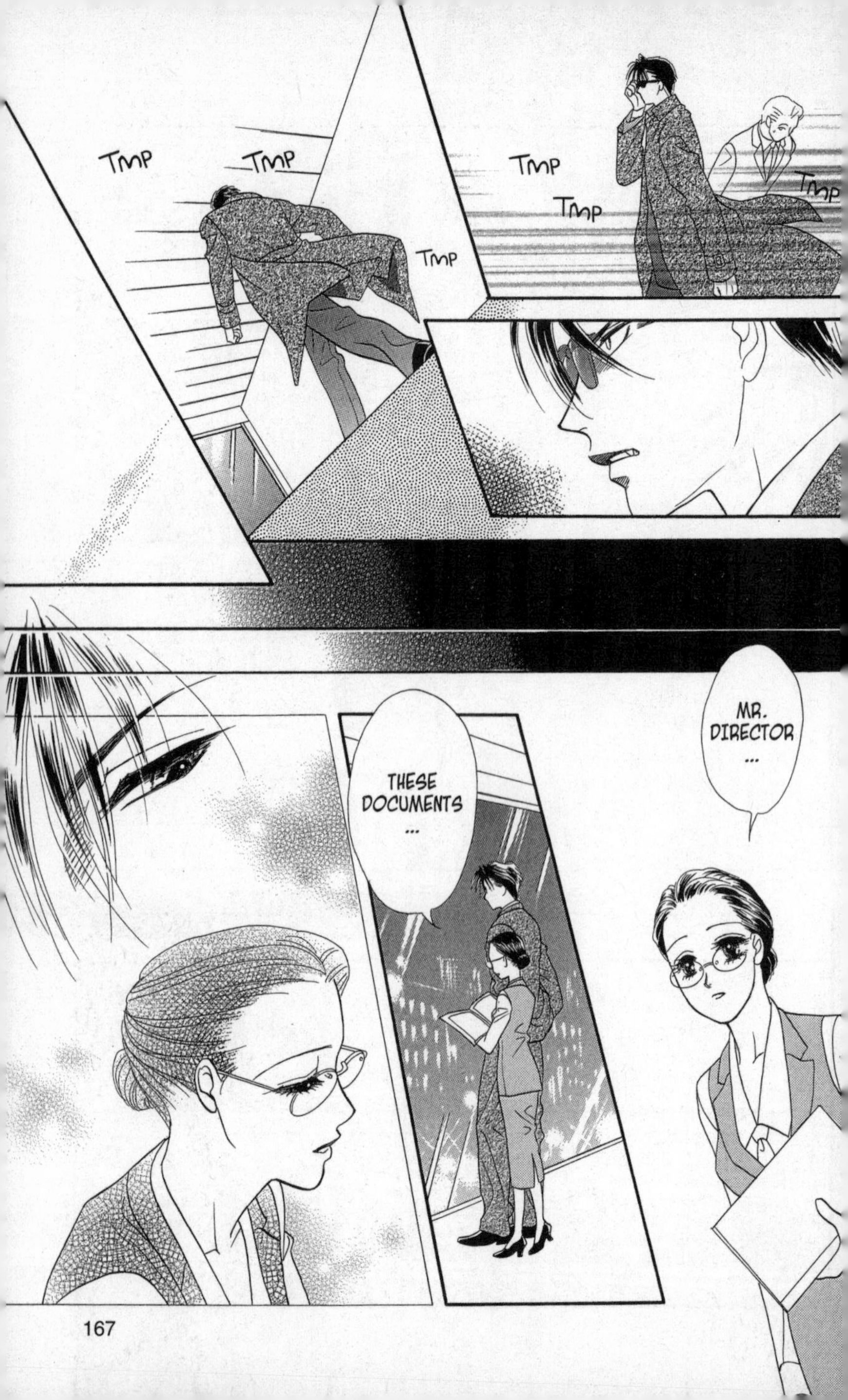
TMP
TMP
TMP
TMP
TMP
TMP
TMP
MR. DIRECTOR ...
THESE DOCUMENTS ...

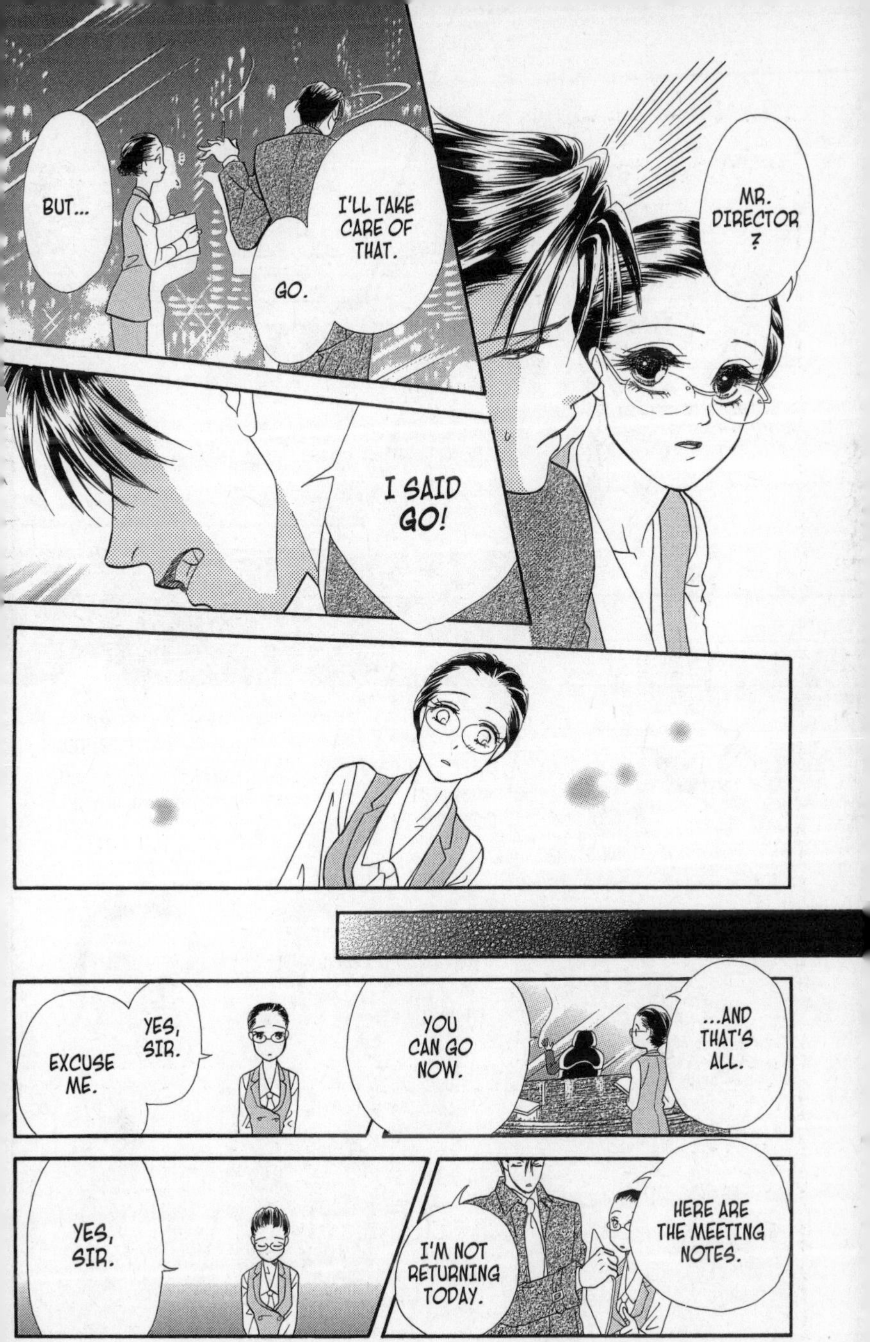
MR. DIRECTOR?
I'LL TAKE CARE OF THAT.
GO.
BUT...
I SAID GO!
...AND THAT'S ALL.
YOU CAN GO NOW.
YES, SIR.
EXCUSE ME.
HERE ARE THE MEETING NOTES.
I'M NOT RETURNING TODAY.
YES, SIR.

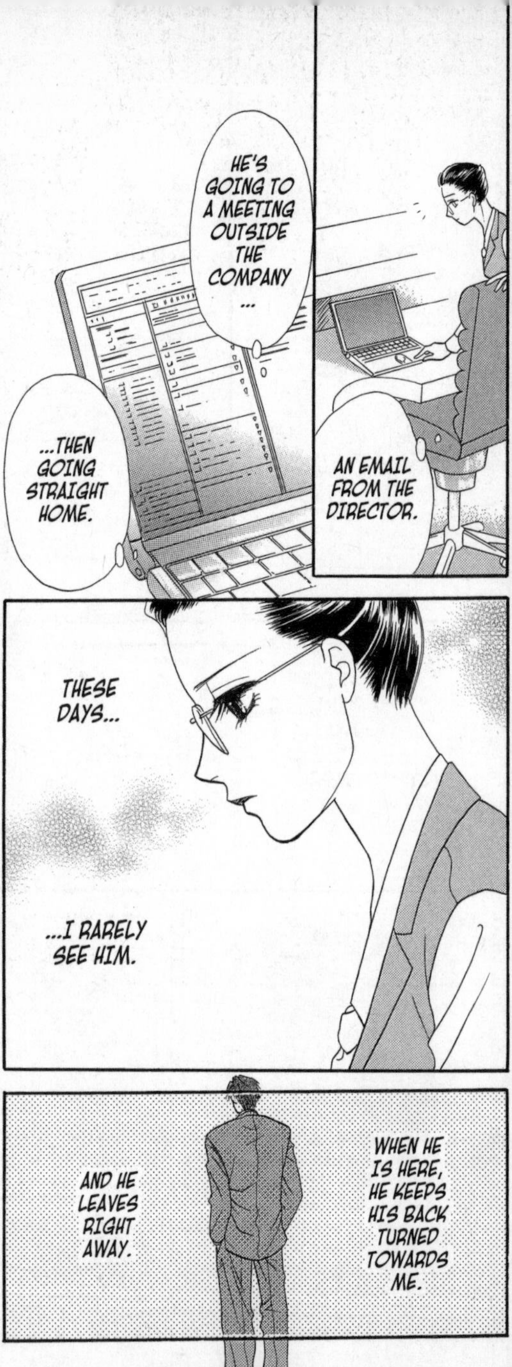
AN EMAIL FROM THE DIRECTOR.
HE'S GOING TO A MEETING OUTSIDE THE COMPANY ...
...THEN GOING STRAIGHT HOME.
THESE DAYS...
...I RARELY SEE HIM.
WHEN HE IS HERE, HE KEEPS HIS BACK TURNED TOWARDS ME.
AND HE LEAVES RIGHT AWAY.

- Moonlight Garden -

I intended to make the dress in the chapter title page really lacy and gorgeous, but after drawing it, I felt that embroidery on the edges was more chic and maidenly.

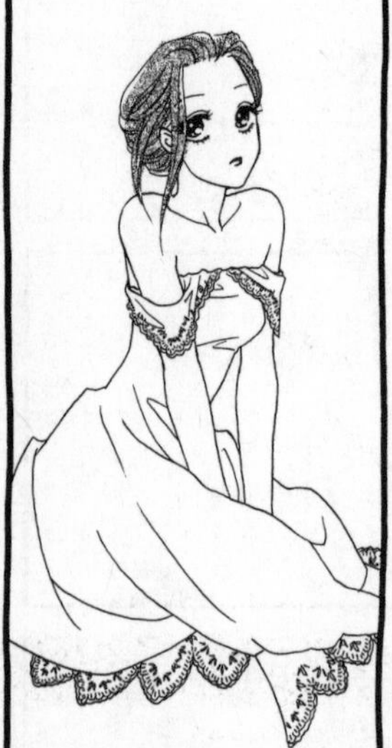

Kaya is always in her uniform. So I thought about putting her in something else... and it turned out to be a dress. Somehow, I can't picture her in everyday street clothes.

Since she's such a workaholic...

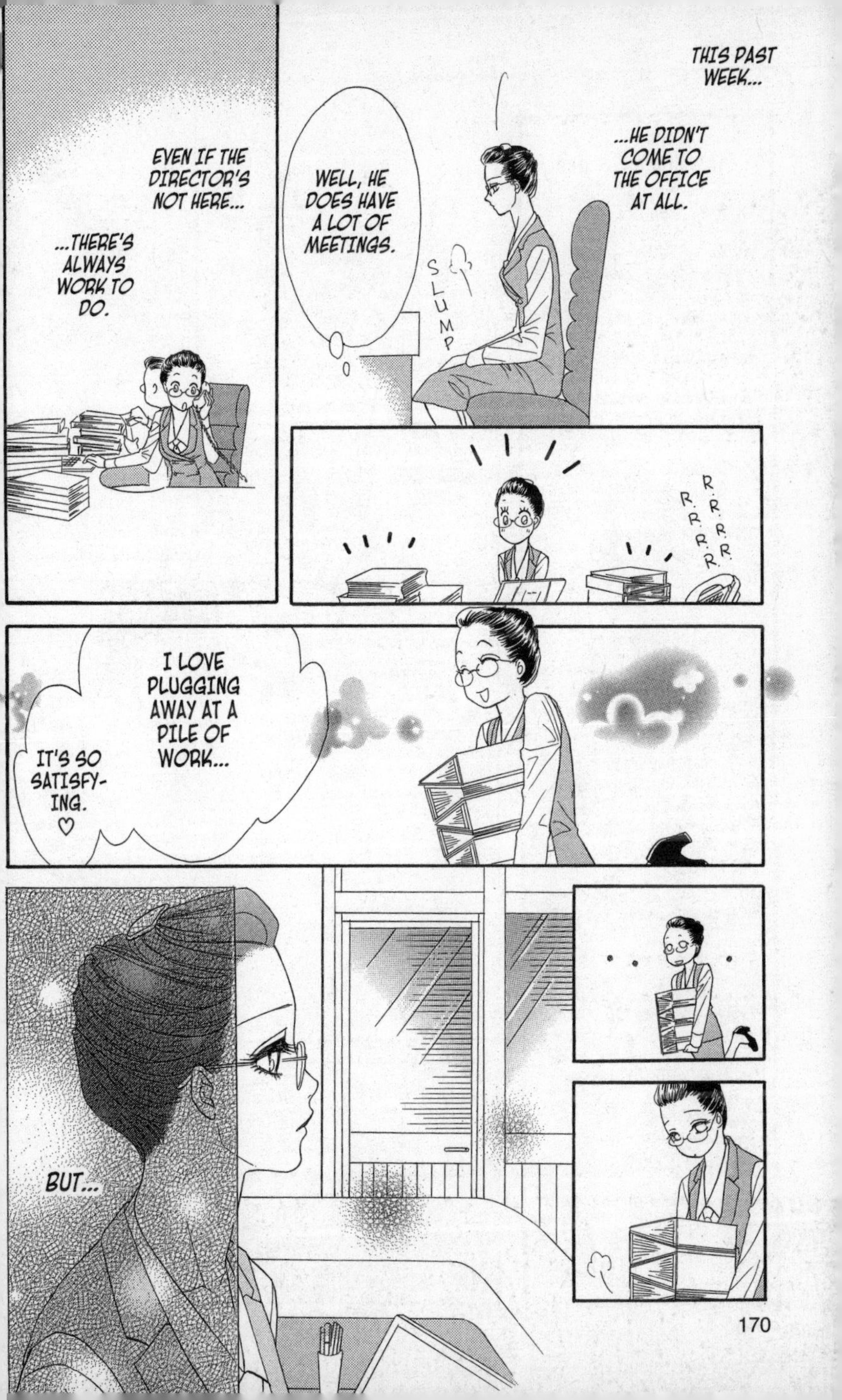
THIS PAST WEEK...
...HE DIDN'T COME TO THE OFFICE AT ALL.
SLUMP
WELL, HE DOES HAVE A LOT OF MEETINGS.
R.R.R.R.R.R.R.R.
EVEN IF THE DIRECTOR'S NOT HERE...
...THERE'S ALWAYS WORK TO DO.
I LOVE PLUGGING AWAY AT A PILE OF WORK...
IT'S SO SATISFYING. ♡
BUT...

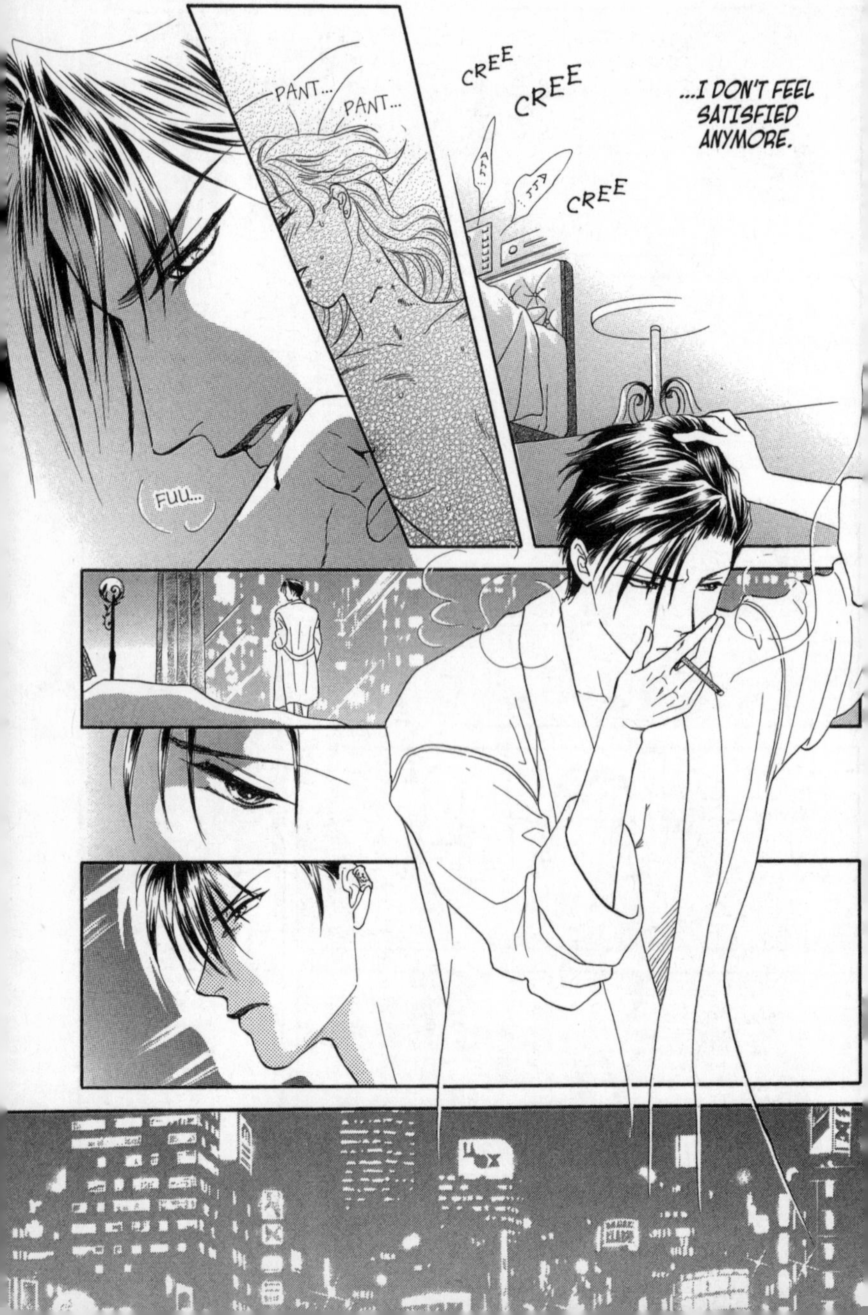
...I DON'T FEEL SATISFIED ANYMORE.
CREE
CREE
CREE
PANT...
PANT...
FUU...

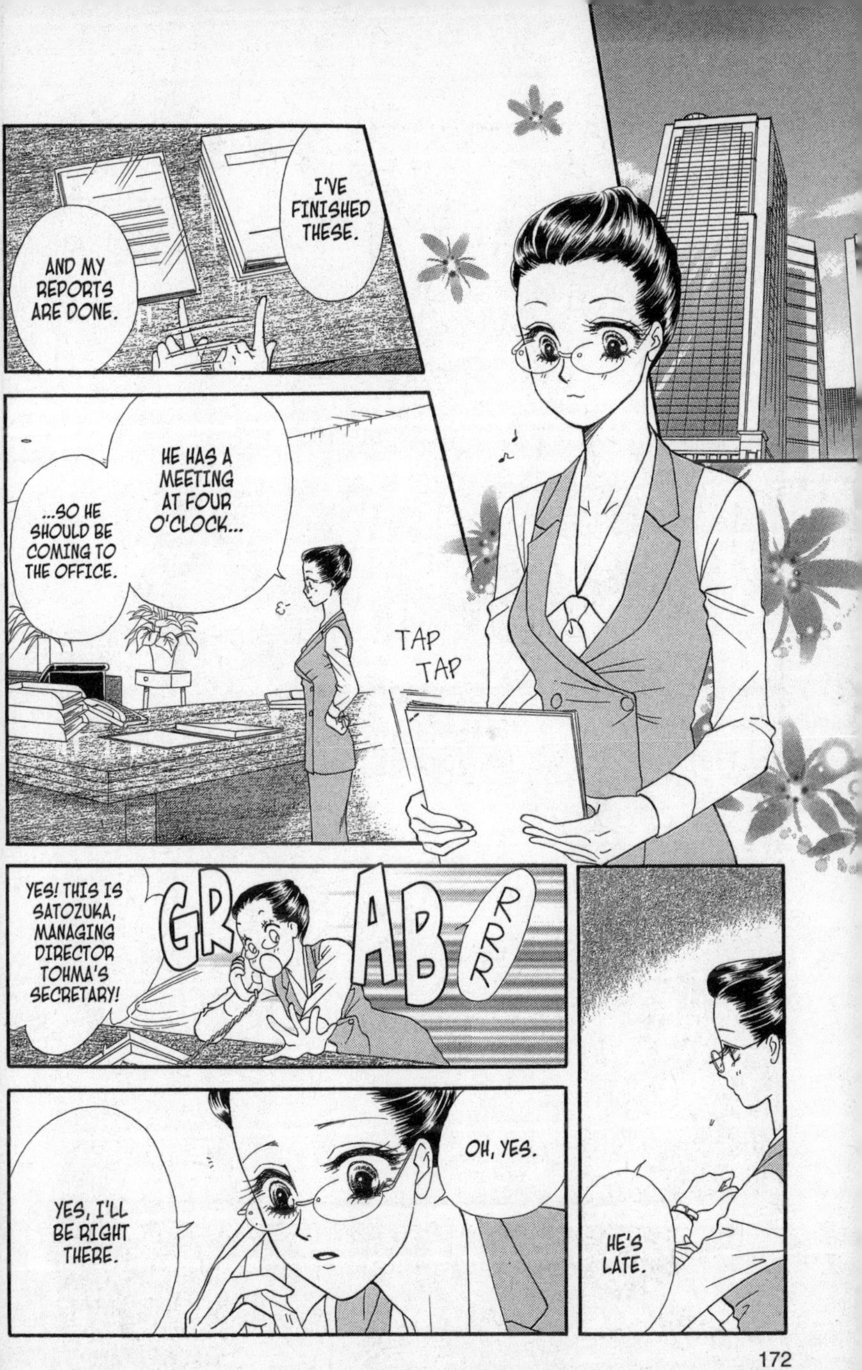
TAP
TAP
I'VE FINISHED THESE.
AND MY REPORTS ARE DONE.
HE HAS A MEETING AT FOUR O'CLOCK...
...SO HE SHOULD BE COMING TO THE OFFICE.
HE'S LATE.
RRR
GRAB
YES! THIS IS SATOZUKA, MANAGING DIRECTOR TOHMA'S SECRETARY!
OH, YES.
YES, I'LL BE RIGHT THERE.

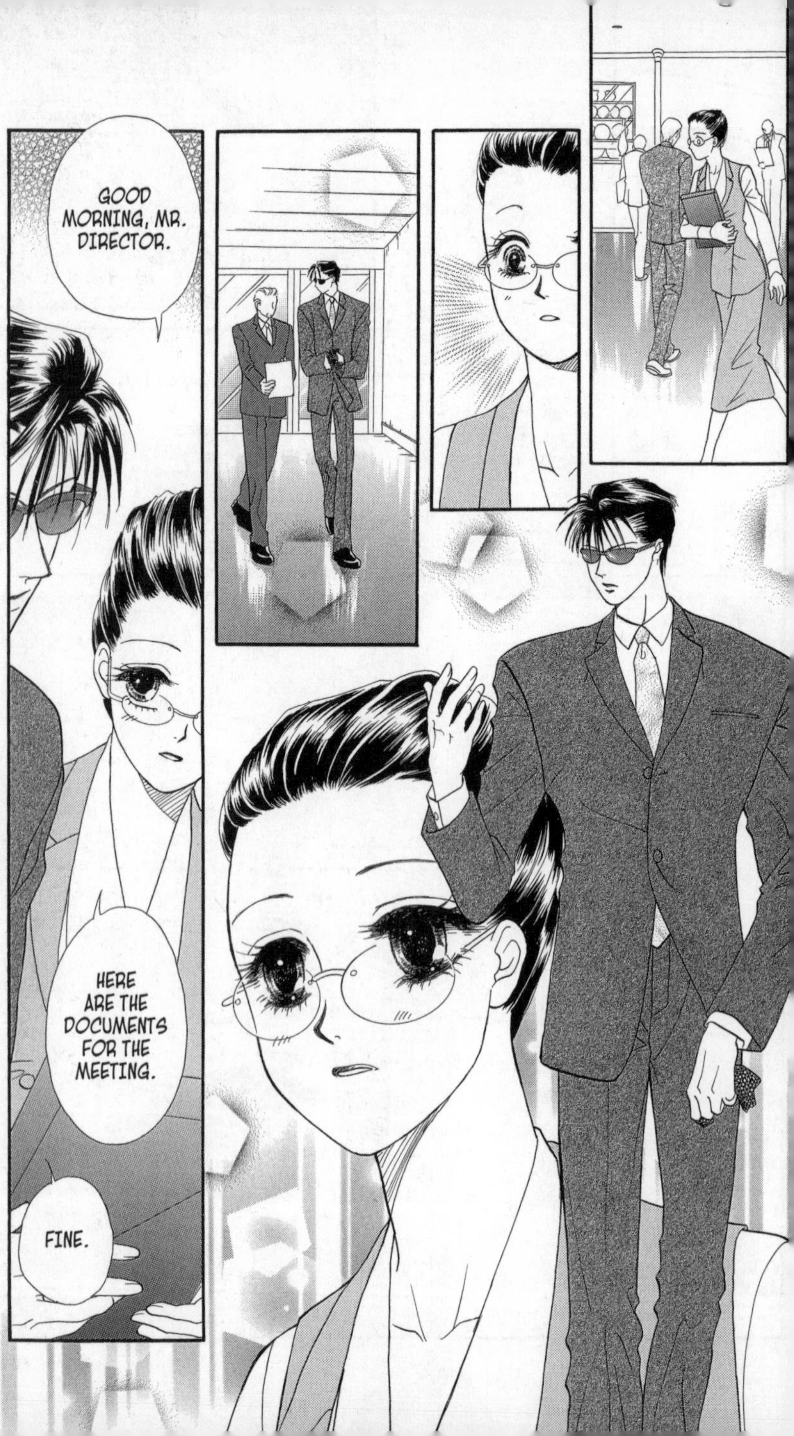
GOOD MORNING, MR. DIRECTOR.
HERE ARE THE DOCUMENTS FOR THE MEETING.
FINE.

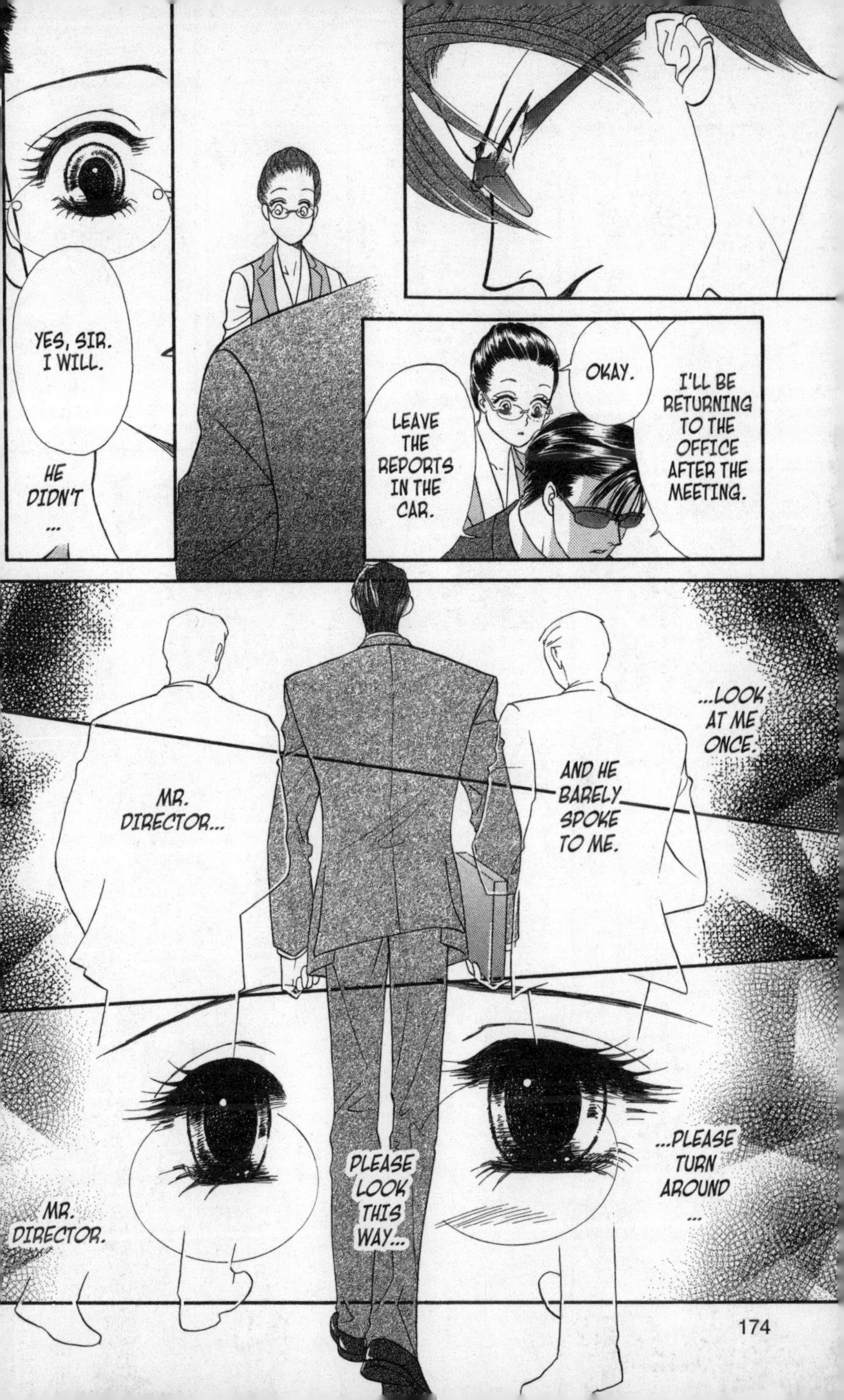
I'LL BE RETURNING TO THE OFFICE AFTER THE MEETING.
OKAY.
LEAVE THE REPORTS IN THE CAR.
YES, SIR. I WILL.
HE DIDN'T ...
...LOOK AT ME ONCE.
AND HE BARELY SPOKE TO ME.
MR. DIRECTOR...
...PLEASE TURN AROUND ...
PLEASE LOOK THIS WAY...
MR. DIRECTOR.

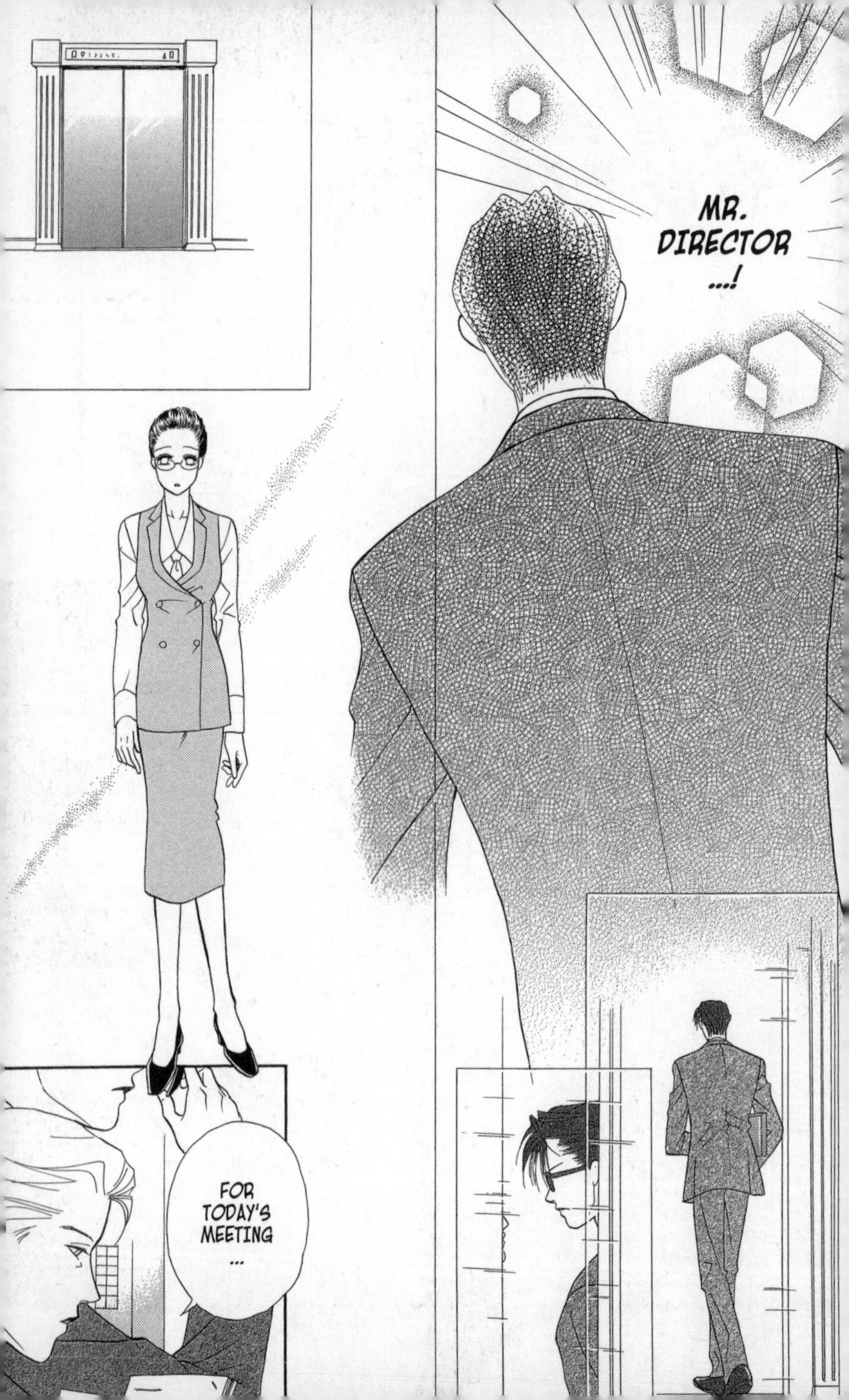
MR. DIRECTOR ...!
FOR TODAY'S MEETING ...

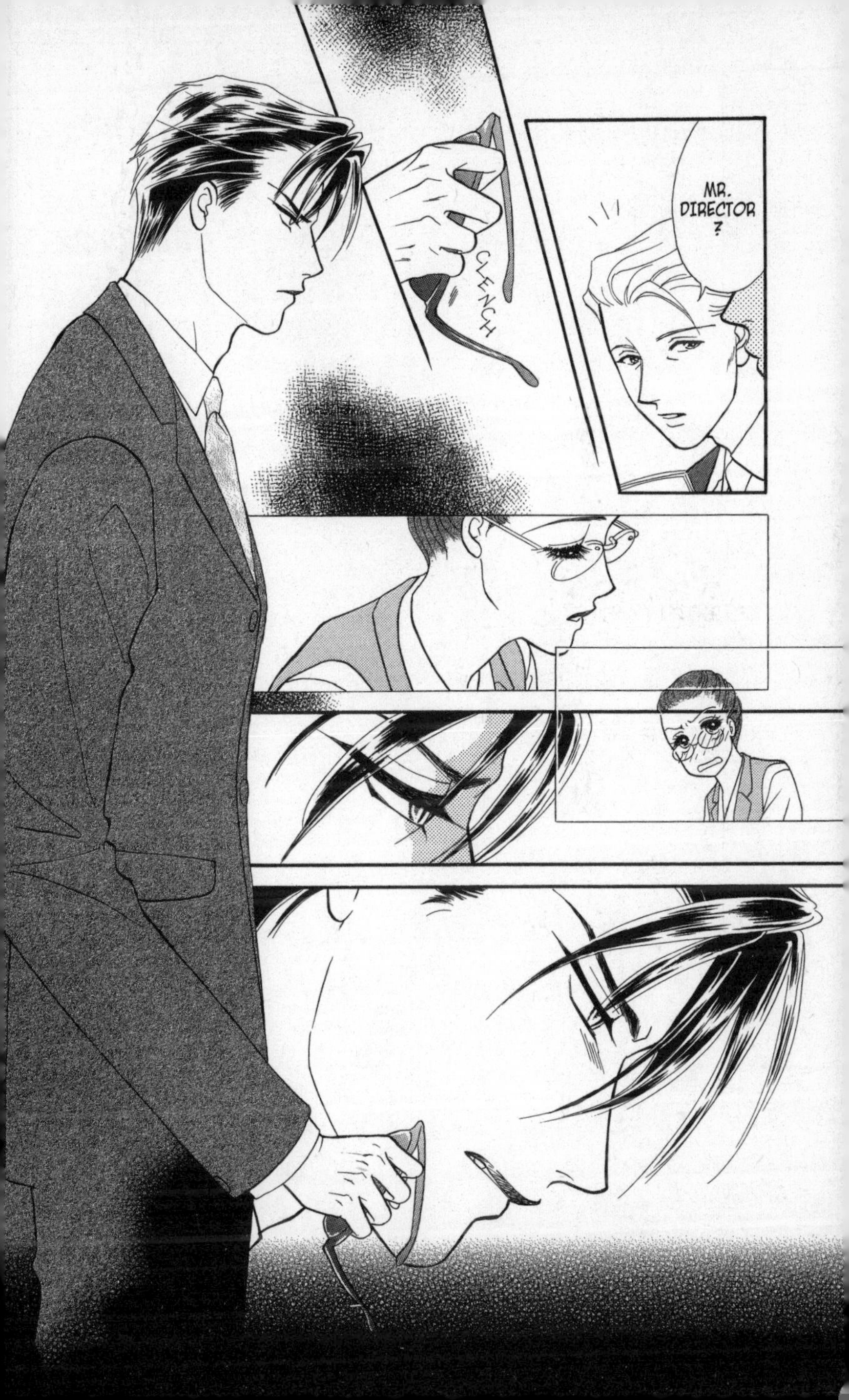
MR. DIRECTOR?
CLENCH

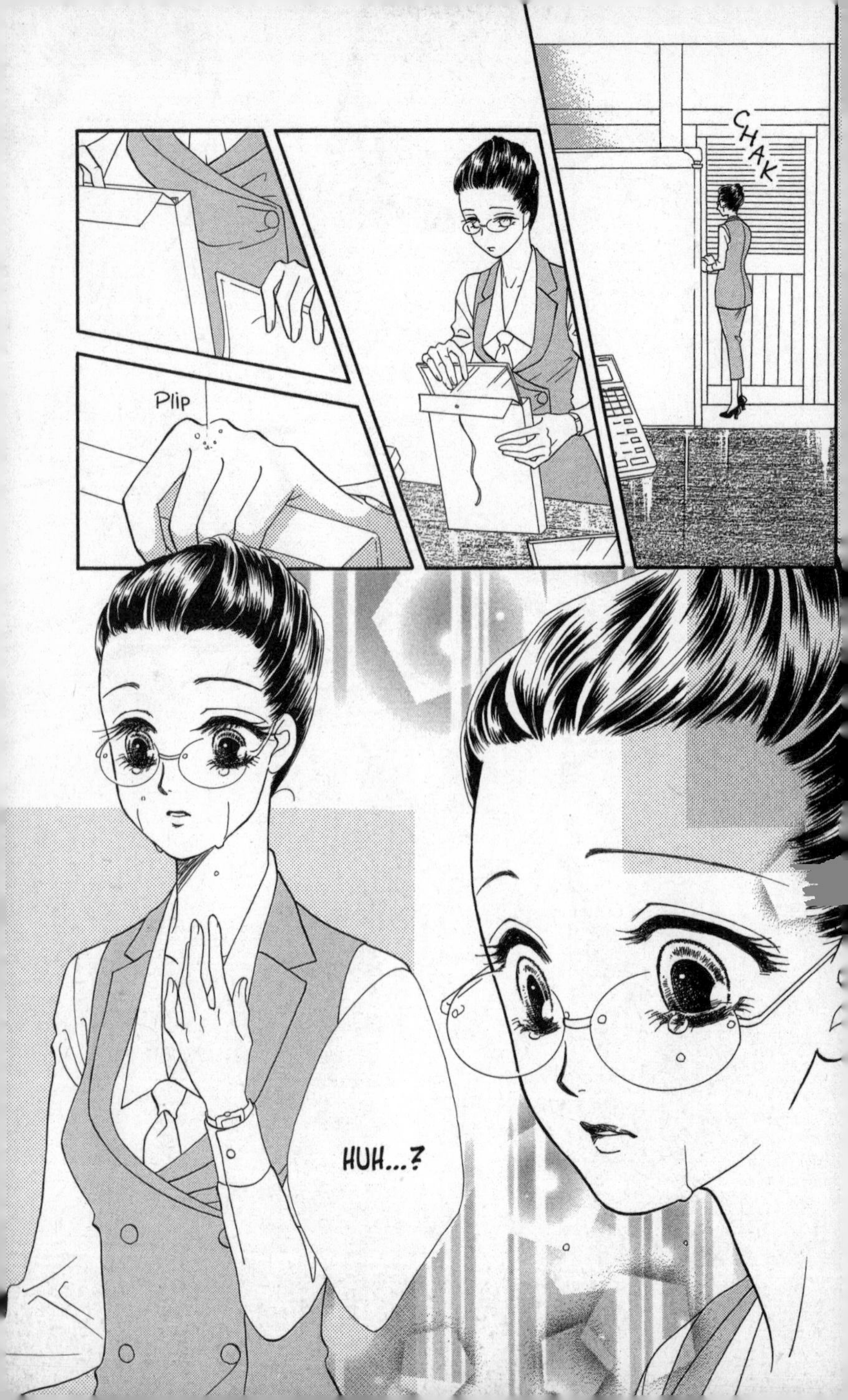
CHAK
Plip
HUH...?

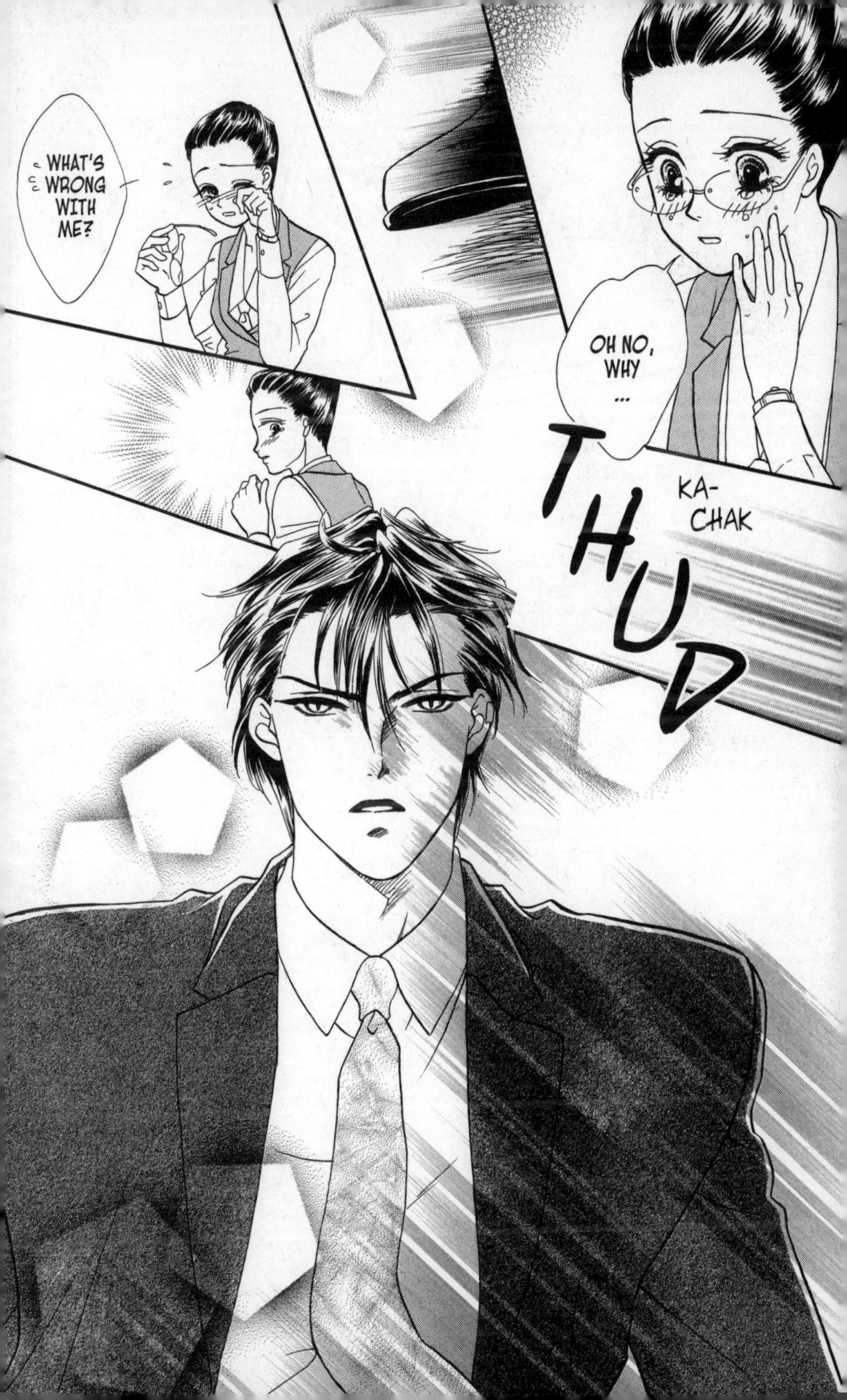
OH NO, WHY ...
WHAT'S WRONG WITH ME?
KA-CHAK
THUD

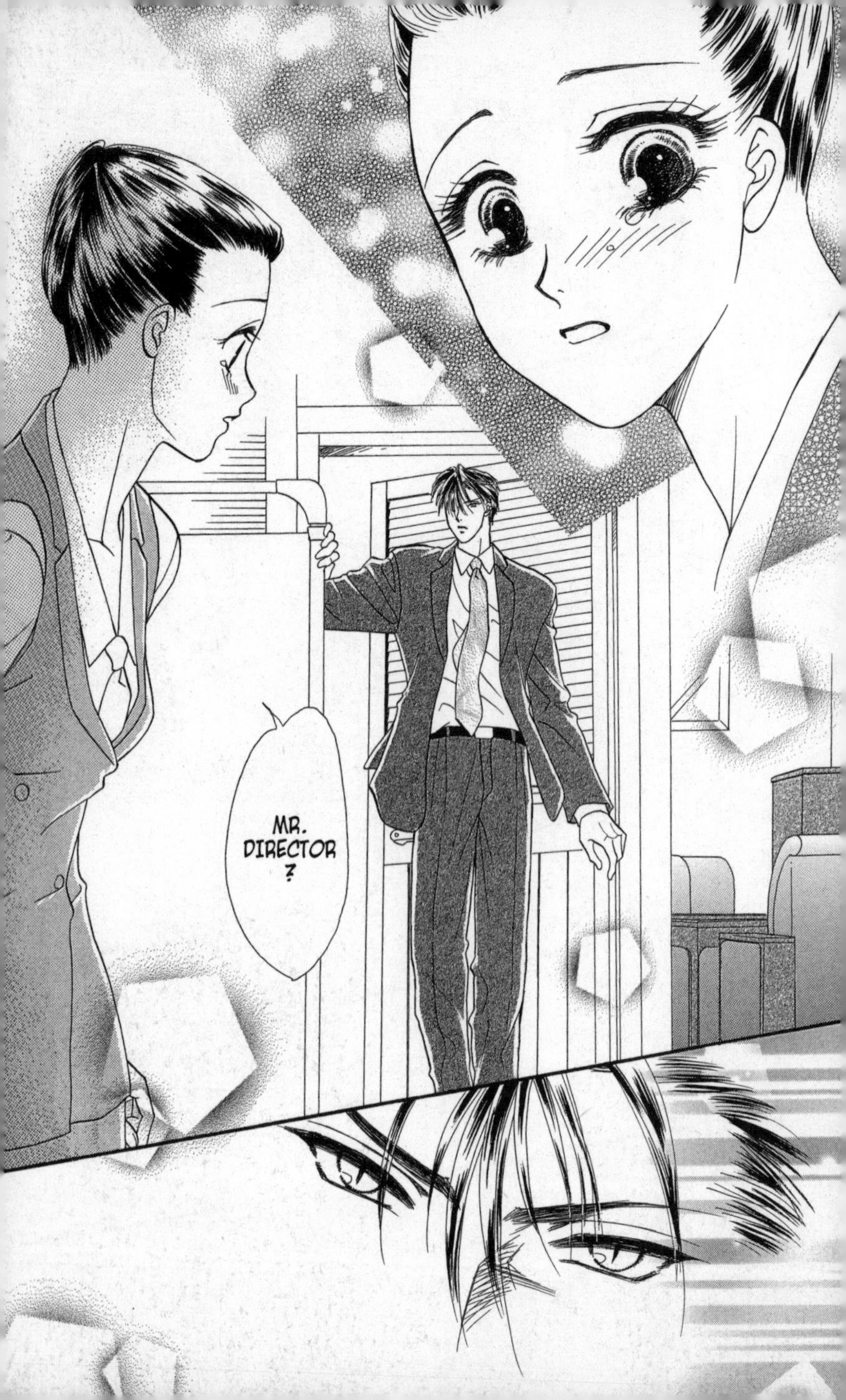
MR. DIRECTOR?

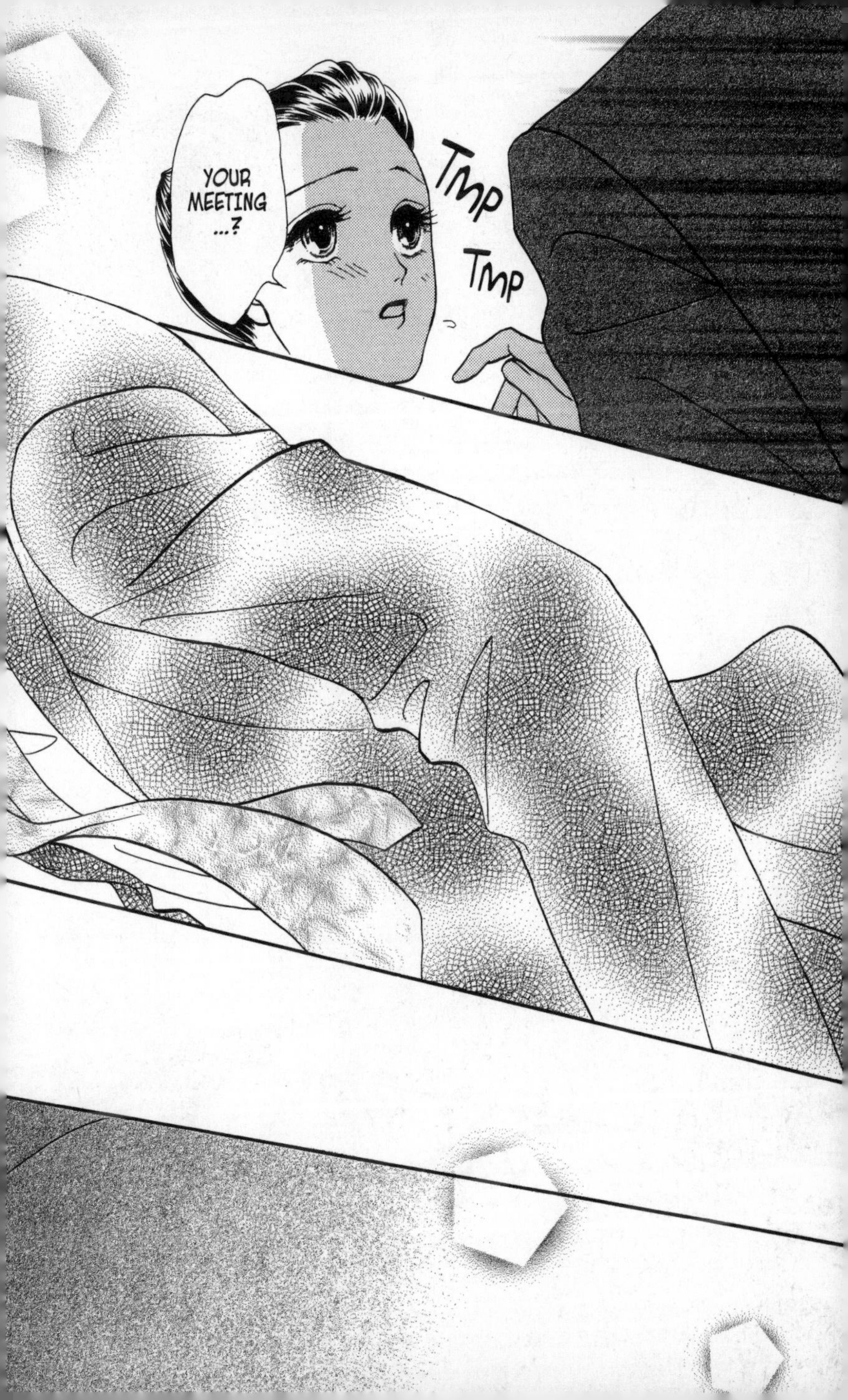
Tmp
Tmp
YOUR MEETING ...?

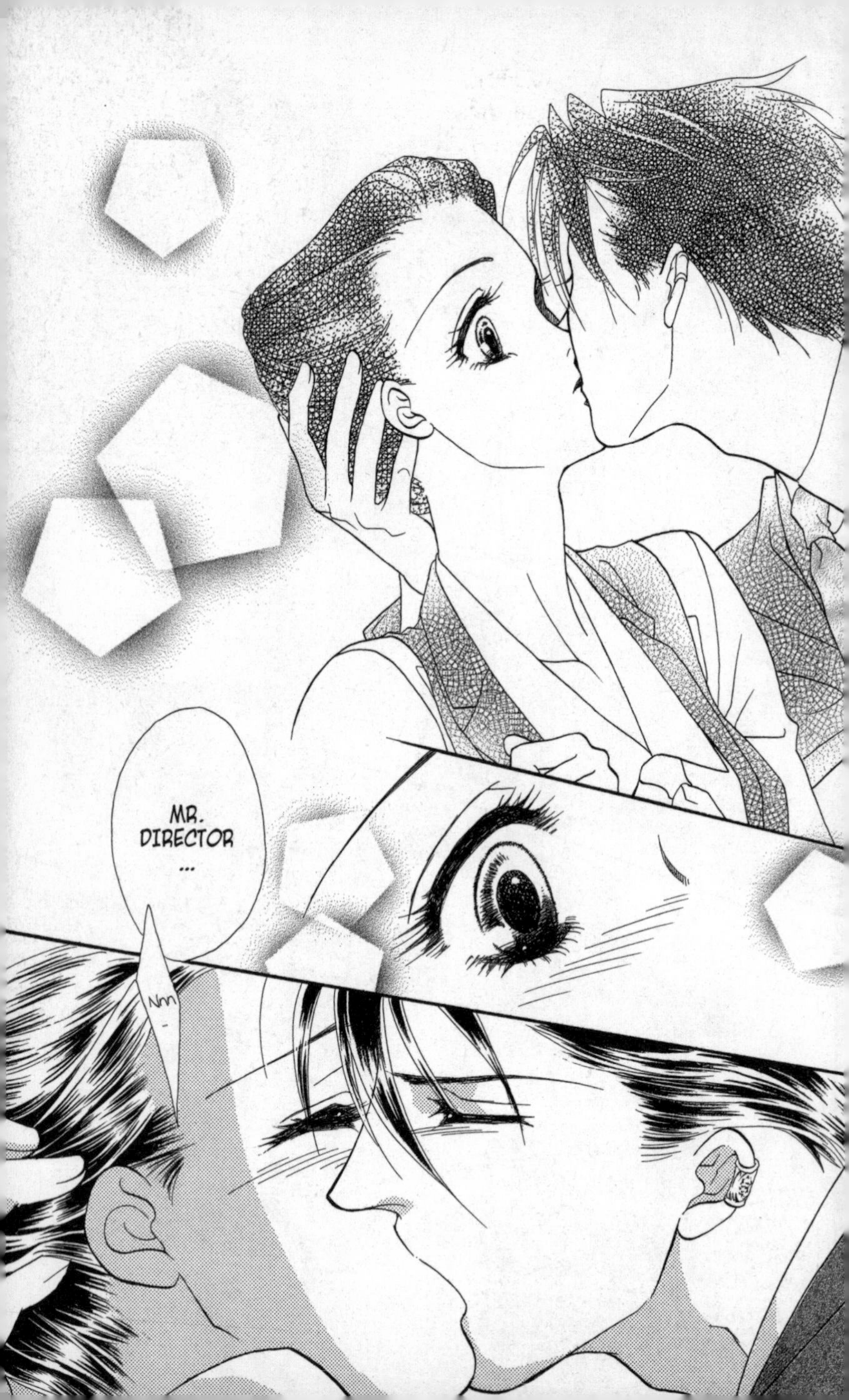
MR. DIRECTOR ...
Nnn -

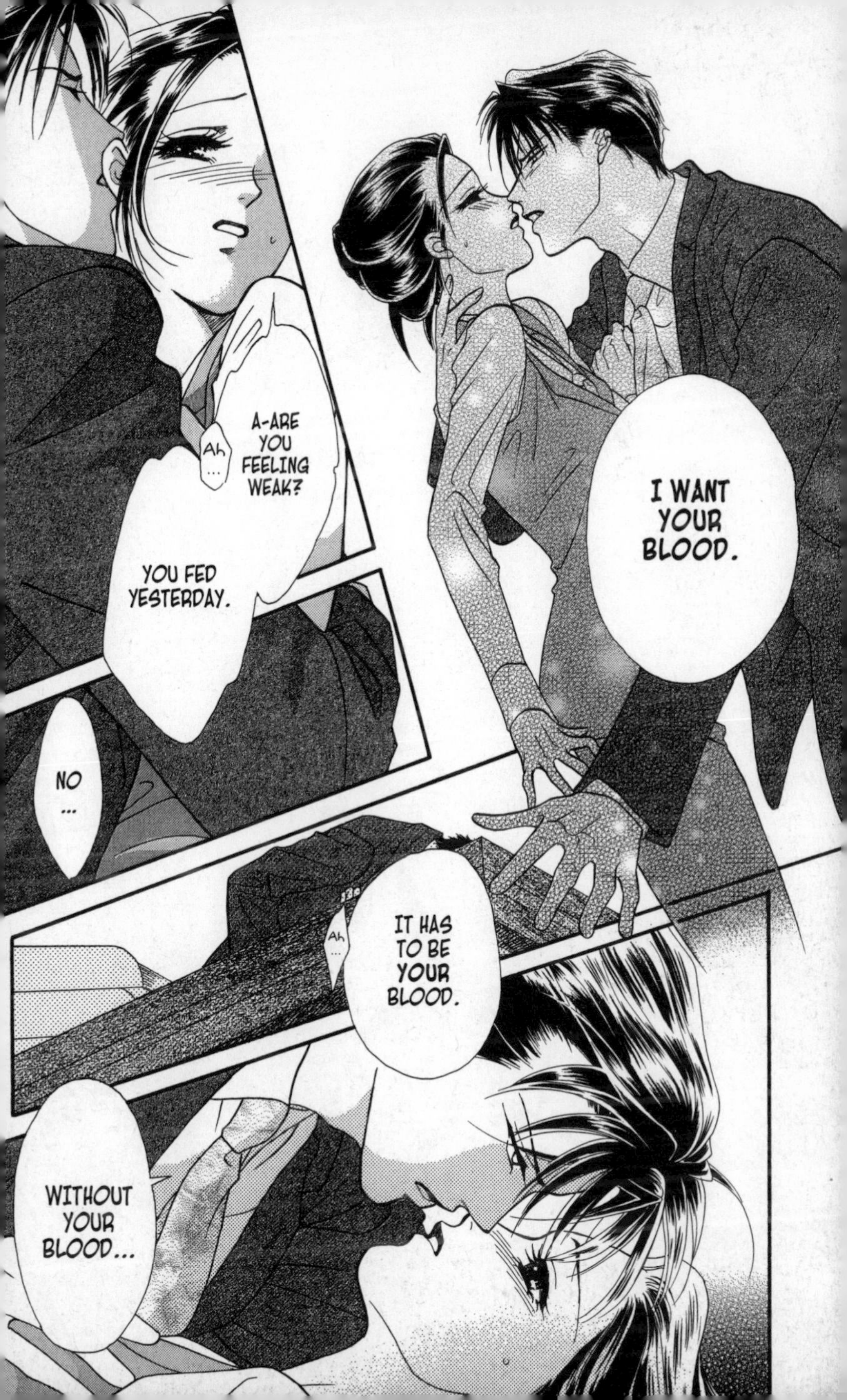

I WANT YOUR BLOOD.
A-ARE YOU FEELING WEAK?
Ah ...
YOU FED YESTERDAY.
NO ...
IT HAS TO BE YOUR BLOOD.
Ah ...
WITHOUT YOUR BLOOD...

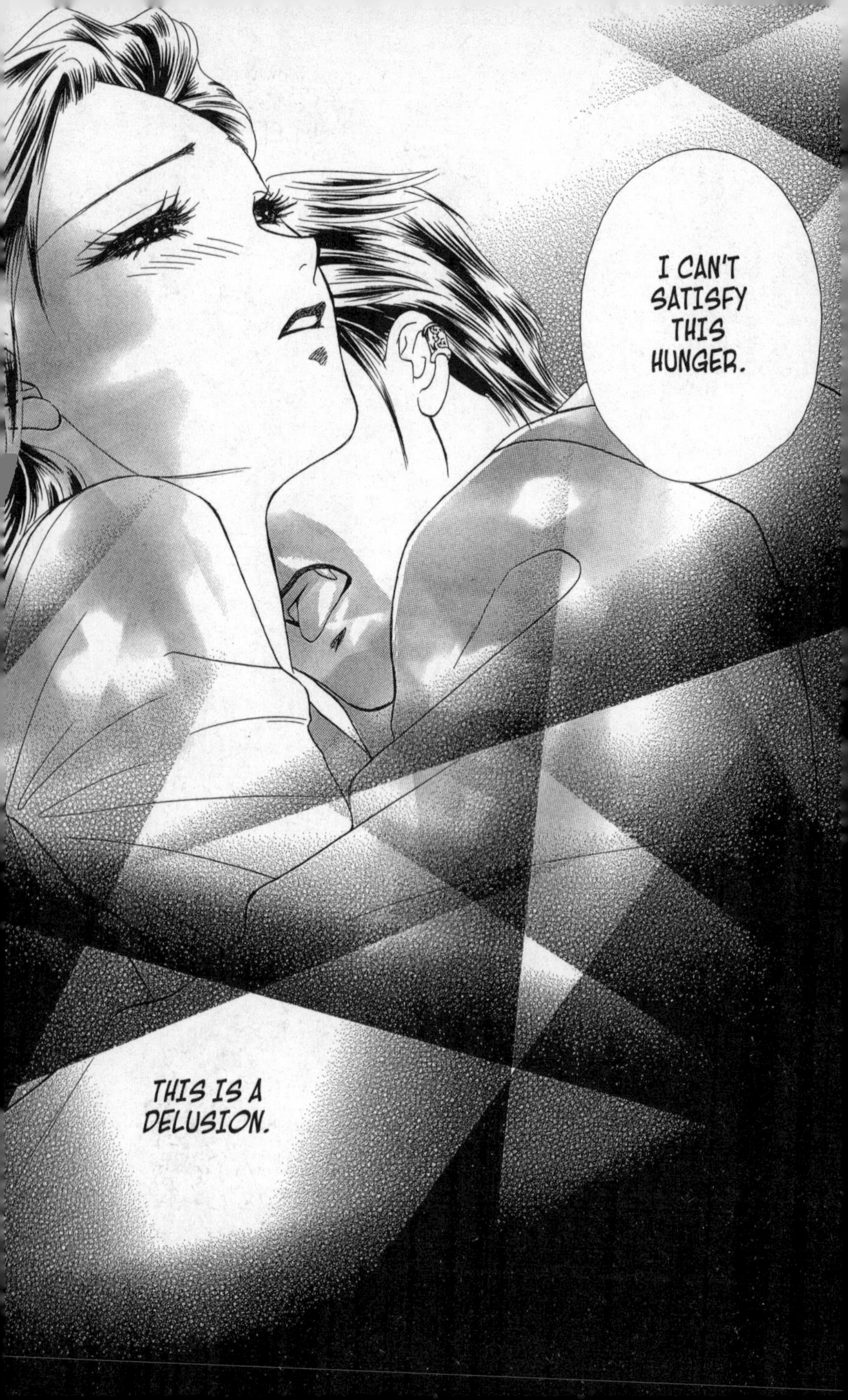
I CAN'T SATISFY THIS HUNGER.
THIS IS A DELUSION.

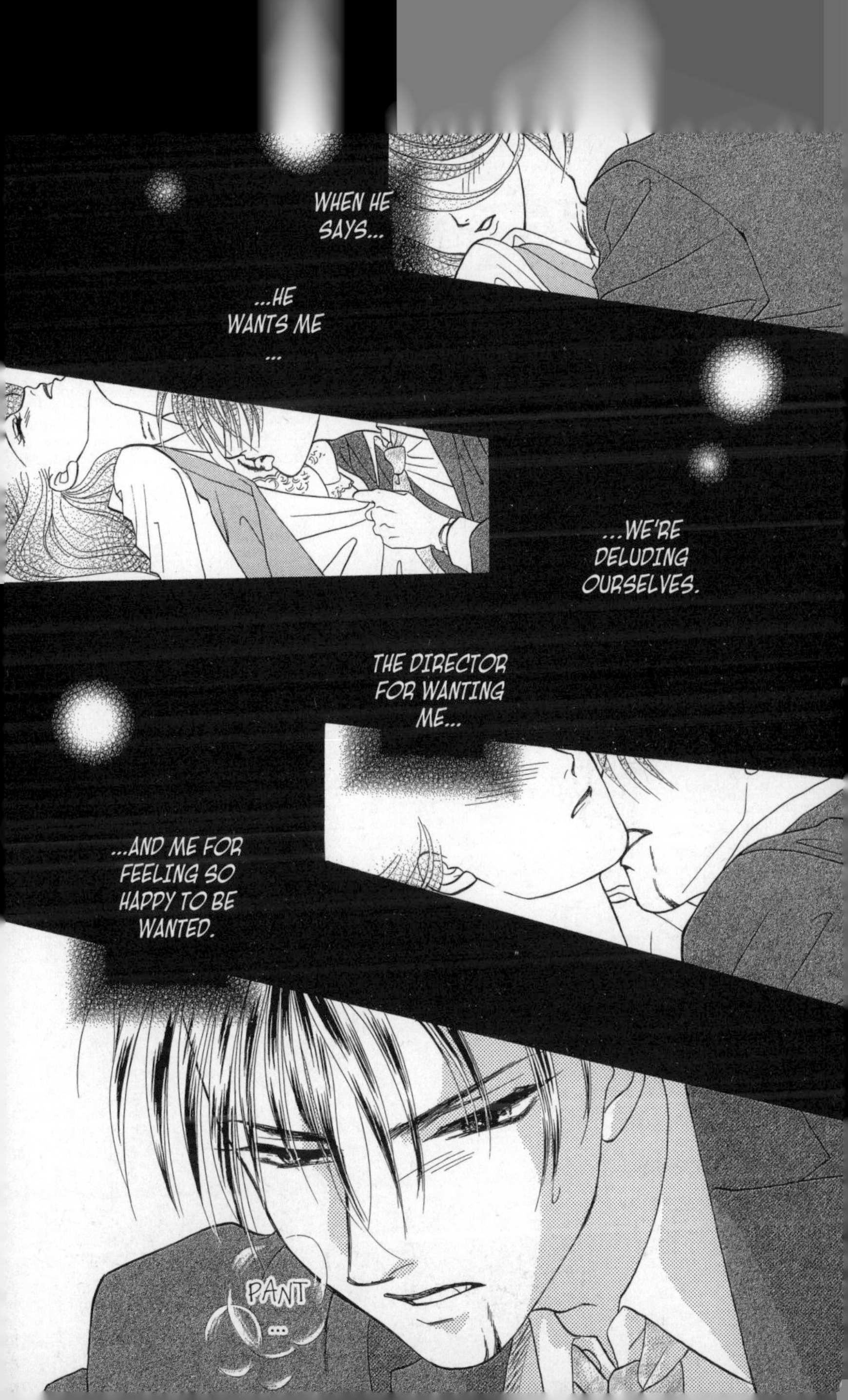
WHEN HE SAYS...
...HE WANTS ME ...
...WE'RE DELUDING OURSELVES.
THE DIRECTOR FOR WANTING ME...
...AND ME FOR FEELING SO HAPPY TO BE WANTED.
PANT ...

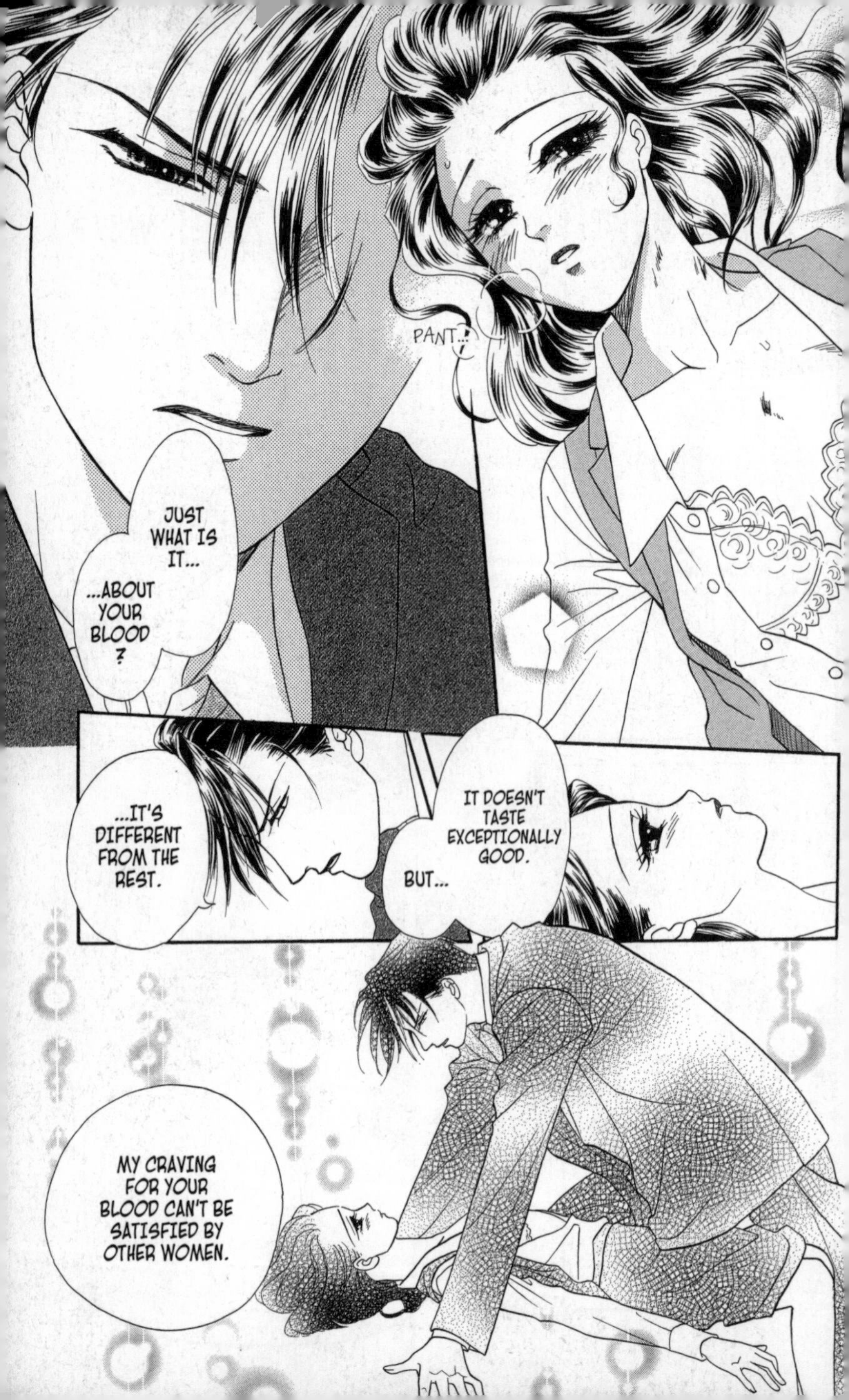
PANT...
JUST WHAT IS IT... ...ABOUT YOUR BLOOD?
IT DOESN'T TASTE EXCEPTIONALLY GOOD. BUT...
...IT'S DIFFERENT FROM THE REST.
MY CRAVING FOR YOUR BLOOD CAN'T BE SATISFIED BY OTHER WOMEN.

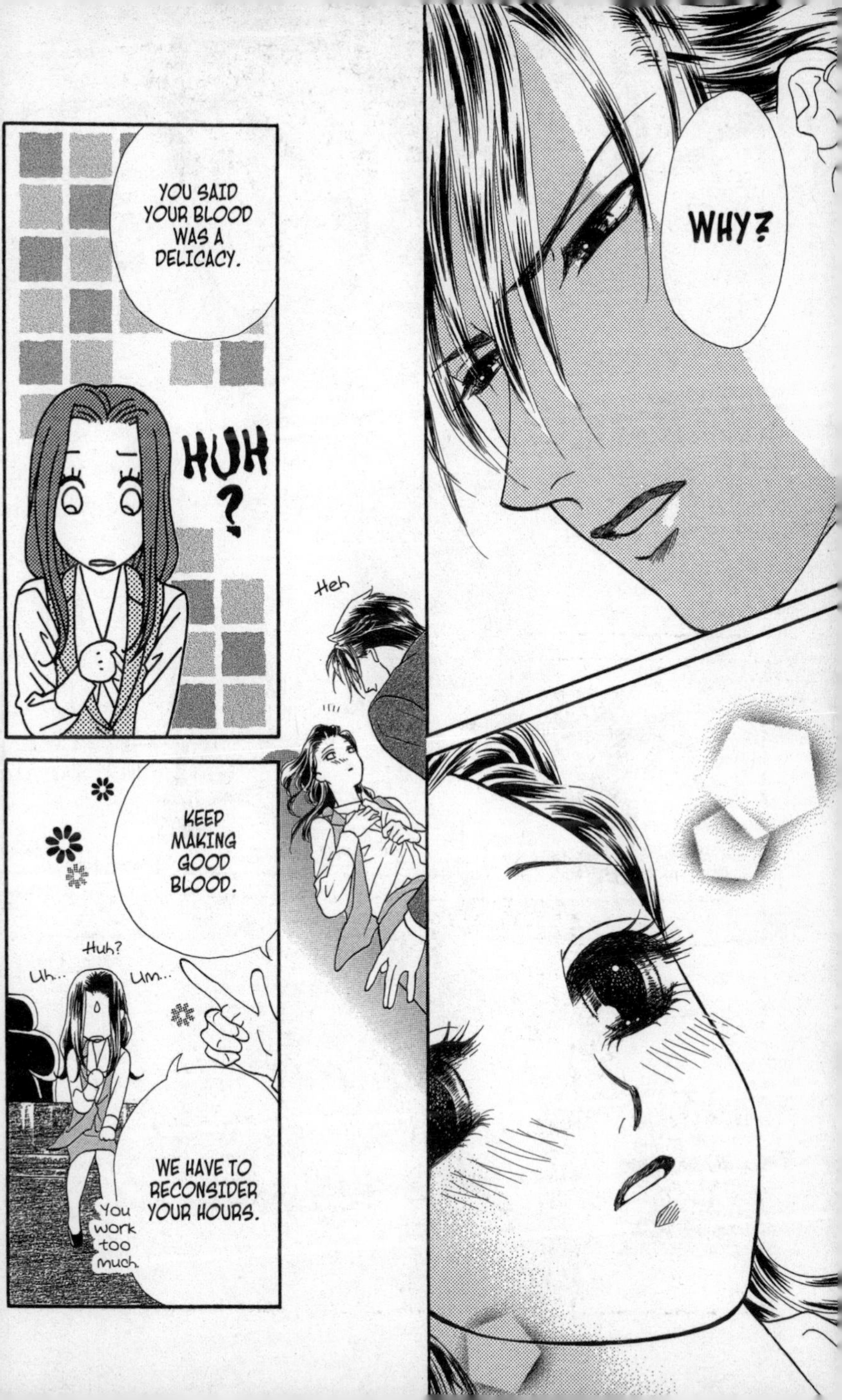
WHY?
YOU SAID YOUR BLOOD WAS A DELICACY.
HUH?
Heh
KEEP MAKING GOOD BLOOD.
Huh?
Uh...
Um...
WE HAVE TO RECONSIDER YOUR HOURS.
You work too much.

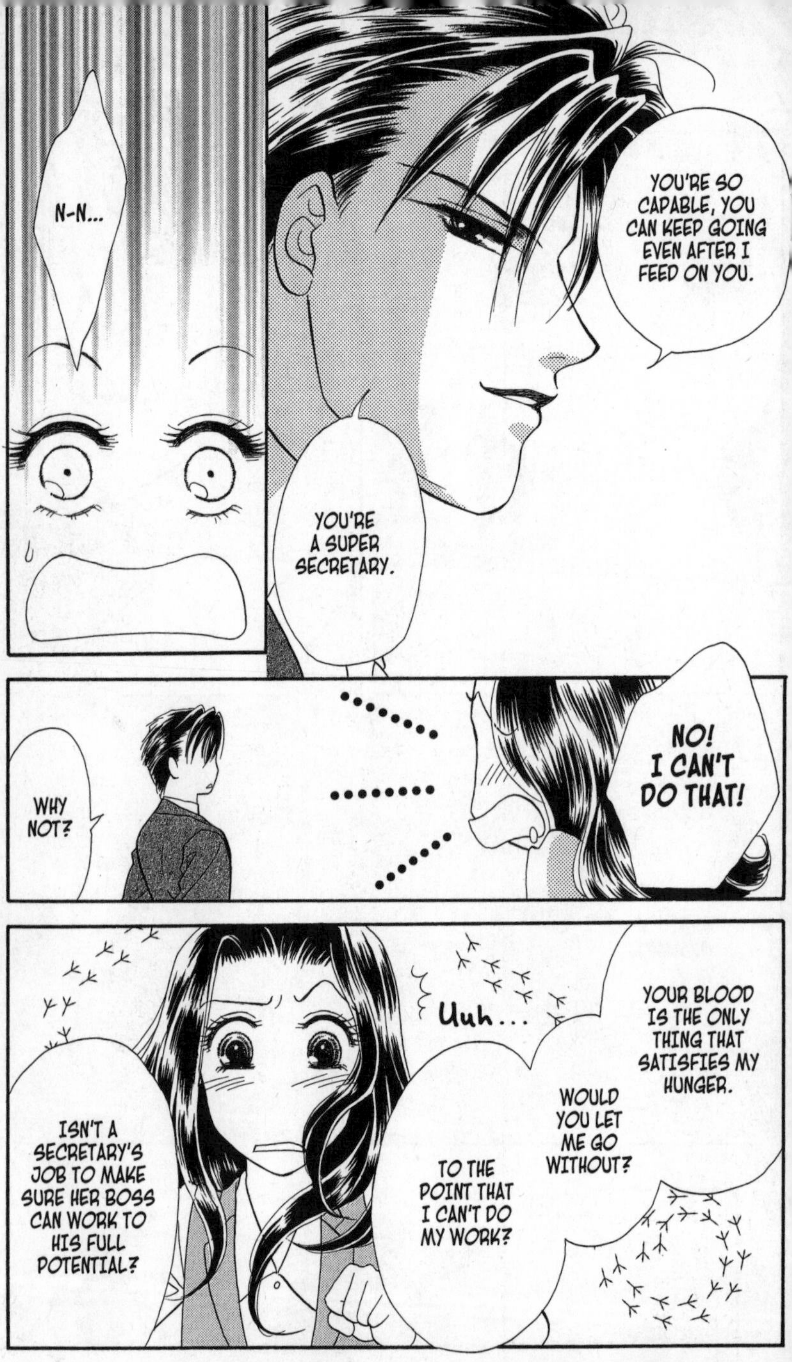
YOU'RE SO CAPABLE, YOU CAN KEEP GOING EVEN AFTER I FEED ON YOU.
YOU'RE A SUPER SECRETARY.
N-N...
NO! I CAN'T DO THAT!
......
WHY NOT?
YOUR BLOOD IS THE ONLY THING THAT SATISFIES MY HUNGER.
Uuh...
WOULD YOU LET ME GO WITHOUT?
TO THE POINT THAT I CAN'T DO MY WORK?
ISN'T A SECRETARY'S JOB TO MAKE SURE HER BOSS CAN WORK TO HIS FULL POTENTIAL?

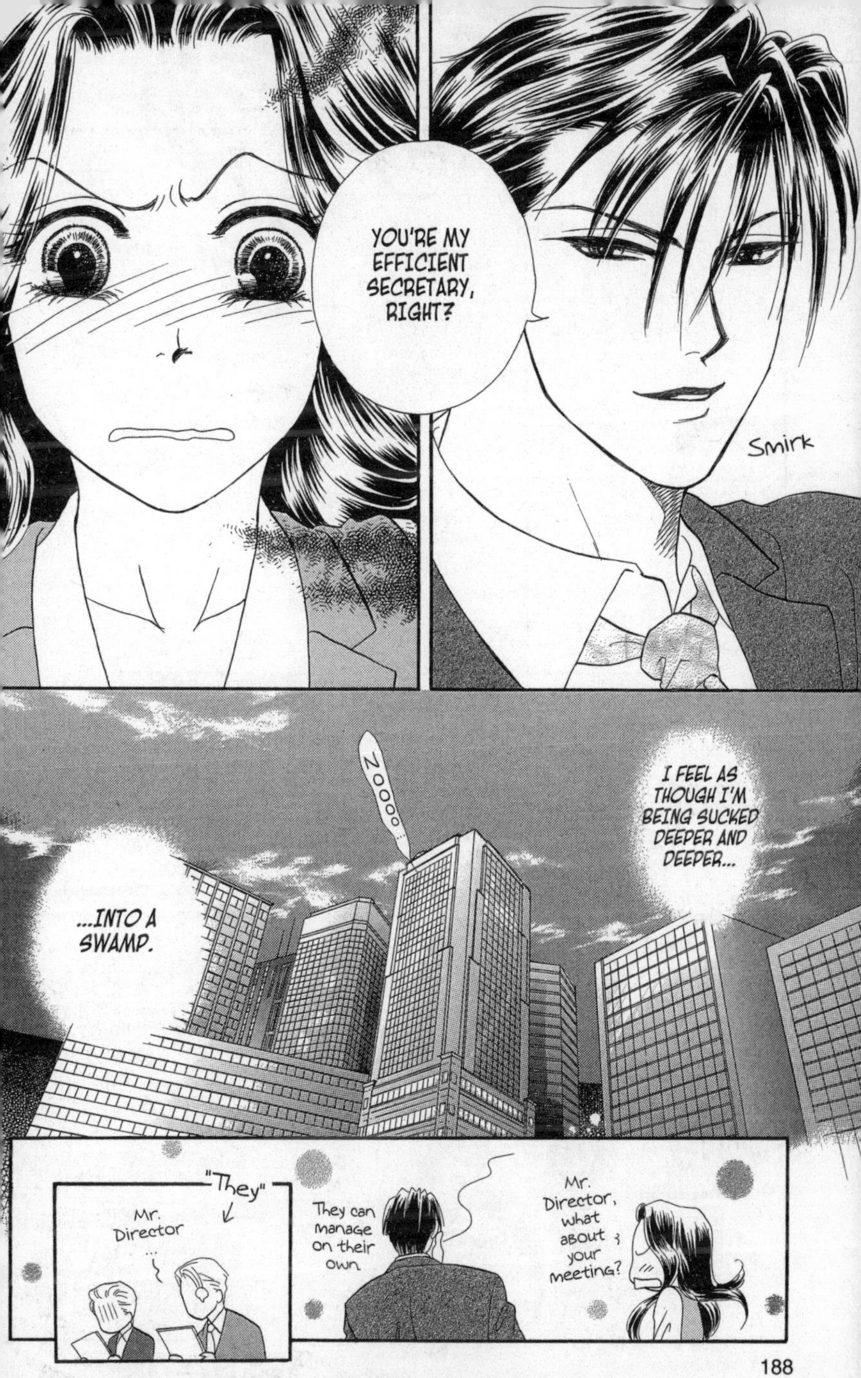
YOU'RE MY EFFICIENT SECRETARY, RIGHT?
Smirk
I FEEL AS THOUGH I'M BEING SUCKED DEEPER AND DEEPER...
Noooo...
...INTO A SWAMP.
Mr. Director, what about your meeting?
They can manage on their own.
"They"
Mr. Director ...

AFTERWORD

Hello! I'm Tomu Ohmi!

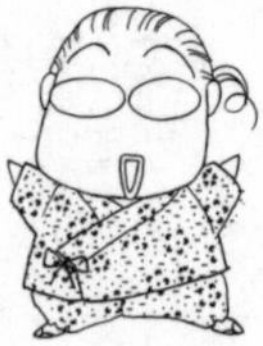

Thank you for picking up my 16th Flower comic!

I hope you enjoyed my new series about a vampire.

I did a piece about a vampire previously, so I have a basic image of vampires.

However, I'm still feeling my way forward with Kaya and Kyohei.

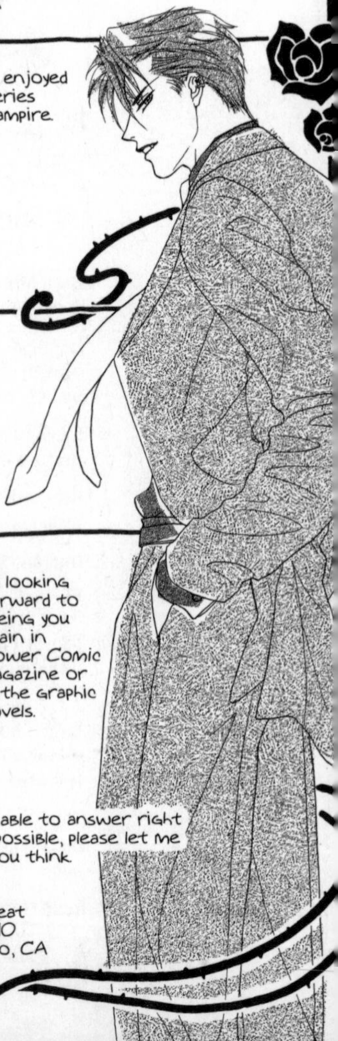

What will happen to Kaya?

What about Kyohei?

I'd be pleased if you follow their journey.

I'm looking forward to seeing you again in *Flower Comic* magazine or in the graphic novels.

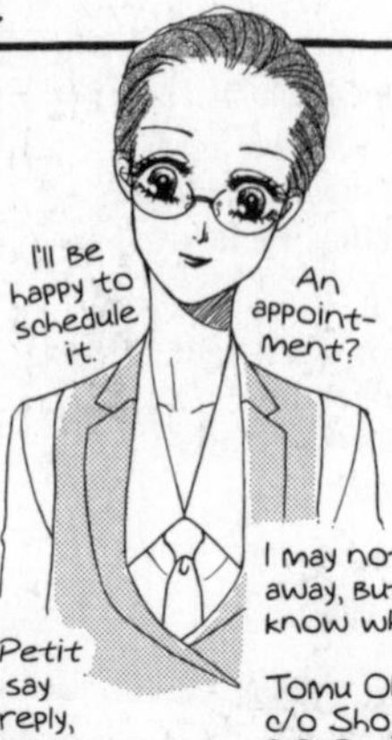

An appointment?
I'll be happy to schedule it.

My thanks to everyone who helped me with this manga, and to all the readers.

I may not be able to answer right away, but if possible, please let me know what you think.

Tomu Ohmi
c/o Shojo Beat
P.O. Box 77010
San Francisco, CA
94107

You can also email your thoughts to *Petit Comics*. I shouldn't say this is in lieu of a reply, but I'd like to send you a New Year's greeting card, so please include your address.

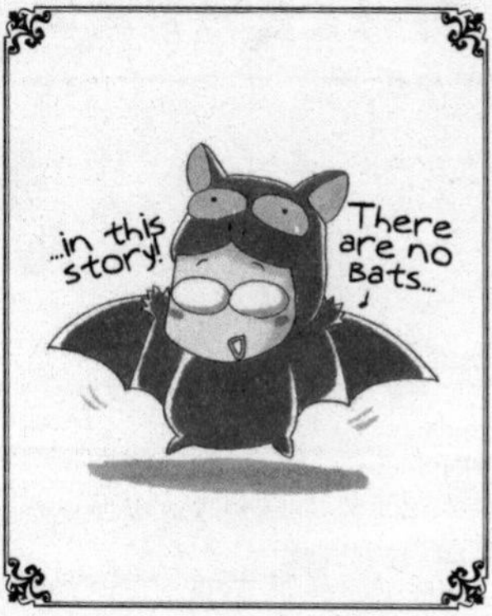
There are no Bats...
...in this story!

Tomu Ohmi Profile

*Born May 25. Gemini. Blood type B. Resides in Hokkaido.

*Debut work: *Kindan no Koi wo Shiyoh* (*Petit Comic* June 2000 issue).

*Likes: Beasts, black tea and pretty women.

*Presently working on *Petit Comic* projects.

*Hurrah! ♥ Sixteen volumes of manga!! Thank you very much for purchasing them! I'm looking forward to meeting you in my future volumes!

After the wolf, it was a tiger, then a bat…rather, a vampire. By the way, bats don't appear in this story. (*laugh*)

This Ohmi work has no beasts, but I hope you enjoy it just the same.

-Tomu Ohmi

Midnight Secretary
Volume 1
Shojo Beat Edition

STORY AND ART BY
Tomu Ohmi

MIDNIGHT SECRETARY Vol. 1
by Tomu OHMI

Original Japanese edition published by SHOGAKUKAN.
English translation rights in the United States of America, Canada, the United Kingdom and Ireland arranged with SHOGAKUKAN.

English Translation & Adaptation/JN Productions
Touch-up Art & Lettering/Joanna Estep
Design/Izumi Evers
Editor/Pancha Diaz

Printed in the U.S.A.

Published by VIZ Media, LLC
P.O. Box 77010
San Francisco, CA 94107

10 9 8 7 6 5 4 3 2 1
First printing, September 2013

www.viz.com
www.shojobeat.com

PARENTAL ADVISORY
MIDNIGHT SECRETARY is rated M for Mature and is recommended for ages 18 and up. This volume contains sex scenes.
ratings.viz.com

This is the last page.

In keeping with the original Japanese comic format, this book reads from right to left—so action, sound effects, and word balloons are completely reversed. This preserves the orientation of the original artwork—plus, it's fun! Check out the diagram shown here to get the hang of things, and then turn to the other side of the book to get started!

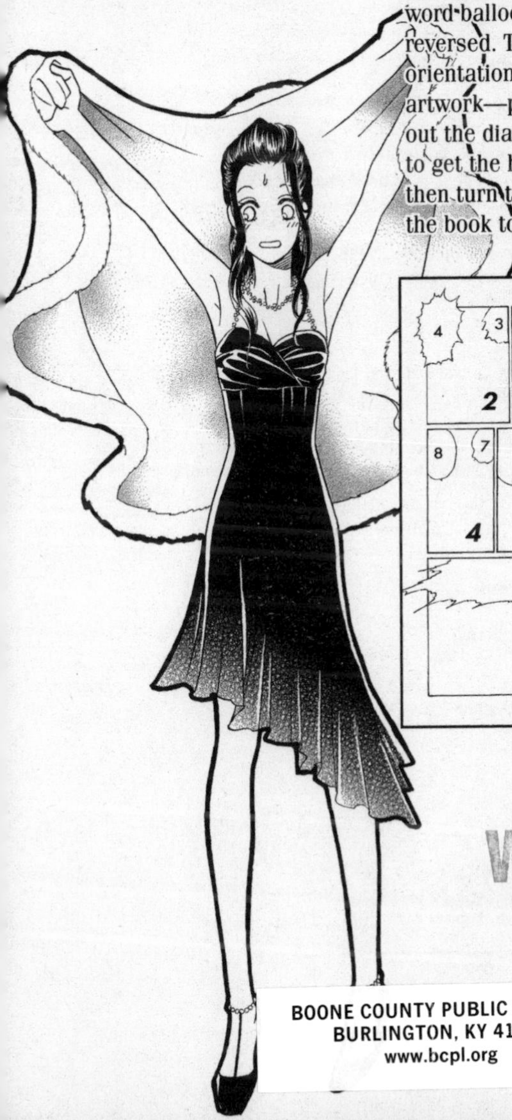

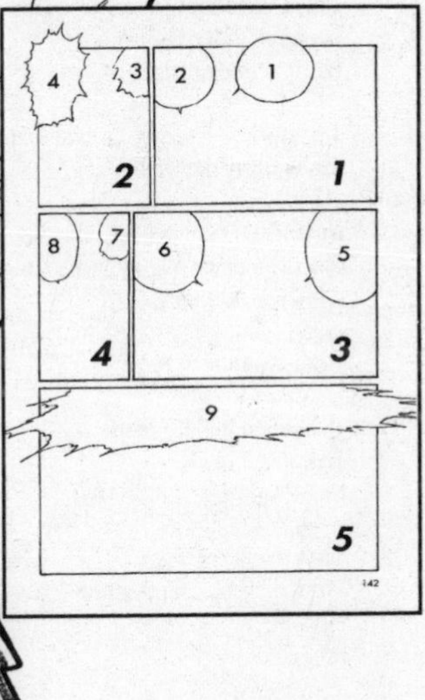
1
2
1
3
4
2
5
6
3
7
8
4
9
5
142